THE
SHENANDOAH VALLEY
BOOK
A Complete Guide

Apple blossoms signal spring in the Shenandoah Valley. Local legend has it that George Washington himself introduced apples to Valley farmers as a cash crop.

THE
SHENANDOAH
VALLEY
BOOK

A Complete Guide

JOAN LEOTTA

Berkshire House Publishers
Lee, Massachusetts

On the Cover and Frontispiece

Front Cover: *The Knob at Mount Jackson in the Shenandoah Valley.* Photo © Shenandoah2000.
Frontispiece: *Apple blossoms in the Shenandoah Valley.* Photo © Shenandoah2000.

THE SHENANDOAH VALLEY BOOK: A COMPLETE GUIDE

Copyright © 2003 by Berkshire House Publishers
Cover and interior photographs © Shenandoah2000 and other credited photographers

ISBN: 1-58157-062-7
ISSN: 1056-7968 (series)

Editor: Kathryn Flynn. Managing Editor: Philip Rich. Design and composition:
Dianne Pinkowitz. Cover design and composition: Jane McWhorter. Maps: Maps.com.
Index: Diane Brenner.

Berkshire House books are available at substantial discounts for bulk purchases
by corporations and other organizations for promotions and premiums. Special
personalized editions can also be produced in large quantities. For more information,
contact:

Berkshire House Publishers
480 Pleasant St., Suite 5; Lee, Massachusetts 01238
800-321-8526

Manufactured in the United States of America

10 9 8 7 6 5 4 3 2 1

*No complimentary meals or lodgings were accepted by the author or reviewers in gathering
information for this work.*

Berkshire House Publishers'
Great Destinations™ travel guidebook series

Recommended by NATIONAL GEOGRAPHIC TRAVELER and TRAVEL &
LEISURE magazines.

. . . a crisp and critical approach, for travelers who want to live like locals.
USA TODAY

Great Destinations™ guidebooks are known for their comprehensive, critical
coverage of regions of extraordinary cultural interest and natural beauty. The
authors in this series are professional travel writers who have lived for many
years in the regions they describe. Each title in this series is continuously updated with each printing, in order to insure accurate and timely information. All
of the books contain over 100 photographs and maps.

Neither the publisher, the authors, the reviewers, nor other contributors accept
complimentary lodgings, meals, or any other consideration (such as advertising) while gathering information for any book in this series.

Current titles available:
The Adirondack Book
The Berkshire Book
The Charleston, Savannah, & Coastal Islands Book
The Chesapeake Bay Book
The Coast of Maine Book
The Finger Lakes Book
The Hamptons Book
The Hudson Valley Book
The Monterey Bay Big Sur & Gold Coast Wine Country Book
The Nantucket Book
The Napa & Sonoma Book
The Santa Fe & Taos Book
The Sarasota, Sanibel Island, & Naples Book
The Shenandoah Valley Book
The Texas Hill Country Book
Touring East Coast Wine Country

If you are traveling to, moving to, residing in, or just interested in any (or all!) of
these enchanting regions, a **Great Destinations**™ guidebook is a superior companion. Honest and painstakingly critical, full of information only a local can provide, **Great Destinations**™ guidebooks provide you with all the practical
knowledge you need to enjoy the best of each region. Why not own them all?

*This book is dedicated to my dear family — my husband Joe,
our daughter Jennie, and our son Joe.
Together, we have driven the Valley's length, explored its heights and
depths, and experienced all so that I could share it with you, the reader.*

Acknowledgments

It took a village to make this book. I am especially grateful to Jean Rousseau, president and publisher of Berkshire House, who granted me the time and support to complete the book; also to Philip Rich, managing editor, for his continual encouragement and guidance. Special thanks also go to Kathryn Flynn, who skillfully edited the entire manuscript and checked many of the facts, and to Dale Gelfand, who reviewed early drafts and made valuable suggestions.

My heartfelt thanks also go out to those who contributed time and reviews, suggestions and fact-checking, among whom are my husband, daughter, son, and many friends; Allison Blake (author of Berkshire House's *The Chesapeake Bay Book: A Complete Guide*); Beverly Bittle, Civil War enthusiast; Dan Casey of *The Roanoke Times*, Karen Diamond of Bath County; Don Riley, Eric Latham, and Elizabeth Lloyd; as well as all of the wonderful people in the Virginia tourism industry, both in the commonwealth offices and at the local level.

Despite our best efforts, some omissions had to be made due to length, and if any errors escaped us or you have suggestions for improvements for future volumes, we hope you will share your findings with us.

Contents

CHAPTER ONE
Valley of the Daughter of the Stars
WELCOME TO THE SHENANDOAH
1

CHAPTER TWO
Getting There and Getting Around
TRANSPORTATION
19

CHAPTER THREE
Entertain the Possibilities
CULTURAL ATTRACTIONS
33

CHAPTER FOUR
The Nature of the Valley
OUTDOOR RECREATION
101

CHAPTER FIVE
Sleep Inn
LODGING
145

CHAPTER SIX
Everything from Soup to Nuts
RESTAURANTS, FOOD PURVEYORS, AND WINE
181

CHAPTER SEVEN
It's in the Bag
SHOPPING
237

CHAPTER EIGHT
Helpful Hints
INFORMATION
264

Introduction

The Shenandoah Valley is ringed with mountains, laced with caves, and strung with jewels of tiny towns and midsized cities — each with a distinct personality. On my first trip to the Valley at age 12, the caves seemed like fairylands, the mountains a springboard to touch the sky. As an adult with my own family, I've roamed the Valley, visiting Civil War battlegrounds, tasting homemade potato chips, eating goat cheese from goats we helped feed, and watching many a stunning sunset, the orange globe descending into the river against a backdrop of deep purple, velvet mountains. My awe of the Valley's beauty and my joy at meeting its people increase with each visit. I return from every visit with tales of new places to see and things to do.

THE WAY THIS BOOK WORKS

This book covers the counties of the Shenandoah Valley from Winchester to Roanoke and the mountain counties of Highland, Bath, and Alleghany. The great parklands of the Valley have their own place within this book, but it is not the purpose of this guide to explore those in detail. Our purpose is to get you to them and to introduce you to the many free resources within their offices that will ensure a magnificent time.

The book is an attempt to offer those who would explore this historic and exceedingly lovely spot a guide to activities, lodging, and food. The word "complete" in the title refers to what could be included within the allotted pages for the series. To list *all* would be impossible. Changes in ownership, hours, and consolidations in the shops and sites of the area continue apace. We tried to be up-to-the-minute as much as possible.

A car is the boon companion for navigating from place to place, but at various times visitors can shift to horse, boat, hiking, and even the air to further acquaint themselves with the beauty of this place.

It is equally simple to see the Valley in depth, over a week or ten days, or to use a segmented approach. Many peruse the Valley a weekend or a few days at a time, slipping in from other major tourism areas like Washington, D.C., or Virginia's beaches, from Richmond or Charlottesville, or from the southeastern mountain states of the U.S.

The layout of the book is by subject, then by county going from north to south (the most commonly followed travel path), followed by the listings for the mountain counties. Any references to prices, hours, names of owners, even the names of museums are cited as they were at the time of writing. The way in which the book interprets lodging and dining pricing and reservation information is noted below.

LODGING

A ll rate ranges are based on rates posted at the time of writing, without dis-count. Rates can change at any time. Many of the inns offer discounts for longer stays and out-of-season stays. The rates are sometimes increased during the leaf season or in May, when spring flowers and college graduations abound. Many also offer AARP, AAA, and other discounts. Be sure to ask when you book.

Rates quoted do not include tax imposed by the state on a per-night basis. We use the following scale to give you an idea of the rates we were quoted when researching the book:

Lodging Rates

Inexpensive	Up to $75	Expensive	$126 to $175
Moderate	$76 to $125	Very Expensive	Over $175

AMERICAN PLAN

S ome of the inns require American Plan or Modified American Plan (inclu-sion of meals, all meals, or just breakfast and dinner) during their high season. Some require it all the time.

MINIMUM STAY

M any inns also require two-night stays on weekends during the spring or fall leaf seasons. Often if you call at the last minute and they have an opening they will override the minimum rule. The hotels listed do not have a minimum. The resorts in the area often have a two-night minimum stay and sometimes require a one-week stay for their timeshare units.

DEPOSITS & CANCELLATIONS

M ost of the properties require at least a credit card number and many im-pose a partial cancellation fee — up to a set number of days — and require a full night's payment for cancellation within 24 hours. The ones with the most stringent policies in this regard are usually the smallest inns, where a cancellation at the last minute means losing one-third or so of the planned income for that night. Be sure to ask about the cancellation policy when you make your reservation.

OTHER CONSIDERATIONS

M ost of the properties do not allow pets, although a few will do so for an ad-ditional fee. Be sure to ask first. If you are traveling with a pet and want to stay somewhere that does not accept pets, most can recommend nearby kennels. While it is true that most inns do not accept children, this is changing. Many that say they do not accept children will consider a child over age 12 — always inquire. Most of the inns charge an additional per-person fee if you have a third person in the room, child or adult.

Many of the inns are jumping on the no-smoking bandwagon. If you are a smoker, inquire when you make your reservation as to the inn's policy in this regard.

You will notice that some of the inns in the mountain counties do not have street addresses. This is not an omission — the towns do not consider it necessary to have numbers on the addresses. Folks pick up their mail from their boxes at the post office.

BOOKING

Most of the properties can be booked by phone or online. Timeshare exchange units are often booked through large international membership groups, or you can call the resort directly to inquire about units that are left open for rental rather than exchange.

RESTAURANTS

Restaurant prices indicate the cost of an individual's meal, which includes appetizer, entrée, and dessert, but does not include cocktails, wine, tax, or tip. Restaurants with a prix-fixe menu are noted accordingly.

Inexpensive	Up to $15	Expensive	$31 to $40
Moderate	$16 to $30	Very Expensive	Over $40

Credit Cards are abbreviated as follows

AE — American Express	DC — Diner's Club
CB — Carte Blanche	MC — MasterCard
D — Discover	V — Visa

Meals are abbreviated as follows:

B — Breakfast	D — Dinner
L — Lunch	SB — Sunday Brunch

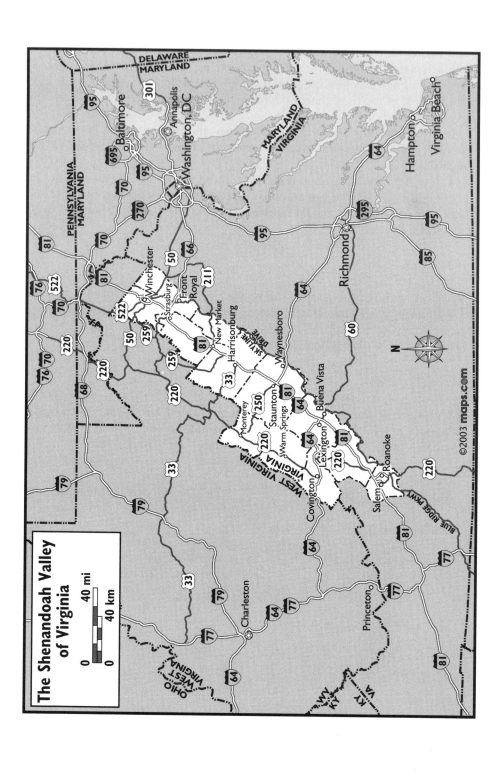

The Shenandoah Valley
of Virginia

©2003 maps.com

CHAPTER ONE
Valley of the Daughter of the Stars
WELCOME TO THE SHENANDOAH

Shenandoah2000

Mountain peaks are known as "knobs" in the Shenandoah Valley. This is the Knob at Mount Jackson in Shenandoah County.

The allure of Virginia's Shenandoah Valley lies both in the incredible beauty of the land itself and in the industry, artistry, and hospitality of the people who have lived there over time. Today's visitors to the Valley are likely to be outdoorsy types lured by the area's breathtaking scenery, history buffs eager to discover its fascinating past, or lovers of the arts drawn to its many cultural pursuits.

The Valley is defined by the state's tourism office as the 13 counties that stretch almost 200 miles from north to south, extending from the city of Winchester in the north downward to Roanoke and Salem. The area is bordered to the east by the Appalachian Mountains and the Blue Ridge, and on the west by West Virginia and the Allegheny Mountains.

THE RIVER FLOWS THROUGH IT

The scope of this book includes the 21st-century version of the geographic Shenandoah Valley in Virginia mentioned above. But today's economic and cultural designation is not the same as the historic and geographic Shenandoah Valley, defined by the river basin and extending northward to Harpers Ferry, West Virginia. The New River Valley city of Roanoke is now considered part of the Shenandoah Valley for tourism and other economic purposes unrelated to the flow of rivers.

The Shenandoah is a south-to-north flowing body of water. And if you find that puzzling, area maps may not be much help to you. Rivers labeled clearly as South Fork or North Fork are still called by local stream or tributary names on some maps. A national park ranger once told me that he couldn't understand the fuss — "After all, the river doesn't care what it's named — neither do the mountains!"

Shenandoah2000

The beauty of the North Fork's twists and turns is evident from a high point near Woodstock, Virginia.

The exact point of origin of the famed Shenandoah is a matter of debate as well. According to most sources, the North Fork of the river begins somewhere in George Washington National Forest, swings through New Market in Shenandoah County and climbs up, flowing around and under Route 11 and Interstate 81 on its way to Front Royal.

The South Fork is less problematic. On most maps, the South River becomes the South Fork of the Shenandoah just outside Port Republic.

THE VALLEY

Nestled between the Allegheny Mountains to the west and the Shenandoah, Blue Ridge, and Appalachian Mountains to the east, the heart of the Valley is only 25 to 40 miles wide. Unlike the towering mountains of the western United States, the encircling ring of the Shenandoah's lower peaks and intersecting line of the Massanutten Mountains are almost always visible from the Valley floor. Reddish Knob, just west of Harrisonburg, is the highest Shenandoah Valley peak at 4,397 feet.

The mountains curve protectively about the Valley and her rivers, and their beauty is quite literally more than "skin" deep. Under the lush farmland and the warm violet of the mountain peaks, the ground is a sort of Swiss cheese. More than 3,000 caves lace the state. Those open to tourists are called "show caves," and eight of them lie in the Valley. Their particular beauty and, in many cases, rare, delicate ecologies are strictly regulated by The Virginia Cave Board, a part of the commonwealth's Department of Natural Resources.

Much of the natural beauty of the Valley is preserved in parks — local, state, regional, and federal. These include the George Washington National Forest, the Shenandoah National Park, the Blue Ridge Parkway, and a variety of others.

One word of warning: Visiting the Shenandoah Valley and her surrounding mountains touches both heart and soul. Many who visit end up consulting the local Yellow Pages for real estate agents.

NATURAL HISTORY

FORMATION OF THE VALLEY

Scientists say the formation of the Shenandoah Valley occurred during the Paleozoic era. They call it a "Wilson cycle," which means that while volcanoes were rumbling and hot spots forming in the earth's crust, the rumbling action shook out the crust of the earth — somewhat like shaking out a blanket after a picnic. With one metaphoric shake the valley filled with water, as a blanket balloons with air. Another caused the water to disappear from the surface. The theory is that much of the water worked its way downward through the limestone, forming the area's many caves and the pools that lie in their depths.

In colonial times the caves were important economic resources, mined for saltpeter (used in making gunpowder) and other minerals such as manganese, iron, lead, zinc, and clay. Today, the economic value of the caves lies primarily in their success as tourist attractions.

Shenandoah2000

Goshen Pass is one of the most beautiful places in the Valley. High stone cliffs reach up to the sky along a riverbank lined with rhododendron.

FAUNA AND FLORA

An occasional black bear still ambles by the road in the Valley's higher elevations, and now and then a fox will poke his graceful red snout out from the roadside bushes, reminding you that this is hunt country. But most wildlife keeps a low profile in a world where the auto tire is a deadlier enemy than the hunting dog. The exception is the deer. When driving anywhere in the Shenandoah Valley, near fields or forest, be on the lookout for deer by the road — especially at dawn and dusk.

Above the farm fields, hawks extend their wings on the hunt for prey. Hiking trails pass through the woods where wild turkeys, quail, doves, and woodpeckers dart among the brush and trees. Cardinals, the state bird, nest in the underbrush and remain in most of the Valley year-round. Birding information can be picked up at most of the Tourist Information Centers in the Valley and from the Virginia Department of Game & Inland Fisheries (804-367-1000; www.dgif.state .va.us; 4010 W. Broad St., Richmond, VA 23230).

Turtles (mostly box turtles) laze about in the streams and rivers in plain view of all. These, frogs, and toads are the benign reptiles of the area. Several vari-

This is my retelling of how the Valley was named, based on the version on the Shenandoah Valley Travel Association Web site: www.svta.org.

Legend of the Daughter of the Stars

When the Ancient Ones gather they tell this tale:

"After the Great Spirit made the world, and found it good, the morning stars looked down and saw a place of wondrous beauty, a silver lake that reflected their own glory. The stars glided through the sky to rest on the blue mountains that circled the lake like an azure crown. They all agreed that this was the most beautiful place they had ever seen.

"As the stars hovered above the quiet waters, their robes of fire lit the mountaintops and the stars sang songs of joy. The stars pledged to gather in that same spot every thousand years.

"At one such gathering, a mighty crash interrupted the singing. One of the great rocks on the mountainside split open, and the silvery lake waters poured through the crack, into the ground.

"As time passed, the now sorrowful stars sought another place of beauty to meet when they came upon the earth. No place seemed as lovely as their lake valley until, one day, the stars spotted another valley with a crown of blue mountains. Instead of a lake the bottom was green, with one shimmering ribbon of river winding through it. This valley was another place of incredible beauty.

"So the stars gathered on the mountaintops as of old. Just before the singing was to begin, one star cried out: 'This green valley is the bed of our own dear, lost lake! The blue crown of mountains is the very same crown we lit with our robes of fire those many years ago!

"The stars were so joyful that they placed the brightest jewels from their own robes and crowns within the valley, giving her more streams and rivers, and declared this valley to be their own child, their daughter.

"Today, we know this valley and its river as the stars named it — *Shenandoah, Daughter of the Stars.*"

eties of poisonous snakes also call the Valley's hiking trails home, including the timber rattlesnake and the copperhead. Hikers can probably avoid snake trouble if they stay on the path, and keep hands and feet out of any hole or overgrown place. Any place that could hide a mouse might be a place where a snake is waiting for its next meal.

Trout is king among the Valley's fish, but the heavy fishing of the streams and inflow of people into the area have rendered the stream ecosystems quite fragile. Area fishing experts and ecologists advise that if you want to eat the fish you catch, trout farms are a better source than the natural streams, which are better suited to catch and release. Besides, the stocked ponds of trout farms are also a fun way to introduce children to the joy of fishing because they will undoubtedly catch something!

Along the roads, even busy Interstate 81, the magnificent display of flowers

---

Preserving Wildlife

The **Wildlife Center of Virginia** (540-942-9453; www.wildlifecenter.org; wildlife@ wildlifecenter.org; PO Box 1577, Waynesboro, VA 22980), located just a half-mile off Interstate 64, is a native wildlife hospital. It's also a center for teaching about wildlife and the environment. Although it's not open on a regular basis, frequent "open house" days give people a chance to see a wildlife rehabilitation center in action. There is no charge, but reservations are required. Call or e-mail for the schedule.

---

and trees paints the countryside an array of colors ranging from the pastel pinks of spring's dogwoods to the deep reds of autumn's leaves.

Virginia's floral wonders also are on view at historic homes, during Garden Week in private homes, and in the several arboretums of the Valley. One of the two largest state facilities is located just outside Winchester, and another large one is located on the James Madison University campus in Harrisonburg. (See Chapter Three, *Cultural Attractions*, for more on the area's arboretums.)

Each season brings its own particular beauty to the Valley through its natural blooms.

Spring comes first to the southern end of the Valley. Driving down from the north, the chill dissipates and the air becomes fragrant with the breath of renewal and blossoms the farther south one travels. Come mid-April, the moun-

Shenandoah2000

Spring brings Mountain Laurel blooms to the high points of the Alleghenies.

tains have changed from the gray of winter to a quilt of white and pink. Day lilies, generally a deep orange, soon fill the shallow roadside ditches, making a vibrant contrast to the area's tall, dark-topped cattails. May brings apple blossoms to the roads along the Valley's many orchards.

The state keeps the center of Interstate 81, the main highway through the Valley, beautiful with an array of seasonally blooming wildflowers. Throughout the summer, their reds and purples and yellows punctuate the deep greens of the grassy median.

In autumn, the change of season proceeds in reverse order, with the northern Valley's trees succumbing first to the touch of Jack Frost and ringing the Valley in a modern crown of fire — a spectacle that is probably the Valley's largest tourist draw.

Even the bleaker days of winter have a beauty all their own. Frost on the roadside grasses glimmers in the sun and the tops of the bare trees shimmer blue-gray in the twilight.

SOCIAL HISTORY OF THE VALLEY

Native American tribes hunted and fished the area for thousands of years before the first Europeans and Africans arrived. In fact, artifacts all over the Valley and the highlands confirm that their communities thrived in the area as early as 8,000 or 9,000 years B.C.

William Pidgeon, an amateur Winchester anthropologist, uncovered ancient Indian burial mounds in the Valley in the 1800s. Arrowheads, bits of pottery, and remains of villages can still be found in streams and caves throughout the Valley, and many local museums have cases filled with arrowheads and other artifacts found by area families.

Most of the early area tribes were the Senedo of Shawnee-Algonquian extraction from whose language the Valley takes its name. One of their centers was in the area now called Meem's Bottom.

The name Shenandoah (there are thirty variant spellings) comes from their tribe, although others also claim it. Some believe that the Valley is named for one of the Iroquois chiefs, Sherando, or from an Iroquois word that means "river through the spruce." Not long before the Europeans arrived, the Iroquois drove out many of the Senedo, taking these rich lands for their own.

Other Eastern Woodland Indians said to inhabit the Valley include Monacan, Tuscarora, Shawnee, Occoneechee, Piscataway, Nahyssan, Oenock, Oustback, Ushery, Massawomack, Pamunkey, and Algonquin. Today only a few Pamunkey and Monacans remain.

By the time the Europeans arrived in Jamestown in 1607, Powhatan had conquered the area and brought the Indians there under his domination. Oral history reports that Captain John Smith explored here before 1610, but the first recorded expedition was in the 1670s by John Lederer.

First Africans

In 1619 the first Africans were brought to Virginia to work the tobacco plantations of the Tidewater area as indentured servants. (It was not until the 1660s that slavery found its way into Virginia's legal codes.) It is not known when they first began to migrate west. By 1776, 40 percent of Virginia's population was of African descent. (Source: *The Story of Virginia, An American Experience*, published by the Virginia Historical Society)

After Powhatan's death, the federation passed to the control of Chief Opecancanough, and English settlers began to explore the areas west of Jamestown. Treaties held for a while, but skirmishes between whites and Indians increased in the coastal areas. In the 1640s the volume of settlers moving west increased, as did violence with the Indian tribes in the area.

In 1669-70, Lederer led one of the first explorations of the upper Valley to leave records. When Thomas Batte and Robert Hallom found the passage west through the Blue Ridge and crossed the Allegheny Mountains near today's Narrows, Virginia, the western areas opened up to settlers in a rush.

The few settlers became many, and just in time. Immigration and overuse of the land in the Tidewater area of the state near the Chesapeake Bay were already making many look west to the fertile valley of the Shenandoah. The English Toleration Act of 1689 made the trip to Virginia even more desirable for French Huguenots, Scotch-Irish, Germans, Quakers, Swiss, Swedes, and Dutch, most of whom poured inland to the fertile lands of the Shenandoah Valley.

The large numbers of Europeans, their superior weapons, and the Indians' susceptibility to European diseases severely reduced Native American populations in the Valley by the mid-18th century. Many of the remaining Indians simply moved west or farther south to avoid contact with settlers.

Meanwhile, a lack of proper mapping contributed to land disputes among the European settlers, creating a demand for surveyors. In the 1750s, Lord Thomas Fairfax sent young George Washington and several others on a month-long trip west across the Blue Ridge Mountains to ascertain the correct borders of the extensive Fairfax crown grants. Washington developed a lifelong love of the area on the trip, and in later years purchased large tracts of property in the western highlands (now West Virginia). Descendents of his nieces and nephews still live in West Virginia.

Native Americans grew increasingly unhappy about the encroachment upon their land, however, and skirmishes became more frequent. In the northern part of the Valley, much of this came to a head in the 1750s with the French and Indian War. At the end of that war, in 1763, a royal proclamation forbade settlement west of the mountains, but Virginians defied this ban. The Valley had served as a jumping-off place for the westward-bound forces of the war, and it continued to be a popular starting point for frontier exploration until the frontier itself moved farther west.

After 1776, when becoming part of a new nation became Virginia's focus, the farmer of the Valley, who also resented the king's stamp tax, joined the force against the British. A vast number of immigrants of varying faiths also hoped that freedom from England would mean freedom from the tax paid to its church.

Trade issues for the young ironworks industry, pottery-manufacturing operations, and vast small farmlands also inspired area residents to throw their support behind the Revolutionary War. And, of course, defying England didn't take a long stretch of mind or action for the Scotch or Irish settlers.

Winchester and the northern part of the Valley saw battles, but most of the fighting was outside the Valley. Native Americans continued to be the most dangerous aspect of life, but they had already begun moving farther south and west by the time of the Revolution.

After the Revolution, the Shenandoah region briefly resumed its role of jumping-off point for much of the exploration of the West. Renowned explorers Lewis and Clark were among those crossing the Allegheny Mountains. Legend has them helping to provision their 1803 trip into the uncharted lands of the Louisiana Purchase with stops in the Valley.

The University of Virginia confirms a stop on the way back as well: "When Meriwether Lewis was returning to President Jefferson in Washington from the expedition, he stopped in Fincastle for the night, perhaps two days." (Clark's wife's family was from Fincastle.) To find out more about this connection and to see a variety of sites about the expedition, see the links section at www.lewis andclarkeast.org.

Shenandoah Telephone Corp.

Winchester's annual apple blossom parade (first weekend in May) celebrates local history and the hope for a good crop.

Though the frontier moved westward, the towns of the Valley still prospered from trade with the West and from the traffic on Route 11, the Valley Pike, a major north-to-south interior route in the early days of our country. Early 19th-century travelers, tradesmen, and those seeking the cures of the hot springs in the west drove the pike and the roads we know today as Route 33, Route 340, and Route 250.

Grain (barley, rye, oats, and wheat), flax, cattle, and trade dominated the economy. The Frontier Culture Museum Web site reports that, by 1850, the Valley produced 22 percent of Virginia's wheat crop, though it had only 9 percent of the state's tillable acreage.

Agriculture was a backbreaking hand and horse affair until one of the great geniuses of the 19th century came along: Cyrus McCormick of Steeles Tavern in Rockbridge County. In 1831, his invention of a reaper mechanized the wheat harvest process. By hand a farmer could reap half an acre in a day. With McCormick's reaper, one person could finish 12 acres in one day. The McCormick family farm and Cyrus' workshop are located just 20 minutes north of downtown Lexington. The workshop, a blacksmith shop, and gristmill are open to visitors year-round without admission fee. (See Chapter Three, *Cultural Attractions.*)

Iron also played a role in the Valley's industry in the first half of the 1800s. The Columbia, Liberty, Caroline, Boyer, and Elizabeth furnaces were among the iron-making operations brought to the Shenandoah by European settlers quick to take advantage of the area's fortuitous conjunction of ore deposits, limestone, and waterpower.

Pottery was another thriving Valley industry in the antebellum years. Salt-glazed pots of Virginia clay stocked the larders of housewives all over the country. Strasburg, in Shenandoah County, became known as Pot-Town due to the abundance of wonderful, utilitarian pottery produced there.

The pig iron and metalworking industries utilized the region's coal and mineral deposits to bring manufacturing to the Valley, and the railroad arrived in the mid-1800s, bringing greater ease to transport, trade, and the exchange of new ideas.

CIVIL WAR

Economic problems of the 1830s forced many farmers to sell their slaves (generally to large slaveholders farther south), and many farmers left the Valley for the more prosperous lands west, north, and south. The various slave rebellions of the 1830s and '40s frightened many white farmers and hardened their view against freedom for slaves. This view was solidified in the atmosphere of fear following John Brown's 1859 raid at Harpers Ferry. (See sidebar at the end of this chapter.)

After months of debate on the issue, the General Assembly of Virginia voted to secede from the Union on April 17, 1861. Many delegates in the far western counties voted against secession, however, and these counties later broke away and formed the new state of West Virginia, loyal to the Union.

Valley of the Shadow

One of the most comprehensive and exciting new looks at the origins of the Civil War in the Valley is an online project run by the Center for Digital History at the University of Virginia. The project, known as the Valley of the Shadow (www .iath.virginia.edu/vcdh/teaching/vclassroom), compares original source material from Augusta County, Virginia, and Franklin County, Pennsylvania, allowing students of all ages to see for themselves the similarities and differences in viewpoints that led to the war.

Shenandoah2000

The gravestones of Soldiers Circle at Prospect Hill Cemetery mark the burials of many of Warren County's Confederate dead. Local lore says Stonewall Jackson directed his artillery campaign in the early days of the Civil War's Battle of Front Royal from this spot.

But the Civil War did far more than reshape the map. From 1861 to 1865, Virginia was bathed in the blood of blue and gray alike, and much of it flowed in the Shenandoah Valley. Both small engagements and major battles were fought here, including Cedar Creek, Brandy Station, Port Republic, and Kernstown.

The northern part of the Valley changed hands often — Winchester alone almost 70 times.

Troops from both sides used the resources and the macadam-paved roads of the Valley to further their cause. The Valley was considered the breadbasket of the Confederacy at the start of hostilities, and its strategic location made it an ideal staging area for any strike on the North, as well as an ideal pathway for a march down to the back door of Richmond.

Confederate General Thomas J. "Stonewall" Jackson taught at Lexington's Virginia Military Institute immediately before the war. His 1862 Valley campaign — which included just one defeat, at Kernstown in March — was one of the major strategic operations of the early days of the war. These victories bolstered the morale and fortunes of the South, but also took a heavy toll on the land.

Jackson died at a field hospital near the site of the Battle of Chancellorsville in 1863. He is buried in a Lexington cemetery now known as the Stonewall Jackson Cemetery.

One of the saddest aspects of the Civil War was that it often pitted friend against friend, brother against brother. Skirmishes in the Valley were not immune to this sorrowful situation. At the Battle of Cedar Creek, for example, generals would gather at the deathbeds of dying friends and West Point classmates serving the other side. At night, the voices of common soldiers crossed the lines, requesting coffee and trading food with those who were their enemies by day.

In 1864 Union General Philip Sheridan swept down the Valley in a campaign known locally as "The Burning." His goal was to crush the area's ability to supply the remaining troops of the South. He largely succeeded. The town of Harrisonburg was burned almost completely to the ground and railroads lay in ruins. Some older buildings still show the marks of the Union flames. (For a list of individual battlefield sites open to the public, see Chapter Three, *Cultural Attractions*.)

When the war ended in April 1865, those who returned to Virginia found charred soil, burned buildings, and devastation so great that, throughout the state (figures for the Valley itself are not available), some 25,000 Virginians existed on Union rations for six months.

Men such as Robert E. Lee hushed voices crying to hold a grudge. Lee himself retired to Lexington to live quietly as the head of Washington College (named Washington and Lee after his death). Along with the rest of the South, Virginia's returning soldiers began to rebuild their lives.

RECOVERY IN THE AGE OF RECONSTRUCTION

Recovery after the Civil War was slow, due partly to wrangling between the new state of West Virginia and her mother state over funds. It was not until 1870 that Virginia was readmitted to the Union.

The role of the railroad in the history of Roanoke and the Valley as a whole is well documented at the Virginia Museum of Transportation.

Joan Leotta

The railroad became the hope for recovery. Once the state's orchards were replanted, trains delivered apples throughout the region. Railways also boosted tourism by transporting spa lovers to "take the cure" at Hot Springs.

The rails also brought prosperity to the tiny settlement of New Lick, a crossroads and new center of industry that would eventually be renamed Roanoke. The railroad hotel built there in the late 1890s still stands — a historic landmark and wonderful place to stay. (See Chapter Five, *Lodging*.)

THE NEW CENTURY

Virginia's return to national prominence came with the election of Woodrow Wilson to the presidency in 1912. Although he was the governor of New Jersey (Wilson attended Princeton and then stayed on as a professor), his administration brought many Virginians to places of prominence in Washington.

Virginians supported the country's entry into World War I with copious enlistments, industrial support of the war effort, and agricultural output to feed the armies.

Just after the "Great War," Democrat Harry Byrd came to power as state governor, a position he would hold for the next 40 years. He presided over the state's Depression years, carefully guiding her to recovery.

Tourism concerns and the need to find a project for the Civilian Conservation Corps brought national attention to the Shenandoah during the Great Depression. But the story of Shenandoah National Park actually begins right at the turn of the century, when a man named George Freeman Pollock inherited a barren piece of mountain land near Luray and called it Skyland. Skyland soon became a popular place to go — especially among Washington, D.C., politicians.

Pollock's dream of a national park came to fruition through his friendship with these politicians. Unfortunately, his dream displaced a number of small

Reliving History

In the last days of the war, the New Market Battlefield was the scene of a struggle of young cadets from the Virginia Military Academy against Union troops.

Shenandoah2000

More than 130 years after it ended, the Civil War's devastation of the Shenandoah Valley now helps build the Valley economy by drawing history-loving tourists to battle sites.

Visitors retrace the brilliant strikes of Stonewall Jackson, or track Philip Sheridan's sweep of the region as he sought to break the last vestiges of Southern strength.

Many battle reenactments are carried out on the sites where the original skirmishes took place, and preservation efforts throughout the Valley mean that battlefield visitors can enjoy the same sweeping views that Union and Confederate scouts viewed.

New Market is one of the most affecting of the Civil War battlefields to visit. Still standing is the farm that sheltered the young Virginia Military Institute cadets, most under age 16, who hoped to protect their beloved Virginia. (General John C. Breckinridge is said to have shouted, "Put the boys in, and may God forgive me for the order!") The young men tried desperately to halt the Union drive, slogging through mud so heavy that the site became known as the "Field of Lost Shoes."

The booklet *Civil War Trails*, available at most visitor centers, maps out these Civil War heritage spots throughout the state. Further information also appears in Chapter Three, *Cultural Attractions.*

To gain an even deeper understanding and appreciation for the battles of the area, try to schedule your visit to coincide with a reenactment. There are reenactors for every period of history, but the Civil War draws the largest numbers of those who want to relive the experience, especially in Virginia. Reenactors research the period, choose a role, buy or make historically accurate clothing and other accoutrements, and several times a year live out the lives of those they portray by acting out a battle or a march. Some are professional historians or teachers. Most are simply folks who share a love of history.

Many women have taken up the hobby as well, portraying nurses, soldiers' wives, shopkeepers, or local farmers' wives. Some even dress as male soldiers, as did many intrepid 19th-century patriots on both sides.

farmers whose families had lived on the land since the earliest European settlers arrived. Only 19 families received permission to remain within the park boundaries; the last of these residents died in 1979.

The Civilian Conservation Corps worked to build the paths (including the Appalachian Trail) into the park, which opened in 1936 and was completed in 1948. Each year thousands of visitors drive the peaks on Skyline Drive from Thornton Gap to Rockfish Gap, where it joins the Blue Ridge Parkway. The CCC also built the sturdy stone guardrails and overlooks that visitors enjoy today.

World War II saw another surge of patriotic enlistments of Valley residents. One of the greatest soldiers of the 20th century, George C. Marshall, was born in Uniontown, Pennsylvania, but educated at VMI in Lexington. (A museum there now offers a panorama of his achievements.) Marshall led men with distinction during the war and was the architect of the European recovery strategy that came to be known as the Marshall Plan.

The area's slow way of life was upended here as elsewhere both by the vast number of people who left to fight the war and never returned, and by the new attitudes and changes brought about by those who did return. The History Museum in Roanoke displays clippings of interviews with soldiers who describe tasting Italian food for the first time, living in the Philippines, or fighting side by side with people of other races and cultures.

Frederick, Clarke, and Warren Counties produced some of the state's 20th-century luminaries, including politician Harry S. Byrd and Arctic explorer Admiral Richard E. Byrd. Country singer Patsy Cline (1932–1963), best known for her tunes "Crazy" and "I Fall to Pieces," was born just north of Winchester. Willa Cather (1873–1947), Pulitzer Prize–winning novelist, also was born near Winchester. She lived in the area until age nine, when she moved to the grasslands of Red Cloud, Nebraska, where most of her novels are set.

THE VALLEY TODAY

The people of the Valley continue to work to preserve its essential character and their lifestyle in the face of local and national change. Rather than being overwhelmed by economic ups and downs, the Valley's people value their past and look forward to the future, exploring the new and blending it slowly into their way of life. Farming, tourism, and industry power the economy of the region.

The main street of 19th-century Lexington, Virginia, is a scenic place to walk, shop, and eat.

While farming still plays a significant role in the economy of the Shenandoah Valley, fruit orchards, vineyards, and small boutique crops are taking over from large wheat, corn, and dairy farms. Cooperatives and cooperation with large corporations dominate many industries, such as apples in Winchester and poultry in Rockingham County.

What was old has become fodder for the antique shops or has made its presence known in a new way. Ironwork in the Valley — important from colonial times — contributes to its industry today mostly through artisan ironwork. Pottery is no longer a humble craft — area potters now produce art objects for display as well as use. Even the ancient sport of jousting is reborn each year at a tournament at Natural Chimneys Regional Park that draws great crowds. (See Chapter Four, *Outdoor Recreation*, for a more complete description.)

Harpers Ferry and the Shenandoah Valley

The view of the Shenandoah River flowing into the Potomac at Harpers Ferry, West Virginia, is one of the great sights in our nation — one that Thomas Jefferson deemed "worth crossing the Atlantic for." But the beauty of the area is not its only asset. From colonial times through the Civil War, Harpers Ferry was key in the commercial and military history of our nation.

The scope of this book is the Shenandoah Valley in Virginia, which means this historic town over the West Virginia line is not included, but its many historical and cultural ties to the Valley merit its mention.

The town's road to an immutable place in our history began in the early 18th century, when luminaries such as Thomas Jefferson and everyday folk like Robert Harper, a Philadelphia builder, recognized its beauty and commercial possibilities. Harper established a ferry across the Potomac, linking the "wild west" of Virginia and its raw materials to the more settled colonial pocketbooks on the other side. Harper also built a gristmill to take advantage of the Valley's grain production.

George Washington had seen the area during his surveying years and, in 1785, as president of the Patowmack Company, he traveled there to assess the town's role in a planned system of canals to bring commerce to the western frontier of Virginia. Almost a decade later, he used his knowledge of the area to name Harpers Ferry as his choice for a site for a federal armory and arsenal.

The fame of the arsenal was such that Meriwether Lewis made it a prime stop when gathering equipment for his 1803 expedition with William Clark. Records show that among the items Lewis purchased were 15 rifles, powder horns, bullet molds, musket locks, gun repair tools, tomahawks, knives, and a collapsible, iron-framed canoe.

The tiny town leapt into the forefront of history when John Brown took possession of the U.S. Armory on Oct. 16, 1859, to arm his planned slave uprising. On Oct. 18, a company of marines retook the armory, and Brown was subsequently tried and hung in nearby Charles Town. But the fire he lit was more explosive than any artillery explosion. His raid is thought by many to have polarized factions thinking about secession.

Thomas J. "Stonewall" Jackson charged into Harpers Ferry just days after the war began and Virginia seceded — April 28, 1861. Jackson took the arsenal and armory under his command and used the area to train Virginia volunteers. When his troops moved out, the Union's moved in, and in the fall of 1862 Jackson thundered back to trap and secure the surrender of 12,500 Union troops inside Harpers Ferry.

This "brilliant victory," as it was called, fueled the spirit of the South for a while, but the town did not remain under Confederate control. Runaway slaves and soldiers from both sides filled the streets of Harpers Ferry during the war, and shells and cannon reduced many of its buildings to rubble. After the war, the government destroyed what was left of the arsenal and floods devastated the town's attempts to rebuild its commerce.

The lack of prosperity that devastated the town worked to preserve it for us. Today's visitors to Harpers Ferry National Park can see the ruins of the old arsenal, Harper's home (the oldest building in town), a John Brown and Civil War museum,

(continued on next page)

as well as Jefferson's Rock, where the Founding Father stood to proclaim the view so wondrous.

THE PARK

HARPERS FERRY NATIONAL HISTORICAL PARK
304-535-6298.
PO Box 65, Harpers Ferry, WV 25425.
Open: Summer: daily 8–6; winter: daily 8–5. Closed Thanksgiving, Christmas, and New Year's Day.
Admission: Car entry $20; Visitor Center entry $5 (valid three days).

From July through September, park rangers offer a number of special education programs. Call or check the Web site at www.nps.gov/hafe/events.htm for details.

If you approach the park from Maryland, you may pass **Kennedy Farm**, the place where John Brown planned his raid on Harpers Ferry. Privately owned, it is nevertheless open to the public. Call 301-432-2666 for hours, fees, and directions.

Visitors also can enjoy a one- to two-hour walking tour that travels past an old cotton mill and other industrial ruins of the once-thriving 19th-century industrial town. The **Virginius Island Trail** begins at the end of the Hamilton Street footpath just outside of the Lower Town. Alternate starting points are along Shenandoah Street at the Randolph Bridge or the Shenandoah Pulp Mill ruins.

Where to Stay

There are a few places to stay in town and in nearby **Shepherdstown, West Virginia**, but the town is less than an hour from **Winchester**, which offers abundant accommodations. See Chapter Five, *Lodging*, for more information.

Want to stay closer to the park, in West Virginia? Contact the **Jefferson County Convention & Visitor Bureau** (304-535-2627, 800-848-TOUR; PO Box A, Harpers Ferry, WV 25425).

CHAPTER TWO
Getting There and Getting Around
TRANSPORTATION

Shenandoah2000

Rockingham County's Mennonites still travel by the old ways. Keep your eye out for buggies, especially near the Dayton Farmer's Market.

Native Americans crisscrossed the Shenandoah Valley on narrow footpaths through the trees. These paths or trails were later widened into roads by pioneers trekking by foot and wagon. This web of roads then spread south and west into the wilderness of the Louisiana Purchase and beyond. In the 1850s, the railroad added to the accessibility of the Valley.

Today the automobile is king. Most visitors travel the Valley by car on many of those same old, well-used roads. Those who fly into the region will likely need to rent a vehicle.

Trains, once the area's premier transportation, still run to the Valley, but in a very limited fashion — and, as with air travel, you will still need a car if you come by train. In the fall leaf season, special trains run from the Washington, D.C., metro area into the mountains, displaying for travelers the unique splendor of autumn in places only accessible and visible from railroad rights-of-way.

Bicycles share the road with cars all over the Valley and equestrians still enjoy miles of trails throughout the area. Motorbikes are becoming a more common sight, and more esoteric means of transport (hot air balloons, World War II planes, etc.) also can be hired for forays above the Valley. (See Chapter Four, *Outdoor Recreation,* for details.) But for general travel, think AUTO.

GETTING TO THE SHENANDOAH VALLEY

G etting to the Valley is the beginning of your adventure in the Shenandoah. The northern entrances are Winchester (most northerly) and Front Royal. These are the main gateways for travelers coming from the Northeast (Washington, D.C., Baltimore, and points north) and from the Midwest via Pittsburgh. These two cities are served by Washington Dulles International Airport (about an hour away) and, for those who have their own planes, a small airport in Winchester (Winchester Municipal).

The second gateway area is Waynesboro/Staunton on Interstate 64. These two towns are in the center of the Valley and are good access points for those coming via Richmond or Charlottesville, or from the southeast via I-95. A small commercial airport near Harrisonburg also serves as an entry to the central part of the Valley.

Roanoke-Salem is the southernmost gateway area. Travelers approaching Roanoke from the south, east, and southwest from such cities as Atlanta can connect with I-81 to begin their tour of the Valley from the south up. Roanoke Regional Airport serves the area.

Trucks — and lots of cars — are a constant on Interstate 81.

Shenandoah2000

BY CAR

From Baltimore, Philadelphia, New York, and other points north on the I-95 corridor: Take I-95 south until you reach Baltimore, where you will take I-695 west toward Towson and I-70. From there merge onto I-70 toward Frederick, going left at the fork in the ramp to I-70 west. Follow I-70 for almost 40 miles until you get to Route 340 west/Route 15 south to Charles Town/Leesburg. Keep left so that you continue west. You'll stay on Route 340 for about 23 miles until the road goes south. Take the Route 340 south ramp headed toward Berryville/Leesburg until you see the signs for Route 7 west. You'll be on Route 7 for about 10 miles, and then you can follow signs to city center/tourism information. There's an information center outside of town by Abrams Delight and another in the center of town. (Note: If you stay on 340 west instead of getting on Route 7, you'll skip Winchester and continue toward Luray.)

From Washington, D.C., and Northern Virginia via Dulles Airport to Winchester: Take the Washington Beltway (I-495) or I-66 to the Dulles Toll Road, Route 267 west. Airport travelers don't pay the toll; however, those taking the road for convenience to Winchester will pay. (From the airport it's a left onto Aviation Drive, then take 267 west toward Leesburg.) Stay on Route 267 for a bit less than 30 miles, then take the turnoff for Route 7 west. Stay on Route 7 for another 35 miles or so. Look for the Kent Street exit and then Boscowan Street. Follow the signs to the Visitor Center and pedestrian area.

From points north and northeast, Northern Virginia, Washington, D.C., to enter at Front Royal: Travelers on I-95 continue to the Washington Beltway, I-495, and head west/south into Northern Virginia. From the Beltway take I-66 west. Continue on I-66 to Linden/Front Royal. There are other local streets to take into town from this exit, but this way you get to stop at The Apple House for apples and barbecue. You can also continue on I-66 until it ends at I-81. Head north on I-81 for Winchester or south to Strasburg and the rest of the Valley.

From Dulles Airport to enter at Front Royal: Take a left onto Aviation Drive, then merge onto the Dulles Toll Road, heading east. Then take Route 28 south toward Centreville. At Centreville take the exit for I-66 west. Take I-66 to Front Royal, and follow directions above.

From the west via Pittsburgh to Winchester and I-81: Take the Pennsylvania Turnpike (I-70/76), a toll road, southeast about 100 miles to the Breezewood exit, where you'll continue on I-70 to Hancock. There you take Route 522 south to Winchester. If you prefer to stay on interstates, continue on I-70 to Hagerstown, then take I-81 south to Winchester.

From Richmond and other points south on the I-95 corridor to Waynesboro and Staunton and I-81: Take I-95 to I-64 west. Waynesboro and Staunton are practically contiguous; signs will direct you. From Staunton you can take I-81 or Route 11 north (toward Winchester) and south (toward Roanoke) to explore the rest of the Valley.

From Atlanta and other interior points in the South to Roanoke on Interstate 81: From I-75 north take the exit for I-85 north. Travel on I-85 for about two miles until you reach Greenville, North Carolina, where you will take I-77 north. It's a long stretch on I-77. After about 130 miles, take the exit for I-81/Route 11. Head toward Roanoke and merge onto I-81. For downtown Roanoke, take I-581 and follow the signs to the airport and then into downtown.

Note: The nearest gateway points to Skyline Drive are Front Royal (both Exits 6 and 13 lead to Shenandoah National Park) and Waynesboro. At Waynesboro, travelers can head north to Skyline Drive or south to the Blue Ridge Parkway. See Chapter Four, *Outdoor Recreation,* for more information on national and state parks.

BY AIR

Whether you fly to *Washington Dulles International Airport, Roanoke Regional Airport* or *Shenandoah Valley Airport,* the small regional airport outside Harrisonburg, you'll still want to have a rental car available unless you intend to stay in just one city. These three airports have both commercial and general aviation. Of the three, Dulles is served by the largest number of major domestic and international airlines.

There are also a number of small general aviation airports in the Valley.

WASHINGTON DULLES INTERNATIONAL AIRPORT (IAD)
703-572-2700.
www.metwashairports.com/Dulles.
45020 Aviation Dr., Sterling, VA 20166.

Commercial airlines:

Air Tran (800-247-8726; www.airtran.com).
Midwest Express (800-452-2022; www.midwestexpress.com).
United Airlines and United Air Express (800-241-6522; www.ual.com).
US Airways (800-428-4322; www.usairways.com).
Alaska Airlines (800-252-7522; www.alaskaair.com).
American Airlines (800-433-7300; www.aa.com).
Jet Blue Airways (800-538-2583; www.jetblue.com).
Northwest Airlines (800-225-2525; www.nwa.com).
Continental Airlines and Continental Express (800-525-0280; www.continental.com).
Delta Air Lines and Delta Express (800-221-1212; www.delta.com).

General aviation services:

Piedmont Hawthorne Aviation (800-926-0150; www.flypiedmont.com).
Signature Flight Support (703-572-0001; www.signatureflight.com).

Parking information:

Call 703-572-4500 (recorded information) or 703-572-4580 (live person). For questions about parking or any ground transportation issue, you can also e-mail IADGround.Transportation@mwaa.com.

Automobile rental:

Alamo (800-327-9633; www.alamo.com).
Avis (800-331-1212; www.avis.com).
Budget (800-527-0700; www.budget.com).
Dollar (800-800-4000; www.dollar.com).
Enterprise (800-736-8222; www.enterprise.com).
Hertz (800-654-3131; www.hertz.com).
National (800-227-7368; www.nationalcar.com).
Thrifty (800-367-2277; just outside airport grounds, reservations required; www.thrifty.com).

Other ground transportation options:

General taxi information (800-578-4111; www.metwashairports.com/ dulles/ground.htm).
Washington Flyer Taxi (703-661-6655, 888-WASHFLY).
General ground transportation (www.metwashairports.com/ dulles/ground.htm).

There are 75 listings for limousine services that serve Dulles. The airport does not endorse any particular one. You can locate them on the Internet through the airport's ground transportation page.

Greyhound Airport Service offers transportation from the airport to various Shenandoah Valley cities. Call 888-BUS-N-FLY for current schedule and rates.

For The Homestead resort: Check with the resort's travel office, 540-839-7648 or 800-838-1766. No regular shuttle service from Dulles, though there is service from the Roanoke airport.

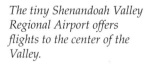

The tiny Shenandoah Valley Regional Airport offers flights to the center of the Valley.

Shenandoah2000

SHENANDOAH VALLEY REGIONAL AIRPORT
(Serving Staunton/Waynesboro and Harrisonburg)
540-234-8304.
www.flyshd.com/airportinfo.htm.
PO Box 125, Weyers Cave, VA 24486.

Commercial airline:

US Airways (800-428-4322; www.usairways.com) Flights go through the hub in Pittsburgh.

General aviation services:

Shenandoah Flight Services (540-234-9789; www.airnav.com/airport/shd/shenandoah_flight_svcs).
Scott Aviation Enterprises (540-234-8900; www.scottavn.com).

Automobile rental:

Avis (800-331-1212; www.avis.com).
Enterprise (800-736-8222; www.enterprise.com).
Hertz (800-654-3131; www.hertz.com).

Taxi:

Harrisonburg City Cab (540-434-2515).
Staunton City Cab (540-886-3471).
Waynesboro City Cab (540-949-8245).

Limousine:

AB Luxury Suburban & Limousine Service (540-248-0597).
A Goff Limo (800-459-5645).
Rodney's Limo & Custom Van (540-885-9895, 540-248-1874).
Valley Limo (540-886-4905).

Renting an Automobile at the Airport

When you make your airline reservation, remember to ask about fly-drive package discounts. When you reserve the car, ask about discounts for AAA, AARP, weeklong rentals, coupons, and any deals that will give you free mileage. Smaller airports may not have all auto models readily available, so if you need a specially equipped car or a minivan, reserve as far in advance as possible.

Be sure to inquire about dropping off your rental vehicle at a different place if you intend to make a one-way trip in either direction in the Valley.

And be aware: Virginia has seatbelt laws that apply to both drivers and passengers, and its speed limits and low-tolerance DUI limits are strictly enforced.

ROANOKE REGIONAL AIRPORT
540-362-1999.
www.roanokeregionalairport.com.
5202 Aviation Dr. NW, Roanoke, VA 24012.

Commercial airlines:

Atlantic Southeast Airlines (Delta commuter carrier; 800-221-1212; www.asa-air.com).
Comair (Delta commuter carrier; 800-221-1212; www.comair.com).
Northwest Airlink (800-225-2525; www.nwairlink.com).
US Airways (800-428-4322; www.usairways.com).
United Express (800-241-6522; www.ual.com).

General aviation services:

Piedmont Hawthorne Aviation (540-563-4401; www.flypiedmont.com/roa).
Executive Air (800-633-8326; www.execair.com).
Hillman Flying Service (540-293-1287).
LC's Flying Service, Inc. (540-362-2501).
Roanoke Aero Services (540-563-5212).
Saker Flying Service (540-293-2448).
Summit Helicopters (540-992-5500).

Automobile rental:

Avis (800-331-1212).
Budget (800-527-0700).
Dollar (800-800-4000).
Enterprise (800-736-8222).
Hertz (800-654-3131).
National (800-227-7368).

Taxi:

Liberty Cab (540-344-1776).
Yellow Cab (540-345-7711).

Limousine:

Roanoke Airport Limousine (800-288-1958, 540-345-7710).
C'artier Limousine (540-982-5466).

Special ground shuttle arrangements have been made with The Homestead resort. For more information or to make reservations, call Homestead's travel office at 540-839-7648 or 800-838-1766.

GENERAL AVIATION

These listings handle only private aircraft. Try www.flyvirginia.com for maps. Call to find out what size craft they can accommodate, hangar fees, conditions, ground transportation, etc.

Winchester Regional Airport (540-662-5786; www.flyvirginia.com/airport/OKV; WRAAOOKV@intelos.net; 491 Airport Rd., Winchester, VA 22602).
Front Royal-Warren County Airport (540-635-3570; www.flyvirginia.com/air port/FRR; Va. Rte. 4, Front Royal, VA 22630).
Sky Bryce Airport (540-856-2121; www.flyvirginia.com/airport/W92; 1982 Fairview Dr., Basye, VA 22810) See Bryce Resort information in Chapter Five, *Lodging*.
Luray Caverns Airport (540-743-6070; www.flyvirginia.com/airport/W45; County Rd. 652, Luray, VA 22835) This airport, between two mountains, is affected by fog more than some of the others.
New Market Airport (540-740-3949; www.flyvirginia.com/airport/8W2; 59 River Rd., Timberville, VA 22853) This airport's mailbox is in Rockingham County, but the actual airport extends into Shenandoah County.
Bridgewater Air Park (540-828-6070; www.airnav.com/airport/VBW; Rte. 727, PO Box 7, Bridgewater, VA 22812) Serves the Harrisonburg area.
Eagle's Nest (540-943-4447; www.airnav.com/airport/W13; Rte. 5., Waynes-boro, VA 22980).
Ingalls Field (540-839-5326; Rte. 703, Hot Springs, VA 24445) For The Home-stead resort.

BY TRAIN

Amtrak (800-USA-RAIL; www.amtrak.com) does not directly serve any of the Valley's gateway cities. Connection stops closest to Roanoke (Clifton Forge) and Winchester (Staunton) are on *The Cardinal*, a Chicago-D.C. train via Indianapolis, Cincinnati, and Charleston. You also can take Amtrak to Washington, D.C., and be just an hour away from Winchester.

Autumn Colors Express is a fall foliage trip from Washington, D.C., to Clifton Forge via Waynesboro. It's run by the Washington chapter of the National Railway Historical Society (www.dcnrhs.org; infor@dcnrhs.org; PO Box 151; Alexandria, VA 22313), but there is no guarantee that the tour will be held every year. Seeing the Valley's beauty by train is not inexpensive, either. Prices can range from around $100 round-trip for a coach seat to about $400 for a prime, dome car seat. If you're willing to drive to Waynesboro, about two hours south of D.C., the Waynesboro-Clifton Forge round-trip fare is about one-third the cost (coach only available on that leg).

GETTING AROUND THE VALLEY

G etting there (no matter where *there* is) is indeed part of the enjoyment of a trip into the Shenandoah. The main highways running north and south in the Valley are Route 11, I-81, which roughly parallels Route 11 without going through most of the towns, Route 340, and Route 42. Route 220 is a north-south scenic route that runs across the mountain counties — a road that seems to run along the top of the world.

The primary east-west roads are Route 250 (the Parkersburg-Staunton Turnpike and also a way into Highland County), I-64, and Routes 55, 211, 33, and 39.

North-South Routes

I-81: This interstate runs through central New York state, down into central Virginia and the Valley, and shoots farther south into Tennessee. The stretch from Winchester to Roanoke is approximately 178 miles — three hours plus — of rolling, four-lane highway. If you want to "make time" and are not a fan of slower, scenic roads for between-point travel, you can take I-81 and still enjoy scenery.

I-81 is the "fast" route, but that fact and its multistate run make it a major north-south commercial trucking route. No matter the time of day or time of year, you *will* share the road with an incredibly large number of tractor-trailer trucks. And be advised: The large number of colleges and universities along the road make late summer, early autumn, and the first two weeks of May extremely heavy traffic times. Fall foliage and college football games also contribute to traffic excesses.

Even if time is a factor for most of your journey, I would highly recommend taking at least a small part of the trip along Route 340, Route 11, Skyline Drive or the Blue Ridge Parkway. Even before you've moved far enough away from the interstate to drown out its incessant hum, the world of the Valley envelops you in calm.

Route 11: One of the oldest paved roads in the state, its importance to early commerce is so strong that its mud and clay were overlaid with macadam in the 19th century. Also known as the Valley Pike, this route runs parallel to I-81 for much of the time and sticks close to the North Fork of the Shenandoah River as it makes its way through the Valley. It winds in charming fashion over hill and dale, near river and farm, through towns and past stores, inns, battlefields, and fantastic restaurants. To save time, one can travel the major distances on the interstate and, once ensconced, travel up and down Route 11, stopping as often as desired along the way.

Route 340: This road runs along the highly scenic South Fork of the Shenandoah River between Berryville and Waynesboro. There are many spots along this route for taking photos of the river and mountains — not marked spots and

Joan Leotta

As one drives along Route 340 from Massanutten in Rockingham County to Jordan Hollow in Page County, the views of the Shenandoah River and her mountains are spectacular.

overlooks, but simply places where you can pull over and pull out the camera. This is another route for those with a lot of time. It's the road to take to Luray and is closer to the Skyline Drive entrance points than either Route 11 or I-81. The upper part of 340 between I-66 and the West Virginia line is an enclave of bucolic small villages with world-class restaurants. Below I-66 the road takes on a more old-fashioned feel, more of a "oneness" with the mountains themselves — perhaps it's the proximity to the river.

Route 42: A north-south road from Timberville to Harrisonburg and then out into the country, parallel to the railroad right of way. Just south of Harrisonburg, take the turnoff for Route 760 (and then Route 767) to see the Natural Chimneys, a venue for jousting and one of the great natural wonders of the Valley. At the town of Goshen the road takes a turn to the west and goes through Millboro, up to Warm Springs and Bacova, to the West Virginia border.

Route 220: The route takes travelers from Highland County, through Bath and Alleghany Counties, curves east/west a smidge (along I-64), and then heads down through Botetourt County to Fincastle, the county seat. Fascinating attractions abound along the old road, from the Monterey and McDowell battlefields to the maple sugar camps of Highland County to the top-of-the-world views that awe travelers on the way to The Homestead resort. Covington's covered bridge and waterfalls and Clifton Forge's railroad museum hold attention along with the road's own natural wonders. After the road turns north-south again and enters Botetourt County, there is a sign for Eagle Rock — definitely worth a stop.

East-West Routes

Route 55: An interesting east-west crossover between Front Royal and Strasburg is provided by Route 55. If you're visiting interior places in the northern half of the Valley, this is an ideal option. The highway continues past Strasburg up into the mountains, too.

Route 211: In the Valley, it extends from Thornton Gap on Skyline Drive, passes Luray, then continues through George Washington National Forest and onto Timberville and Broadway.

Route 33: Provides another entry point (at Swift Ridge Gap) to Skyline Drive. It runs through Page and Rockingham Counties and is a scenic route to take from the Harrisonburg/Massanutten resort area to Shenandoah National Park or to Hawksbill in Stanley.

I-64: This is the primary route for travelers from Richmond and Charlottesville who want to reach the Valley via Staunton/Waynesboro. I-64 then turns south (joining 81) and heads east-west again from Lexington, making it a main access road to the mountain counties. The cities of Covington and Clifton Forge are part of the trip, along with wonderful views of countryside and mountains.

Route 250: If you want to head west from Staunton to Monterey in Highland County (the sugar festival is a must!), then take Route 250, also known as the Parkersburg-Staunton Turnpike.

Route 39: To enter the mountain counties through the wondrous Goshen Pass, leave I-64 just beyond Lexington for Route 39 and proceed west on that road through Goshen and up to Millboro Springs, Route 220, and The Homestead resort.

TRAFFIC, ROAD CONDITIONS, AND MAPS

For up-to-date information on the state of the roads (in leaf season you'll really be glad you called), maps, and other details, use **Travel Shenandoah** or the **Virginia Department of Transportation** (VDOT) **Highway Helpline**.

Travel Shenandoah, 800-578-4111 or www.travelshenandoah.com, is a free, real-time traffic and tourism information service for Virginia's I-81 corridor. It is the first in a planned statewide family of similar services.

VDOT's Highway Helpline (800-367-ROAD; TTY users call 800-432-1843) covers the entire state. For more specific information on a particular road or county, call the appropriate VDOT regional office:

Staunton District VDOT (540-332-9075; stauntoninfo@vdot.state.va.us; Commerce Road, PO Box 2249, Staunton, VA 24402) This office covers most of the Shenandoah region: Alleghany, Augusta, Bath, Clarke, Frederick, Highland, Page, Rockbridge, Rockingham, Shenandoah, and Warren Counties.

Salem District VDOT (540-387-5320; saleminfo@VirginiaDOT.org; 731 Harrison Ave., PO Box 3071, Salem, VA 24153) This office covers many counties, including Botetourt and Roanoke in the Shenandoah Valley.

The best statewide maps of the area are free. Two resources are the **Virginia Department of Transportation** (804-786-5731, TTY 800-828-1120; www.vdot .state.va.us; 1401 E. Broad St., Richmond, VA 23219) for road maps and the **Virginia Tourism Corporation** (www.virginia.org) for an assortment of specialized maps and other tour information. If you wait until you drive to the state border, be sure to stop at a welcome center for a map.

The two most frequently requested statewide driving maps are the *Official State Transportation Map* and *A Map of the Scenic Roads in Virginia*. Specialized tour maps (Civil War routes, antiquing maps, winery routes, black history tours, etc.) are published by the tourism corporation and private groups. They are generally free and widely available at state and local tourism offices, chambers of commerce, and economic development offices. (See Chapter Eight, *Information*.)

Get Out Your Compass

When folks today speak of the northern part, or "top" of the Valley, they generally mean the northernmost counties: Frederick, Warren, and Clarke. But if you look at older maps of the area, you might think your world has been turned upside down.

From colonial times until the modern era, river flow took precedence, as rivers were often the best bet for traveling. Since the Shenandoah River flows north, the "upper valley" was the upstream end of the river — what we call the middle to lower part of the Valley today. The very lowest part of today's Valley, speaking north to south, is actually not geographically a part of the Shenandoah Valley at all. Salem and Roanoke lie in the New River Valley.

Wonder how many rivers there are in the Valley basin? Do many of them — the Sherando, Gerando, Sherundo and Gerundo — seem to be in the same place? Don't worry — they're all the Shenandoah. The South Fork forms at Port Republic in Rockingham County and flows up the eastern side of the Massanutten Mountains through Page County. The North Fork begins around Timberville and flows up on the west side of the mountains, meeting with the Potomac at Harpers Ferry.

Confused yet? Well, how about the disappearing mountains? If you've been enjoying an old map or a Civil War novel that refers to North and South Mountains, you might wonder why they don't appear on a modern map. They are not invisible. They're simply "hidden" in the guise of new names — North Mountain is Massanutten and South Mountain is the Blue Ridge range along the Valley counties.

Ready to proceed? Keep your map handy, but don't worry. In this book, north is geographic north, and all names for sites are the ones found on modern maps.

ALONG THE WAY

Almost 2,000 miles of Virginia road sport little blue signs with a cardinal. These designate the road as scenic to call attention to the particular beauty of perhaps lesser-known places.

Virginia has a number of scenic roadside overlooks, including those found

Confederate breastworks from Fort Edward Johnson. (Highland County).

Joan Leotta

along the Blue Ridge Parkway and Skyline Drive. Aptly named "waysides," they often mark gems of historic interest. The following waysides and scenic overlooks are my particular favorites in the Shenandoah:

Visitors from Texas surely will want to see the **Sam Houston Wayside,** which marks the birthplace (March 2, 1793) of this hero with a huge piece of pink Texas granite. The wayside is on the right side of Route 11 north, 100 yards off I-81.

Just northwest of Monterey on Route 250 is a **scenic overlook** that appears to be on the top of the world. From here you can look out onto the Jackson River and beyond into West Virginia. According to the marker, the pass below is one that George Washington used to survey western lands in 1756.

The **Confederate Breastworks** are also along Route 250. Here, Confederate soldiers constructed a long, trenchlike fortification to guard and protect the way through the Shenandoah Mountains during the early part of the Civil War. The breastworks are right alongside the road. If you have time for a short hike, a well-marked trail yields incredible beauty in the form of rare wildflowers, majestic trees, and spectacular vistas across the Cowpasture River Valley.

Falling Spring surprises drivers along Route 220 about seven miles north of Covington. Here, 7,000 gallons of water a minute plunge over a sheer 200-foot bluff to the rocks below. Roadside signs note its immediacy, but we drove past and saw the falls in the mirror the first time! Parking is limited — be sure to park at an approved spot, since the road is winding and narrow — but the sight is well worth the stop.

Another spot of incredible beauty is **Goshen Pass** on Route 39, one of the places where pioneers trekked through a gap in the mountains to head west. Goshen Pass is without a doubt one of the most magnificent places to be experienced in the state. Here, the Maury River is shielded on one side by a rock "wall," and trees stand guard by the walking path. **Goshen Roadside** is part of the state park system. It offers a bathroom (when it's open) and a place to picnic (always open).

Two of Virginia's remaining eight covered bridges are in the Valley:

Meem's Bottom Bridge (Exit 269 off I-81 in Shenandoah County) Follow Route 730 from the exit to Route 11, then go north 0.9 mile to Route 720. You will find the bridge a few hundred yards down Route 720 west, four miles north of New Market and two miles south of Mount Jackson. You can drive over this bridge, over the North Fork of the Shenandoah River, and stop at either end to snap pictures.

Humpback Bridge (Exit 10 off I-64 just outside of Covington) This James River bridge, constructed in 1858, is restricted to pedestrian traffic. Its humpback design element supposedly gave it more strength. In 1929 a modern steel truss bridge nearby replaced it as the main transport over the James. The Humpback languished until 1954, when the Covington Chamber of Commerce and Covington Professional Women's Club joined forces to restore and preserve it. The small park has benches and an ample gravel parking area, making this an easy-to-reach oasis of calm.

Shenandoah2000

One of the two covered bridges in the Valley, the Meem's Bottom Bridge at Mount Jackson, was rebuilt after a 1976 fire and still carries traffic.

CHAPTER THREE
Entertain the Possibilities
CULTURAL ATTRACTIONS

Shenandoah2000

Belle Grove Plantation House played the important roles of Union headquarters and hospital during the nearby battle of Cedar Creek.

Using the word "culture" to describe this set of attractions is simply a way of organizing. This chapter covers the historic sites and homes, museums, gardens, battlefields, universities, festivals, and libraries in the Valley. Within each category the attractions are grouped by area. With a few exceptions (arboretums, for example), activities that are primarily sport or outdoor or enjoyment of nature are grouped under *Outdoor Recreation*, the next chapter.

The listings are by category, arranged from north to south. Categories containing more than a dozen entries are subdivided by county. Where there are fewer than a dozen, they are listed in north-to-south order. Directions are general; call for details.

ARBORETUMS AND PUBLIC GARDENS

STATE ABORETUM OF VIRGINIA
540-837-1758.

The State Arboretum, also known as Blandy Experimental Farm, consists of 700 acres containing more than 8,000 varieties of trees and shrubs. If

www.virginia.edu/~blandy
/home.html.
400 Blandy Farm Lane,
Boyce, VA 22620.
About 10 miles southeast of
Winchester at Rtes. 50 and
340.
Open: Daily dawn to dusk.
Admission: Free.

you like flowers and plants and are visiting the Valley, take some time to stop here. One of its outstanding features is the Virginia Native Plants Trail, a fascinating floral time machine. Not only will you see plants that are in the state today, you can experience the fragrances and loveliness that enchanted colonial-era settlers.

Another spectacular feature is a row of 300 ginkgo trees. In the fall, the yellow fan-shaped leaves of that row have an almost otherworldly beauty about them. Activities for families and plant lovers of all ages make this a truly fun place to visit. The Web site offers a bloom calendar.

**EDITH J. CARRIER
ARBORETUM**
540-568-3194.
www.jmu.edu/arboretum.
Nicholas House, MSC 7015,
Harrisonburg, VA 22807.
Exit 245 from I-81; enter the
James Madison University
campus and follow signs.
Open: Daily dawn to dusk.
Admission: Free; call for
guided tours Mon.–Fri.
9–5.

Spring and fall are the two most spectacular times for visiting this mostly outdoor facility due to the abundance of deciduous trees and flowering shrubs. This small arboretum's springtime strengths include its bulbs as well as its shrubs. (In fall, JMU sponsors a sale of those same bulbs).

Walls of oaks along the roads provide a majestic backdrop for autumn drive-throughs. In spring their buds are a backdrop for banks of Virginia's state flower/tree, the dogwood, a spindly lower-story tree that brings some of the first color to the hills.

The noteworthy herb garden and a swampy bog garden offer a look at some less familiar plants. The Sinclair Garden, a highly stylized array of Japanese plants, rhododendrons, and more, provides an elegant place to relax.

Its natural amphitheater acts as a venue for stage and music groups. When there is no special activity, the area seems a fairy hideaway. Trails meander down from the amphitheater through the various well-marked varieties of woodland flora on display.

Check ahead, especially if you're seeking solitude. The area can get quite crowded around the time of plant and bulb sales and during other university activities, requiring parking at another part of campus.

**MILLENNIUM GROVE
ARBORETUM**
540-234-9261, Ext. 2349, or
888-750-2722, Ext. 2349.
www.br.cc.va.us/arbor
etum.
Box 80, Weyers Cave, VA
24486.
Use Exit 235 from I-81;
follow signs to Blue Ridge

This arboretum, begun in 1987, is a true living museum and research unit. Studies on the trees keep the facility connected to the farming community. In addition, the site maintains samples of all of the native and naturalized plants now grown in Virginia.

The Millennium Grove, which commemorates 25 events in state history, is one of the top draws here. Each tree (grown from seed) in the grove is a de-

Community College and arboretum.
Open: Daily dawn to dusk.
Admission: Free.

scendent of a living witness to history. Be aware, however, that the selection of events and trees was based on availability of the natural matter in spring 2000, when the grove was installed, and not upon a particular effort to include some historical events while excluding others.

The first tree (by event chronology) is the Berkeley Plantation 1619 white ash. This tree welcomed the first settlers from England and witnessed their first Thanksgiving. The George Washington holly from Mount Vernon commemorates the role he played as first president and as the "Father of American Landscaping." The collection's Brompton white oak is a descendent of the 1862 witness to the battle at Fredericksburg, one of Lee's greatest victories. The most contemporary tree in the collection is a 1963 crab apple, descended from the tree that shades the grave of President John F. Kennedy in Arlington, Virginia.

BOXERWOOD GARDEN
540-463-2697.
www.boxerwood.com.
webmaster@boxerwood
.com.
963 Ross Rd., Lexington, VA 24450.
Open: Mar. 15–Nov., daily dawn to dusk; guided tours Tues.–Sun. 9–4, call for appt.
Admission: $5.

This little arboretum and nature center complex includes 15 acres of trees and native and exotic plants. Of special note are its magnolias, dogwood, rhododendrons, azaleas, and Japanese maples. Each plant/tree/shrub is carefully labeled, making the self-guided tour informative.

The nature center segment of the complex is divided into several habitats — woodland, meadow, wetlands, and pioneer forest, all with marked walking paths to help visitors enjoy them. The educational focus is on gaining a greater understanding of how various plant and landscape features act in different environments.

It takes about an hour to see the grounds. There is no concession area on-site, but picnics are permitted.

DABNEY COLLEGE ARBORETUM
540-863-2800, 877-733-7522.
www.dl.vccs.edu.
Dabney S. Lancaster Community College.
1000 Dabney Dr., Clifton Forge, VA 24422.
Open: Daily dawn to dusk.
Admission: Free.

A summer highlight of this two-acre, campus-based education arboretum is the wisteria-covered arbor at the entrance. Nine separate gardens occupy the site with more than 700 labeled plants for visitors to enjoy.

Other gardens of note in the Shenandoah Valley area are those at the **Glen Burnie House** in *Winchester*, Frederick County (see "Historic Houses & Sites"), and the **Buffalo Springs Herb Farm** (see Chapter Seven, *Shopping*) near *Raphine* in Rockbridge County.

Private homes often open up in the spring for charity-sponsored garden shows. Check with the local tourism office to see if your spring visit coincides with one of these tour opportunities.

ARTS AND CRAFTS CENTERS

This section covers those galleries and centers that are either sponsored by a local government entity or university. Admission to these sites is free. Other art galleries and local crafts are found in Chapter Seven, *Shopping*. Art museums are in this chapter under the heading "Museums."

Blue Ridge Arts and Crafts Center (540-635-9909; brac@shentel.net; 301 E. Main St., Front Royal, VA 22630) Wander in for a constantly changing exhibition of the ouevre of local visual artists. The center offers pamphlets and brochures on their sponsored musical and theater programss and on other area performing arts events. The center also offers classes in the arts. Open: Tues.–Fri. 10–4, Sat. 10–2.

The Art Group (540-477-4131; www.theartgroup.org/exhibiti.html; tag@shentel .net; 5906 Main St., PO Box 676, Mount Jackson, VA 22842) The Art Group is a nonprofit cooperative of Shenandoah Valley artists. Its members sponsor workshops and performing arts events in the community. You can preview the artist of the month and learn about activities at its Web site. Resident and visiting artists' works are displayed for viewing and sale throughout the building. Open: Mon., Thurs., Fri., Sat. 10–5, Sun. 12–5.

Arts Council of the Valley (540-801-8779; www.valleyarts.org; PO Box 1057, Harrisonburg, VA 22803) Nonprofit group supports local cultural arts programs, area artists, and arts organizations, but has no specific exhibit/sales space as of this writing. Some member pieces are displayed in Court Square Theater in downtown Harrisonburg, where the council sponsors many performing arts activities.

Also in Harrisonburg are two galleries specializing in the work of students and faculty:

Eastern Mennonite University Hartzler Library Art Gallery (540-432-4175; third floor of Hartzler Library, 1200 Park Rd., Harrisonburg, VA 22802) Call for hours.

James Madison University, Sawhill Gallery (540-568-6407; Duke Hall, Harrisonburg, VA 22807) Enter main gate and follow the signs. Call for hours.

ARTISAN CENTER OF VIRGINIA
540-946-3294, 877-508-6069.

ACV is a nonprofit visual arts organization led by a professional staff and a volunteer board of trustees. ACV opened a 3,500-square-foot retail and

www.artisanscenterof
virginia.org.
ACV@nexet.net.
601 Shenandoah Village Dr.,
Waynesboro, VA 22980.
Open: Mon.–Sat. 10–6,
Sun. 12:30–5:30.

exhibition gallery at the Waynesboro Village shopping mall in June 2000.

The center is as much a showcase/museum as a store. Various Virginia artists are featured in a section of the space, while the rest of the room is devoted to a variety of art. All is for sale, but browsers are welcome to simply drink in the beauty, too. Pottery, porcelain, oil paintings, photography, weavings, and jewelry are well represented. The staff is knowledgeable about the various genres and the artists.

The center is a short walk from the P. Buckley Moss Museum and an outlet mall — one parking spot gets you to all three.

STAUNTON AUGUSTA ART CENTER
540-885-2028.
saartscenter@aol.com.
1 Gypsy Hill Park, Staunton, VA 24401.
Open: Wed.–Fri. 10–5, Sat. 10–2; Mon. and Tues. by appt.

The center offers classes for children and seniors and holds six six-week shows each year (closed for two weeks in between exhibits) along with special May and Christmas shows. Call ahead to see if there is going to be a show during your visit.

ARTS COUNCIL OF THE BLUE RIDGE
540-342-5790.
www.theartscouncil.org.
info@theartscouncil.org.
20 Church Ave. SE,
Roanoke, VA 24011.

ACBR does not have a gallery to visit, but the group sponsors juried events, including a city art show. ACBR also offers a variety of services for local artists and showcases many performing artists from the community. If you're interested in the cutting edge of art in the Roanoke area, contact this group before or during your visit. Local newspapers and the tourism office carry material on the council's performing arts programs.

THE ALLEGHANY HIGHLANDS ARTS COUNCIL
540-962-6220.
ArtsCo@aol.com.
185 N. Maple Ave.,
Covington, VA 24426.

Geared more to the performing arts, the council also works with visual artists. It features touring performers, dance, comedy, drama, and student series, as well as performances of the Alleghany Highlands Chorale and Orchestra.

ALLEGHANY HIGHLANDS ARTS AND CRAFTS CENTER
540-862-4447.
www.alleghanyhighlands
.com/arts.htm.

Located in downtown Clifton Forge, the center offers locally made crafts and art, including watercolors, oils, pottery, weavings, and photos that share space with history exhibits. There are many

439 E. Ridgeway St., Clifton
   Forge, VA 24422.
Open: May–Dec., Mon.–Sat.
   10–4:30; Jan.–Apr.,
   Tues.–Sat. 10–4:30.

small, lovely items here (in both size and price), as
well as large works of art.

BATTLEFIELDS AND CIVIL WAR REENACTMENTS

Shenandoah2000

In October, Cedar Creek's fields fill with reenactors recalling the thunder of cannon and hooves of the famous cavalry encounter of 1864.

During the Civil War, hardly an inch of the Shenandoah Valley was not traversed by a foot soldier or a cavalry steed outfitted in either blue or gray. Countless lives were lost and reputations established or ruined as valiant military actions were fought on this scenic ground.

Strategically, the Shenandoah Valley represented the granary of the Confederacy and the pathway to and from the North. As a result, it was not unusual for towns in the Valley to change hands during the war. Winchester, for example, is said to have passed from Confederate to Union hands and vice versa at least 72 times!

This critical area was the scene of two major campaigns: Jackson's Valley Campaign of 1862 and the Campaign of 1864. Today, the sites of the area's battles, actions, and skirmishes form an informative, scenic, and historically important visitor "tourground."

In this section we have tried to cover the major battlefields, how to visit them, and the contacts and/or dates for reenactments. For true history buffs, the following Web site lists even the lesser-known skirmishes: www.angelfire.com/va3/valleywar/battle/figure7.html.

Virginia Civil War Trails maps are available at all visitor centers, online at www.civilwar-va.com, or by calling 888-CIVIL-WAR. **The Civil War Trail** allows visitors to follow the Valley Campaigns of 1862 and 1864; 40 individual sites are marked.

Another source of information is the **Shenandoah Valley Civil War Information Center** located in the Kurtz Building at 2 N. Cameron St. in Winchester. Call 540-722-6367.

Living history reenactments are frequently held on both the major and lesser-known battlefields, often close to the battle anniversary date. The Web sites listed below offer more information on the art of reenacting. Local tourism offices (see Chapter Eight, *Information*) also will be able to inform visitors of activities taking place during their visit.

Material in this chapter is listed county by county, north to south. The sidebar "Month by Month" listings below will give you a quick reference to battle dates (and possible reenactments) to facilitate your planning.

Remember that not all battlefield properties are in public hands. Some are still privately held, and the privacy and property rights of the owner must be respected.

Web sites of interest include:

> www.cwc.lsu.edu/cwc/links/reenacts.htm
> www.highlandcounty.org
> www.svta.org
> www.civilwar-va.com

Month-by-Month Listing of Larger Valley Engagements

Mar. 2 — Waynesboro	July 20 — Rutherford's Farm
Mar. 23 — Kernstown I	July 24 — Kernstown II
May 8 — McDowell	Aug. 16 — Guard Hill Front Royal
May 13 — New Market	
May 23 — Front Royal	Sept. 3–4 — Berryville
May 25 — Winchester	Sept. 19 — Opequon
	(a.k.a. Winchester III)
June 8 — Cross Keys	Sept. 21–22 — Fisher's Hill
June 9 — Port Republic	
June 13–15 — Winchester II	Oct. 9 — Tom's Brook
June 17–18 — Cool Springs	Oct. 19 — Cedar Creek
(Clarke County)	

FREDERICK, CLARKE, AND WARREN COUNTIES

Mosby Heritage Area (Rte. 50, Clarke County) There are many markers along this roadway commemorating Colonel John Singleton Mosby's activities here. The road is now a four-lane highway, but a smaller version traversing roughly the same area was in place during the Civil War and was a major thoroughfare for troops and Mosby. The preservation society has declared the entire site a heritage area.

Cool Spring (Rte. 7, east of Berryville, Clarke County) Be on the lookout for the state historical markers that tell about the pursuit of Confederate General Jubal Early after his foray into the suburbs of Washington, D.C. On July 18, 1864, Early was able to turn back the Union forces, including those led by future president Rutherford B. Hayes. Cool Spring, a large plantation, was located nearby and gives this action its name.

Front Royal

Front Royal in Warren County saw some of the bloodier episodes of the Civil War, and the infamous Mosby-Sheridan feud had its origins here. Colonel John Mosby's men shot a Union officer who had fallen from his horse. In retaliation, when Union General Philip Sheridan captured six of Mosby's men, he had George Custer execute them instead of holding them as prisoners of war. Before execution they were paraded through the streets of the town with nooses around their necks. The men were hanged in the town and are buried in Stonewall Cemetery. Additionally, the following markers note activity within the town:

Battle of Front Royal Marker and Map (Rtes. 55 and 340/522 at Riverton) Two markers give a brief account of the Battle of Front Royal.

Mosby's Men Markers (Near the Twi-Lite Motel and on Guard Hill, just off Route 66 on N. Royal Ave.) These markers indicate where Mosby's men were hanged.

Confederate Monument (In front of the courthouse in the Market Square) Dedicated on July 4, 1911, to the memory of those who fought for the Confederacy, the monument is a lovely example of turn-of-the-century sculpture. The courthouse itself is an interesting building, but it is not open for tours.

Brother Against Brother Marker (Chester and Royal Aves.) Here a battle took place between two regiments from the same state fighting for different causes. Maryland, a border state, had both Northern and Southern sympathizers, more than enough to support regiments for both sides. At the noted corner in Front Royal, the First Maryland Regiment, C.S.A., fought the First Maryland Regiment, U.S.A.

For information on other significant area sites, see "Museums" later in this chapter.

Winchester and Kernstown

Winchester, in Frederick County, was the site of three battles either in the town itself or on its edge, and nearby Kernstown was the site of two. Winchester was of critical importance, as it was the major transportation hub of the Valley and the northern end of the Valley Turnpike, a macadamized road running south to Staunton. This "pike" represented the north-south corridor for the shipment of supplies and the rapid movement of troops.

There is no fee to see any of these sites. For more detail, see www.winchester va.com or stop at a **Visitor Orientation Center**. The Winchester center is on Rte. 11 south of town. The Kernstown sites are on farmland run by the **Kernstown Preservation Group** (PO Box 1327, Winchester, VA 22601). Follow the brown signs from downtown Winchester for Opequon Church and Kernstown Battlefield. Centers are open Apr.–Oct., Sat. 10–4, Sun. 12–4.

First Winchester: Fought on May 25, 1862, the First Battle of Winchester occurred midpoint in Stonewall Jackson's brilliant series of victories in the Valley. Following the capture of Front Royal, Jackson moved toward Winchester. Retreating Union troops deployed in an attempt to halt the Confederate pursuit. Bowers Hill and Camp Hill saw heavy fighting, and the Union line was enfiladed and eventually collapsed. The Union forces then retreated through Winchester and northward. Today the only area left easily accessible is on Camp Hill south of Key Street and on Bowers Hill behind Handley High School.

Second Winchester: In preparation for an invasion of the North, General Robert E. Lee ordered Richard Ewell to attack Federal forces at Winchester. In the ensuing three-day battle, June 13–15, 1863, Ewell defeated and routed the Federal troops under Robert Milroy. This defeat of the Union forces culminated in the capture of approximately 3,000 Union troops at Stephenson's Depot and fueled high hopes for the invasion of the North, hopes which would be dashed at Gettysburg.

Third Winchester: The Third Battle of Winchester occurred on Sept. 19, 1864, and is often referred to as the Battle of Opequon. It is of particular significance because it is the largest battle of the Civil War in the Shenandoah Valley. Casualties were extreme in this hard-fought battle, which marked the beginning of the rise of Union General Philip Sheridan in the Valley and the decline of Confederate dominance.

First Kernstown: Fought March 23, 1862, this is part of Jackson's Valley Campaign. Many historians consider this to be the only battle "lost" by Jackson during the campaign. The vulnerability of Washington, D.C., became evident, forcing a reassignment of Union troops westward from the peninsula, thus compromising the Peninsula Campaign against Richmond. The area of the most intense fighting at the first battle of Kernstown was near the Glass House. Much of the property is preserved as it was, but it is not open to the public. Instead, roadside markers present the battle action.

Second Kernstown: This part of the 1864 Valley Campaign was fought on July 24, 1864, and is considered the Confederate victory that forced General

Ulysses Grant to re-organize Union troops in one district under the command of Sheridan. Heavy fighting took place on Pritchard's Hill and in the vicinity of Opequon Church. Roadside signs tell the history of the battle. The Opequon Church is still standing and wayside exhibits in the parking lot interpret both battles of Kernstown. While the church building is not generally open for tours, one can certainly stroll through the graveyard.

Other sites in or near Winchester include:

Rose Hill (March 23, 1862) Take Amherst St. west out of the city and turn left on Merriman, then go about three miles to a marker that describes the action where Confederate infantry defended a wall until they ran out of ammunition. The property is part of the Glen Burnie development

Rutherford's Farm (July 20, 1864) Just outside of Winchester on Rte. 11. William Averell's Union troops defeated Stephen Ramseur's Confederates here in a sudden assault. Ramseur withdrew toward Winchester. Confederates assumed a defensive position at Fisher's Hill following this defeat.

Stephen's City (historic Newtown) Go south on Rte. 11 from Winchester and look for the roadside marker. Stonewall Jackson's troops saw action here just before the 1862 Battle of Winchester. Area buildings later became hospitals for Union troops. Markers tell the story.

Middletown

CEDAR CREEK BATTLEFIELD AND FOUNDATION
540-869-2064, 888-628-1864.
www.cedarcreekbattlefield
.org.
8437 Valley Pike, PO Box 229, Middletown, VA 22645.
Open: Apr.–Nov., daily 10–4. Call ahead other times of the year.
Admission: Museum $2. Access to battlefield is free; self-guided tour book is $6. Call ahead to reserve guided tours ($25/vehicle).

On the morning of Oct. 19, 1864, just before dawn, Jubal Early's Confederate troops left their trenches just south of Cedar Creek to surprise the Union troops who were encamped just north of the creek. This attack resulted in the retreat of the Union forces to a position west of the Valley Pike. A Union stand on Cemetery Hill resulted in heavy casualties, but it also broke the momentum of Confederate assaults.

Upon General Philip Sheridan's arrival from Winchester, Union troops were re-organized and Sheridan himself rode his line in an act of leadership now referred to as "Sheridan's Ride." Union cavalry on both flanks of the Confederate line attacked. A general assault on the Confederate center of the line met stiff resistance, and continued pressure caused the Confederate forces to fall back across Cedar Creek. Early lost most of his artillery when the bridge at Spangler's Mill collapsed.

Further pursuit by Union cavalry ended at Fisher's Hill with a heavy Confederate loss of cannon, wagons, men, and battle flags. Rarely has any battle swung so drastically as Cedar Creek, moving from a stunning Confederate success to a complete Union victory by the end of the day. This was Sheridan's last major battle of the 1864 Valley Campaign, and was one of the two largest battles fought in the Shenandoah.

This Union victory is considered pivotal since it raised Union morale and, along with General William Sherman's campaign to Atlanta, gave a needed boost to President Lincoln's bid for re-election. Cedar Creek is considered the battle that sealed the defeat of the Confederacy in the Shenandoah Valley.

The small on-site museum has many battle relics. Locally made craft items and a great selection of Civil War books make the gift shop a worthwhile stop as well. The staff is very knowledgeable and is glad to talk about the battle.

Each October, large-scale reenactments are held on the property, which is now owned by a preservation foundation. The view, unchanged since the battle, makes this a special stop.

SHENANDOAH COUNTY

Strasburg

STONEWALL JACKSON MUSEUM AND CRYSTAL CAVERNS
(a.k.a. Hupp's Hill Battlefield Park & Study Center)

(See listings under "Museums" in this chapter and "Caves" in Chapter Four, *Outdoor Recreation*.)

STRASBURG TRAIN STATION / MUSEUM
540-465-9197.
440 E. King St., Strasburg, VA 22657.
Open: May–Oct., daily 10–4.
Admission: Adults $2.

This is where Stonewall Jackson returned locomotives to the service of the Confederacy after hijacking them in Harpers Ferry in April 1861.

Other sites south of Strasburg include:

Fisher's Hill Marker: Just south of Strasburg, not far from the intersection of I-66 and I-81, this marker commemorates the place where, in the fall of 1864, the forces of Philip Sheridan and Jubal Early fought. Five Medal of Honor recipients and two future U.S. presidents, William McKinley and Rutherford B. Hayes, fought here. The 215-acre site in the hamlet of Fisher's Hill is owned by The Civil War Preservation Trust and cared for by The Strasburg Guards. A self-guided walking tour (follow the green signs) is open to the public without charge. Follow signs from Exit 298 off I-81 to Strasburg along Rte. 11 after the Stonewall Jackson Museum.

Edinburg Mill: Two Civil War Trails signs in the parking lot of the mill on Rte. 11 describe the action. This 1850 mill survived the Sheridan-ordered burnings of late September-early October 1864. The mill's Stoney Creek also was used by Confederates earlier in the war as a defensive line to delay the Federal advance on Valley Pike.

Narrow Passage: Just south of Woodstock on Rte. 11, this is where Stonewall Jackson ordered Jedediah Hotchkiss to make a map of the Shenandoah Valley on March 26, 1862.

Mount Jackson: A bit farther south on Rte. 11, it housed a Confederate hospital complex.

Rude's Hill: Near the Meem's Bottom covered bridge (See Chapter Four, *Outdoor Recreation*), Stonewall Jackson camped here in 1862 and Jubal Early halted the "Woodstock Races" here in 1864. (See Tom's Brook, below.)

Tom's Brook: Take Exit 291 off I-81; Civil War bugle markers guide you to the spot. On Oct. 9, 1864, Union and Confederate cavalries clashed, causing Confederates to flee in what was referred to by Valley residents and Union troops as the "Woodstock Races." Two former West Point roommates, Tom Rosser, C.S.A., and George Custer, U.S.A., fought each other here.

New Market

NEW MARKET BATTLEFIELD STATE HISTORICAL PARK AND HALL OF VALOR MUSEUM
540-740-3101.
www4.vmi.edu/museum/nm.
8895 George Collins Parkway, PO Box 1864, New Market, VA 22844.
Open: Daily 9–5.
Admission: Adult $8, children 6–13 $4, under 6 free.

One admission fee covers entrance to the battlefield site and to the Hall of Valor Museum, a $2 million facility built by VMI alumni. The award-winning 45-minute film, *Field of Lost Shoes*, a powerful part of the presentation, memorializes each Virginia Military Institute student who died in this battle. This film is a particularly affecting tale for teens, since 247 teen-age VMI students were among the soldiers on this field.

The park covers about 280 acres, some adjacent to the steep bluffs overlooking the North Fork of the Shenandoah River. Also included is the Bushong Farm wheat field, where the boys of VMI charged a Union cannon for the glory of the Old South. Here, the young men learned both the glory and horror of war.

On May 15, 1864, the cadets and regulars together climbed the fences of the Bushong Farm and then advanced through a field so muddy that their shoes were pulled from their feet. The wheat field came to be known as "The Field of Lost Shoes." The Confederate charge continued to the top of Bushong's Hill, where the Southerners overran the Federals and drove them from the field. The cadets even captured a cannon, a feat visitors can pretend to duplicate by charging across a field still regularly planted with wheat. Ten cadets died and 47 were wounded in the action. (Overall there were 600 Southern casualties and 800 Northern.)

The Hall of Valor Museum has been operating since 1970. Its discovery room helps younger visitors become familiar with Civil War history through the use of hands-on activities.

PAGE COUNTY

Barbee Monument (E. Main St., Luray) This statue of a suffering Confederate soldier stands in the downtown area near the courthouse. The artist, Herbert Barbee, a 19th-century Italian-trained sculptor, grew up in Luray. An adjacent store and stagecoach stop, Calendine, was his workshop.

White House Bridge (Rte. 211 west; outdoor marker) White House Bridge takes its name from the small white Kaufmann House just west of the present-day bridge over Rte. 211. The bridge's moment in history came when Stonewall Jackson sympathizers burned it at 4am on June 2, 1862, in an attempt to keep Union forces from overtaking him. Jackson then defeated both John Fremont and James Shields separately at Cross Keys and Port Republic.

ROCKINGHAM COUNTY

Cross Keys and Port Republic

Cross Keys (June 8, 1862) and **Port Republic** (June 9, 1862) **Battlefields:** Both are noted with roadside markers within a few miles of each other along Rte. 659 (from Exit 245 off I-81). These battles were decisive victories during Stonewall Jackson's 1862 Valley Campaign.

Cross Keys: Union General John Fremont was defeated here. Private foundations in Cross Keys own about 100 acres of the original battlefield. In addition to its importance in Jackson's overall strategy, the tactics used at Cross Keys are still studied.

Port Republic: Stonewall Jackson defeated the rest of the Federal wing from the Cross Keys operation here. The house in which General Turner Ashby lay in state is still standing with appropriate interpretative displays. A small museum in Port Republic is open Sunday afternoons and by appointment. (Call 540-249-3156.) A set of street-side interpretive signs along the river in Port Republic describe the activity in town during the battles — especially helpful when the museum is not open.

Harrisonburg, Dayton, Bridgewater, Grottoes

Ashby Marker at Port Republic Road is located just off I-81's Exit 245. Most of the town was burned during Sheridan's march through the Valley. This marker notes a skirmish on June 6, 1862, which cost the South one of its noted officers: Turner Ashby. (See sidebar.)

Grand Caverns in Grottoes (See "Caves" in Chapter Four, *Outdoor Recreation*) made a natural hiding place for soldiers of both sides. Many signed the walls, the most famous being that of W.W. Miles, simply because it is the most visible. Cave tour guides no longer point to the other signatures for fear of vandalism. Legend says Stonewall Jackson took a break here during the June 1862 Port Republic battle.

Who was Turner Ashby?

Turner Ashby, a Confederate officer, enjoyed a phenomenal career trajectory. In less than 14 months he had been promoted from captain of a small volunteer company of cavalry to brigadier general. By all accounts the man was truly brave, energetic, cool, resourceful, and, at the same time, gentle and highly ethical. He was 32 and unmarried when the war started. Stories tell of a swath of Southern belles swooning when the handsome, modest, and charismatic Ashby came to town. He was said to embody the ideal blend of sincere charm and concern for those around him. Ashby died not long after being shot on June 6, 1862, and rests now in Winchester's Mount Hebron cemetery.

Shenandoah Valley Heritage Museum in Dayton (see "Museums") has an electronic map outlining the 1862 Valley Campaign. Call 540-879-2681 for current operating hours. Fee charged.

In **Bridgewater**, Civil War markers throughout town detail its role as a Confederate logistics center. Stonewall Jackson attended church here as he moved through on May 18, 1862.

AUGUSTA COUNTY

Staunton

Staunton's Depot area played a key role in transporting grain, arms, and munitions to and from Richmond and this central Valley area via the Virginia Central Railroad. When Union Major General David H. Hunter entered Staunton on June 6, 1864, he established his headquarters at **The Virginia Hotel** (which stood on the northeast corner of Greenville Avenue at New Street) and converted the rails that were left into a Union supply line.

The current railroad station is the third one on this site; one was destroyed in the war, another in an accident with a train. A Civil War Trails interpretation is often given downtown at the station, Augusta Street and Middlebrook Avenue.

Other Staunton spots of interest include:

Trinity Episcopal Church, built in 1861. Many Confederates worshipped here, including Robert E. Lee.

Thornrose Cemetery's Confederate Section, built in 1849. A monument of a soldier, impressive limestone retention walls, and cast-iron urns lend somber elegance to this, the last resting place of Generals Thomas L. Rosser, Jubal Early, and Fitzhugh Lee, a governor of Virginia and nephew of General Robert E. Lee.

Waynesboro

On March 2, 1865, a small Confederate force under Jubal Early was defeated by Philip Sheridan at Waynesboro. Civil War interpretation is available at the Plumb House; call 540-942-6644 for a schedule.

BOTETOURT AND ROANOKE COUNTIES

Most of the action raged east or west of these counties, but several of the area's natural springs did play an important role. In addition to their obvious use as a source of fresh water, Botetourt Springs and Big Cook Springs in Bonsack, near modern-day Vinton, have a role in legend. Local history says that there were two blanket factories in the area. One was burned and the other saved by promising to stop supplying the Confederates — a promise made but not kept!

MOUNTAIN COUNTIES: HIGHLAND, BATH, AND ALLEGHANY

McDowell Battlefield in Highland County lies just east of the town of McDowell along a trail accessible from Rte. 250. On May 8, 1862, Confederate forces staved off attacks made by town-based Union forces. This was the first victory for Stonewall Jackson in the 1862 Valley Campaign. A Civil War Trails sign just across the Bullpasture River on the south side of the road marks the battle location.

The town of **Monterey,** also in Highland County, was a strategic post on the Staunton-Parkersburg Pike, now Rte. 250. Federal troops retreated through the town after the Battle of McDowell. The county courthouse offers battle information.

Camp Alleghany, in Alleghany County, was the scene of a Confederate winter camp. It is located just off Rte. 250 on the West Virginia border. It was attacked unsuccessfully on Dec. 13, 1861. Parts of the camp are preserved and interpreted by the Monongahela National Forest through its West Virginia office. Call 304-636-1875 for information.

The **Confederate Breastworks** pull-off along Rte. 250 seems to be on top of Shenandoah Mountain. The pull-off is just large enough to allow several cars to park, and a short loop trail along the remnants of the breastworks is well marked. The detailed information even includes pictures. The adjacent observation area offers a spectacular view of the Cowpasture River Valley below.

CINEMA

This section lists the major movie theaters in the Valley. For '50s nostalgia, try one of the Valley's two drive-in movie theaters in Winchester and Lexington. Call ahead for prices, which vary according to the time of day and, sometimes, the movie being shown.

FREDERICK COUNTY

Stephens City Family Drive-In (540-665-6982; www.driveinmovie.com; on Rte. 11, one mile south of Stephens City) Operational since 1957, it includes a playground for little ones. Daily Memorial Day–Labor Day, weekends only in spring and fall.
Carmike Cinemas Apple Blossom 6 (540-665-0012; 1850 Apple Blossom Dr., Winchester).
Carmike Cinemas Center 6 Cinemas (540-678-1225; 601 E. Jubal Early Dr., Winchester).

WARREN COUNTY

Royal Cinemas (540-622-9997; 117 E. Main St., Front Royal).

SHENANDOAH COUNTY

Daulke's Community Theater (540-459-2221; 136 N. Main St., Woodstock) A privately owned, first-run movie house. It has three screens and makes its own luscious popcorn.

PAGE COUNTY

Page Twin (540-743-4444; 33 E. Main St., Luray).

ROCKINGHAM COUNTY

Regal Cinemas 14 (540-434-7733; 381 Universal Blvd., Harrisonburg).

AUGUSTA COUNTY

Dixie 4 Cinema (540-885-6772; E. Beverley and Market Sts., Staunton) Still showing movies at the time of this writing, but there are plans afoot to turn it into an arts center.
Regal Cinemas Staunton Mall Cinemas (540-885-3082; Rte. 11 South, Staunton).

ROCKBRIDGE COUNTY

Hull's Drive-In (540-463-2621; www.hullsdrivein.com; Rte. 11 four miles outside of Lexington, use Exit 55 from I-64 or Exit 195 from I-81) When the owner died after 48 years in business, the community rallied to keep the screen going. Open weekends, Apr.–Oct. Call or check Web site for schedule.
State Theater (540-463-3424; 12-14 Nelson St., Lexington).
Valley Cinema (540-261-7292; 2275 Beech Ave., Buena Vista).

ROANOKE COUNTY

Grand Carmike (540-725-9800; 4302 Electric Rd., Roanoke).
Valley View Grande 16 Cinema (540-362-8989, 4730 Valley View Blvd. NW, Roanoke).
Salem Valley — Carmike (540-389-0444; 1700 Apperson Dr., Salem).

ALLEGHANY COUNTY

Covington Movies 3 (540-963-8888; 139 N. Maple Ave., Covington).

CLASSICAL AND FOLK DANCE

FREDERICK COUNTY

Shenandoah Conservatory: Part of Shenandoah University. (See "Music.")

PAGE COUNTY

Plains Promenaders Square Dance Club (540-896-7913; Luray).

ROCKINGHAM COUNTY

James Madison University: Harrisonburg. (See "Music.")

ROANOKE COUNTY

Roanoke Ballet Theatre (540-345-6099; 541 Luck Ave., Suite 318, Roanoke, VA 24011) Venue used is often Shaftman Performance Hall. (See "Music.")
Veryovka Ukrainian Dance Company (804-792-6965; Danville Arts and Humanities, PO Box 3581, Danville, VA 24543) Singers, dancers, and musicians form this group, based just south of the Valley. They often perform Ukrainian folk songs and ballads in Roanoke accompanied by an orchestra of guitars, balalaikas, and bayans.

COLLEGES AND UNIVERSITIES

FREDERICK COUNTY

Shenandoah University (540-665-4500, 800-432-2266; 1460 University Dr., Winchester, VA 22601) This 125-year-old university attracts students from throughout the region and across the globe to 60 different programs of study. The main campus is in Winchester, and the Health Professions Building is on the campus of the Winchester Medical Center and Northern Virginia Campus in Leesburg.

Lord Fairfax Community College (800-906-5322; www.lf.vccs.edu/AboutUs/middle.shtm; 173 Skirmisher Ln., Middletown, VA 22645) LFCC is a dynamic institution providing accessible, comprehensive, and affordable education. Founded in 1970, LFCC is a nonresidential, two-year public institution with campuses in Middletown and Warrenton. It's one of 23 institutions in the Virginia Community College System.

ROCKINGHAM COUNTY

James Madison University (540-568-6211; www.jmu.edu; 800 S. Main St., Harrisonburg, VA 22807) JMU is a state university with 4,000-plus students. Founded in the early 1900s as a teacher's college, it now boasts one of the premier technology programs in the state and a well-thought-of business school, as well as excellent theater and graphic arts departments. Events held in the campus theater and football stadium are often open to the public.

Eastern Mennonite University (540-432-4000; www.emu.edu; 1200 Park Rd., Harrisonburg, VA 22802) This private liberal arts school with 1,400-plus students is a Mennonite college founded in 1917. Many campus facilities offer programs that are open to the public. These include the EMU Hartzler Library Art Gallery and the EMU Hostetter Museum of Natural History (540-432-4175).

Bridgewater College (540-828-8000; www.bridgewater.edu; 420 E. College St., Bridgewater, VA 22812) This small, private liberal arts college was founded by a member of the Church of the Brethren in the 1880s. There are 1,000 students enrolled in the school's more than 30 degree programs.

Blue Ridge Community College (540-234-9261; One College Lane, PO Box 80, Weyers Cave, VA 24486) This comprehensive two-year institution is part of the Virginia Community College System. Blue Ridge offers diverse programs of instruction. Also home to a great historic arboretum.

AUGUSTA COUNTY

Mary Baldwin College (800-468-2262; www.mbc.edu; admit@mbc.edu; Frederick Avenue, Staunton, VA 24401) This four-year women's liberal arts college is on its way to becoming a university. Founded as Augusta Female Seminary in 1842, it was later renamed for one its first students, Mary Julia Baldwin. The school offers a coed master's in education program, and since 1995 has been the home of the Virginia Women's Institute for Leadership.

ROCKBRIDGE COUNTY

Southern Virginia University (800-229-8420, 540-261-8421; www.southern virginia.edu; admissions@southernvirginia.edu; One University Hill Dr., Buena Vista, VA 24416) This school grew from a women's college in the 1890s to full university accreditation in 2001. A liberal arts school with just under 500 students, it was reorganized in 1996 to become a college of the Church of Jesus Christ of Latter-day Saints.

Virginia Military Institute (540-464-7000, 540-464-7230; www.vmi.edu; Lexington, VA 24450) VMI is the nation's oldest state-supported military college. Today, as at its founding in 1839, its 1,200 cadets pursue bachelor's degrees in 13 disciplines in the general fields of engineering, science, and liberal arts. The university also is home to two wonderful museums — the Marshall Museum and the VMI Museum.

Washington and Lee University (540-463-8710; www.wlu.edu; admissions@ wlu.edu; Lexington, VA 24450) Washington and Lee, a liberal arts college and law school, was founded in 1749 as Augusta Academy, became Liberty Hall Academy in 1776, Washington Academy in 1798, and Washington College in 1813. It's the ninth-oldest university in the United States and George Washington himself was one of the school's major donors. Robert E. Lee served as president from 1865 until his death in 1870. The Lee Chapel was built during his tenure and his name was added to the college's name after his death. General Lee and most of his family are buried in the chapel.

ROANOKE COUNTY

Roanoke College (540-375-2500; www.roanoke.edu; 221 College Lane, Salem, VA 24153) The 74-acre campus of this Lutheran college has an open gateway into the town and a number of fine tree-lined walking paths. The art gallery, library and theater in F.W. Olin Hall for Arts and Humanities often offer programs open to the general public. Check with the school and local sources for more information.

Hollins University (800-456-9595; www.hollins.edu; 7916 Williamson Ave., PO Box 9707, Roanoke, VA 24020) Just outside of downtown Roanoke, Hollins, founded in 1842, is a distinguished liberal arts university with nationally recognized programs in creative writing, art, dance, and psychology. Women only for undergraduate, but coed graduate programs in English and creative writing, liberal studies, and more.

Virginia Western Community College (540-657-VWCC; www.vw.cc.va.us; info center@vw.vccs.edu; PO Box 14007, Roanoke, VA 24038) A community college that serves traditional students and students already in the workforce. Its 70 acres in Roanoke are divided into north and south campuses by Colonial Avenue.

ALLEGHANY COUNTY

Dabney S. Lancaster Community College (540-863-2800, 877-733-7522; www.dl
.vccs.edu; 1000 Dabney Dr., Clifton Forge, VA 24422) Lancaster is a two-year
college on a 117-acre plot of land bounded on three sides by the Jackson
River. The college has a small two-acre arboretum on the property. Among
the school's more unique offerings is its recently begun golf operations and
facilities management program.

HISTORIC HOUSES & SITES

This section lists historic homes and sites not designated as museums in their
title. Some of them may have museums on-site.

FREDERICK, CLARKE, AND WARREN COUNTIES

Daniel Morgan Homes

The Winchester-Frederick Historical Society (540-662-6550; www.winchester
history.org/winchesterhistory) coordinates periodic tours of the homes of Daniel
Morgan located throughout the tricounty area. Morgan was a Revolutionary War
soldier who built homes in the area. Saratoga, where he lived for a time, is in private
hands in Clarke County. His Winchester home, where he died in 1802, was built for
his daughter that same year, and many of his documents are on display there. Call
the society to learn when the tours are offered.

Winchester

GLEN BURNIE HISTORIC HOUSE & GARDENS
888-556-5799, 540-662-1473.
www.glenburniemuseum
.org.
801 Amherst St., Winchester,
VA 22601.
Open: Apr.–Oct., daily 10–5
(later in the summer).
Admission: Adults $8;
senior citizens, children,
and students $6; $5 for
gardens only. Groups of
ten or more receive
discounts with advance
reservations.

Six generations of the Winchester-area Wood/
Glass family have lived here and furnished this
gorgeous house with many of the fine antiques on
display. Glen Burnie, a Scottish word for "valley with
stream," is the name given the 1,200 acres by James
Wood, surveyor and *paterfamilias*. Wood made a gift
of some of his land to make Winchester the first En-
glish-speaking settlement west of the Blue Ridge.
Wood was a compatriot in arms to George Washington during the French and Indian War. His 1832 marriage joined the Glass family to the property.

Glen Burnie's role in 19th-century history was ce-
mented when it came under fire during the first and
second battles of Winchester in the Civil War.

Its collection of 18th- and 19th-century art includes a portrait of George Washington by Rembrandt Peale as well as furniture from throughout the life of the home. On the lower level a miniature house shows the entire structure and *all* rooms, including upstairs rooms not open to the public. The scale house is fully furnished as well.

But there is no miniature substitute for the gardens, which are a must-see. Twenty-five acres of varied displays show off a Japanese garden, an herb garden, a European-style sculpture garden, and folly buildings, among others. The rose garden and boxwood garden are also particularly exciting for anyone interested in 18th-century gardening. An orientation video prepares visitors for the 60-minute guided tour of the house and gardens.

Glen Burnie has targeted late 2003 to begin expansion from its current status as a historic house into a new facility, the Museum of the Shenandoah Valley. The foundation literature describes the transformation this way: "Today Glen Burnie tells the story of one family — in 2003 it will tell the story of the entire Valley."

Other sites of interest in Winchester:

Handley Regional Library and Archives (540-662-9041; www.hrl.lib.state.va.us/ handley/default.asp; reference@hrl.lib.state.va.us; 100 W. Piccadilly St., PO Box 58, Winchester, VA 22604) The archives are run jointly by the Winchester-Frederick Historical Society and the library, but they're closed on Sunday and Monday even though the library is open daily. The archives are a popular place for visitors who want to explore possible genealogical links to families in the Valley. The building itself is a lovely example of Greek Revival architecture, with a small Greek temple-like portico at the Piccadilly St. entrance.

Winchester National Cemetery (540-662-4868; 401 National Ave., Winchester, VA 22601) Open dawn to dusk for visitation. The cemetery was established in 1866 and is the final resting place for more than 4,000 Union dead. The 4.89-acre site north of Woodstock Lane is divided into sections named for states. Just south of Woodstock Lane on National Avenue is the Stonewall Cemetery.

Stonewall Cemetery (540-662-4868; National Ave., Winchester, VA 22601) On the south side of the street are the graves of 829 Confederate unknowns and some who have been identified. A Web site, members.rogers.com/civil warus/confederate.html, gives details of the soldiers on both sides who gave their all for their beliefs over 130 years ago.

Mount Hebron Cemetery (540-662-4868; 305 E. Boscawen St., Winchester, VA 22601) Holds many 19th-century graves as well as Civil War dead and prominent folk of 20th-century Winchester. Most notable from the 20th century is Harry Flood Byrd (1887-1966), a U.S. senator from Virginia from 1933 to 1965.

Patsy Cline Sites: Country-western singer Patsy Cline was born on Sept. 8, 1932, in Gore, just outside Winchester. A brochure at the visitor center notes Cline-related sites and suggests a driving tour that takes you by the diner where she was a waitress (Triangle), the drugstore where she worked

(Gaunt's), and radio station WINC, where she got her start. Cline died in a plane crash in 1963 and was elected to Country Music Hall of Fame posthumously in 1973. A bell tower marks her grave in Shenandoah Memorial Park (540-667-2012; 1270 Front Royal Pike, Winchester, VA 22602). Two streets, Patsy Cline Blvd. and the Patsy Cline Memorial Highway, honor her. The Web site www.patsycline.com tells more about her.

Willa Cather Sites: Pulitzer Prize-winning novelist Willa Cather (1873-1947) was also born in Gore. A roadside marker notes the house (no tours). She moved to Red Cloud, Nebraska, when she was nine and set most of her books in that area. She is best known for *O Pioneers* and *Death Comes for the Archbishop*. She set a children's book, *Sapphira and the Slave Girl*, in Winchester.

Spottswood (Spotsy) Poles House (530 Fremont St., Winchester; view from outside only) Poles, known as the Ty Cobb of the Negro League, batted .444 in 1911 and stole 41 bases in 60 games. He won a Purple Heart in France in World War I and retired from sports in 1923.

Middletown

BELLE GROVE PLANTATION
540-869-2028.
www.bellegrove.org.
336 Belle Grove Rd.,
Middletown, VA 22645.
One mile south of town on Rte. 11.
Open: Apr.–mid Nov.,
Mon.–Sat. 10:15–3:15, Sun. 1:15–3:15.
Admission: Adults $5, children $2.50. Call about discounts for seniors and groups.

Belle Grove, built in 1794 by Revolutionary War Major Isaac Hite, is a National Historic Trust Site. For 70 years the Hite family entertained luminaries such as Thomas Jefferson and James and Dolly Madison. During the Civil War, the house was Philip Sheridan's headquarters and a hospital. More than 1,300 Confederate prisoners were held on the grounds near the house.

In one of the war's many ironies, officers who had been friends at West Point met on the field on opposing sides during the Battle of Cedar Creek nearby. Confederate Major General Stephen Ramseur was mortally wounded in the battle and taken to Belle Grove Plantation. Ramseur called for his West Point roommate, Union General George Armstrong Custer, who sat by Ramseur's bedside until he died.

During the annual Cedar Creek reenactment, many locals take on the role of the Frederick Ladies Relief Society and roam Belle Grove's grounds in period dress. Cedar Creek and Belle Grove have been joined together as a National Park site, but they will continue to operate separately for a while.

Front Royal

BELLE BOYD COTTAGE/ WARREN COUNTY HERITAGE SOCIETY
540-636-1446.

Belle Boyd is probably one of the most famous women of the Civil War, and many of her personal items are on display here. Boyd's aunt took

Shenandoah2000

This cottage is the home of Belle Boyd, the young Confederate spy who charmed Union soldiers into spilling secrets that she passed on to Stonewall Jackson.

101 Chester St., Front Royal, VA 22630.
Open: Mon., Tues., Thurs., Fri. 12:30–3.
Admission: $2 donation per person requested.

her in after she roiled the town of Martinsburg (now in West Virginia) with her pro-Confederate activities. She flirted and danced her way into the confidence of Front Royal's Union soldiers and then delivered the information to Southern troops. "La Belle Rebelle," as she was called, later married a Union soldier and moved to England. In her later years she lectured in England and the United States.

The cottage is directly behind the house that serves as heritage society headquarters. The tiny building was rescued from its many lives as a storeroom, apartment building, and military headquarters, and moved to the current site in 1971.

Other Front Royal sites:

Prospect Hill Cemetery (Prospect St.) From the hill now known as Soldier's Circle, where 276 men representing all 13 Confederate states are interred, Stonewall Jackson directed his troops during the May 23, 1862, Battle of Front Royal. John Mosby's statue greets visitors at the entrance to this cemetery, which holds six of his rangers, executed in Front Royal in September 1864. The cemetery is open dawn to dusk; admission is free.

Warren County Courthouse Lawn (Main St. and Royal Ave.) This site has monuments to area soldiers who served in the Civil War, World Wars I and II, the

Korean War, and Vietnam. Front Royal's walking tour lists places of African-American, Revolutionary War- and Civil War-era interest.

Millwood

The Burwell-Morgan Mill still grinds grain as it did 200 years ago when grain was king in the Valley and mills were a common site along the streams.

Shenandoah2000

BURWELL-MORGAN MILL
540-837-1799, off-season 540-955-2600, mill site 540-837-1799.
15 Tannery Lane, PO Box 282, Millwood, VA 22646.
Open: Apr.–Oct., Thurs.–Sat. 10–5, Sun. 12–5.
Admission: Donation requested.

This 1785 stone and clapboard building has been restored (with wooden gears from 1750) to the time when Lieutenant Colonel Nathaniel Burwell of Carter's Grove built it and hired Brigadier General Daniel Morgan, a Revolutionary War hero, to run it.

Through the early 19th century, the local economy was based in large part on the mill. Today, its wheel turns and the stones grind meal and flour on a limited basis for tourists. A gift shop on-site sells the ground products.

HISTORIC LONG BRANCH
540-837-1856, 888-558-5567.
historic@historiclongbranch.com.
830 Long Branch Ln. (Rtes. 624 and 626), PO Box 241, Millwood, VA 22646.
Open: Apr.–Oct.; grounds, daily 8–6; mansion, weekends only.
Admission: Adults $6, seniors $5, children under 12 $3. Discounts for groups.

Built by Robert Burwell with tobacco money in 1805, the house passed through several hands until Henry Z. Isaacs, a Baltimore textile executive and horse breeder, made it a museum in the 1990s. The spiral staircase is breathtaking and that feature alone is worth the house tour. House and grounds are used widely by the community.

The Shenandoah Valley Astronomical Society joins Historic Long Branch once a month for an evening of sky viewing. The Shenandoah Valley Hot Air Balloon and Wine Festival also is held on the grounds each October; check for details at the Web site, www.historiclongbranch.com/balloon fest/balloon.htm.

Long Branch's house and grounds are home to many local festivals, including those of the Valley's Astronomical Society and local hot air balloon enthusiasts.

Courtesy of Long Branch

SHENANDOAH COUNTY

Basye-Orkney

ORKNEY SPRINGS HOTEL
540-856-2141.
53 Orkney Springs Rd., Orkney Springs, VA 22845.

This turn-of-the-century hotel is the site of the Shenandoah Valley Music Festival, now in its third decade of performances. No air conditioning — at the time of its construction, opening two doors and a window was air conditioning enough. Still open to guests.

Mount Jackson

Meem's Bottom Covered Bridge (See "Along the Way" in Chapter Two, *Transportation*) On Rte. 11 just outside Mount Jackson.
Historic Union Church (Main St.) The church was built around 1812 and its graveyard contains the remains of many who fought in the Civil War.
Widow Kip's Country Inn (355 Orchard) An 1830s building with interesting architecture.

Woodstock

Walking down Main Street will take you by the Lutheran church, home of Revolutionary War hero John Muhlenberg, "The Fighting Parson." He settled in Woodstock in 1772, and served in Washington's Eighth Virginia as commander of the German regiment.

The Union Church in Mount Jackson was once used as a Civil War hospital. Many of the soldiers who found healing there left their signatures on the walls, still visible today.

Shenandoah2000

Other Woodstock sites include:

Woodstock Tower: From this tower on a trail just outside of town you can see the seven bends of the Shenandoah River.

Shenandoah County Courthouse: The oldest still in use west of the Blue Ridge — built in 1795. It's a walk-by attraction in the center of town.

PAGE COUNTY

Luray

MASSANUTTAN ONE-ROOM SCHOOLHOUSE
540-743-3915.
Xerkel St., Luray, VA 22835.
Open: By appt. only.
Admission: Free.

This one-room schoolhouse from the 19th century has 16 desks — the original double variety — and a 100-year-old cast-iron stove. The teacher's desk is handmade and the flagpole in the school was used during the Civil War.

PAGE COUNTY COURTHOUSE
540-743-4142.
116 S. Court St., Luray, VA 22835.

This 1834 Roman Revival-style courthouse was completed by two of Thomas Jefferson's builders, Malcolm F. Crawford and William P. Phillips. This is an outside-view only unless you have court business.

Other sites of interest near Luray:

Willow Grove Mill: A typical 19th-century mill two miles south of Luray on Business 340. This is a drive-by site.

Mauck Meeting House: This historic home of one of the area's leading families is open by appointment only. Located on Rte. 766. Call 540-743-3915.

Calendine (see Barbee Monument under "Battlefields and Civil War Reenactments") and **Stevens Cottage** (a satellite office for the Chamber of Commerce in summer): An 1800s building on E. Main St. that had many uses over the years, including a printing office.

ROCKINGHAM COUNTY

The **Turkey Statue/Marker** on Rte. 11 as you cross the county line pays homage to the noble turkey — Rockingham's "cash cow," the mainstay of the county's agricultural income base.

Harrisonburg/Dayton

If you're interested in architecture, you might want to contact the **Vernacular Architecture Forum** (www.vernaculararchitecture.org; PO Box 1511, Harrisonburg, VA 22803), which has a lot of information about everyday buildings in the area. Most of the sites in this town are listed elsewhere in this chapter.

Colonial patriot Daniel Harrison's house also served as a fort to protect nearby settlers from Indian attacks near today's city of Harrisonburg.

Shenandoah2000

DANIEL HARRISON HOUSE
540-879-2280.
N. Main St., Dayton, VA 22821.
Open: May–Oct., weekends 1–4; special events the rest of the year.
Admission: Free.

The circa 1749 stone house we see today was Fort Harrison (for whom Harrisonburg is named). A secret tunnel allowed the settlers to reach a nearby spring, even during Indian attacks. This is one of the sites spared during the Civil War.

AUGUSTA COUNTY

Staunton/Waynesboro

Woodrow Wilson was the first Southern president to be elected after the Civil War.

Courtesy Woodrow Wilson Birthplace Foundation

WOODROW WILSON HOUSE
Woodrow Wilson Birthplace Foundation
540-885-0897, 888-496-6376.
www.woodrowwilson.org.
woodrow@cfw.com.
18-24 N. Coalter St., PO Box 24, Staunton, VA 24402.
Open: Mar.–Oct., daily 9–5; Nov.–Feb., Mon.–Sat. 10–4, Sun. 1–4. Closed Thanksgiving, Christmas, and New Year's Day.
Admission: Adults $6.50, students $4, children 6–12 $2. Guided tour lasts 1½ hours, last tour begins 1 hour before closing.

This is the boyhood home of Woodrow Wilson, 28th president of the United States (1913–1921), who championed the Versailles treaty that ended "the war to end all wars." Wilson was the first Southerner to be elected president after the Civil War.

The house is nestled within Gospel Hill, one of Staunton's five National Historic Districts. A 1933 boxwood garden surrounds the house, setting it off from the town, and a guided tour offers an authentic picture of family life in pre-Civil War Shenandoah Valley. The museum also includes an overview of Wilson's public life, from his study in Princeton, New Jersey, where he was a professor, to his historic World War I peace efforts. A computer archive offers 1850s newspapers, historic photographs, Civil War rosters, and more.

A free one-hour guided walking tour of Staunton leaves from the house at 10am each Saturday, June–Oct., or call the Historic Staunton Foundation (540-885-7676) for a brochure detailing a self-guided walking tour.

The Fishburne Military School (540-946-7700; www.fishburne.org; 225 S. Wayne Ave., Waynesboro, VA 22980) is a grand old structure with great grounds. This is one of the country's oldest military schools for high school students.

ROCKBRIDGE COUNTY

Lexington

ROCKBRIDGE HISTORICAL SOCIETY
540-464-1058.
www.rockhist.org.
Campbell House, 101 E.
  Washington St., PO Box
  514, Lexington, VA 24450.
Open: Mid-Apr.–Oct.,
  Tues.–Sat. 10–1.
Admission: Free.

Many artifacts from the Victorian period and a collection of clothing and photographs spanning the 20th century tell the story of Rockbridge County through the lives of its residents.

An adult-sized cradle harks to the 1784 capture by Shawnee Indians of an eight-year-old child, Mary Moore. She was sold as a slave to a tribe in Canada. She returned to Virginia at age 15, but in subsequent years she relived the horror of her experience in vivid dreams that awakened her. The adult-sized rocking cradle on view was made to help comfort her.

Pottery from the valley forms another interesting part of the exhibit. Several pieces attributed to the Firebaugh Pottery and the Rockbridge Baths Pottery are part of the collection, as are two pieces of Caddo Indian pottery that date back to about the sixth century.

LEE CHAPEL
Washington and Lee
  University, Lexington, VA
  24450.

See "Museums."

STONEWALL JACKSON HOUSE
540-462-2552.
www.stonewalljackson.org.
8 E. Washington St.,
  Lexington, VA 24450.
Open: Varies by season; call
  ahead.
Admission: Adults $5,
  children under 18 $2,
  under 6 free.
Handicap Access: Call
  ahead for alternative tour
  arrangements.

The house has been restored to the period just before the Civil War, when Jackson lived there with his second wife, Anna Morrison. The tour tells of Jackson's life as a math teacher at VMI, his accomplishments as a general, and the role of the house as a hospital during and after the war. Much family furniture has been returned to the home, so it's easy to imagine Jackson reading the Bible or correcting papers at his desk. The home's small garden is still a place of respite as it must have been for the Jackson family.

The house is a short walk from the main part of VMI. Changing exhibits of period items such as quilts, historic uniforms, and more are displayed. The bookstore on the lower level is wonderful and a great source of books on the Civil War. (Note: The house is scheduled for closure to install a new fire protection system sometime between November 2003 and March 2004. Be sure to call to see if it's open.)

Also in Lexington: **Stonewall Jackson Memorial Cemetery** (S. Main St.; open daylight hours) The cemetery grew around the old Lexington Presbyterian Church, which was built on the edge of town in 1789. The site of the old church can be seen in the cemetery beside Main Street near the Preston family plot.

Steeles Tavern

CYRUS McCORMICK FARM
540-377-2255.
www.vaes.vt.edu/steeles/
mccormick/mccormick
.html.
Shenandoah Valley
Agriculture Research and
Extension Center.
McCormick Farm Cir., PO
Box 100, Steeles Tavern,
VA 24476.
From I-81, head east on Rte.
606 to border of
Rockbridge and Augusta
Counties.
Open: Daily 8:30–5.
Admission: Free.

Cyrus McCormick, inventor of the mechanical wheat reaper, first demonstrated his invention to the public in July 1831, when he was only 22. The family's Walnut Grove farm is now a livestock research center run by Virginia Tech. Because it remained in the McCormick family until 1954, many buildings and artifacts are original to the family.

The property's mill is where McCormick worked on his invention. The blacksmith shop and workshop areas of the farm are also interesting, and demonstrate what the creativity of one individual can bring to the world. Today's children, "techies" one and all, should be able to identify with young Cyrus, who wanted to do things better — and did!

Raphine

WADE'S MILL
540-348-1400, 800-290-1400.
www.wadesmill.com.
info@wadesmill.com.
55 Kennedy, Raphine, VA
24472.
Exit 205 off I-81, then west
on Rte. 606.
Open: Apr.–mid Dec.,
Wed.–Sat. 10–5; also Sun.
1–5 in Apr., May,
Sept–Dec.

This water-powered gristmill is on the National Register of Historic Places. It was built around 1750 by one of the Valley's Scotch-Irish settlers, Captain Joseph Kennedy, whose family owned the mill for about 100 years. They sold it to the Wade family in 1882. Today the inside of the mill is restored to the Wade era.

Seeing the mill in operation and tasting some of its production (buckwheat, bread flour, cornmeal, and more are sold in the gift shop) are tangible reminders of a life gone by. What's more, the history of the mill is a microcosm of the Valley's own history and life today — old charm, hospitality, fun, and an awareness and sampling of sophisticated associations beyond the Valley. The current miller and his wife, Jim and Georgie Young, operate a wonderful kitchen shop here as well. (See Chapter Seven, *Shopping*.)

NATURAL BRIDGE   See "Theater" in this chapter and Natural Bridge Caverns under "Caves" in Chapter Four, *Outdoor Recreation.*

Glasgow

The **Frank Padgett Monument** is an open-air, 900-pound stone monument in Glasgow Park that can be seen from dawn to dusk. Glasgow, just north of Natural Bridge on Rte. 130, was a busy river port in the early 19th century. Frank Padgett, a slave who worked on the boats, lost his life saving victims of an icy winter storm in January 1854. A local captain who witnessed the effort erected the monument.

BOTETOURT COUNTY

Buchanan

JAMES RIVER VISITOR CENTER
804-299-5496.
www.blueridgeparkway.org.
Milepost 63, Blue Ridge
 Parkway.
Open: May–Oct., daily 9–5.
Admission: Free.

Most of the visitors to Virginia associate the James River with her capital city of Richmond, where the James is an integral part of the cityscape. But in the early days, before railroads became the favored mode of transport, engineers built locks to move freight along the river. Canals as a way west were a short-lived economic idea, though, as roads and railroads soon overtook them.

The restored lock that can be seen here was part of a 200-mile canal system running from Richmond across the Blue Ridge to Buchanan. The other highlights of this wayside visitor center are a footbridge across the James River and a trail leading to the Kanawha Canal lock exhibit.

Also in Buchanan: **Buchanan Walking Tour and Swinging Bridge** (540-254-1212) Here you can see one of the country's few swinging bridges — this one over the James River.

Fincastle

Historic Fincastle (540-473-3077; www.hisfin.org; PO Box 19, Fincastle, VA 24090) This historic town has a lot to see on its walking tour, most notably the jail. The inside of the jail is rarely open, but you can learn a lot about the town at the Fincastle Museum. (See "Museums.")

James Matten Early Cabin (540-473-3077; www.hisfin.org; PO Box 19, Fincastle, VA 24090) This reconstructed 18th-century cabin is open only by appointment.

Botetourt County Courthouse (540-473-8274; 1 W. Main Courthouse Sq., Fin-

This jail has been a center of the Fincastle community since the early 1800s.

Shenandoah2000

castle, VA 24090) Built on the site of the original, this is also a site for histori-cal records. Make an appointment to use those. Courthouse is open Mon.–Fri. 8:30–4:30, but it is a working building, so call if you want to do more than simply walk in and take a quick look.

ROANOKE COUNTY

Roanoke

Center in the Square (540-342-5700; One Market Sq., Roanoke, VA 24011) This five-story former furniture warehouse is the center of cultural activity in Roanoke. The History Museum and Historical Society of Western Virginia, the Art Museum of Western Virginia, the Science Museum of Western Virginia and Hopkins Planetarium, opera, ballet, and Mill Mountain Theater all call it home. There is a small admission fee for most of the museums, but their gift shops are free. Most of the museums are closed on Monday and some have limited oper-ation on Sunday and Tuesday as well. Roanoke's historic farmer's market in the City Market Building and local art galleries complete the excitement in the central downtown area, a wonderful place to stroll and shop. Eateries that range from hole-in-the wall to elegant in price and décor offer a wide variety of ethnic and southern Virginia delicacies. (See Chapter Six, *Restaurants.*)

Historic Farmer's Market (540-342-2028; 310 First St., Roanoke, VA 24011) The market is the oldest one in continuous use in Virginia (since 1866). It is a col-lection of stalls and little shops with local and other produce, as well as won-derful food products from all over Virginia, the United States, and the world.

Mill Mountain Star Overlook (540-342-6025, 800-635-5535; 114 Market St., Roanoke, VA 24011) The star is the symbol of Roanoke, and area residents have found it a perfect spot for marriage proposals since it was put up in 1949. From the overlook you can enjoy the same wonderful view of the Valley that Native American legend says enchanted the real stars in ancient times. The 100-foot-tall steel star is lit from dusk to midnight in various color combinations ranging from plain white light through fancy displays of red, white, and blue.

Roanoke County Courthouse (540-387-6211, 305 E. Main St., Salem, VA 24153) Open Mon.–Fri. 8:30–5:30. This is the place to come for historical and genealogical resources.

Fire Station Number 1, just across from Center in the Square, is a historic landmark built to look like Philadelphia's Independence Hall. The station is still operational, but is also open to tours. Enter the fire station from the Church Avenue doors. It is open Mon.–Sat. 7:30–5.

The **Hotel Roanoke**, now a property owned by Doubletree and managed by Virginia Tech, is a crown jewel of the railroad hotel era and a landmark building in Roanoke since its construction in the 1890s. It is still a wonderful place to stay. (See Chapter Five, *Lodging*.)

Salem

The **Historic District Walking Tour** directs visitors past many of the town's historic churches and homes. Maps are free at the Visitor Center (540-375-3004; 1001 Roanoke Blvd., Salem, VA 24153). The **Williams-Brown House Store** (see "Museums") houses the museum for the area.

The **City of Salem Courthouse** (540-375-3067; 2 E. Calhoun St., Salem, VA 24153; open Mon.–Fri. 8:30–5) is a lovely building to look at, as well as a repository of historical and genealogical records. Call ahead to use those.

HIGHLAND, BATH, AND ALLEGHANY COUNTIES

Monterey (Highland)

This town is so small and friendly that folks here use PO boxes — no street addresses. The Maple Museum, a replica of an old-time sugarhouse, is one mile south of Monterey. (See "Museums.") There is good eating, fine shopping, and lots of entertainment at the Highland Cultural Center in the heart of town. Highland Adventures (see Chapter Four, *Outdoor Recreation*) offers tours of local caves and customized canoe trips into the great outdoors.

Monterey's **Sugar Camps**, in town and to the north and south, are vast fields of tapped maple trees and open and indoor fires heating iron pots of sugar sap. Their modern steel sugaring facilities are open two weekends a year during the Highland County Sugar Festival, the southernmost maple sugar and syrup making venture in the United States.

Hot Springs–Warm Springs (Bath)

Jefferson Pools (540-839-5346; Rte. 220 north of Warm Springs) There are two covered pools here (one for women, one for men) run by The Homestead. A reservation is required for a complete treatment (soaking and a massage). You'll need a major credit card to make your reservation if you're not a guest at the hotel. Open daily 10–6.

Bacova (540-839-2521; near the junction of Rtes. 621 and 39 in George Washington National Forest) This tiny town's claim to fame is the Bacova mat factory and the tiny church converted to an art gallery. (See Chapter Seven, *Shopping*.)

The Homestead (800-833-1766; www.thehomestead.com; Rte. 220, PO Box 2000, Hot Springs, VA 24445) This hotel is one of the most historic in the United States. (See Chapter Five, *Lodging*, for details.)

Clifton Forge (Alleghany)

Chesapeake and Ohio Historical Society (540-862-2210; www.cohs.org, www .chessieshop.org; 312 E. Ridgeway St., Clifton Forge, VA 24422) This is THE place for railroad buffs. It's at the end of the street with a good view of the old tracks, but the tiny society office is easy to miss. Railroad logos, Chessie memorabilia (authentic and reproduction), and a rack of cards fill the gift shop front. The archives are full of photos and drawings, which visitors can peruse with an appointment. Open Mon.–Sat. 10–4.

Covington (Alleghany)

Alleghany County Courthouse (540-965-1720; Main St., Covington, VA 24426) Open Mon.–Fri. 9–5.

Alleghany Highlands Genealogical Society (540-962-3074; 1011 N. Rockbridge Ave., Covington, VA 24426) Do you have a budding family historian in your group? If so, this may be the place to visit. Open Tues., Thurs., and Fri. 10–3.

Longdale Furnace Historic District (540-862-0892; longdale@symweb.com; Exit 35 off I-64) There are many artifacts here — remnants of the time when this site forged iron items needed for the farm and the Civil War. The nearby B&B was once the home of the local ironmaster, William Firmstone.

HORSES

Virginia is horse country! Most of the entries related to horses are for riding, but we don't want you to miss Virginia's paean to this noble beast, the showplace for horse events in this part of the state: the Virginia Horse Center.

VIRGINIA HORSE CENTER AND HORSE CENTER FOUNDATION VIRGINIA HORSE CENTER AMERICAN WORK HORSE MUSEUM (at same site)
540-464-4300, 540-463-2194.
www.horsecenter.org.
info@horsecenter.org.
PO Box 1051, Lexington, VA 24450.
From Rte. 11 take Rte. 39 (Maury River Rd.) and follow for about a mile.
Open: Museum open when there are events at the center; check schedule.
Admission: Event price varies; museum admission free.
Handicap Access: Call first.

The Virginia Horse Center is a place for education, recreation, and competition. The research facilities of the foundation, the workhorse exhibits of the museum, and the performance/exhibition ring successfully cover the role of the horse in Virginia's history and contemporary society.

The center's state-of-the-art barns can stable about 600 horses. From the grandstand, visitors can enjoy events in the arenas and rings, and there's also a cross-country course. When the center is open for events, visitors can peruse the museum as well. There may be a minimal charge for some events at the center, but normally there is none. For information and schedules, call or check the Web site.

MUSEUMS

FREDERICK, CLARKE, AND WARREN COUNTIES

Winchester

ABRAM'S DELIGHT HOUSE MUSEUM
540-662-6519.
www.fortedwards.org/cwffa/abrams.htm.
1340 S. Pleasant Valley Rd., Winchester, VA 22601.
Open: Apr. 1–Oct. 1, Mon.–Sat. 10–4, Sun. 12–4.
Admission: Adults $3.50, seniors and students $3, children $1.75, family $8.75.

This 1754 structure has the distinction of being the oldest still-standing house in the northern part of the Valley. The house and grounds act as a mnemonic bridge from our modern era to the time when the Shawnee lived in the meadows nearby and watched the first Europeans ride up to their camp.

Local lore tells that Abraham Hollingsworth, a Quaker, saw a group of Shawnee Indians camped beside a bountiful spring, and in talking to them, declared the property, "A delight to behold." He then purchased 582 acres (including the land by that spring) from the Indians for a cow, a calf, and a piece of red cloth. Hollingsworth built a log home on the property and a mill beside the spring. He then brought his family from Cecil County, Maryland (an already thriving European settlement) to this new land on the frontier.

Shenandoah2000

Abram's Delight, built in 1754 by Isaac Hollingsworth, one of Winchester's first European settlers, displays period furniture and glimpses of the early-American way of life.

The family prospered, and Abraham's son, Isaac, built the elegant stone house that is known today as "Abram's Delight." The log cabin and stone house both remain.

The west wing of the stone house was added about 1800 and the house was redecorated and property improved last in the 1830s. The stone house is decorated with period antiques to create the same warm, welcoming atmosphere for today's visitors that guests would have enjoyed in the early 19th century. While the stone home presents a view of affluent life in that time, the log cabin next door represents the way most settlers would have lived in the early 18th century, when Winchester was on the frontier of European settlement in the North American New World.

Note: The offices of the **Winchester-Frederick County Historical Society** are currently located on the second floor of the stone house.

GEORGE WASHINGTON OFFICE MUSEUM
540-662-4412.
32 W. Cork St., Winchester, VA 22601.
Open: Apr. 1–Oct. 31, Mon.–Sat. 10–4, Sun. 12–4.
Admission: Adults $3.50, seniors and students $3,

This log office is a link to a phase of George Washington's life (1755-1756) when he was a surveyor and then a young colonel in the Virginia militia serving with the British regulars during the French and Indian War. The museum's collection is a small but exquisite display of some of Washington's personal effects and surveying equipment, as well as other historic memorabilia.

children $1.75, family $8.75.

Among the exhibits is a scale model of Winchester circa 1755 that shows Washington's fort. It's interesting to see the old layout of the town before walking the center area yourself.

Block Ticket

In season it's possible to obtain a block ticket to see Abram's Delight, Stonewall Jackson's headquarters, and George Washington's office, three of the most important historic sites in the city of Winchester. Abram's Delight is just a smidge far for walking, so see it first and then park near the downtown walking mall and visit the other two spots. Block tickets cost $10 for adults, $4 for seniors and students age 7 to 18.

OLD COURTHOUSE CIVIL WAR MUSEUM
800-662-1360.
PO Box 215, Winchester, VA 22604.
Entrance on Loudoun St. walking mall.
Open: Fri.–Sat. 10–5, Sun. 1–5.
Admission: $3.

The fun of this museum is that the items are primarily from local battles and skirmishes, or from the closets of local residents. It depicts, through pictures, letters, and artifacts, the story of the common soldier, the volunteer nature of the armies, and the technological advances of weapons in the Civil War. If you are in Winchester and are a fan of the Civil War, don't miss it.

The Discovery Museum is a hands-on delight. Children are especially fond of the dinosaur displays.

Shenandoah2000

SHENANDOAH VALLEY DISCOVERY MUSEUM
540-722-2020.
www.discoverymuseum.net.

The exhibits here were developed according to the motto, "To touch is to explore, to explore is to discover, and to discover is to learn."

One of the exhibits features things a child might

information@discovery museum.net.
54 S. Loudoun St., Winchester, VA 22604.
Open: Mon.–Sat. 9–5, Sun. 1–5.
Admission: $4 per person, free to members.

find on a local nature hike. Other stimuli for the imagination include a hands-on archeology display in which children can "dig" for fossils, and a play hospital emergency room.

This Winchester building is where Stonewall Jackson planned the Valley campaign of 1862. Today Jackson memorabilia and Civil War relics are on display.

VA Tourism Corp.

STONEWALL JACKSON'S HEADQUARTERS MUSEUM
540-667-3242.
415 N. Braddock St., Winchester, VA 22601.
Open: Apr.–Oct., Mon.–Sat. 10–4, Sun. 12–4; Nov.–Mar., Sat. 10–4, Sun. 12–4.
Admission: Adults $3.50, seniors and students $3, children $1.75, family $8.75.

The house is described as a Hudson River Gothic Revival home. Built around 1854, it briefly served as Jackson's headquarters during the 1862 Valley Campaign. At that time the house was owned by Lieutenant Colonel Lewis Moore and Confederate sympathizers. The house is now a museum displaying Jackson's personal prayer table, initialed prayer book, and many other bits of Jackson memorabilia. Jackson wrote about the house in letters to his wife, describing the walls of the office as "papered with elegant gilt paper," a remnant of which has been reproduced as a part of the restoration.

Stephens City

STONE HOUSE MUSEUM
540 869-1700.
stonehouse@shentel.net.
805 Fairfax St., Stephens City, VA 22655.

This regional museum is in the process of expanding and will soon be known as the Historic Stephensburg Museums. Its exhibits tell the story of the Valley Pike (Rte. 11), including original har-

Open: Jun.–Aug.,
   Thurs.–Sat. 10–4, Sun. 1–5;
   Sept.–Oct., Fri.–Sat. 10–4.
Admission: Adults $2,
   children over 6 $1, family
   $5.

nesses, wagons, and wagon-making equipment. It also displays a model of the town as it was in 1790 and is the starting point for a walking tour of Stephens City. The nonprofit Stone House Foundation looks out for the interests of local history and maintains the museum.

Front Royal

**WARREN RIFLES
   CONFEDERATE
   MUSEUM**
users.erols.com/va-udc/
   museum.html.
540-636-6982.
95 Chester St., Front Royal,
   VA 22630.
Open: Daily 12–4, Apr.–Oct.,
   or by appt.
Admission: $4.

This museum offers a wonderful collection of guns, many of which were used by local citizens in the Civil War. The amazing variety is due to the fact that military guns were not standardized until late in the war, and then only on the Union side.

The collection also includes a large number of personal items such as letters, buckles, belts, and cases that belonged to citizen soldiers and notables such as Turner Ashby, Stonewall Jackson, Robert E. Lee, and Jubal Early. There is also a fine collection of women's dresses and various Belle Boyd memorabilia. The museum's book racks offer a wide variety of Civil War selections, including a lot of hard-to-find local information.

Berryville

The **Clarke County Historical Association Museum & Archives** (540-955-2600) includes artifacts from many of the area's notables, including Revolutionary War hero Daniel Morgan. Call for an appointment and directions, as it was in the process of moving to a new location at the time of this writing.

SHENANDOAH COUNTY

Strasburg

**MUSEUM OF AMERICAN
   PRESIDENTS**
540-465-5999.
www.waysideofva.com/
   presidents.
museuminfo@waysideofva.
   com.
130 N. Massanutten St.
   (Rtes. 55 and 11),
   Strasburg, VA 22657.
Take Exit 298 off I-81.

Virginia is the birthplace of eight presidents. While only Woodrow Wilson was actually born and raised in the Valley, many others, including some nonnative Virginians, spent quite a lot of time here.

The eclectic display offers samples of Thomas Jefferson's writing (he owned the Natural Bridge for a while) and George Washington relics (his first job was as a surveyor in the Valley). Herbert Hoover and Franklin Roosevelt enjoyed the cool breezes of

Open: May–Oct., daily 10–5; Nov.–Apr., Fri.–Sun. 10–5 (call first). Closed Thanksgiving, Christmas Eve and Day, New Year's Day, and Easter.

the Blue Ridge in summer and are also represented here.

STONEWALL JACKSON MUSEUM
540-465-5884.
www.waysidefoundation
.org.
museuminfo@wasideofva
.com.
Hupp's Hill, 33231 Old Valley Pike, Strasburg, VA 22657.
Open: End of May–Labor Day, daily 10–5; off-season, daily 10–4. Closed Thanksgiving, Christmas, New Year's Day, and Easter.
Admission: Adults $3, seniors and children $2, under 6 free. For museum and cave: Adults $8, children and seniors $6.

This very child-friendly museum is part of an estate established in the 1750s by George F. Hupp. The grounds include the Crystal Caverns and are just down the road from the Hupp's Hill battlefield.

Cases of artifacts are on display, and a large number of items can be handled by visitors. There are even wooden horses for the children to ride, dress-up period clothing, and "Discovery Boxes" to explore different topics of Civil War-era life.

Combine your visit here with a visit to the caverns, which served as a party place for the Revolutionary War-era Hupp family and as a hiding place for many Civil War soldiers from both sides. Before the war, local history says, Hupp's Hill caves were an important stop on the Underground Railroad.

Be sure to also visit the hill itself, where the Confederates tried to hold off Union troops on Oct. 13, 1864. Original battle entrenchments can still be viewed.

For more on this area, see Crystal Caverns under "Caves" in Chapter Four, *Outdoor Recreation*.

Woodstock

WOODSTOCK MUSEUM AND TOWN HALL
540-459-5518; or Chamber of Commerce, 540-459-2542.
137 W. Court St., PO Box 741, Woodstock, VA 22664.
Open: Hours vary; call ahead.
Admission: Free.

The Woodstock Museum National Historic Site is just one of the local buildings you can stroll by in this pocket-sized town. It was built to be the town hall in 1853 and served as the original 1879 council chambers. Galleries in the museum interpret Woodstock from 10,000 B.C. to the present. The building was completely restored in 1993–1995 and now offers a wide variety of programs and services.

Edinburg

EDINBURG MADISON DISTRICT MUSEUM
40-984-8521.

A bit of everything has been gathered from the local area, which is rich in history from prehis-

5107 Center St., Edinburg, VA 22824.
Open: Weekends only, 1–4.
Admission: Free.

toric through modern times. No fee, but be sure to call ahead, even in season. There is no phone in the museum itself at this writing; the phone is in the municipal office.

New Market

NEW MARKET BATTLEFIELD MILITARY MUSEUM
540-740-8065.
www.newmarketmilitary
museum.com
georga@shentel.net.
9500 George Collins Pkwy., New Market, VA 22844.
Open: Mar. 15–Oct. 31, daily 9–5.
Admission: Adults $8, children 6–13 $4, children under 6 free.

Take a virtual tour of Bushong Farm, where the battle took place, or walk it yourself. The farmhouse later served as a hospital. (You can combine this with a visit to New Market Battlefield State Historical Park.)

BEDROOMS OF AMERICA MUSEUM AND POTTERY
540-740-3512.
9386 S. Congress St., New Market, VA 22844.
Open: Mon.–Fri. 10–4, Sat. 10–4:30, Sun. 12–4:30.

This is a fun stop if you'd like to learn how folks slept in the Valley over its history. The structure itself is a restored 18th-century building, used as a headquarters by General Jubal Early during the Civil War. There are 11 different rooms of authentic furniture from circa 1650 through the Art Deco of the 1930s. A shop is attached to the museum. (See Chapter Seven, *Shopping.*)

PAGE COUNTY

CAR & CARRIAGE CARAVAN MUSEUM
540-743-6551.
www.luraycaverns.com.
970 U.S. Hwy. 211 West, PO Box 748, Luray, VA 22835.
Open: Daily 9–5.
Admission: Adults $5, children $3.50.

Part of the Luray Caverns complex of things to see, the museum offers joint tickets with other cavern sites. (See "Caves" in Chapter Four, *Outdoor Recreation.*) Seventy-five restored antique cars await, including a 1908 Baker electric, a 1913 Stanley Steamer, and a restored 1892 Benz still in operating condition. Cars owned by the rich and famous add to the interest — Rudolf Valentino's 1925 Rolls Royce is a heartthrob of an auto. You also can see a coach from 1725 and a real Conestoga wagon, the vehicle of choice in America's trek westward.

Luray's Car & Carriage Caravan Museum displays examples of wheeled transportation from the Valley's history.

Courtesy Luray Caverns

Exploring the Culinary History of Page County

The **Page County Historical Society** offers this Web site for those who want to recreate the county's historic dishes: www.rootsweb.com/~vagspc/recipes.htm. The Web site allows you to peek into the Valley's family recipe boxes.

PAGE COUNTY HERITAGE MUSEUM
540-743-3915.
Rte. 766, Luray, VA 22835.
Open: May–Oct., Sat. 10–4,
   Sun. 12–4. Other times by
   appt. only.
Admission: Free

Small collection of local artifacts with many everyday life items.

ROCKINGHAM COUNTY

Harrisonburg/Dayton/Bridgewater/Port Republic

VIRGINIA QUILT MUSEUM
540-433-3818.
www.folkart.com/~latitude
   /museums/m_vqm.htm.
301 S. Main St.,
   Harrisonburg, VA 22801.
Open: Mon., Thurs.–Sat.
   10–4, Sun. 1–4. Closed on
   major holidays.
Admission: Adults $4,
   seniors and children 12–18
   $3, children 6–12 $2.

Appropriately located in the heart of a tradi-tional Mennonite quilt-making community, this museum fills the role of quilting display, re-source, and educator. There are scads of documents here on quilts and quilting, and they regularly offer classes, including one-day seminars. Call ahead for the schedule. The gift shop is well stocked with quilting supplies and books, too.

REUEL B. PRITCHETT MUSEUM
540-828-5462.
Cole Hall (ground floor), Bridgewater College, Rte. 257, Bridgewater, VA 22812.
Open: Hours vary; call first.
Admission: Free.

Reuel Pritchett was a farmer and preacher of the Church of the Brethren in White Pine, Tennessee, and an avid collector of many, many things. From autographs to Bibles, from the American West to China, if he liked an item, he bought it. At his death he chose to share his unusual items with others, willing his eclectic collection to Bridgewater College. His lusterware glass, rare books (including a Venetian three-volume Bible dating from 1482), a land deed signed by Thomas Jefferson, and other items await.

SHENANDOAH VALLEY FOLK ART AND HERITAGE CENTER MUSEUM
540-879-2616.
www.heritagecenter.com.
382 High St., PO Box 715, Dayton, VA 22821.
Open: Mon.–Sat. 10–4. Closed all major holidays and in bad weather.
Admission: $5.

The heritage center is home to and operated by the Harrisonburg-Rockingham Historical Society, an organization that has existed for more than 100 years. Many of the volunteer staff are former professors from the several higher education institutions in the area and can answer most questions about local history. Changing exhibits provide information on various aspects of local life, and the electronic map in the museum anteroom allows you to track the Civil War campaigns of the Valley. The gift shop is filled with booklets, books, local art, and crafts, including lovely pottery and freshly ground wheat and other grains from Wade's Mill.

PORT REPUBLIC MUSEUM
540-249-3156.
PO Box 82, Port Republic, VA 24471.
Take Exit 245 off I-81, follow signs for 11 miles.
Open: Sun. 1:30–4.
Admission: $1.

The museum has artifacts of local history and one room devoted to Turner Ashby, the young hero known as the Black Knight of the Confederacy. Born in 1828, Ashby was beloved by the people of the area for his kind and heroic nature. He was mortally wounded on Port Republic Road in Harrisonburg.

The Port Republic Battlefield is a mile and a half downriver from the village. The Association for the Preservation of Civil War Sites has established a short interpretive trail there, with signage at the "coaling" that overlooks the battlefield. Coaling refers to the site of the placement of Federal guns. Some of the fiercest fighting of the war took place in an effort to gain or keep control of these guns. The Society of Port Republic Preservationists, Inc. runs the museum.

AUGUSTA COUNTY

Staunton/Waynesboro

The Frontier Culture Museum just north of Staunton is a living history facility that includes several types of homes built in that area by colonial-era farmers from various European countries.

Shenandoah2000

FRONTIER CULTURE MUSEUM
540-332-7850, Ext. 124.
www.frontiermuseum.org.
info@frontiermuseum.state.va.us.
1290 Richmond Road, PO Box 810, Staunton, VA 24402-0810.
Open: In season, daily 9–5; Dec. 1–mid Mar., daily 10–4. Closed on Thanksgiving, Christmas, certain days in Jan., and during severe weather. Call ahead to be sure it's open.
Admission: Adults $8, children $4; discounts for groups, seniors, and students. Extra for guided tour.

Allow about two and a half hours for a guided tour and about three hours to see everything on your own. If you're pressed for time, at least see the free Visitor Center overview film and visit the great gift shop, which contains wonderful books and historic crafts. There is free on-site parking but, as of this writing, no meal facilities. You can bring your own picnic or snacks to munch on.

The museum is living history, a three-dimensional recreation of cultural diversity over the past three centuries. Actual rebuilt farms show the different approaches to agriculture and various home styles. The period farmhouses were dismantled in Europe and brought over, then rebuilt here and their fields plowed and planted in the historically appropriate style. They represent: a German farm, c. 1700–1750; an Ulster (Scotch-Irish) farm, c. 1700-1830; and an English yeoman farm, c. 1675–1700.

A slightly later "American" farm of the early colonial era was brought from Eagle Rock. This farm shows in its building and style how the ideas from the other three groups influenced what we have come to call "American." Costumed interpreters "populate" the site and demonstrate crafts of the era, including blacksmithing, carpentry, and others. Check the Web site for information on special student tours and exhibitions.

ALUMNI HOUSE & MUSEUM
Augusta Military Academy
540-248-3007.
Valley Pike (Rte. 11), Fort
  Defiance, VA 24438.
Open: Apr.–Oct., Thurs.–Sun.
  10–5; Nov.–Mar., Wed.,
  Sat., Sun. 10–5.
Admission: Free.

This museum, located eight miles north of Staunton, chronicles local and military history. The building itself is a great gingerbread Victorian that appears to be the kind of place Louisa May Alcott and her Little Women may have inhabited, so it's no surprise that the house has an author's room. The museum's virtual tour is amazing in detail and ease of use, and its games are a good way to help children learn to appreciate museum exhibits.

Other sites in Staunton:

The 116th Regimental Museum (540-332-3945) is located in the armory in Gypsy Hill Park. The Local Sun Trust Bank on W. Beverley St. between Central Ave. and Augusta St. has a tiny **Museum of Banking** in its main office. Open during normal banking hours: Mon.–Thurs. 9–2, Fri. 9–6. Admission is free. The 1930 Beaux-Arts-style banking hall is worth seeing just for its own beauty!

The **Jumbo Museum** on N. Augusta St. downtown is a local firehouse that's usually open on weekdays. It offers a free viewing of the only surviving 1911 Robinson pumper fire engine. Call 540-332-3150 to confirm that it's open. **The Statler Brothers Museum** on Thornrose Avenue near Gypsy Hill Park is a renovated schoolhouse containing memorabilia of these country music stars and a gift shop. It's free and is open Mon.–Fri. 10:30–3:30.

Waynesboro

P. BUCKLEY MOSS MUSEUM
540-949-6473.
www.p-buckley-
  moss.com/museum.html.
150 P. Buckley Moss
  Museum Dr.,
  Waynesboro, VA 22980.
Open: Mon.-Sat. 10–6, Sun.
  12:30–5:30.
Admission: Free.

This 18,000-square-foot museum, store, and foundation for the promotion of the arts is the fruit of the career of P. Buckley Moss. Moss' slim Amish figures dash across paper while riding in horse-drawn buggies, skating on ponds, and in general enjoying family fun. She also records many of the wonderful old buildings of the Valley.

Fans of her thin, stylized figures will enjoy this retrospective of work from her school days through today. It's also interesting to learn that she accomplished all of this despite a learning disability that would seem, at first blush, to be at cross purposes with worldwide success.

The gift shop on the lower level is a gold mine for collectors of her work since it carries a full range of her current offerings as well as many items that are considered out of print. Several times each year the artist comes to Waynesboro for signings. Contact the museum to see if your visit will coincide with one of hers.

ROCKBRIDGE COUNTY

Lexington

The Lee Chapel at Washington and Lee University is the final resting place of General Robert E. Lee.

Shenandoah2000

LEE CHAPEL & MUSEUM
540-463-8768.
Washington and Lee
  campus, Lexington, VA
  24450.
Open: Apr.–Oct., Mon.–Sat.
  9–5, Sun. 1–5; Nov.–Mar.,
  closes at 4. Call first as
  chapel is closed during
  weddings.
Admission: Free.

Lee died on Oct. 12, 1870, and was buried beneath the chapel. Eventually the chapel became a memorial to the entire Lee family; the remains of his wife, mother, father ("Light-Horse Harry" Lee), all of his children, and other relatives are now buried in the crypt as well. His beloved horse, Traveler, is buried in a plot beside the chapel entrance.

Lee's office and the Lee Museum are on the lower level. The office is preserved much as Lee left it for the last time on Sept. 28, 1870.

Donations from the family resulted in the impressive collection of art exhibited here. The portrait gallery displaying the Washington-Custis-Lee Collection and the exhibition tracing the history of Washington and Lee University provide many insights into Lee family ties and their role in shaping the rich heritage of Virginia. The museum shop is a good place for those looking for books and other materials on the Lee family.

MARSHALL MUSEUM
540-463-7103, Ext. 231.
www.marshallfoundation
  .org.

The Marshall Museum is on the parade grounds of the Virginia Military Institute. Photos and blurbs on the walls of the museum reveal a lot about this great statesman's personal style.

George C. Marshall's heroic exploits are preserved at this museum on VMI's campus — both his work as a soldier (World War II general) and in peacetime as author of the Marshall Plan.

George C. Marshall Museum, Drawer 1600, Lexington, VA 24450.
Open: Daily 9–5 except Thanksgiving, Christmas, and New Year's Day.
Admission: Adults $3, children 7–18 $1.

George Catlett Marshall (1880–1959) was born in Pennsylvania, but chose VMI as his springboard to a military career. He served with distinction during World War I in combat and as an aid to General John Pershing. By the time World War II began, this career officer had hopscotched from service in China to overseeing the Civilian Conservation Corps to teaching at the War College. During World War II, Franklin Roosevelt made him a general and chief of staff.

At the end of the war Marshall resigned from the Army but continued to distinguish himself as a civilian, first in the peace talks and then as Harry S Truman's secretary of state. His Marshall Plan outlined the rebuilding of Europe and is credited with regenerating Europe's economic strength after the war. He received the Nobel Peace Prize for his efforts in 1953.

That Nobel Prize is on display at the museum, part of its collection of Marshall's flags, medals, and awards. There is also a small but good bookstore with many materials on Marshall and other aspects of military operations during World War II.

Shenandoah2000

Lexington's Virginia Military Institute (VMI), now a state university, has trained and inspired military leaders throughout its more than 200-year history.

VIRGINIA MILITARY INSTITUTE MUSEUM
540-464-7232.
www4.vim.edu/museum.
Jackson Memorial Hall, lower level.
Open: Daily 9–5. Closed holidays in correlation with VMI.
Handicap Access: Call for arrangements.
Admission: Free.

At 140 years, this is one of the oldest museums in the Valley. It is widely known for its collections that honor the traditions of the institute and the accomplishments of its graduates in war. Many famous graduates have contributed personal items — this includes Stonewall Jackson (professor, not graduate), George Marshall, and even General George S. Patton. One exhibit traces a cadet's life at school from the very beginning, including a replica of a cadet room in the VMI barracks.

Henry M. Stewart Jr. of the VMI class of 1935 donated a collection of over 350 different patent office models relating to firearms, as well as hundreds of antique guns and rifles. The collection includes a Lewis and Clark air rifle that accompanied the storied pair on their exploration of the Louisiana territory. This rifle was state-of-the art when purchased in 1803.

Portraits of famous graduates, sculptures, and other art hang in the museum. Some are works by such art luminaries as Norman Rockwell, Julian Scott, Moses Ezekiel, N.C. Wyeth, and Edwin Forbes. There is also a new exhibit on the role of VMI grads in Vietnam.

The gift shop (also accessible online) contains many hard-to-find books and items with a military link.

CYRUS McCORMICK
FARM

See "Historic Houses & Sites."

Natural Bridge

THE WAX MUSEUM
800-533-1410, 540 291-2121.
PO Box 57, Natural Bridge,
VA 24579.
Open: Daily 9–dark.
Admission: Adults $17,
children $7 (includes cave
and museum).

This is a hall of heroes rather than horrors (as are many wax museums). The 170 or so life-sized replicas enhanced with light and sound include George Washington, Thomas Jefferson, Robert E. Lee, and Daniel Boone. The tour also shows how the figures are made.

AMERICAN WORK
HORSE MUSEUM
540-463-2194.
One mile west of I-64 and
I-81 interchange.

Includes oddities such as a treadmill for horses! Open when Virginia Horse Center is open. See listing under "Horses."

BOTETOURT AND ROANOKE COUNTIES

Fincastle

BOTETOURT COUNTY
MUSEUM
540-473-8394.
Courthouse Square,
Fincastle, VA 24090.
Open: Tues., Thurs., Sat.
10–2, Sun. 2–4.
Admission: Free.

The museum is in an 1806 building containing many artifacts dating back to the 1770s. There is also a wonderful collection of Native American arrowheads and other fragments of early human life dug from nearby Eagle Rock.

Daily living is the focus of this museum's exhibits — quilts, clothing, glassware, and pottery. The museum bookstore offers a great array of local history pamphlets and booklets, many of which delve into the fascinating connection between the town and the Lewis and Clark expedition. (Clark married Julia Hancock of Fincastle upon his return.) One of the more popular souvenirs is a map that shows Botetourt County extending to the Mississippi River.

The museum also contains a very moving display of World War I uniforms and memorabilia on what would have been the upstairs porch of the building that houses the museum. The Botetourt County Historical Society runs the museum in Courthouse Square.

Roanoke

**HISTORY MUSEUM /
HISTORICAL SOCIETY
OF WESTERN
VIRGINIA**
540-342-5770.
www.history-museum.org.
PO Box 1904, Roanoke, VA
24008.
One Market Square, third
floor.
Open: Tues.–Fri. 10–4, Sat.
10–5, Sun. 1–5.
Admission: Adults $2,
seniors and children 6–17
$1, 5 and under free.

The permanent exhibit shows the history of southwestern Virginia from prehistoric times to the present. There is an actual bead necklace of the type that gave the city of Roanoke its name. (The name means "shell" and refers specifically to the type of shell used for wampum or currency among the Native Americans who lived in the area.)

The town's first name was Big Lick, referring to its role in the cattle industry, but Roanoke came into its own as a railroad town in the late 19th century. Call ahead to arrange for or take advantage of a planned tour of the area's historic buildings, local churches, and other area historic sites. These guided tours are offered periodically and prices vary.

Visitors enjoy participating in science through the many hands-on exhibits in Roanoke's Science Museum of Western Virginia.

Courtesy of the Roanoke Valley Convention and Visitor's Bureau

**SCIENCE MUSEUM OF
WESTERN VIRGINIA**
540-342-5718.
www.smwv.org.
One Market Square,
Roanoke, VA 24011.
Open: Tues.–Sat. 10–5, Sun.
1–5. Closed major
holidays.
Admission: Adults $6,
children 3–12 $4, under 3
free. Discounts for seniors
and groups. Additional
fee for MegaDome and
planetarium.

The gift shop for this museum is reason alone to visit — an incredible variety of items to fascinate anyone with even a minimal interest in science. Many hands-on exhibits are both local and global in their presentation. Permanent exhibits cover geology, weather, and local ecology. Sure to pique the interest of even the most jaded youngster.

The Harrison Museum of African-American Culture often celebrates the contribution of African Americans through festivals as well as exhibits.

Roanoke Valley Convention and Visitors Bureau

HARRISON MUSEUM OF AFRICAN-AMERICAN CULTURE
540-345-4818.
www.harrisonmuseum.org.
523 Harrison Ave. NW, Roanoke, VA 24016.
Open: Tues.–Sun. 1–5.
Admission: Free.

This museum is located on the ground floor of the 1916 building that served as the first high school for African Americans in Roanoke. Permanent exhibits focus on the art of Roanoke's African-American citizens and their contributions to the city's history.

The museum also serves as a repository for oral history research and a center for promoting African-American pride through heritage activities held throughout the year, most notably the Henry Street Heritage Festival on the last Saturday in September.

The museum store is a good place to shop for gift items, and brochures here detail other area sites of interest to African Americans, including the Booker T. Washington National Monument (540-721-2094; 12130 Booker T. Washington Highway/Rte. 122, south of Roanoke).

VIRGINIA MUSEUM OF TRANSPORTATION
540-342-5670.
www.vmt.org.
303 Norfolk Ave., Roanoke, VA 24016.
Open: Daily, except closed Mon. in Jan.–Feb. Also closed Thanksgiving and Christmas. Hours vary widely; call first.
Admission: Adults $6, children $4. Discount for seniors.

If things on wheels fascinate, or if you love the circus, make sure that you stop at this museum. Antique carriages, cars, trucks, buses, trolleys, and trains are exhibited along with a wonderful miniature circus train display. In fact, the circus train exhibit room is a miniature not just of a circus train, but of the entire big top in action.

Antique cars and bikes are given their due, but trains are the stars here. Magnificent engines dating from the days of steam through contemporary times are on display. What's more, many are restored and guests can climb aboard.

Another room of special interest is the oral history area, where statements from African-American rail workers can be heard and visitors can see a life-sized model of a loading platform and small depot/station. The gift shop is loaded with train memorabilia and posters.

The To The Rescue Museum honors the work of rescue workers.

Julian Stanley Wise Foundation

TO THE RESCUE MUSEUM
540-776-0364.
TTRescue@juno.com.
428 Electric Rd., Roanoke, VA 24018.
Open: Tues.–Sun.; hours vary.
Admission: Adults $2 (EMTs half price), children over 5 $1.

This tiny museum is a storefront in the Tanglewood Shopping Mall on the outskirts of town. Interactive exhibits give a good idea of what volunteer rescue services do. Call before going, as it's manned by volunteers.

CATHOLIC HISTORICAL SOCIETY MUSEUM OF THE ROANOKE VALLEY
540-982-0152.
400 W. Campbell Ave., Roanoke, VA 24016.
Open: Tues. 10–2, or by appt.
Admission: Free.

Exhibits here chronicle the history of the Roman Catholic faith in southwestern Virginia using artifacts from the area's various parishes. There is also a good Catholic bookstore and religious article store attached.

VIRGINIA'S EXPLORE PARK
540-427-1800.
www.explorepark.org.
jevans@explorepark.org.

This 1,100-acre environmental, historical, and recreational park offers absolutely first-rate living history exhibitions. Costumed interpreters live out various tableaux of Virginia life from A.D. 1000

Milepost 115 (just beyond Mill Mountain Park), Blue Ridge Parkway, PO Box 8508, Roanoke, VA 24014.
Open: May–Oct., Wed.–Sat. 10–5, Sun. 12–5. Open some weekends in Apr.; call ahead.
Admission: Adults $8, children $4.50.

to 1850. This is one of the places in the Valley where the contributions of African Americans are featured prominently: One of the eras depicted — the river commerce era of southwestern Virginia — highlights the role of the African-American bateaux workers.

Salem

THE SALEM MUSEUM
Williams-Brown House.
540-389-6760.
www.salemmsueum.org.
info@salemmuseum.org.
801 E. Main St., Salem, VA 24153.
Open: Tues.–Fri. 10–4, Sat. 12–5; closed Sun.–Mon.
Admission: Free; paid personal tours can be arranged.

The Williams-Brown House, a 19th-century building, has been a residence, a post office, and a general store. The house is on the National Register of Historic Places and maintains a historic herb garden. Native American and Civil War relics from nearby sites are displayed alongside contemporary artwork and mementos of daily life from Salem's history.

The Water Street community, the heart of the African-American community from about 1860 on, is well documented in photos and stained glass windows from since-demolished churches. Local artist Walter Biggs also recreated scenes from Water Street to fill in details of daily life for museum visitors. You can pick up a Salem walking tour map here and a map of the area's biking trails.

THE MOUNTAIN COUNTIES

Highland County

THE MAPLE MUSEUM
540-468-2550.
One mile south of Monterey on Rte. 220.
Open: Year-round; call Highland County Department of Tourism (540-468-2347) for hours.
Admission: Free.

The interior of this replica of an old-time sugarhouse provides an overview of the methods, tools, and equipment used to make maple sugar and syrup from the time of the Native Americans through the present day. If you're there during the sugar time in March, you also can visit an actual sugar camp; obtain a list and directions from the Highland Chamber of Commerce during the festival. Some sugaring is also done during the week anytime from February through the festival dates in March.

MUSIC

Note: This section deals mostly with "classical" music. Other types of music are included in "Other Miscellaneous Entertainment."

SHENANDOAH CONSERVATORY
540-665-4600.
www.su.edu/conservatory.
1460 University Ave.,
  Winchester, VA 22601.

The conservatory is part of Shenandoah University (see "Colleges"). Classical music, jazz, and even opera are offered by students and guest professionals throughout the academic year. Information can be found on the university Web site. There is also a summer music theater festival (see "Theater").

MASTERWORKS CHORUS
540-459-5640.
www.masterworkschorus
  .bravepages.com.
PO Box 752, Woodstock, VA
  22664.

This northern Shenandoah Valley regional oratorio and choral society is dedicated to performing inspirational and entertaining choral literature. The chorus holds two major concerts annually and its approximately 12-woman *camarata* group performs for paid functions throughout the year. Check Web site for information on concert locations, times, and ticket prices.

SHENANDOAH JUBILEE EXPRESS SHOW
540-778-1993.
www.shenandoahjubilee
  .com.
Shows held at 8 p.m.
  Fridays at Skyland Resort
  in Shenandoah National
  Park.
Admission: $10.

This is a musical revue-type show. It's more pop than classical, but lots of fun. Also performed monthly at the American Celebration museum located adjacent to Shenandoah Caverns.

JAMES MADISON UNIVERSITY
540-568-7000, 540-432-4582.
www.jmu.edu.
Exit 245 off I-81,
  Harrisonburg, VA 22807.

The Music Department sponsors classical and other music productions by students and professional guest artists. One of the more popular offerings is the Masterpiece Season Series held in JMU's Wilson Hall. Another one to look for is the Shenandoah Valley Bach Festival held each summer in Lehrman Auditorium. Check the university Web site for up-to-date information.

ROANOKE SYMPHONY ORCHESTRA AND CHORUS
540-343-9127, 866-277-9127.
music@rso.com.

The Roanoke Symphony Orchestra, founded in 1953, is the largest professional orchestra in Virginia west of Richmond. A number of the season's concerts feature the Roanoke Symphony Chorus with

Jefferson Center, 541 Luck Ave, Suite 200, Roanoke, VA 24016.

the orchestra. The symphony's education programs include concerts for elementary and middle school students, a youth symphony, a junior strings training orchestra, and a youth harp ensemble. Summertime music festivals often round out the program.

OPERA ROANOKE
540-982-2742.
wckrause@operaroanoke .org.
Jefferson Center, 541 Luck Ave., Suite 209, Roanoke, VA 24016.

Opera Roanoke, founded in 1977, offers English translations projected right above the stage, a great help for following along, no matter the language being sung! One big advantage for those who want to learn more about opera is that the director gives previews of the storyline 30 minutes before each performance, open to all ticket holders.

SHAFTMAN PERFORMANCE HALL
540-345-2550.
info@jeffcenter.org.
Jefferson Center, 541 Luck Ave., Roanoke, VA 24016.

This 1,000-seat hall is often the performance space for the Roanoke Ballet Theatre, Opera Roanoke, and the Roanoke Symphony Orchestra as well as other classical, family, and contemporary performances. The space is also rented for entertainment, private, and corporate events.

ROANOKE CIVIC CENTER
540-981-1201.
www.roanokeciviccenter .com.
710 Williamson Rd. NW, Roanoke, VA 24030.

This is another major performance venue in Roanoke within walking distance of downtown. Major concerts and touring Broadway shows share schedule time with conventions. Star City GRITS, the Valley's women's road cycling team, is headquartered here as well.

OLIN HALL
540-375-3454.
Roanoke College, 221 College Ln., Salem, VA 24153.

Call for schedule of musical events.

SALEM CIVIC CENTER
540-375-3004.
1001 Boulevard, PO Box 886, Salem, VA 24153.

A variety of performances and special shows grace this 21,000-square-foot venue, which seats up to 7,000 for sporting events. Many national shows come here, where tickets are cheaper than they are closer to Washington, so it pays to check if you're planning a visit.

GARTH NEWEL MUSIC CENTER
877-558-1689 (tickets) or 540-839-5018.

Chamber music performed by critically acclaimed artists resounds over the 114 rolling acres of the Garth Newel Center year-round. (Garth

www.garthnewel.org.
office@garthnewel.org.
PO Box 240, Warm Springs,
VA 24484.

Newel means "new home" or "new hearth" in Welsh.) The piano quartet is the in-house group, but musicians from all over the world are often guest performers. Among the more spectacular offerings are the annual summer Adult Chamber Music Retreat and the Music Holiday Weekends held in the spring, fall, and summer. The center's performance venue, Herter Hall, is a converted 1920s horse show ring, updated for acoustics, with a décor that retains the look and feel of a 1924 estate. Outside, there are 20 acres for walks and picnics.

ALLEGHANY HIGHLANDS ARTS COUNCIL
540-962-6220.
185 N. Maple Ave.,
Covington, VA 24426.

The council sponsors events in various venues, and is a source for information on local and notable touring performers in music, drama, comedy, and dance. The council also sponsors student series during the school year and the annual series of performances by the Alleghany Highlands Chorale and the Alleghany Highlands Orchestra.

THEATER

For more than 30 years, Middleton's Wayside Theatre has offered a full season of live theatrical productions.

Shenandoah2000

FREDERICK, CLARKE, AND WARREN COUNTIES

Wayside Theatre (540-869-1776; 7853 Main St., PO Box 229, Middletown, VA 22645) This is a wonderful place to see excellent live theater. Intimate, historic space, close to D.C. The tickets are only $12–$13 per person and the performances are wonderful. They offer classes and children's programming as well. Occasionally used as a music venue for area vocal groups and orchestras, especially during the holidays.

Winchester Little Theatre (540-662-3331; 315 W. Boscawan St., Middletown, VA 22601) Occasionally produces plays. Call for schedule. Winchester Visitor Center also will have schedule.

SHENANDOAH COUNTY

The **Valley Educational Center for the Creative Arts** (540-984-4229; 508 Picadilly St., Edinburg, VA 22824) and the **Woodstock Community Theatre** (540-459-2221; 136 N. Main St., Woodstock, VA 22664) are the focal points for theater arts activity in Shenandoah County.

ROCKINGHAM COUNTY

Court Square Theater (540-433-9189, Court Square, Harrisonburg, VA 22801) Although there are some theatrical productions here, the majority of the activity here is musical — folk and country.

University Theater, James Madison University (540-568-7000; www.jmu.edu; Harrisonburg, VA 22807) Many University Theater events are open to the public; check the Web site for details. The University Masterpiece Theater season brings national and international theater and art to campus. Check with the box office.

Valley Playhouse (540-432-0634; 107 E. Water St., Harrisonburg, VA 22801) A community theater — lots of fun and reasonably priced tickets. Prices vary.

AUGUSTA COUNTY

SHENANDOAH SHAKESPEARE BLACKFRIARS THEATER
540-885-5588.
www.shenandoahshake speare.com.
sse@shenandoahshake speare.com.
11 E. Beverley St., Suite 31, Staunton, VA 24401.

This theater is a recreation of Shakespeare's indoor, winter theater at Blackfriars in London. It's open year-round for Shakespeare productions, as well as for special musical and theatrical events, tours, and educational programs. The touring company, **Shenandoah Shakespeare Express,** is currently the most active touring Shakespeare company in the world.

Seeing a show here is an experience that takes you back to the time of the bard. Not only is the set-

Shenandoah2000

The play's the thing at Staunton's Blackfriars Theatre, where the building and the actors emulate the look and style of Shakespeare's own winter theatre in London.

Performances: Daily evenings and 2 to 3 matinees a week. Tickets: $10–$20.

ting authentic, but the production techniques follow those used by Shakespeare insofar as is possible. The troupe uses universal lighting, doubles up on parts, and disregards gender in casting. (In the bard's time the cast was all men. In a modern twist on that idea, women play men's roles and vice versa.) Popular ditties of the day often punctuated Shakespeare's plays, and that tradition carries on here as well.

NEW DIXIE THEATRE
540-885-6772.
www.newdixietheatre.org.
125–127 E. Beverley St., Staunton, VA 22401.

This nonprofit organization envisions developing and operating The Staunton Performing Arts Center in this historic building. At this writing it serves as a movie house, but may soon be restored to live performances. The outside is a must-see, with its absolutely fabulous ceramic artwork.

OAK GROVE THEATER
540-248-5005.
www.oakgrovetheater.org.
info@oakgrovetheater.org.
212 Hendren Ave., Staunton, VA 22401.

The actual theater space for this community group is an outdoor grove just 2.1 miles west of Rte. 11 on Rte. 612 (Quick's Mill Road) in Verona. Check the Web site for the schedule and audition notices.

The **Waynesboro Players** (540-949-7464) is a community group with just a phone number — no set venue, but they offer live theater in various community spots.

ROCKBRIDGE COUNTY

LIME KILN THEATER
540-463-3074.
www.theateratlimekiln.com.
14 S. Randolph St.,
  Lexington, VA 24450.
Open: Apr.–Oct. for shows;
  call for schedule.
Admission: Varies by type
  of performance.

The ruins of a 19th-century lime quarry and kiln create a magical setting in which locals and visitors can enjoy music and dramatic performances. The entire area only seats 388, with some tent seating available for those who don't want to take a chance on a sudden Shenandoah shower soaking them. The Lexington Visitors Bureau (540-463-3777; 106 E. Washington St.) and the theater's Web site list performances.

**LENFEST CENTER FOR
  PERFORMING ARTS**
540-463-8000.
www.wlu.edu.
Washington and Lee
  University, Lexington, VA
  24450.

This is a year-round venue with hours and schedules that vary widely. Both professional and student productions ranging from music to theater are held here. Schedule on Web site and at Lexington Visitors Bureau (540-463-3777; 106 E. Washington St.)

Other Rockbridge County theatrical venues include:

Natural Bridge Drama of Creation (800-533-1410; Natural Bridge, VA 24578) Since 1927, each night (weather permitting) Apr.–Nov. and on weekends in winter, a music and light show has illuminated the beauty of the bridge for visitors.

The Monacan Indian Village at Natural Bridge is a living history display of life in the Valley before the Europeans came.

Mary Ann Puglisi

Monacan Indian Village (800-533-1410; Natural Bridge, VA 24578) Living history/theater is open from spring to late fall at Natural Bridge Caverns. Descendants of the original tribe work in the exhibit, showing visitors what life was like in the early days.

BOTETOURT AND ROANOKE COUNTIES

Attic Productions (540-473-3216; www.atticproductions.info; PO Box 695, Fincastle, VA 24090) Local theater group. Call for schedule and venue.

DUMAS DRAMA GUILD
540-345-6781.
tap@taproanoke.org.
PO Box 2868, Roanoke, VA 24011.

This is an African-American theater company offering a full season of performances using local actors. The group works with young people through its Youth on the Yard Organization (YOYO), an after-school drama education program for children in kindergarten through 12th grade. These productions feature original performances written, directed, and acted by the students.

MILL MOUNTAIN THEATRE
800-317-6455, 540-342-5740.
www.millmountain.org.
MMTmail@millmountain.org.
One Market Square, Second Floor, Roanoke, VA 24011.

This professional regional theater operates year-round, mounting productions on two stages in Center in the Square. Dramas, musicals, comedies, a new play competition, and educational and drama enrichment programs are available to all. In addition, there are often free lunchtime one-acts, and the Mill Mountain Players tour throughout Virginia. For performance dates, hours, and prices, call or check the Web site.

RENAISSANCE THEATRE FESTIVAL AND VIRGINIA WESTERN THEATRE
540-857-7327.
www.vw.vccs.edu/theatre.
bmccleary@vw.vccs.edu.
Virginia Western Community College; 3099 Colonial Ave, SW, Roanoke, VA 24015.

Children are welcome at the one and only completely free theater in the Roanoke area. (Donations are accepted, but no one is ever pressured to give.) The finest in classic, contemporary, and new plays are presented. For performance dates and times, see the Web site.

Other venues include:

The Crime Scene Murder Mystery Dinner Theater (540-427-7267, 866-576-0553; mystery2go@aol.com; 4468 Starkey Rd., Roanoke, VA 24014) The Crime Scene is an interactive murder mystery dinner theater. Dinner comes with just "desserts," or at least a lot of laughs for perpetrators of murder and mayhem onstage. Shows Friday and Saturday nights at the Holiday Inn Tanglewood.

Showtimer's Theatre (540-774-2660; 2067 McVitty Rd., Roanoke, VA 24018) This is the oldest continuously performing community theater in Virginia.

Stonewall Theatre (540-862-7407; ahchamber@aol.com; 510 Main St., Clifton Forge, VA 24422) This turn-of-the century opera house in the historic district is now a performing arts center. More than 500 seats for the Virginia Opry and other music events.

For **Olin Hall** at Roanoke College and other venues in Salem, see "Music."

OTHER MISCELLANEOUS ENTERTAINMENT

These events and entertainment happenings are just a sample of what can be found by contacting local tourism offices. (See Chapter Eight, *Information*.)

At the gazebo in *Front Royal* there are free concerts every Friday night during the summer — everything from calypso to rock to bluegrass. The gazebo is near the Visitor Center.

In *Winchester*, **First Friday** takes place on the first Friday evening of every month except January and May. All of the stores and galleries stay open until 9, and there is music on the streets.

In *Woodstock,* **Chappalino's** offers an open-mic night every Monday. Call 540-459-7332 for information.

In *Basye/Orkney Springs*, Shenandoah County's Shenandoah Valley Music Festival (www.musicfest.org) is the Valley's largest summer musical event. Symphony, folk, jazz, and big band concerts are presented on five select summer weekends. See Web site for dates and dollars.

Luray offers two summer programs: The **Bluemont Series** of free summer concerts on Saturday nights in Luray Park on Main Street (check with the tourism office, 888-743-3915, for schedule) and the **Luray Singing Tower** (540-743-6551) in a park opposite Luray Caverns, Rte. 211 and Rte. 340 bypass. The latter are free concerts offered spring through fall on a 47-bell carillon. Call for schedule.

In *Harrisonburg,* the *Daily News Record* and its online version, www.dnronline.com, will give you the latest on pubs and places of interest. The large student population means that there are plenty of club venues in the area, but they change frequently. **Dave's Downtown Taverna** (540-564-1487) and the **Little Grill** (540-434-3594) also offer open-mike nights.

In *Staunton,* several restaurants occasionally sponsor acoustic music. As of this writing, **L'Italia Restaurant's Pompeii Lounge** (540-885-0102; www.stauntonweb.com/litalia.html; 23 E. Beverley St.) provides live music on weekend nights in the lounge, and you can frequently hear acoustic music at **Brooklyn's Deli** (540-213-2150; 7 S. New St.). A good source for uncovering acoustic music happenings in Staunton is **Queen City Acoustic** (540-886-5362), which offers contemporary folk music on selected Thursdays. Call for venue and times. In addition, there are concerts in **Gypsy Hill Park** throughout the summer. The **Stonewall Brigade Band** plays every Monday evening, and on Thursdays you can hear **Jazz in the Park.**

Also in Staunton is the **Statler Brothers Complex** (540-885-7297; www.statler brothers.com, statlers@cfw.com; Thornrose Avenue, PO Box 2703, Staunton, VA 24402). The Statler Brothers do perform here, and their Web site provides their touring schedule. Free tours of the center are offered Monday through Friday at 2pm. Gift shop open weekdays 10:30–3:30.

In *Lexington,* **Southern Inn Restaurant** (540-463-3612) offers live music on Thursday and Friday nights. **Washington and Lee University** also sponsors other music events.

Two *Roanoke* restaurant venues occasionally offering live music were: **The Club at Fiji Island** (540-343-6751; Franklin Rd.) and **The Coffee Pot** (540-774-8256; 2902 Brambleton SW). The Coffee Pot is a Roanoke institution. Folks who listened to music here in their teens and are now in their 50s return and join new listeners in their teens. The eclectic audience is part of the fun.

In *Monterey,* **The Highland Center** (540-468-1922; highcent@cfw.com; PO Box 556, Monterey, VA 24465) provides a varied schedule of music and community events, including professional performances and shows by local children. It is a real center of activity within the community.

At **The Homestead** in *Hot Springs* (800-838-1766; www.thehomestead.com; PO Box 2000, Hot Springs, VA 24445), entertainment is provided for guests. The Homestead is known for its theme weekends and wonderful entertainment. Check the Web site — many shows are open to the public.

ZOOS AND DINOSAURS

Places to see real animals of the present and replica animals from the past include:

Shenandoah Valley Discovery Museum (540-722-2020; www.discovery museum.net; 54 S. Loudoun St., Winchester, VA 22604) See listing under "Museums" in this chapter.

Wilson's Wild Animal Park (540-662-5712; www.wilsonsanimalpark.com; 985 W. Parkins Mill Rd., Winchester, VA 22602) Enjoy more than 200 mammals, birds, and reptiles. A South American capybaras, one of the largest rodents in the world, is a resident. Closes in winter for the comfort of the animals. Open May–Oct., daily 10–5, until 6 on weekends. Admission is $4, free for children under age 3.

Dinosaur Land (540-869-2222; www.dinosaurland.com; 3848 Stonewall Jackson Highway, White Post, VA 22663) Besides wandering through huge replicas of favorite prehistoric beasties, visitors can stop by a gift shop loaded with Native American-style gifts and dino-goodies. It's a piece of kitsch, truly fun and great for toddlers. Open Mar.–Dec., 9:30–5:30 daily.

Deauville Fallow Deer Farm (540-856 2130; deer1@shentel.net; 7648 Crooked Run Rd., Basye, VA 22810) You can pet the deer at Alex and Gail Rose's farm in Shenandoah County. The chickens are another wonderful sight — many different and very colorful varieties in a pen in back. If you're there when they're gathering eggs you'll see that the eggs are different, too! Call for hours.

Luray Reptile Center and Dinosaur Park (540-743-4113; www.lurayzoo.com; reptiles@lurayzoo.com; 1087 Hwy. 211 W., Luray, VA 22835) Eighty different kinds of snakes, including exotic black mambas, are waiting to thrill and enthrall. Turtles, lizards, and an alligator snapping turtle that weighs 180 pounds make visitors wonder if Jurassic Park could be far behind. These real animals are scary enough for me! Open daily 10–5; in winter, call to confirm. Admission: adults $6, children $5.

Virginia Safari Park (540-291-3205; 229 Safari Ln., Natural Bridge, VA 24578) Located just off I-81 at Exit 180, this is Virginia's only drive-through zoo and safari gift shop. It's a great place to stop if you have little ones or simply can't get enough of exotic animals. There's a real African safari feel here, with the visitor being in the "cage" (one's own car) and the animals on the loose all around. Open: Apr.–Oct.; 9–6 daily, Nov.–Mar. 9–5 weekends only.

Mill Mountain Zoo in Roanoke County (540-343-3241; www.mmzoo.org; info@mmzoo.org; off Parkway Spur Rd., PO Box 13484, Roanoke, VA 24034) This 3.5-acre zoo, located just up the road from the Roanoke Star, includes exotic animals such as a Siberian tiger, red pandas, and snow leopards. A wildflower garden highlights local flora. Special events and educational programs are held for children of all ages. Open daily on varying schedule. Admission: adults $6, children $4. Additional fee for Zoo train ride.

FESTIVALS AND OTHER SEASONAL EVENTS

The following festivals and events are usually held annually. Multiple weekend events are listed in the beginning month with a notation about continuance. Recurring single-day/weekend events are listed below by month, except winery events and Civil War reenactments. For wineries, see Chapter Six, *Restaurants, Food Purveyors, and Wine* and for their festivals check with the **Virginia Wine Marketing Office** (804-786-0481; www.virginiawines.org; PO Box 1163, Richmond, VA 23218). For Civil War reenactments, see "Battlefields and Civil War Reenactments" earlier in this chapter.

Listings are given in this order: event name, contact number, location, and notes, if any. Many events charge admission fees. For additional festivals, exact festival dates, and a weather forecast for your travel dates, check www.svta.org or call 877-VISITSV.

Be aware that May is the time for university graduations in the Valley and fall is the time for college football as well as harvest festivals.

JANUARY

Birthday Convocation for Robert E. Lee (540-463-3777; Washington and Lee University, Lexington).

Fort Harrison Twelfth Night (540-879-2280; Daniel Harrison House, Dayton) Usually held Jan. 6.

Winterfest (800-838-1766; www.thehomestead.com; The Homestead, Hot Springs) Activities for the community as well as resort guests.

FEBRUARY

African-American Heritage Month (540-332-7850; Frontier Culture Museum, Rte. 250 W., Staunton).

Groundhog Day at Mill Mountain Zoo (540-343-3241; Mill Mountain Zoo, Roanoke).

President's Birthday Party (540-465-5884; Museum of American Presidents, Strasburg).

Presidents Day Weekend (540-883-0897; Woodrow Wilson House, Staunton).

Presidents Day Weekend Open House (540-662-4412; George Washington's Office Museum, Winchester).

MARCH

Augusta County Arts and Crafts Expo (540-337-2552; Fishersville).

Battle of Waynesboro Commemoration (540-942-6644; Waynesboro High School, Waynesboro).

Highland County Maple Festival (540-468-2550; various locations in Monterey) Usually held on two weekends.

Shenandoah Valley Spring Arts and Crafts Sale (540-879-9417; Harrisonburg Fairgrounds) Held third or fourth weekend in March.

St. Patrick's Day Parade and Celtic Festival (540-853-2889; www.roanokespecial events.org; Jefferson St., Roanoke).

Wildlife Center Open House (540-942-9453; Waynesboro).

Women's History Month Celebration (540-885-0397; Woodrow Wilson House, Staunton).

MARCH–APRIL

Easter Traditions (540-332-7850; Frontier Culture Museum, Staunton).

Outdoor Easter Services (540-291-2121; usually held at sunrise at Natural Bridge) May be in March or April; depends when Easter falls.

APRIL

Historic Garden Week (540-644-7776) Usually held on the second or third weekend in April all over Virginia.
Riverfest (540-942-6720; Waynesboro).
Victorian Spring Festival (540-332-3867; Staunton).
Vinton Dogwood Festival (540-983-0613; Vinton).
Virginia Beef Expo (540-992-1009; Rockingham County Fairgrounds, Harrisonburg).
Virginia Fly Fishing Festival (540-942-6705; Waynesboro).
Wildlife Center Open House (540-942-9453; Waynesboro).
Wool Days (540-332-7850; Frontier Culture Museum, Staunton).

MAY

Garden Fair at the Arboretum of Virginia (540-837-1758; www.virginia.edu/~blandy; Boyce).
International Bird Migration Day at Mill Mountain Zoo (540-343-3241; www.mmzoo.org; Roanoke) Usually held in early May.
Memorial Day Horse Fair and Auction (540-434-4482; Rockingham County Fairgrounds, Harrisonburg).
Microwbrew Festival (540-869-2028; Belle Grove Plantation, Middletown) Usually held in early May.
Middle Mountain Momma (540-977-4335; Douthat State Park, Millboro) A mountain bike race.
Roanoke Festival in the Parks (540-342-2640; various locations in and around the city).
Shenandoah Annual Food and Business Fair (540-434-0005; www.rockinghamcountyfair.com; Rockingham County Fairgrounds, Harrisonburg).
Shenandoah Apple Blossom Festival (800-230-2139; www.sbaf.org; Winchester) One of the largest events in the Valley. Usually held the first full weekend in May.
Strawberry Festival (540-342-2028; Roanoke) Early May.
Virginia Wine and Mushroom Festival (540-835-5185; Front Royal) Usually second or third weekend in May.

JUNE

Bike Festival at Explore Park (540-427-1800; www.exploresingletrack.com; Roanoke) Clinics on bikes, bike demos, and rides on park trails.
Blue Ridge Garden Festival (800-842-9163; www.explorepark.org; Explore Park, Roanoke).
Maury River Fiddler's Convention (540-261-7321; www.glenmaurypark.com; Buena Vista).
Natural Chimneys National Jousting Hall of Fame Joust (540-249-5705; Natural Chimneys Regional Park, Mount Solon).

NBHA Virginia Championship (540-463-3777; Virginia Horse Center, Lexington).
Shenandoah Valley Pow Wow (540-477-9616; Silver Phoenix Indian Trading Post, Quicksburg) In Shenandoah County near Mount Jackson.
Summer Nights at the Frontier Culture Museum (540-332-7850; Staunton) Songs, dances, storytelling, and more to entertain the family. Held all summer long; call for specific events and fees.

JULY

Annual Butterfly Count (540-999-3282; Shenandoah National Park) Call for details.
Annual Raft Race (800-654-1714; Stuarts Draft).
Beach Music Festival (540-261-7321; www.glenmarypark.com; Buena Vista).
Douthat Arts and Crafts Fair (540-862-8100; Douthat State Park, Millboro).
Hot Air Balloon Rally (540-463-3777; Virginia Military Institute, Lexington).
Rockbridge Regional Fair (540-463-6263; Virginia Horse Center, Lexington).
Salem Fair (540-373-3004; www.salemfair.com; Salem).
Shenandoah Bach Festival (540-432-4582; James Madison University campus, Harrisonburg).
Shenandoah Valley Bike Festival (540-438-8063; Harrisonburg).
Shenandoah Valley Christmas in July (540-879-9412; Harrisonburg) An arts and crafts event.
Shenandoah Valley Music Festival (540-459-3396, 800-459-3396; www.music fest.org; Orkney Springs Hotel, Orkney Springs) Multiple weekends through September.
Summer on the Farms (540-332-7850; Frontier Culture Museum, Staunton) Usually held on an early weekend.

AUGUST

Appalachian Folk Festival (540-427-1800; Explore Park, Roanoke).
Highland County Fair (540-468-2550; Monterey).
Jousting Tournament (540-249-5705; Natural Chimneys Regional Park, Mount Solon).
Massanutten Hoo-Ha (800-207-MASS; Harrisonburg) One of the largest and oldest mountain bike races in existence.
Rockbridge Community Festival (540-436-3777; www.lexingtonvirginia.com; Lexington).
Rockingham County Fair (540-434-0005; Rockingham County Fairgrounds, Harrisonburg).
Shakespeare Festival at Blackfriars Theatre (540-885-5588; Staunton).
Shenandoah County Fair (540-459-3867; www.shencofair.com; Woodstock).
Virginia Mountain Peach Festival (540-342-2028; www.downtownroanoke .org; Roanoke).

SEPTEMBER

A Taste of History (540-332-7850; Frontier Culture Museum, Staunton).
African-American Heritage Festival (540-332-3972; Staunton).
Appalachian Folk Festival (800-842-9163; Explore Park, Roanoke).
Blue Ridge Oktoberfest and Chili Cook-off (540-635-3185; www.frontroyal chamber.com; Front Royal).
Constitution Day (540-465-5884; www.waysideofva.com; Museum of American Presidents, Strasburg).
Edinburg Ole Time Festival (540-984-9492; Edinburg).
Grand Caverns Annual Bluegrass Festival (540-249-5729; Grand Caverns Regional Park, Grottoes).
Labor Day Festival (540-261-7321; www.glenmaurypark.com; Buena Vista).
Olde Salem Days (540-375-4046; Main St., Salem).
Rockbridge Mountain Music and Dance Festival (540-463-5214; www.rock bridgefestival.org; Glen Maury Park, Buena Vista).
Visiting Artist Series (540-722-2020; Shenandoah Valley Discovery Museum, Winchester) Held on second weekend of each month, Sept.–Jun.

OCTOBER

Affair in the Square (540-342-5700; Roanoke).
Apple Day Celebration of Appalachian Heritage (540-862-8100; Douthat State Park, Millboro).
Arborfest (540-837-1758; State Arboretum, Boyce).
Belle Grove Halloween Storytelling (540-869-2028; www.bellegrove.org; Middletown).
British Car Festival (540-942-6644; Waynesboro).
Ghost Walk (540-332-3962; Staunton).
Holiday Lantern Tours (540-465-8660; Strasburg) Guides dressed in 19th-century apparel lead tours through the Crystal Caverns under Hupp's Hill.
Holidays in History (540-332-7850, Frontier Culture Museum, Staunton).
Monacan Indian Living History Reenactment (800-533-1410; Natural Bridge).
New Market Heritage Fall Festival (540-740-3212; New Market).
Roanoke Bicycle Festival (540-774-1012; Roanoke) Road and trail rides, food and fun.
Shenandoah Fall Foliage Bike Festival (757-229-0507, 540-332-3865; Staunton) Weekend of on- and off-road events for biking the back roads of the Valley near Staunton.
Shenandoah Valley Hot Air Balloon Festival at Long Branch (888-558-5567; Winchester).
Zooboo (540-343-3241; Mill Mountain Zoo, Roanoke).

NOVEMBER

Christmas at Fort Harrison (540-879-2272; Dayton).

Food for the Table (540-332-7850; Frontier Culture Museum, Staunton).

Living History Days at Belle Grove (540-869-2028; www.bellegrove.org; Middletown).

Roanoke Valley Mineral and Gem Show (540-375-3004; www.salemcivic center.com; Salem).

DECEMBER

Belle Grove Candlelight Christmas (540-869-2028; Middletown).

Candlelight Tours of Woodrow Wilson House (540-885-0897; Staunton).

Christmas Remembered (540-463-2552; Stonewall Jackson House, Lexington).

Dickens of a Christmas (540-342-2028; Roanoke) Several weekends in December.

Horse's Christmas (540-261-7321; Glen Maury Park, Buena Vista).

Old-Fashioned Christmas Weekend (540-463-7191; downtown Lexington) Usually the first full weekend in December.

Ringing of the Bells (540-473-3077; Fincastle) New Year's Eve in the Town Square.

Waynesboro First Night (540-942-6644; Waynesboro) First Night celebrations are town-wide New Year's Eve events — no alcohol, but plenty of entertainment, food, and good company for the whole family. They are spreading throughout the country. Get your tickets early!

Winchester First Night (540-662-4135, 800-662-1360; Winchester) First Night celebrations are a family approach to New Year's Eve — lots of entertainment at venues around the city.

Woodrow Wilson Birthday Party (540-885-0897; Woodrow Wilson House Museum, Staunton) Dec. 28.

CHAPTER FOUR
The Nature of the Valley
OUTDOOR RECREATION

Shenandoah2000

Kayaking is a popular water activity in the Valley. Many outfitters rent kayaks and give instruction.

Opportunities for outdoor recreation in the Shenandoah Valley could — and do — fill several specialized volumes. The activities suggested here form a representative sample. Tourism offices in each part of the Valley (See Chapter Eight, *Information*) and your accommodation host will have additional activity listings for you.

Deciding which categories should fall under Chapter Three, *Cultural Attractions*, and which should go in this chapter was difficult. My goal was to place the information where you, the reader, would be most likely to look for it — so, formal gardens and arboretums are under culture, while parks and caves are in this chapter. If my line of thinking on the topics is not the same as yours, referring to the index should resolve any problems.

In exploring the great outdoor spaces of the Valley, I enlisted the help of friends and local Boy Scout troops along with Dan Casey, outdoor columnist for

The Roanoke Times, Allison Blake, author of Berkshire House's *The Chesapeake Bay Book*, and the owners of several outfitters in the Valley.

BASEBALL

Salem has a minor league team, but another place to spot future stars is the summer season of the NCAA teams that play in the Valley. The major leagues sponsor this league and others like it around the country to get a look at the students' abilities with a wooden bat. (They use metal bats during the school year.) What makes this league extra special is that it is an outgrowth of an early 1900s league, so the town-to-town rivalries have had lots of time to develop.

The Valley League plays a 40-game schedule in June and July, and seeing one of the games is a lot of fun if you're a fan of America's pastime. Check these numbers and Web sites for ticket information, game schedules, and directions to the stadiums. Contact information for each club also appears. The best way to keep up on the league is on the Internet. Team information on the Web:

www.valleyleaguebaseball.com

www.frcardinalbaseball.com/links.htm (This page links to all the other teams.)

Directions to all of the fields: www.valleyleaguebaseball.com/direct.htm

CLUB ADDRESSES

Covington Lumberjacks (540-962-7867; www.covingtonlumberjacks.com; cov jacks@intelos.net; 315 W. Main St., Covington, VA 24426).

Front Royal Cardinals (540-635-6498; www.frcardinalbaseball.com; sminkeen @shentel.net; PO Box 995, Front Royal, VA 22630).

Harrisonburg Turks (540-434-5919; www.harrisonburgturks.com; hbgturks@ vaix.net; 1489 S.Main St., Harrisonburg, VA 22801).

Luray Wranglers (540-743-3338; www.luraywranglers.com; luraywranglers@ hotmail.com; 1203 E. Main St., Luray, VA 22835).

New Market Rebels (540-740-4247; www.rebelsbaseballonline.com; nmrebels@ shentel.net; PO Box 902, New Market, VA 22844).

Staunton Braves (540-886-0905; www.stauntonbraves.com; sbraves@hotmail .com; 14 Shannon Place, Staunton, VA 24401).

Waynesboro Generals (540-949-0370; www.waynesborogenerals.com; jim_critzer @hotmail.com; PO Box 615, Waynesboro, VA 22980).

Winchester Royals (540-667-9227; www.winchesterroyals.com; jimphill@shentel .net; PO Box 2485, Winchester, VA 22604).

MINOR LEAGUE BASEBALL

Salem Avalanche (540-389-3333; www.salemavalanche.com; info@salemava lanche.com; PO Box 842, Salem, VA 24153) Admission is only $7 for box seats at Salem Memorial Stadium and $4 for general admission. Children and seniors pay $1 less on each. The Web site offers the schedule and a seating chart for the 6,500-seat stadium. An extra bonus is the wonderful view of the mountains — it's lovely whether or not the home team wins.

BALLOONING

Hot air balloons are a peaceful way to float over the Valley.

Joan Leotta

One of the more unusual ways to enjoy the sights of the Valley is to see it from above — via hot air balloon. These outings are expensive, running about $175 per person at the time of this writing. Two of the area's well-known companies are:

Blue Ridge Hot Air Balloons (877-RIDE-AIR, 540-622-6325; www.rideair.com; balloon@rideair.com; Front Royal, VA 22630).

Shenandoah Hot Air Balloons (540-636-2150; www.flyballoons.com; balloon @shentel.net; Front Royal, VA 22630).

BICYCLING

Zipping about the Valley on two wheels is popular among exercise lovers and sightseers alike. A number of biking clubs organize rides up and down the Valley and offer current information on area trails, races, and safety.

The Virginia Department of Transportation publishes the *Virginia Bicycling Guide* and *Virginia Bicycle Facility Resource Guide*. You can obtain it by phone, 800-835-1203, or online (another source for trail and event information and bike road safety tips) at virginiadot.org/infoservice/bk-default.asp and www.virginiadot.org/infoservice/bk-proginfo.asp.

Dan Casey, outdoor columnist for *The Roanoke Times* newspaper, contributed much of the information for this section. Dan and his family are avid bikers. He has this general advice: "With preparation, the Shenandoah Valley is suitable for almost year-round road or mountain biking. But beware — temperatures will often hit the 90s in July and August, or drop as low as the high teens in December and January. Stay in the lower parts of the Valley in the depths of winter, away from the ice that's often found in higher-elevation roads.

"Cycling in the Valley can be as easy or as challenging as any cyclist wants to make it. Riders who wish to avoid huffing, puffing, and leg cramps should stick to the rolling central Valley along Route 11 and the local roads that connect to it. In most places this highway is two lanes wide with a wide shoulder. Local maps can help you find smaller and more cycle-friendly roads. There are many that crisscross Route 11.

"For challenging rides with absolutely gorgeous views, nothing beats the Blue Ridge Parkway, which snakes along for hundreds of miles along the spine of the Blue Ridge Mountains on the Valley's eastern edge. Mile for mile, the grades are among the toughest of any road in the country — but all that work is worth it. On clear days, the parkway uncoils as an unending series of dazzling 60-mile views, blooming mountain meadows, brilliant foliage, brawny rock outcroppings, and blue-gray peaks. On hazy days, the views won't be as spectacular, but visitors will understand immediately why this easternmost line of the Appalachian peaks is called the Blue Ridge."

Many of the trails run through more than one county, so the information on the trails, contact information, and area clubs is divided into two main parts: the northern half of the Valley (Frederick, Clarke, Warren, Page, and Shenandoah Counties), followed by the central and southern Valley and mountain region (Rockingham, Augusta, Rockbridge, Botetourt, Roanoke, Highland, Bath, and Alleghany Counties).

Visitors to Roanoke who would rather rent a bike than take one with them on their drive through the Valley can contact **East Coasters Cycling and Fitness** (540-774-7933; 4341 Starkey Rd., Roanoke, VA 24014).

NORTHERN VALLEY

Club Resources

Many of these clubs do not publicize phone numbers, but offer information via the Internet. In the northern part of the Valley, bicycling along Skyline Drive offers many of the same breathtaking opportunities as the Blue Ridge does farther south.

Virginia Bicycling Federation (www.vabike.org; PO Box 5621, Arlington, VA 22203) This organization is located in Northern Virginia, but has links to groups all over the state and information about biking events online.

Potomac Pedalers Touring Club, Inc. (www.bikepptc.org) This organization lists bike routes for the northern Valley, and for Maryland and Washington, D.C., as well. Most of the routes are intended for experienced cyclists. The Web site contains a disclaimer that those who ride the routes are responsible for their own safety and reminds users that many of the routes are also used by autos and trucks and have no special bike lanes.

Winchester Wheelmen Bicycle Club (540-667-6703; PO Box 1695, Winchester, VA 22604).

Babes on Bikes (www.babesonbikes.org) This organization covers biking issues from the female viewpoint.

Trails

Skyline Drive (540-999-3500; www.nps.gov/shen; Shenandoah National Park, Luray, VA 22835) Mile zero is at Rte. 66 at Front Royal. You can pick up maps at the first visitor center. The deer are very tame and you may see bears — please DO NOT feed them. They may appear cuddly, but they are wild animals. There are numerous small trails along the way and opportunities for paddling and hiking. This is one of the most popular tourist routes for cars, especially on weekends and during the fall foliage season, so don't be surprised to see bumper-to-bumper traffic.

Front Royal's Happy Creek Trail (in town) This is a quarter-mile trail, level and well marked, and a great one to introduce small children to hiking and biking. The trail begins at Main Street at the Happy Creek Bridge.

Winchester's Jim Barnett Park (540-662-4946; off Pleasant Valley Rd., Winchester) Bike trails can be found throughout the facility. For dirt bike enthusiasts, a BMX track is open dawn to dusk daily. This sanctioned track is the only one in the state offering nighttime racing. Call for race schedule.

CENTRAL & SOUTHERN VALLEY AND THE MOUNTAIN COUNTIES

Club Resources

Blue Ridge Bicycle Club, Inc. (www.blueridgebicycleclub.com; PO Box 13383, Roanoke, VA 24033).

Milepost Zero Bike Club (www.milepostzero.homestead.com) This is a major advocacy group for building bike trails. The Web site describes many trail opportunities.

The Shenandoah Valley Bicycle Club (www.svbikeclub.homestead.com; PO Box 1014, Harrisonburg, VA 22803) Sponsors excursions into neighboring counties.

Trails

Rockingham County: There is a nice, short (4-mile) loop called the Blueberry Trail that begins on County Road 625 just west of Harrisonburg. The trail has a 540-foot climb (just after Union Dam) and a subsequent roller coaster-like descent. This is listed as one of the three top rides in the state in the *Virginia Cycling Book*. The annual Shenandoah Bicycle Festival is located in Bridgewater. Call the Rockingham/Harrisonburg Visitor Center (540-434-2319) for the exact dates of this 20- to 100-mile ride.

Augusta County: This is one of the Valley's great bike ride areas. The Shenandoah Fall Foliage Festival each October in Staunton takes riders on the winding roads of Augusta and Rockingham Counties during the peak of the leaf beauty. The festival offers rides for beginners and experienced riders alike. Experienced riders can choose the 100-mile Apple Butter Century. Another great ride in the area is the Reddish Knob trail, equally popular with hikers. This trail brings you to a 3,000-foot overlook in George Washington National Forest. Call 540-828-2591 for more information on the Knob trail.

Botetourt and Roanoke Counties: Carvins Cove in Roanoke and Botetourt Counties is a 13,000-acre watershed that drains in the city of Roanoke, the city's chief reservoir. The area is open to the public and is studded with bike trails suitable for any skill level of mountain biker. Beginners should stick to the 4.5-mile dirt road that runs along the reservoir's east side. The area is open year-round from dawn to dusk. The city distributes maps of the trails and you can get them at the tourism office or from the Carvins Cove office. Call 540-563-9170 for directions from where you are. If you're on I-81, take the Plantation Road/Hollins exit and follow Plantation south to Route 11. Then make a left. Pass Hollins College and make another left onto state Route 648, Reservoir Road. This road dead-ends at the Cove parking lot.

City of Roanoke: Inside the city of Roanoke is a challenging and unique bike ride on Prospect Road. This shady, closed-to-traffic former toll road goes up Mill Mountain to a large, neon-lighted star that is the symbol of the city. Beneath the icon is an overlook which offers a wonderful view of the city of Roanoke, about 1,000 vertical feet below. Then you can zoom back to town, two miles, downhill all the way. The total ride is about six miles, including the two across the Walnut Bridge before the climb begins.

Botetourt County: In Botetourt County, try the Springwood Loop that begins at the county courthouse in historic Fincastle, a 33-mile, gently rolling circuit along beautiful byways through the towns of Buchanan and Lithia. There are no great climbs, so this loop is suitable for all skill levels. To get to Fincastle, take I-81 to Route 220. Take Route 220 north for 12 miles. Turn right at the sign for the courthouse, one block up on your right.

The mountain counties (Highland, Bath, and Alleghany): Set on a forested area north of Clifton Forge in Virginia's Douthat State Park is the mountain-biking Mecca of the Alleghany Highlands. Forty miles of twisty, single-track trails snake through the wooded hollows and up pristine peaks in this Depression-era Civilian Conservation Corps creation. Follow Big Stony Run up Middle Mountain to Tuscarora Overlook (elevation 3,000 feet) for a stunning view of the park's 70-acre lake far below. Maps are available from the park's main office (540-862-8100) and all of the trails are marked with signs. The interpretative biking trails are also open to hikers. The U.S. Forest Service owns Highland County's bike areas and there are no mountain bikes allowed.

BOWLING

OK, so it's not *outdoor* recreation, but the Valley has its rainy days, too. Here, then, is a list of bowling alleys for those occasions.

Frederick, Clarke, and Warren Counties

Royal Oak Lanes (540-636-3113; 430 Remount Rd., Front Royal).
Northside Bowling Lanes (540-667-1470; N. Loudoun St., Winchester).
T Bowl Lanes (540-652-8126; Hwy. 340 N., Shenandoah).

Shenandoah County

Signal Knob Lanes (540-465-5400; 35 Brandy Ct., Strasburg).
Shenandoah Lanes (540-477-2341; 5904 Main St., Mount Jackson).
Mountain View Lanes (540-459-5400; 750 E. Reservoir Pl., Woodstock).

Page County

Luray Bowling Lanes (540-743-3535; 55 W. Main, Luray).
T Bowl Lanes (540-652-8126; Hwy. 340 N., Shenandoah).

Rockingham County

Valley Lanes (540-434-8721; 3106 S. Main St., Harrisonburg).

Augusta County

Staunton Bowling Lanes (540-885-1655; 831 Greenville Ave., Staunton).

Rockbridge County

Lexington Lanes (540-464-2695; 98 Northwind Ln. , Lexington).

Rockbridge and Botetourt Counties

AMF Hilltop Lanes (540-366-8879; 5918 Williamson Rd. NW, Roanoke).
Viking Lanes (540-342-6753; 2727 Franklin Rd. SW, Roanoke).
Lee-Hi Lanes (540-389-0000; 1830 Apperson Dr., Salem).
Vinton Bowling Center (540-344-2055; 1200 Vinyard Rd., Vinton).

CAMPING

Shenandoah2000

Camping by the James River is popular in summer.

If camping is your preference, the campgrounds of Virginia offer many choices. Private campgrounds, state parks, and national parks — including Shenandoah National Park, Blue Ridge Parkway, and George Washington National Forest — all offer a variety of accommodations, from tents to cabins.

Many, indeed most, of the campgrounds are open only from April to October. There are a few that stay open for hardy winter camping. While camping can be a very inexpensive proposition, be advised that prices of some of the lodge facilities can rise to the expensive level. There are hundreds of choices. Here we have included information on a few of the better known or highly recommended private and public campgrounds in the Valley and mountain highlands.

Check with local tourism offices and the private campground sources noted below to see when these sites are open.

PRIVATE CAMPGROUND RESOURCES

There are two main sources for information about the many private campgrounds in the Shenandoah. These private associations will send you campground guides, including the camps of their members and the state park campsites in the area. They are:

Virginia Campground Association (540-697-2431; www.virginiacampgrounds .org; PO Box 2020, Louisa, VA 23093) This group can send you a directory of campgrounds and RV parks in Virginia. Its material contains information on state parks and private campgrounds. The listings are informative as to the type of showers, if there are data ports, swimming, fees, and other important information.

Virginia Hospitality and Travel Association (804-288-3065; www.vhta.org; 2101 Libby Ave., Richmond, VA 23230) This is the home of **The Campground Association of Virginia,** another private organization that will send you a campground directory which includes its members and state park information, as well as other travel information on the Shenandoah Valley.

STATE RESOURCES

Virginia State Parks (800-933-PARK, 804-786-1712; www.dcr.state.va.us/parks; pco@dcr.state.va.us; Department of Conservation and Recreation, 203 Governor St., Suite 213, Richmond, VA 23219) For reservations, call 800-933-PARK, 804-225-3867 in Richmond, or e-mail resvs@dcr.state.va.us. Payment can be made by American Express, Visa, or MasterCard over the phone. The Web site and printed materials also include full information on the parks and their facilities for travelers with disabilities. The TDD number for hearing-impaired callers is 804-786-2121.

NATIONAL RESOURCES

There are three different National Park options in the Shenandoah Valley: Shenandoah National Park, the Blue Ridge Parkway, and the George Washington National Forest. See the campground sampler below and "Parks" later in this chapter for details on each, and contact the appropriate office to reserve space, if necessary.

For a list of campgrounds open year-round, visit the Web site at www.south ernregion.fs.fed.us/gwj/cgwinter.htm. From there you can access a privately compiled *U.S. National Forest Campground Guide* to make your selections.

Darrell Little

Staying in the Shenandoah National Park cabins gets you close to nature — even winter has a stark beauty that bears noticing.

CAMPGROUND SAMPLER

Candy Hill (540-662-8010, 800-462-0545; 165 Ward Ave., Winchester, VA 22602) Open year-round. Five inexpensive cabins and 105 campsites on 23 acres. All come with water and electricity. The camp allows cats, dogs, and campfires. Occasional trolley tours take quick trips — to local orchards during apple-picking season, for example.

Creekside Campground (540-984-4229; escamp@shentel.net; 108 Palmyra Rd., PO Box 277, Edinburg, VA 22824) This is another site on historic ground — in use by settlers since 1817 and Native Americans before that. There are 25 RV sites and a number of tent sites here, and it's very close to the many sights of Shenandoah and Page Counties.

Elizabeth Furnace Recreation Area in George Washington National Forest (Lee Ranger District, 540-984-4101; www.southernregion.fs.fed.us/gwj; 109 Molineu Rd., Edinburg, VA 22824) Features a 30-unit family campground and three group sites. This area offers showers, drinking water, and grills. It has a trail that takes you on a learning tour of the Civil War-era iron industry, as well as nature trails and access to Passage Creek, a trout-fishing stream. Reservations are required. For more information on other sites in George Washington National Forest, contact the National Park Service (202-205-8333; PO Box 96090, Washington, DC 20090).

The Country Place Campground (540-743-4007, 877-547-8600; www.country place.com; 100 Fort Liscomb Rd., Luray, VA 22835) On 35 wooded acres with a private Shenandoah River beach. Some riverfront cabins, canoes, and bikes to rent along with a "base camp" for fans of group camping, such as Boy Scout troops.

Yogi Bear Jellystone Park Campground (540-743-4002, 800-420-6679; Hwy. 211 E., Luray, VA 22835) Hubert Fry, a Scout leader in Fairfax, says he loves to come here with his family because there are many activities on-site to entertain them — mini-golf, swimming, a playground, water slides, and a fishing pond, to name just a few. He also likes the proximity of the grounds to Thornton Gap on Skyline Drive, making it a good base for hiking there.

Shenandoah National Park (540-999-2243, 800-778-2851; www.nps.gov/shen/ 1b1.htm; 3655 U.S. Route 211, Luray, VA 22835) There are five different campgrounds in this park. Big Meadows and Dundo (group only) require reservations; Mathews Arm, Lewis Mountain, and Loft Mountain fill on a first-come, first-served basis. Inexpensive cabin and tent rentals, too. Minimum stays apply. ARAMARK Virginia Sky-Line Company (800-999-4714 or 540-743-5108; PO Box 727NP, Luray, VA 22835) is the contact for reservations for Shenandoah National Park sites.

Sherando Lake (contact point is the George Washington National Forest, Pedlar Ranger District, 540-291-2188; PO Box 10, Natural Bridge Station, VA 24579) The site is 12 miles south of Waynesboro, and it's one of the most popular spots in the area, offering 65 campsites and lots of natural beauty. All campsites are open Apr. 1–Oct. 31. Take the Blue Ridge Parkway to mile 16, then go 4.5 miles on Rte. 814.

Blue Ridge Parkway Campgrounds (828-298-0398 for general information; www.nps.gov/blri/camp.htm; mailing address is 199 Hemphill Knob Rd., Asheville, NC 28803) All parkway campgrounds are open from Apr.–Oct. 31 except Peaks of Otter, and are filled on a first-come, first-served basis. Campgrounds include Otter Creek at mile 60.9 (tent and RV sites), Peaks of Otter at mile 86 (tent and RV sites), and Roanoke Mountain at mile 120.5 (tent and RV sites). A park guide, available at the main office, can tell you what facilities are available at each site. Information is also available at the Friends of the Parkway Web site, www.blueridgefriends.org, and the Blue Ridge Parkway Foundation, www.brpfoundation.org.

Douthat State Park (800-933-PARK, 540-862-8100; www.dcr.state.va.us/parks/ douthat.htm; Route 1, PO Box 212, Millboro, VA 24460 for the offices and Douthat Road/Route 629 in Clifton Forge for the park itself) The site is beautiful and offers many different sorts of accommodations. It is one of the parks built by the Civilian Conservation Corps, opening on June 15, 1936. In 1986, on its 50th anniversary, this park was recognized as a Registered Historic District. In 1998, Douthat won the Virginia Lakes and Watersheds Association award for best-operated and maintained dam, and the following year it received the Centennial Medallion from the American Society of Landscape Architects. There is a lodge for those who don't want to camp (rates are moderate) and inexpensive sites for those who do. There aren't many tent sites, but there are more than 50 RV sites in the park. The lake itself is 50 acres large and the park has more than 4,400 acres for hiking, birding, fishing, and other fun. The park also has a lakeside restaurant and a gift shop, as well as its own small grocery store.

Claytor Lake (800-933-PARK for reservations, 540-643-2500 for park; www.dcr .state.va.us/parks/claytor.htm; 4400 State Park Road, Dublin, VA 24094) A 4,500-acre state park in the New River Valley, just off I-81 at Exit 101. Take State Park Road 660 to the park entrance. This park has the only full-service marina in the state park system and has handicapped-accessible camping. The Visitor Center, Howe House, is a historic home.

CAVES

Each of the Valley's eight public or "show" caves offers visitors a chance to see wonderful hanging stalactites and growing stalagmites. Formations such as the famous Luray stalagmite organ and cave animals such as bats and salamanders are found there, too. Amenities such as electric lights were installed well before people realized that such fixtures could damage a cave's ecosystem. Since the passage of the Virginia Cave Protection Act of 1979, they can no longer be added.

More on Caves

H.H. Douglas, *Caves of Virginia,* and J.R. Holsinger, *Descriptions of Virginia Caves,* describe the detail of the area's show and wild caves. Data also is on file with the Virginia Speleological Survey, affiliated with the National Speleological Society (NSS).

If you are a dedicated speleologist, you know that visiting a wild cave — no light, no paths, and deep chasms — calls for special knowledge and equipment. In Virginia, where 95 percent of the wild caves are on private land, permission of the landowner also is needed.

Contact Rick Lambert's Highland Adventures in Monterey at 540-468-2722 for more information. E-mail nss@caves.org to be put in contact with Virginia caving groups.

When visiting caves, even in the hottest summer months, wear a sweater, as the temperature in the caves remains at around 50 to 56 degrees year-round. Tours are guided, so be prepared to wait a bit if you arrive just after a tour has left. Once a year, usually in October, the caves of Virginia and neighboring states participate in Cave Week to highlight the beauty of this underground resource.

The caves are listed in order of their location off I-81, from north to south, starting with those near Front Royal. Most offer group discounts. Prices listed are subject to change.

SKYLINE CAVERNS
800-296-4545.
www.skylinecaverns.com.
Rte. 340 just off Rte. 66,
    Front Royal.
Directions: From Front
    Royal, take Rte. 340 south
    1 mile past entrance to
    Skyline Drive.
Open: Daily; schedule
    varies by season.
Admission: Adults $12,
    children $7, under 6 free.
    Coupons and discounts
    available.

Anthodites, the orchids of the mineral kingdom, are one of this cave's best-known features. A "Painted Desert" and "Fairy Lake" are among other fabulous sights in this cave, discovered in 1937 by geologist Walter S. Amos. Children are fond of the "wishing well" in the cave and enjoy the miniature train ride next to the cave, with its very own mini horseshoe curve.

You can easily combine a visit to Skyline Caverns with sightseeing on **Skyline Drive.** Enter at Front Royal and take Skyline to the next gap. Exit on 211, see Luray, and return to Front Royal via I-81. Or take Skyline to the first lookout, turn around, and then take Rte. 55 from Front Royal to Elizabeth Furnace Recreation Area for hiking in **George Washington National Forest.**

**CRYSTAL CAVERNS AT
    HUPP'S HILL**
540-465-5884.
www.waysideofva.com.
Rte. 11, Strasburg.
Directions: I-81 to Exit 298;
    take Rte. 11 (Valley Pike)
    south for 1 mile; entrance
    on right.
Open: Daily 10–5; closed
    Christmas.
Admission: Adults $8,
    children, seniors $6. AAA
    discounts and others; ask
    when purchasing tickets.

In the 1750s, the Hupp family was among the many "Dutch" (German) émigrés who moved in to farm the "Great Valley of the Shenandoah." The family is said to have held parties in the large underground rooms. Native American artifacts have been uncovered in the caverns.

Located near several Civil War battle sites, the cave was a place where soldiers of both sides hid from opposition troops. Both sides also used the cave to store ammunition at one time or another. The family opened it as a tourist attraction in May 1922. Andy, a unique species of freshwater crustacean, makes his home in the cavern.

You easily can combine this visit with a call at the **Stonewall Jackson Museum** on-site or other caverns nearby.

**SHENANDOAH
    CAVERNS**
www.shenandoahcaverns
    .com.
540-477-3115, 800-4-CAVERN.
261 Caverns Rd., Shenandoah
    Caverns, VA 22947.

Shenandoah Caverns and their partner, American Celebration Museum, make a popular combination. Especially fun to see is the "bacon" formation (keep on the lookout for eggs) and the diamond cascade, a calcite crystal formation. The Cardross Castle formation, which resembles a Scot-

Exit 269 off I-81.

Open: Daily beginning at 9, closing time depends on season. Closed Christmas.

Admission: Combination tickets are $17.50 for adults and $12.50 for children. Inquire about single-exhibit tickets. A number of discounts are honored.

tish castle, is another popular formation. The caverns have been a tourist attraction since their 1884 discovery, and the entrance was once an inn, kept cool by the breezes from below.

Leave some time to visit the museum, where you can enjoy parade floats of the past.

Courtesy Luray Caverns

Visitors still thrill to the beauties under the ground in Shenandoah's Luray Caverns.

LURAY
540-743-6551.
www.luraycaverns.com.
970 U.S. Hwy. 211 West, PO Box 748, Luray, VA 22835.
From I-81 take Exit 264 and then Rte. 211 east.
Open: Daily on a seasonal

In addition to wonderful formations such as "Totem Poles," the "Wishing Well," and "Dream Lake," Luray boasts the world's only stalacpipe organ. Designed by a Mr. Leland of Springfield, Virginia, a mathematician and electrician, the organ is appropriately located in the cavern's Cathedral Room. Short demonstrations are offered frequently.

schedule. Tours begin every 20 minutes.
Admission: Adults $16, seniors over 62 $14, children $7 (includes Carriage and Car Museum on-site). Discounts available.

Concerts are given on the site's freestanding 47-bell carillon from March through October; call 888-743-3915 for a schedule. The owners of the cave also operate two nearby hotels and a golf resort. Luray was designated a Registered Natural Landmark in 1974.

ENDLESS CAVERNS
540-896-2283, 800-544-2283.
www.endlesscavern.com.
From I-81, take Exit 264 or 257 onto Rte. 11; follow signs to New Market.
Open: June 15–Labor Day, daily 9–7.
Admission: Adults $12, children 3–12 $6.

This cave was found in 1879 by a couple of young boys on a hunting trip. It was developed for tourism, and most of its sights, like "Fairyland," were cataloged in the 1920s. The tour here is a bit longer than that of the others — an hour and fifteen minutes. There are still authorized explorations going on in the cave. In 1991 a new, large room was discovered and a mammoth tooth found!

One of the unique features of this cave is its spring. The cave owners bottle and sell the water, touting it as one of Virginia's finest.

GRAND CAVERNS
888-430-CAVE.
PO Box 478, Grottoes, VA 24441.
Exit 235 from I-81. Follow signs on Route 256 through the town of Grottoes to the cave.
Open: Apr.–Oct., daily 9–5; weekends only in winter; closed on Christmas and New Year's Day.
Admission: Adults $13.50, children $7. Call for group rates and discounts. Groups should make an appointment. Reservations preferred.

This cave, now operated by the Regional Park Authority, has been open to tourists continuously since 1806. During the Civil War, many of those "tourists" were soldiers of both sides who left their signatures as graffiti souvenirs for future visitors. The signatures are treated as historic documents and most are not pointed out, but one, "W.W. Miles," is so easily seen that guides use it as the reference point for telling of the cave's history. Many say that Stonewall Jackson gave his men time off to visit the cave's spectacular 280-foot-long and 70-foot-high cathedral hall during a lull in the Port Republic fighting. This cave is owned and operated by four governmental entities and is the only publicly operated show cave in the group.

NATURAL BRIDGE CAVERNS
800-533-1410.
www.naturalbridgeva.com.
Exit 175 from I-81, about 5 miles north on Rte. 11 to Natural Bridge.
Open: Caves Mar.–Nov. only; grounds year-round.

The Natural Bridge, one of the Natural Wonders of America, would be well worth the visit even if there weren't a wonderful cave, nature trail, and even a wax museum on-site. The Natural Bridge is 215 feet high and 90 feet wide — "As high as Niagara, as old as dawn" is what they say about this National Historic Landmark. The adjacent caverns are known for their enormous cathedral rooms and

Natural Bridge is a slim slice of rock spanning two cliffs –and it still bears traffic! But to get a view of the arch itself, you need to pay and take the walking trail.

Shenandoah2000

Admission: Adults $17, children $7 for combination ticket.

a wonderful "flowstone" formation that looks for all the world as if a sorcerer has frozen a cresting wave for our benefit. Tours take about 40 minutes.

There are numerous sites to see at the caverns, including the nature trails, "Drama of Creation" (see "Theater" in Chapter Three, *Cultural Attractions*), and a wax museum. To see everything would take a whole day. Be sure to allow time to take the Cedar Creek Trail to discover the Lost River and Lace Falls.

The latest addition to the area's family of exhibits is the Monacan Indian living history exhibit. For many years this tribe, one of the first in the Valley, was forgotten. Only in the late 1960s did the tribe's descendents gain recognition. The tribe works closely with the museum on various programs. The activities go on during the spring and summer, but the outbuildings can be toured year-round.

DIXIE CAVERNS
540-380-2085.
www.dixiecaverns.com.
5753 Main St., Salem, VA
    24153.
Exit 132 off I-81.
Open: Daily 9–6.

This cave is just fifteen minutes outside of Salem/Roanoke. Its spectacular formations include a "Magic Mirror" area and a number of flow formations shaped in various directions, including one called "Turkey Wing."

If you're in the market for items for your garden,

Admission: Adults $7.50, children 5–12 $4.50, under 5 free. Discounts for various memberships and visitors at Dixie Cavern Campsites.

be sure to save room in your trunk for an item from Dixie Caverns Pottery. Rock hounds will be entranced by The Rock and Mineral Shop, which also offers enough low-priced items to start a child out on rock collecting without breaking the family budget.

GOLF

Courtesy Luray Caverns

Golf has become a popular sport in the Valley. This golfer is teeing off near Luray.

Golf is year-round in the Valley, even in the mountains, weather permitting. This is a sampling of courses open to the public in the Shenandoah Valley. For a more complete listing, check the Web site www.virginiagolf.com or www.svgcgolf.com.

At the time of this writing, the courses listed do not require visitors to be accompanied by a member and all the courses listed offer at least 18 holes. Fees vary by time of year and day of the week, but be aware that weekend and weekday are relative terms. Call to see if Fridays and holidays are charged at weekend or weekday rates. All fees listed are subject to change.

Golf packages are available at many locations — some resorts of the Valley have their own courses, and hotels and inns often pair up with courses for special deals. Be sure to check with your accommodation of choice and on the tourism and golf Web sites. The listing is north to south by county or county group.

Winchester and Frederick County

Carper's Valley Golf Club (540-662-4319; 1400 Millwood Pike, Winchester, VA 22602) This is a long 18-hole course — yardage 6,125/4,930, par 71/70 — designed by Ed Ault. Greens fees with cart are $35 on weekends, $27 on weekdays. There are three lakes on the course — two are hazards and one is for beauty.

Jackson's Chase At Pine Hills Golf Club (540-635-7814; 65 Jackson's Chase Drive, Middletown, VA 22645) This is one of the newest golf courses to the Shenandoah Valley — it opened in April 1998. The yardage for this par 72, 18-hole course ranges from 5,809 to 6,600 yards. Weekday fee is $50 with cart and $33 without. Add $5 for weekends and holidays. This course is on historic property and displays a cannonball on-site that is reputed to have been shot by Stonewall Jackson's troops. The course's signature hole, the 11th, has a wonderful view over the water and Cedar Creek Battlefield.

Front Royal; Warren and Clark Counties

Shenandoah Valley Golf Club (540-636-4653; 134 Golf Club Circle, Front Royal, VA 22630) Located 8 miles north of Front Royal, this is 27 holes of Virginia's best golf by designer Buddy Loving. Its scenic beauty and four-star rating by *Golf Digest* led to its status as host to many golf championships. Yardage ranges from 2,454 to 3,304. Greens fees are separate from cart and vary by the day of week and time of day.

Front Royal Country Club (540-636-9061; 902 Country Club Rd., Front Royal, VA 22630) *Virginia Golfer* calls Front Royal Country Club one of the state's premier 9-hole layouts. (Golfers play each hole twice from different tee boxes, creating 18 distinct holes.) Four holes border the beautiful Shenandoah River, including the dramatic par-5 17th, which features a tee shot on the river's edge.

Bowling Green Country Club North (540-635-2024) and **South** (540-635-2883; one mailing address for both: 838 Bowling Green Rd., Front Royal, VA 22630) Both courses can be found on the same road; North is on the hill, South is below. Each of these 27-hole courses was designed by Lynnwood Morrison and both are operated by Nellie Morrison. The North course is a showplace of flowers, with its fourth hole an island surrounded by greenery and flowers. The signature hole on the South course is the 16th, where the view from the tee box features mountains, farm silos, and peaceful beauty all around. The North course is slightly longer and has a par of 71. Par on the south is 70.

Shenandoah County

Bryce Resort Golf Club (540-856-2124, 800-821-1444; Rte. 263, PO Box 3, Basye, VA 22810) This 18-hole, par-71 course is a long one (6,261/5,240 yards) and earned a three-star rating in Fodor's. Cart fee is included in greens fees, which range from $24 to $45 (discounts for those staying at the resort). Architect Ed Ault designed the course, which Stony Creek winds through. Watch for deer!

The Shenvalee Golf Resort (540-740-3181; Rte. 11, PO Box 930, New Market, VA 22844) Rod Smith and Ed Ault designed the three 9-hole courses, known as Creek, Olde, and Miller. Folks play combinations of the three. Bobby Jones played here in 1927, and other distinguished players have trod its links as well. It caters to golf groups, with lodging on-site. The view from the third hole on Creek/Miller is judged "best" by many golfers.

Page County

Caverns Country Club Resort (888-443-6551; Airport Road, PO Box 748, Luray, VA 22835) This 18-hole, par-72 course designed by Mal Purdy offers a wonderful view of the Shenandoah River from the first tee. Reserve at least a week in advance. Greens fees range from $37 on weekdays to $48 on weekends (with cart).

Rockingham County

Massanutten Resort Golf Course (540-289-4941; Rte. 644, McGaheysville, VA 22840) This 18-hole course was designed by Frank Duane and Richard Watson. Greens fees range from $40 to $50 with a cart. Fairways are tight on this par 72/73. There are lots of deer in the area, so golfers often see them, even though the course runs along main roads in the resort. Views of the Valley are spectacular from most of the greens.

Heritage Oaks Golf Course (540-442-6502, 680 Garbers Church Rd., Harrisonburg, VA 22801) This course is inside Harrisonburg, owned and operated by the city. Designed by Bill Love, it's one of the flatter courses in the valley and as such is easier to walk. Fees range from $18 to $22 without a cart. From the white tees the yardage is 6,324.

Augusta and Rockbridge Counties

There are no public courses in Rockbridge County, but many courses are within a one-hour drive or less. The Lexington Golf and County Club in Rockbridge was not open to general play at the time of writing. The two open-to-the-public courses listed below are in the city of Staunton in Augusta County, only a few minutes from Lexington.

Gypsy Hill Golf Course (540-332-3949; in Gypsy Hill Park, Staunton) The greens fees for this 18-hole, par-71 course are $15 on weekdays and $17 on weekends; carts are an extra $11. The first nine holes of this course were built in 1912 and it was redesigned into 18 in 1956. It's a challenging course with a lot of trees, deer, and curving holes that make you think before you swing. Yardage range is 4,436 to 5,899.

Ingleside Golf Resort and Conference Center (540-248-7888; 1410 Commerce Road, Staunton) The signature hole is the 13th, with three ponds and a great view of the surrounding hills. Greens fees range from $38 to $40 with cart. Par is 72; yardage ranges from 5,340 to 6,405.

Botetourt and Roanoke Counties

There are golf packages designed just for this area, thanks to partnerships between public and private courses and great places to stay. For reservations, call 877-GOLF-MTN. Two of the courses located closest to the cities of Roanoke and Salem are listed below.

Countryside Golf Club (540-563-0391; One Countryside Rd. NW, Roanoke, VA 24017) Just a few minutes from downtown and only two miles from the airport, this course is a great one if you're dropping into the Star City. Designed by Ellis Maples on an old dairy farm, this par-71 (all tees) course offers four sets of tees and five challenging par-3 holes that are over 200 yards long. Course yardage ranges from 5,185 to 6,815.

Hanging Rock Golf Club (540-389-7275, 800-277-7479; 1500 Red Lane, Salem) This one is highly rated and considered a great value, and it's also only nine miles from Roanoke. Be sure to call in advance for your tee time for this par-72/73 Russell Breeden design that offers a great mountain location and challenging layout. Hanging Rock was voted "Best in Area" by the readers of *The Roanoker* magazine, 1994-2000, and received a 3½-star rating from *Golf Digest* for Places to Play 2000-2001. Greens fees vary according to time of day and day of the week, but are generally in the $25 to $45 range. Call at least one day in advance for weekdays. The course yardage is 6,828/4,463.

The Mountain Counties: Bath

The best golf in the mountain counties can be found in Bath County.

The Homestead is a storied resort course in Hot Springs that is open to the public. There are actually three courses there: **The Cascades**, **The Lower Cascades**, and **The Old Course**. Prices vary for each. The 1892-founded Old Course is the most walkable of the three, as well as the least expensive. Call 800-838-1766 for reservations, or visit the Web site, www.thehomestead.com. The local numbers listed below are for the individual course pro shops.

The Cascades (540-839-7994) This 18-hole course, par 70/71, has greens fees ranging from $75 to $150, plus a $20/person cart fee. The course was designed by William Flynn and is ranked 53rd among America's top 100 courses (1999-2000). Has had a recent upgrade besides! Tough and fast.

The Lower Cascades (540-839-7995) This used to be the place to go if you wanted to spot Sam Snead. Greens fees are $45 to $95, with a $20 cart fee for this Robert Trent Jones course.

The Old Course (540-839-7739) Greens fees range from $45 to $90. Rarely crowded and may be the best bet for a scratch golfer.

HIKING

Shenandoah2000

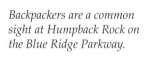

Backpackers are a common sight at Humpback Rock on the Blue Ridge Parkway.

Casual walkers, dedicated naturalists, and enthusiastic hikers will all find trails, vistas, and species to enjoy in the Valley. The resources here guide you to favored trails in the region. Local tourism and park offices can provide you with maps and directions to hiking trials within your range of comfort. If longer hikes (more than a half-day), exploring wild caves, or foraging for wild crops are your interest, consider hiring a guide who can resolve the problems of private property permissions and get you back again. Local outfitters and many of the places that feature hiking maps (see "Maps" sidebar) can tell you how to hire a guide. For hiking trails in the Valley's national, state, regional, and local parks, check with local tourism agencies (see Chapter Eight, *Information*) and refer to the section on parks in this chapter.

Many biking and riding trails also do double duty as hiking routes. Dan Casey's recommendations for biking dress earlier in this chapter apply to hiking as well. Dan also contributed several of the recommendations for this section.

One valuable tip: Take your own water. It's not advisable to drink out of any of the streams in any park, no matter how clean they appear.

Maps

If you're going to hike without a guide, even on public property, take a good map. National and state parks often sell maps in their offices. The U.S. Geological Survey makes the GSPS Maps, available where listed below. (Some of these places also may carry parkland maps.)

Geological Association of JMU (540-433-6722; James Madison University Geology Department, Miller Hall, Harrisonburg, VA 22807).
Wilderness Voyagers (540-434-7234; 1544 E. Market St., Harrisonburg, VA 22801).
Blue Ridge Office Products (540-463-3432; 788 N. Lee Hwy., Lexington, VA 24450).
The Best Seller, Inc (540-463-3714; 29 W. Nelson St., Lexington, VA 24450).
Blue Ridge Outdoors (540-774-4311; 4362 Electric Rd., Roanoke, VA 24018).
CMT Sporting Goods Co., Inc (540-343-5533; 3473 Brandon Ave. SW, Roanoke, VA 24018).
Malcolm Blueprint and Supply (540-342-6703; 1725 Maiden Lane SW, Roanoke, VA 24015).
Architectural & Engineering Supply (540-387-1773; 803 Eighth St., Salem, VA 24153).
The Bookstack (540-885-2665; 1 E. Beverley St., Staunton, VA 24401).
Drafting Technical Supplies (540-387-2200; 594 Roanoke St., Salem, VA 24153).
Artz Hardware (540-465-3121; 181 W. King St., Strasburg, VA 22657).
Rockfish Gap Outfitters (540-943-1461; 1461 E. Main St., Waynesboro, VA 22980).
Winchester Realty Supply (540-670-5500; 28 W. Piccadilly St., Winchester, VA 22601).

FAVORITE HIKES, NORTH TO SOUTH

Frederick, Clarke, Warren, Shenandoah, and Page Counties

Besides the tourism offices and park information offices, the **Potomac Appalachian Trail Club** (703-242-0693; 118 Park St. SE, Vienna, VA 22180) is a wonderful source of information on hiking in the Valley, especially in the northern part. Most of the best hiking trails in this area are along Skyline Drive or are mapped by the Appalachian Trail folks.

Rockingham, Rockbridge, and Augusta Counties

Reddish Knob is the hands-down favorite hike for folks at James Madison University. The various clubs and individuals use a variety of trails to make it to the 3,000-foot peak and look down on the campus. The hike takes about four hours if you are fit. The best source of information on the trails is the George Washington National Forest Dry River District, 540-828-2591.

The Chessie Nature Trail is great for families with children. The well-marked, easy path offers many chances to see wildlife and features great views, including vistas that include the Maury River. It's located on Rte. 608 just off Rte. 60 outside Lexington. For information on this trail, call 540-464-7221 or write to the VMI Foundation, PO Box 932, Lexington, VA 24450.

The Buena Vista River Walk along the Maury River in Buena Vista is an easy 2.5-mile walk that has wonderful scenery. It's a lot like a city sidewalk, which makes it ideal for people with disabilities to navigate in wheelchairs. Benches along the path make it easy for those who need to rest along the way. The path is also well-marked, allowing those who want a shorter walk to go halfway and then turn around and head for home. Nearby parking off 21st Street across the railroad tracks is another convenience.

Page, Rockbridge, Augusta, Botetourt, and Roanoke Counties

White Oak Canyon Trail is located in the Central District of Shenandoah Park near Skyland Lodge along the Skyline Drive. Hikers can pick up this popular but challenging trail near mile marker 42.6 on Skyline. A 4.6-mile walk (one-way) down a long series of switchbacks into a deep canyon takes hikers past six spectacular waterfalls ranging in height from 35 to 86 feet. The total elevation drop is 1,025 feet. For a shorter hike (4.5 miles total), follow the trail to the first waterfall and turn around. For more information, contact the National Park Service (540-999-3500; www.shenandoah.national-park.com/hike.html; PO Box 209, Luray, VA 22835).

Devil's Marbleyard is a destination that takes you though a 200 million-year-old field of fractured quartzite, an eight-acre clearing of bright gray, jagged boulders in an otherwise thick forest. It is one of the Valley's more unusual rock formations. The hike itself is a 1.4-mile gentle climb from the trailhead parking lot. The elevation gain is about 500 vertical feet. This hike is part of the Jefferson National Forest (540-291-2189; Glenwood Ranger District, PO Box 10, Natural Bridge Station, VA 24579). Call for directions to the trailhead.

City of Roanoke (See the Prospect Road biking trail entry.) Call Roanoke Parks and Recreation for more information, 540-510-4340.

McAfee Knob in Roanoke County takes you past one of the common poster images of the Appalachian Trail in Virginia: the spectacularly pointed rock formation (elevation 3,200 feet) that juts into thin air like a diving platform. At the top, a sweeping view awaits — 270 degrees that takes in the Catawba Valley and North Mountain to the west, Tinker Cliffs to the north, and the Roanoke Valley to the east. The buildings of downtown Roanoke gleam in the sunlight when it's not too hazy. The climb itself is a steady one of 1,200 vertical feet over 3.5 miles. It doesn't take a professional hiker to make the climb. The trail is marked with white blazes that direct you toward the knob (peak). Just off I-81 at Exit 141. For more information or directions, call the Appalachian Trail Conference, 540-544-7388.

Nature Hikes

For information on spotting Virginia wildlife and birding trails, contact the **Virginia Birding and Wildlife Trail** (804-367-4335; birdingtrail@dgif.state.va.us; 4010 W. Broad St., Richmond, VA 23230). Another site, good for tips on introducing children to nature in Virginia, is www.vanaturally.com.

The **Andy Layne Trail** in Botetourt County, dedicated in 2001, goes up Scorched Earth Gap, around the high rocky formations of Tinker Cliffs on the back side of Tinker Mountain. Tinker is a volcano-shaped peak north of Roanoke that is easily seen from I-81. This is a difficult ascent, going up 1,700 feet over 2.8 miles, and should be attempted only by those in good condition. Near the top it joins the Appalachian Trail and you continue on that to Fincastle. From I-81 take the Daleville exit. Call 540-544-7388 for directions and information.

The Mountain Counties: Highland, Bath, and Alleghany

There are miles and miles of hiking trails in this area's state and regional parks and the George Washington National Forest. Roadside stops with short loop trails are also plentiful.

Rock Climbing

If it is a sheer face of rocks that entices you, then trek into West Virginia for really fertile ground. There are few good rock climbing opportunities in the Shenandoah Valley. One recommended by Chuck Walker of Rockfish Gap Outfitters is **Raven's Roost** (milepost 10 on the Blue Ridge Parkway). Check the Appalachian Trail, Skyline Drive, and Blue Ridge Parkway resources for more information on rock climbing. If this is your passion, then you'll want a copy of the book *Rock Climbing Virginia, West Virginia, and Maryland* by Eric J Horst (Globe Pequot Press, Guilford, CT 06437), which features 1,200 sites in the three states.

HORSEBACK RIDING

Virginia is horse country, and there are stables throughout. The best thing to do is to ask your accommodation owner for the names of the stables nearest to your destination.

A mecca for horse lovers is the Virginia Horse Center in Lexington (540-464-2951; www.horsecenter.org; info@horsecenter.org; PO Box 10151, Lexington, VA 24450), a place to watch horse shows, see a museum, and learn about horse care. (See Chapter Three, *Cultural Attractions*.)

Shenandoah2000

Many of the area's stables organize trail rides of varying lengths for visitors.

Some of the riding stables in the northern part of the Valley combine riding and water trips for a wonderful day of outdoor fun. We have listed just a few of the stables in the area. Guided rides usually run from $25 to $30 an hour. Call ahead to reserve on the weekends, and be sure to wear close-toed shoes and long pants when you ride.

One great place to ride is the Shenandoah National Park, which has more than 150 miles of horse trails. See the Web site at www.us-parks.com/US_National_Parks/shenandoah/shenandoah_horseback_riding
.shtml.

If you want to bring your own horse into the Valley, be sure to call ahead to find out whether nearby stables will accept your animal for temporary boarding and whether you are allowed to bring your horse on their guided rides. The Shenandoah National Park is one place where you will NOT be able to keep your own horse overnight.

SAMPLING OF VALLEY STABLES

Frederick, Clarke, and Warren Counties

Indian Hollow Stables at Shenandoah River State Park (800-270-8808, 540-636-4756; www.frontroyalcanoe.com/horse.htm; Daughter of the Stars Drive, PO Box 235, Bentonville, VA 22630) Affiliated with Front Royal Canoes for combination trail ride/canoe days.

Highlander Horses (540-636-4523; 5197 Reliance Rd., Front Royal, VA 22360).

Marriott Ranch (540-364-2627; 5305 Marriott Lane, Hume, VA 22639) Technically, this one isn't in the Valley, but it's so close to it that many upper Valley inns recommend it to guests who want to ride.

Shenandoah National Park (540-999-2210; 3655 U.S. Hwy. 211 East, Luray, VA 22835) Stables at mile 41.7 and 42.5.

Fort Valley Riding Stables (540-933-6633, 888-754-5771; www.fortvalleystable.com; 299 S. Fort Valley Rd., Fort Valley, VA 22652).

Shenandoah Trail Rides (540-636-6061).

Skyline Ranch Resort (540-636-6061; 751 Mountain Rd., Front Royal, VA 22630) Take Rte. 340 south, then right on Rte. 619 for 5 miles.

Camelot Farms Inc. (540 955-5000; 101 S. Buckmarsh St., Berryville, VA 22611).

Shenandoah County

Dear Bought (540-984-8861; 1693 Swover Creek Rd., Edinburg, VA 22824).

Dream App's The Starks (540-740-8314; 88 Turkey Knob Rd., Quicksburg, VA 22847).

Emmanuel Equine Facility (540-465-9361; 850 Junction Rd., Strasburg, VA 22657).

Page County

Farmhouse Restaurant At Jordan Hollow Farm (540-778-2285; 326 Hawksville Park Rd., Stanley, VA 22851).

Rockingham County

Mountain Run Kennels and Stables (540-269-2273; Keezletown, VA 22832).

Woodstone Meadows Stables (540-289-6152; Hwy. 644, McGaheysville, VA 22840).

Mountaintop Ranch (540-298-9542; 1030 Mountaintop Ranch Rd., Elkton, VA 22827).

Augusta County

Star B Stables (540-885-8855; starb@ntelos.net; 2926 Barterbrook Rd., Staunton, VA 24401).

Boxley Stables (540-885-3466; Rte. 11, Staunton, VA 24401).

Oak Manor Riding Stables (540-234-8101; Rte. 1, Weyers Cave, VA 24486).

Rockbridge County

Rock 'n' Horse Stable (540-291-2381; P.O. Box 369, Natural Bridge Station, VA 24569).

Fancy Hill Farm (540-291-1000; www.fancyhillfarm.com; Pat@fancyhillfarm
.com; 100 Equus Loop, Natural Bridge, VA 24578).

"Hoofbeats"

Hoofbeats (540-291-HOOF; www.hoof-beats.com; 20 Liberty Lane, Liberty Hill
Farm, Natural Bridge, VA 24578) is a nonprofit organization that offers therapeutic
horseback riding and horsemanship instruction to people with disabilities or serious illnesses. Riding is fun for many, but for these folks it's more than fun. For them,
riding makes life more exciting and often makes them better able to physically and
emotionally deal with daily life. The organization also offers riding instruction for
able-bodied individuals, and its headquarters is open for visitors (mostly groups)
by appointment.

Sunrise Stables (540-463-4766; www.sunrisestables.com; 62 Freshwater Ln.,
Lexington, VA 24450).

Lazy Acres Equestrian Center (540-463-5658; Rte. 39 West, Lexington, VA
24450).

Botetourt and Roanoke Counties

Centura Equine Center (540-989-6567; 8127 Martins Creek Rd., Roanoke, VA
24018).

Pineview Stables (540-366-0900; 7349 Old Mountain Rd., Roanoke, VA 24019).

Lakeland Stables (540-366-0857; 8232 Enon Dr., Hollins, VA 24019).

Pennley Innerprise-Stables (540-473-3497; RR2, Fincastle, VA 24090).

Pleasant Hill Stables (540-774-0315; 4919 Pleasant Hill Dr., Roanoke, VA 24018).

The Mountain Counties: Highland, Bath, and Alleghany

River Ridge Ranch (540-996-4148; Va. Rte. 1, Box 119-1, Millboro, VA 24460).

The Homestead (540-839-5500, 800-838-1766; www.thehomestead.com; U.S.
Hwy. 220, Hot Springs, VA 24445).

HUNTING AND FISHING

HUNTING

Hunting is highly regulated on the public lands of the Valley. If you want to
hunt the private lands, contact a guide through one of the sources listed
here.

Virginia has hunting seasons for everything from small game to bears. Information on state rules and seasons can be found by contacting the Virginia Department of Game and Inland Fisheries (804-367-1000; www.dgif.state.va; gifweb@dgif.state.va.us; 4010 W. Broad St., Richmond, VA 23230). The Web site also gives information on managed hunts and special events such as urban archery opportunities.

License!

Before hunting or fishing in the commonwealth, be sure to get a license. This isn't hard to do, even if you live out of state. You can obtain the license ahead of time online (see directions on the Web site), and in person at the Department of Game and Inland Fisheries office, 127 Lee Hwy., Verona, VA 24482; 540-248-9360. In 2001, the department entered into an agreement with Bass Pro Shops, giving those who need a Virginia license another option. Call 800-986-2628, but be forewarned: The shop adds a processing fee ($3.95 at time of writing).

FISHING

Are they waiting for trout on those lines? Fishing is a popular sport on the Valley's waterways.

Shenandoah2000

Hundreds of rivers and streams liberally lace the mountains and the lowlands of the Valley. Fly-fishing is king, and most lake fishing here is in manmade lakes stocked for fishing. The Web site www.vaflyfish.com is a good source of general information.

While the tourist offices can often tell you where you may legally fish on a nearby river or stream, you might want to hire a guide or at least consult with one. (See listing of outfitters below.) Many of the guides and outfitters also sell licenses and maps.

Several "wise men of the water" shared their knowledge for your benefit:

The ecosystem in the Valley streams and rivers is fragile. Guides urge catch-and-release for stream fishing and trout farms for take-home, eating fish.

Scott Bunten of Reel Time Fly Fishing in Lexington calls the Jackson River "the best trout stream in the entire state." He also recommends that those who want to fly-fish should ask local outfitters for the names of pay-to-fish spots. Escatawba Farms (www.Escatawba.com), near Lexington, comes highly recommended. For more recommendations, contact the local tourism office. Check local phone directories for guides and outfitters who can give you the latest information on where to go and what fish are in season at the time of your visit. You also can find guides through the Web site located at www.rivers mallies.com/guides/guides_va.html.

SAMPLING OF OUTFITTERS

Frederick, Clarke, and Warren Counties

Feathered Hook Outfitters (540-678-8999; asmittle@earthlink.net; 3035 Valley Ave., Suite 105, Winchester, VA 22601) The shop owner, Wes Smittle, makes "hard body poppers" and sells them in his shop. Guides, equipment. and information on where to go are all available here.

Thornton River Fly Shop (540-987-9400; Main Street, PO Box 530, Sperryville, VA 22740).

Turkey Mountain Outfitters (540-987-9134; Main Street, PO Box 276, Sperryville, VA 22740).

Page County

Shenandoah River Outfitters (800-6CANOE2, 540-743-4159; www.shenandoah river.com; canoes@shenandoahriver.com; 6502 S. Page Valley Rd., Luray, VA 22835) Outfitting and guide services on scenic South Fork of Shenandoah River. Canoe, kayak, tube, fish. Tent campground, cabins available.

Shenandoah Lodge (800-866-9958; flyfish@shentel.net; 100 Grand View Dr., Luray, VA 22835).

Long's Hunting and Fishing Outfitter and Guide Service (866-422-6637, 540-743-7311; 3095 U.S. Hwy. 211 E., Luray, VA 22835) Weekdays after 7pm, weekends anytime.

Shenandoah County

Murray's Fly Shop (540-984-4212; www.murraysflyshop; commurrays@shentel .net; 121 Main St., PO Box 156, Edinburg, VA 22824) Harry Murray is known throughout the Valley for his equipment and wisdom and the numerous books he has written.

Rockingham County

Blue Ridge Angler (540-574-3774; 1756 S. Main St., Harrisonburg, VA 22801).
Wilderness Voyagers (540-434-7234; 1544 E. Market St., Harrisonburg, VA 22801) Canoe and camping rental, shuttle service, hiking trips, retail outlet.
Woodstone Meadows Equine Center (540-289-6152; Rte. 1, PO Box 110-L, Mc-Gaheysville, VA 22840) Trail rides in Massanutten Mountains.

Augusta County

Rockfish Gap Outfitters (540-943-1461; www.rockfishgapoutfitters.com; 1461 E. Main St., Waynesboro, VA 22980) Equipment, great know-how, and tips.

Rockbridge County

Reel Time Fly Fishing & Outfitter (540-462-6100; www.reeltimeflyfishing.com; 23 W. Washington St., Lexington, VA 24450) Scott Bunten and others here have expertise in fly-fishing beyond Lexington, into the mountain counties, northward toward Winchester, and south into the New River Valley (Roanoke and Salem). Ask about equipment, buy equipment, find guides, and rely on their good judgment!
Kelly's Corner (540-463-5452; Rte. 60 west/Midland Trail, Lexington, VA 24450).
Llewellyn Lodge Outdoors (540-463-3235; 603 S. Main St., Lexington, VA 24450).

Botetourt and Roanoke Counties

Blue Ridge Outdoors (540-774-4311; 4362 Electric Rd., Roanoke, VA 24018) Another old-time outdoor store that can refer you to guides and stocks what you need to catch the big one!

The Orvis Sporting Goods store in Roanoke is one place to stock up on fishing equipment and stylish sporting outfits and accessories.

Mount Rogers High Country Outdoor Center (540-677-3900; PO Box 151, Troutdale, VA 24378) Wilderness adventures, sightseeing, pack trips, and wagon rides. Trips originate at livery base camp on Rte. 603.

Orvis Company Store (540-345-3635; www.orvis.com; Market Square, 19 Campbell Ave. SE, Roanoke, VA 24011) This venerable old Vermont retailer is the apex for outdoor clothing and equipment. You also can order online.

Mountain Counties

Highland Adventures (540-468-2722; highland@cfw.com; PO Box 151, Monterey, VA 24465) This is *the* place to contact for rock climbing guides, caving (wild caves), foraging, as well as hiking, fishing, and hunting guides.

The Outpost (540-839-5442; 2 Cottage Row, PO Box 943, Hot Springs, VA 24445) Fishing equipment, information, maps, permits to fish four-mile-long stocked Cascades Stream at The Homestead, state licenses, clothing.

JOUSTING

Natural Chimneys Regional Park (Upper Valley Regional Park Authority, 540-350-2510, 540-249-5729; PO Box 478, Grottoes, VA 24441) Yes, there is jousting in the world today. Although it's the state sport of nearby Maryland, one of the largest and oldest continuously held tournaments is held in this park at the end of each summer. Call for information.

MAZES

Feel like getting lost in the Valley? Try these sites on for size:

The Garden Maze (540-743-3915; 970 U.S. Hwy. 211 West, Luray) Part of Luray Caverns' attractions, this green maze is a one-acre ornamental garden and mental challenge rolled into one. The eight-foot-tall trees are four feet wide, making it impossible to peek over the edge. There are more than 40 decision points — but don't worry, if you really get lost (or just tired), you can climb an elevated platform to see your way out! Fee is $5 for adults, $4 for children. Open when the Luray Caverns are open.

Maize Quest (540-477-4200; vamaze@cornmaze.com; Wissler Road, Mount Jackson) Open from Aug.–Oct. on a varying schedule, so call ahead. The maze is carved into a harvested cornfield just down the road from the Meem's Bottom covered bridge. Right after the corn is harvested (usually by the beginning of August), the site opens and stays open through the spooky nights of October. College students and high-schoolers are especially fond of the flashlight nights, trying to find their way through the maze in the dark. This is a franchise operation, but the only corn maze in the Valley as of our writing. Cost is $6 for adults and $5 for youth.

MINIATURE GOLF

The major resorts in the Valley have miniature golf on-site, and many are open to use by other visitors. Miniature golf is gaining in popularity, so check the local phone book to see if more have popped up. Below is a sampling of the mini golf courses in the Valley.

Frederick, Clarke, and Warren Counties

Appleland Sports Center (540-869-8600; 4490 Valley Pike, Stephens City).
Shenandoah Miniature Golf (540-888-4407; Rte. 522 North, Winchester).

Shenandoah and Page Counties

Stony Creek Lilliputt (540-856-8044; Rtes. 263 and 836, Basye).
The Klub House Miniature Golf (540-984-3191; 101 Mini Court S., Edinburg).

Rockingham County

Roth Miniature Golf (540-433-5388; 3050 S. Main St., Harrisonburg).
The Bull Pen (540-433-2243; 1945 Deyerle Ave., Harrisonburg).
Valley Golf Center (540-432-9040; 141 Carpenter Lane, Harrisonburg).

Augusta County

Ingleside Resort and Conference Center (540-248-7888; 1410 Commerce Rd., Staunton).

Rockbridge County

Long's Campground (540-463-7672; 82 Campground Lane, Lexington).

Botetourt and Roanoke Counties

Putt Putt Golf and Games (540-366-3660; 6801 Peters Creek Rd. NW, Roanoke).
Drive-a-way Golf Center (540-389-0995; 1832 Apperson Dr., Salem).
Harbourtown Golf (540-721-4873; Rte. 122, Moneta, just south of Roanoke).

Mountain Counties

Miniature Golf at The Homestead (800-452-2223; U.S. Hwy. 220, Hot Springs).

PAINTBALL AND GO-KARTS

(Hours and fees vary widely)

PAINTBALL

Skyline Paintball (540-465-9537; 363 Radio Station Rd, Strasburg).
Pointblank Paint Ball (540-564-0002; 1084 Virginia Ave., Harrisonburg).
All-Terrain Paintball (540-464-3378; Rte. 11, north of downtown Lexington).

GO-KARTS

Bandit Racing (540-662-7711; 128 Windy Hill Lane, Winchester).
Griffith Specialties (540-433-2408; 510 Waterman Dr., Harrisonburg).
The Bull Pen (540-433-2243; 1945 Deyerle Ave., Harrisonburg).
Specialized Cycle Service (540-337-1159; Rte. 340 South, Stuarts Draft).
Thunder Valley Indoor Go Cart Track (540-387-9477; 1865 Dillard Drive, Salem).

PARKS

From city parks to national parks, you have it all in the Shenandoah Valley. For city park contacts, use the local tourism offices. (See Chapter Eight, *Information*.) State, regional, and national park information related to recreational use is listed here, along with a few specific points of interest for visitors. The activities in these parks are so extensive that they issue large booklets of their own. I recommend that you visit these sites for more detailed information.

The parks of the Valley offer a wide variety of activities. The larger centers have boating, tennis, swimming, hiking, and more. The smaller parks often offer tennis, picnicking, great views, and sometimes even hiking and boating opportunities. Whatever your interest, one of these parks can fill the need.

Some information on hiking, camping, boating, and other recreational activities is also covered in those topic sections in this chapter. The purpose of this section is to make you aware of the extent of park resources in the Valley and provide you with the information you need to contact them about further recreational possibilities.

LOCAL PARKS

Local tourism offices (see Chapter Eight, *Information*) will give you a listing of their town, city, and county parks. For example:

Lake Arrowhead (540-743-6475; 45 E. Main, Luray) A 120-acre all-season recreational area operated by the town of Luray.

Town of Front Royal Parks (540-635-7750; Chimney Field Park on Common-wealth Ave. and Municipal Park at Bing Crosby Rd. and Eighth St.).
Frederick County Parks & Recreation (540-665-5678).
Clarke County Park (540-955-5140; downtown Berryville).

VIRGINIA STATE PARK SYSTEM — HIGHLIGHTS IN THE SHENANDOAH

For highlights on state parks in the Shenandoah region, visit the Web site, www.dcr.state.va.us/parks. For information on availability of overnight accommodations, particular park amenities, or to make a reservation, you can reserve online or call 800-933-PARK (in Richmond, call 804-225-3867). Below are some of the Valley's state parks.

Sky Meadows State Park (540-592-3556; two miles south of Paris on Rte. 710 west, off Rte. 17 north) has rolling pastures and scenic vistas for your hiking enjoyment. Mount Bleak House offers a view of how a middle-class family lived during the 1850s. A bridle path and access to the Appalachian Trail.

Raymond R. "Andy" Guest Jr./Shenandoah River State Park (540-622-6840, 800-933-PARK; www.dcr.state.va.us/parks/andygues.htm; shenandoahriver@dcr .state.va.us; PO Box 235, Daughter of Stars Drive, Bentonville, VA 22610) The park, one of the state's newest, offers visitors 1,604 acres with 5.6 miles of river frontage.

Douthat State Park and Lake (540-862-8100, 800-933-PARK; www.dcr.state .va.us/parks/douthat.htm; Route 1, PO Box 212, Millboro, VA 24460) These 4,493 acres embrace some of Virginia's most outstanding mountain scenery. All facilities are open from Memorial Day through Labor Day. Visitors can dine at the Lakeview Restaurant, camp from March through December, swim, boat, play tennis, rent cabins, use biking trails and playgrounds, enjoy nature programs, and take night canoe tours.

Goshen Pass (www.lexingtonvirginia.com/goshen_pass.htm) is a wayside stop on Rte. 39 west in Goshen. Maintained by the Virginia Department of Transportation.

VIRGINIA REGIONAL PARK SYSTEM

Some of the highlights in the Valley include:

Grand Caverns Regional Park — Grottoes (540-249-5705; from I-81, exit 235 east to Grottoes) These caverns have been open to the public since 1806, making it America's oldest show cave. During the Civil War, both Union and Confederate troops passed through here. Park includes tennis, trails, swimming, and miniature golf. Open Apr.–Oct., daily 9–5

Natural Chimneys Regional Park (540-350-2510; c/o Valley Regional Parks, 94

Shenandoah2000

The pillars of Natural Chimneys in Mount Solon rise up against the sky like cathedral towers.

Natural Chimneys Lane, Mount Solon, VA 22843) The castle appearance of the Chimneys may well have inspired the creation of the Natural Chimneys Jousting Tournament, America's oldest continuously held sporting event. The park also includes seven natural limestone towers, nature trails, a swimming pool, and campgrounds.

NATIONAL PARKS

There are two large national parks and the parks of the National Forest System in the Valley. Several of the battlefields (see Chapter Three, *Cultural Attractions*) are also federal parks. The enormous acreage of these parks could

---

When you are in a national park:
- Do not disturb any plant life.
- Remember that metal detectors are prohibited.
- You need a valid Virginia fishing license to fish and must abide by the state seasonal rules.
- Do not feed the animals.
- The speed limit on most of Skyline Drive is 25 mph and the speed limit in the parks is 45 mph.
- Haze (mostly from auto exhaust) has become as much of a problem in summer as ice and snow in winter. Call the park you're planning to visit for weather conditions.

make short work of a week or even a month of vacation. But thanks to their many entrances and proximity to many other points of interest in the Valley, it is possible to sample these parks, even on a daytrip. The listing of contacts and blurbs of favored places in each parkland area are given for your convenience in planning. For detailed information on the services, camping, sights, and activities of each area, contact the parks.

**SHENANDOAH
NATIONAL PARK
(AND SKYLINE DRIVE)**
540-999-3500.
www.nps.gov/shen.
3655 U.S. Hwy. 211 E.,
Luray, VA 22835.
Directions: The four entry
stations to the park are:
Front Royal (at its
northernmost point via
Rte. 340 or Rte. 55);
Thornton Gap (at mile 33
— accessible via Rte. 211
near Luray); **Swift Run
Gap** (at mile 65.7 via Rte.
33 near Harrisonburg);
and **Rockfish Gap** (at
mile 105, which is also at
the beginning of Blue
Ridge Parkway, via I-64).
Open: The drive is open
year-round, weather
permitting. Other
activities and facilities are
open on a seasonal basis.
Admission: $10/vehicle to
enter park — good for
one week on same car.
Annual pass available.
National Park Golden
Pass honored. Daily
individual fee (includes
bicycle) is $5/person.
There are additional fees
for lodging, camping, and
other activities. Call
ahead.

More than 500 miles of trails lace the area, including 101 miles of the Appalachian Trail in the 195,000-acre park. The 105 miles of Skyline Drive extend from Front Royal to I-64 in Waynesboro and can be made nonstop in about four hours, but there are many overlooks and sights you won't want to miss. For example, the mile 17.1 overlook offers a look at Stony Mountain, and Hogback, at mile 20.8, offers one of the best views of the Shenandoah River. For country music fans, a view of Rockytop Ridge is possible from Big Run Overlook at mile 81.2.

Hiking is probably the single most popular activity in the park. There are almost 60 well-marked trails. Maps are available at the Visitor Center, as well as at the stores noted in "Maps" earlier in this chapter. **Snead Farm Trail** at mile 4.6 offers a choice of 1.4 miles out and back, or a 3-mile loop with views of the cellar, barn, and stone foundation of the farmhouse. Many visitors enter the park at **Old Rag** at mile 31.5. This 5- to 7-mile strenuous hike climbs 500 feet, offers spectacular views, and is one of the most popular trails in the park. **Story of the Forest Nature Trail**, an easy 2-mile paved loop at mile 51 (at the Harry Byrd Visitor Center), is a self-guided introduction to the area's wildlife and plants.

There are three visitor centers where one can buy books, obtain maps, and enjoy ranger-led programs. Please note that not all centers/shops/posts are open year-round. The centers are: **Dickey Ridge** at mile 4.6, **Harry Byrd** at mile 51, and **Loft Mountain** at mile 79. Snack food is available at the visitor centers.

There are also three lodges: **Skyland, Big Meadows,** and **Lewis Mountain Cabins**. These vary greatly in cost, types of amenities, and time of year they're open. Most are open March through October. Reservations should be made by calling 800-999-4714 or online at www.visitshenandoah.com. Each of the lodges offers food and a gift shop.

You can make campsite reservations by calling 800-778-2851 or 540-999-3500. If you want to camp in the back country, you will need to get a permit from Park Headquarters, 540-999-3500. Headquarters is located between Thornton Gap and Luray on Rte. 211, open Monday through Friday.

BLUE RIDGE PARKWAY
828-298-0398.
www.blueridgeparkway.org.
400 BB&T Building,
  Asheville, NC 28801.
Local contact: Friends of the
  Blue Ridge Parkway.
800-228-7275.
PO Box 20986, Roanoke, VA
  24018.
Directions: Enter at
  Waynesboro from I-64 at
  mile one or at several
  points along the way. Last
  stop in the Valley is near
  Roanoke in Mill
  Mountain Park.
Open: Weather permitting.
Admission: None for entry;
  there are fees for camping
  and other activities.

The entire Blue Ridge Parkway is 459 miles long, stretching from Waynesboro to the Great Smokies. Milepost numbering begins with 0 at the Rockfish Gap entry point just outside Waynesboro. The section covered here includes only miles 1–120, from Waynesboro to Roanoke.

The Blue Ridge Parkway itself is the park; the lands surrounding it remain in private hands. Most of the road runs across mountaintops (from 600 to 6,000 feet in elevation), but the lowest elevation on the parkway is in the Valley, near the James River Visitor Center around mile 62: 649 feet. (The highest elevation in Virginia is not far away at Apple Orchard, around milepost 75: 3,950 feet.)

Even though many of the activities associated with the Blue Ridge are on private adjoining land, pockets of park-run activities and overlooks can be found along the way. There are many marked trails and historic sites operated by the park at overlooks and other stopping points. Many hikes have a trailhead at an overlook, including the short (1.6-mile) Falling Water Cascades National Scenic Trail at mile 83.4. Check with the various information centers at park entry points and visitor centers, including:

Rockfish Gap Tourist Information Center (540-943-5187; Rte. 250 at Parkway Access, milepost 0) Exhibits and all services free.

Humpback Visitor Center (540-943-4716; mile 5.8) Offers a trail with exhibits of the life of the mountain folk before the parkway.

James River Visitor Center (804-299-5496; mile 63.6) Has an easy self-guided trail that traces the restored canal locks on the James River.

A word of warning from the parkway Web site:

". . . because the Blue Ridge Parkway was designed for motor travel, bicyclists should exercise caution, have reflectors, and riders should wear high-visibility clothing and helmets. Avoid the Blue Ridge Parkway during fog and periods of low visibility. Long-distance travelers should plan their overnight stays, and be sure to have plenty of water and food."

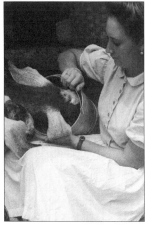

This farm girl reenactor at Humpback Visitor Center on the Blue Ridge Parkway shows visitors what life was like before the area became parkland.

Shenandoah2000

Peaks of Otter Visitor Center (540-586-4357; mile 86) Offers a living history demonstration on summer weekends at an 1880 homestead, the Johnson farm.

Visitor centers are open 9–5 daily in the summer; other times of the year, call 540-857-2490 for hours.

Camping and lodges are open from May to November, with fees charged on a per-night basis. Parkway campers wishing to camp outside of regular campgrounds must apply for a free permit from the Rocky Knob Visitor Center by calling 540-745-9662 or dropping by at mile 169. The **Otter Creek Campground** and **Peaks of Otter Lodge** (540-586-1081, 800-542-5927) are two such accommodations within the bounds of the Valley segment of the parkway.

Note: Just off the parkway and just to the east of the counties that make up the Valley is **The Greenbriar**, one of Virginia's premier resorts. (See Chapter Five, *Lodging*.) It is reached by traveling down the parkway just a bit from Waynesboro. Wineries and other sights are nearby.

Parkway visitors won't want to miss **Virginia's Explore Park** (800-842-9163; mile 115), a great interpretive site. And **Mabry's Mill** (mile 176.2), a quarter-mile walk into the history of the mill era and the most photographed spot on the Blue Ridge Parkway, is just below the Valley segment.

Be sure to pick up a copy of *Blue Ridge Magazine, Parkway Milepost* and the *Blue Ridge Parkway Information Guide*, available at every visitor center and entrance. For those wanting to take a virtual tour in advance, try www.virtual blueridge.com.

GEORGE WASHINGTON NATIONAL FOREST
540-433-2491.
www.southernregion.fs.fed. us/gwj.
Harrison Plaza,
Harrisonburg, VA 22801.

The U.S. Forest Service divides the area into districts for purposes of administration and management. (See below for addresses and highlights of the Valley districts.) The service also publishes a large book outlining all the offerings in the Valley, and its Web site provides the most current informa-

Shenandoah2000

Light and shadow play on the water at the North Mountain Falls in George Washington National Forest.

Southern portion known as:
George Washington and Jefferson National Forest
540-265-5100.
5162 Valleypointe Parkway, Roanoke, VA 24019.
Open: Year-round in many areas, weather permitting. Some activities are seasonal.
Admission: No fees to enter the area, but fees charged for use of facilities and for some maps.

tion on the area's seasonal and year-round activities.

The vast expanse and many elevations of the forest make it easier to plan your trip by considering which district you will be visiting. District offices are open year-round, but the visitor centers keep only seasonal hours. The list below notes the offices within the scope of this book.

Lee Ranger District (540-984-4101; 109 Molineau Rd., Edinburg, VA 22824) Two of the outstanding fun spots in this district are the Elizabeth Furnace Recreation Area and the ATV trails at the Taskers Gap/Peters Mill Run ATV Complex. The latter features 21 miles of trail. A variety of loop trail opportunities and difficulty levels for both ATVs and motorbikes are available. Some routes also are open to full-sized four-wheel drive vehicles. Users must stay on designated trails. There aren't many ATV opportunities in the parks, so if you're an ATV user, mark this one.

Massanutten Visitor Center (540-740-8310; 3220 E. Lee Hwy./Rte. 211, New Market, VA 22824) Open 8–4:30 daily, mid-Apr.–Oct. Be sure to visit Toma-hawk Pond on Runion Creek. It has a universally accessible trail and it's stocked with tasty fish!

Sherando Lake (540-949-0918; Lyndhurst) Offers camping, shower houses, hik-ing, biking, swimming, picnic tables, grills, fishing, and canoeing

Gaithright Information Center (540-962-1138; PO Box 432, Covington, VA 24426) Gaithright Dam offers many wonderful opportunities for boating and other water fun, mostly in Bath County.

Warm Springs Ranger District (540-839-2521; Rte. 2, PO Box 30, Hot Springs, VA 24445) This is a very important sector of the forest, and about 50 percent of Bath County is in the forest. Lake Moomaw, a 2,630-acre lake, is almost com-pletely surrounded by the national forest. Gaithright Dam on the Jackson River and Lake Moomaw provide some of the best outdoor recreation oppor-tunities in Bath County.

Natural Bridge Visitor Center (540-291-1806; PO Box 10, Natural Bridge Sta-tion, VA 24579) Opportunities primarily in Rockbridge County.

SKATING

Most of the skating is roller-skating, but there is one ice-skating rink in Roanoke. The skating rinks are listed north to south.

Mac's Roller Rink (540-869-2129; 5030 Front Royal Pike, Front Royal).
Winchester Skating Rink (540-667-6464; Rte. 7, east of I-81, Winchester).
Stoney Creek Roller Rink (540-984-4022; 3418 Stoney Creek Rd., Edinburg).
Skatetown USA (540-433-1834; 100 Miller Circle, Harrisonburg).
Skatetown Staunton (540-885-3798; 1311 Barterbrook Rd., Staunton).
Skate Center of Roanoke Valley (540-989-2000; 4121 Brandon Ave. SW, Roanoke).
Star City Roller Skating Center (540-362-9500; 140 Hershberger Rd. NW, Roanoke).
Olympic Roller Skating Center (540-890-2250; 1620 E. Washington Ave., Vinton).

The best opportunity for year-round ice skating in the Valley is:

The Ice Station (540-260-1505; www.theicestation.com; 3710 Tom Andrews Rd., Roanoke).

SKIING

Unless you own your own mountain, the way to enjoy the snow on the slopes, with ski or snowboard, is at one of the area resorts: Bryce, Mas-sanutten, and The Homestead. Prices vary widely according to day or half-day,

Shenandoah2000

Massanutten, Bryce, and The Homestead are three of the Valley's largest ski resorts. These Bryce skiers are enjoying the view of the mountains as they schuss down the slopes.

weekday or weekend, equipment rental, and need for lessons. Check for special package rates. Rentals are also available at these sites.

The Homestead (800-838-1766; www.thehomestead.com; U.S. Rte. 220, PO Box 2000, Hot Springs, VA 24445) Skiing, tubing, and outdoor ice skating.
Massanutten Resort (540-289-9441; www.massresort.com) Fourteen slopes and tubing.
Bryce Resort (800-821-1444; www.bryceresort.com; PO Box 3, Basye, VA 22810) Eight slopes and grass skiing on those same slopes in the summer!
Wintergreen Resort (804-325-2200; www.wintergreenresort.com; Rte. 664, PO Box 706, Wintergreen, VA 22958) Just outside of the Valley, but near enough to be mentioned here, this area offers 17 slopes and trails.

SWIMMING

Most of the larger counties and towns in the Valley have at least one public swimming facility. Ask the local tourism board, local park offices, or your host. There is generally a small fee to use the public pools. There are far too many to even attempt a sampling.

TENNIS

Most of the larger towns also have at least one public tennis facility with courts free on a first-come, first-served basis. Check with the local tourism office and local parks and recreation offices for locations, possible fees, and availability during your stay. But be aware that the tightening of public budgets has meant fewer funds for municipalities and recreation facilities all over the state. As with the swimming pools, there are far too many to even begin a sampling.

WATER
BY CANOES, KAYAKS, AND TUBES

The **Virginia Professional Paddlesports Association** (888-42FLOAT; www .vappa.com) is the best resource for information on canoe, tube, raft, kayak, and other water sport activities in the lakes, streams, and rivers of the Valley.

While Apr. 1–Oct. 31 is the main season, water activity on the Shenandoah and the other Valley waters can be almost year-round. Most river sporting activity is on the South Fork of the Shenandoah. When planning a trip, remember that the Shenandoah flows south to north — the opposite of what we think of as up and down. Whitewater is limited in the Valley

Outfitters (see sampling under "Hunting and Fishing") are a good source of equipment, guides, information on the best water entry points, shuttle service to and from points of entry, water condition updates, safety tips, and general river lore.

Be sure that each member of your party wears a Coast Guard-approved life jacket when pursuing any type of water activity. Children under age five or under a certain size need specially fitted life jackets. Many outfitters simply do not take children that young on trips. One outfitter noted: "We get people who want to take infants, but that is simply not safe."

According to the staff of the Front Royal Canoe Company, the most commonly made mistake among visitors is to overestimate the length of time and river they can handle at one time. Many of those who think they can boat 20 miles in four hours often end up far from their take-out point, calling for help as darkness settles on the Valley.

Prices vary widely, but it is usually cheaper to go during the week than on the weekend. During the summer, call ahead to reserve for weekend trips. Some outfitters charge per person; others charge per boat with a limit on the number of people that can go in the boat. Most of the self-guided trips last three to five hours, including travel to and from.

> **Boating in the George Washington National Forest**
> **Parking and Admission Passes**
>
> **Naturally Yours Passport Plus** ($50) Good for parking and admission to all state parks. The pass also entitles holders to a 10 percent discount on camping, all state park merchandise, equipment rentals (may not apply to concessions not operated by the park), and shelter and amphitheater rentals. Those purchasing this pass also receive exclusive cabin specials, quarterly newsletters, special announcements, and a Virginia State Park bumper sticker.
>
> **Naturally Yours Parking Passport** ($30) Good for parking and admission for one park of your choice (indicate park on the application). Boat launching requires a separate pass (see next entry), so if you are going to the lakes, be sure you've gotten one of these and allowed for it in your vacation budget.
>
> **Naturally Yours Passport Plus for Boaters** ($125) Good for boat launching at all Virginia state parks plus all the benefits described above for the Naturally Yours Passport Plus.
>
> **Naturally Yours Park/Launch Passport** ($105) Good for the boat launches and parking at all parks. (This pass differs from the Passport Plus Pass in that no discounts or other benefits are included.) Those with a disability passport do not have to pay a fee and there are discounts for senior citizens. Call in advance to make sure you have the right information with you to obtain these discounts.

When renting, be sure to ask about shuttle service and extras like picnics, combination trail ride and canoe trips, and more. Be sure to let them know if you are a beginner. Many outfitters include a few minutes of orientation and paddling lessons for beginners when they drop them off at the water. Guides are generally only for multiple-day trips.

Since the river flows through several counties, the boat/canoe rental companies and outfitters are listed here alphabetically, rather than by county, as in the other sections of the book.

Front Royal Canoe (540-635-5440, 800-270-8808; www.frontroyalcanoe.com; frcanoe@rma.edu; PO Box 473, Front Royal, VA 22630) Ninety-nine percent of their trips are self-guided. They offer some trips as short as 90 minutes, and they also run a combination trail ride/canoe trip. The riding portion includes trails along the river. The stables (see "Horseback Riding") also offer trail rides only.

James River Basin Canoe Livery (540-261-7334; canoevirginia.com; information@ canoevirginia.com; 1870 E. Midland Trail, Lexington, VA 24450) Serves James, Maury, and New Rivers; Balcony Falls also is in their area.

Massanutten River Adventures (540-289-4066; www.canoe4u.com; MassanuttenRiver@aol.com; Resort Drive, McGaheysville; mail: 2185 Mockingbird Lane, Elkton, VA 22827) Covers the Shenandoah River. They have a separate number for those staying at the Massanutten Resort: 540-289-4978.

River Rental Outfitters (540-635-5050; PO Box 145, Bentonville, VA 22610).

Shenandoah River Outfitters (800-6CANOE2, 540-743-4159; www.shenandoah river.com; canoes@shenandoahriver.com; 6502 S. Page Valley Rd., Luray, VA 22835) Serves South Fork of Shenandoah from Front Royal to Luray.

Shenandoah River Trips (800-RAPIDS-1; www.shenandoah.cc; 4fun@shenandoah .cc; Rocky Hollow Road, Bentonville, VA 22610) Serves South Fork of Shenandoah. Emphasizes the rapids, but offers a range of trips.

Virginia Outdoor Center (877-PLAY-VA2; info@PlayVA; 3219 Fall Hill Ave., Fredericksburg, VA 22401) Serves Rappahannock, James, and other rivers. Also offers mountain hikes and climbing.

WHATEVER! OTHER ASSORTED OUTDOOR ENTERTAINMENT OPTIONS

Horseshoe pits, basketball and volleyball courts can be found at **Criser Road Park in Front Royal.**

Llama Treks, Applewood Inn (540-463-1962; Buffalo Bend Road, Lexington) This is a charming inn and a place to try touring the mountains Andes-style!

Quail Ridge Sporting Clays (540-463-1800; Rte. 3, Box 116A, Lexington).

Wilson's Pet Farm (540-662-5715; just off of Rte. 50 on Rte. 644, Winchester) Follow the signs to this petting zoo situated on approximately 5 acres. Visitors are able to interact with the animals through petting and feeding. Open: 10–5 weekdays, 10–6 Sat. and Sun. May–Labor Day; 10–6 holidays and weekends Apr., Sept., and Oct.

WWII Fighter Rides (800-809-5282; 615 Airport Rd., Winchester).

CHAPTER FIVE
Sleep Inn
LODGING

One of the premier resorts in the United States, The Homestead, in Hot Springs, Virginia, offers spa relaxation and sporting fun (golf, tennis, skiing, and more) all year long.

Throughout the Valley there are many inns, hotels, and motels. Their accommodations range from basic no-frills rooms to suites that offer kitchens and the most modern amenities. No matter what your preference, you should be able to find the perfect place to lay your head.

Major chains represented in the Valley can be contacted on their 800 numbers. Most have handicapped-accessible units. Be sure to ask about special features like a wheelchair-accessible shower. Even the historic homes can often accommodate the handicapped in first-floor rooms. Ask first.

The several chain locations mentioned in this book are included because of outstanding features. Inns not fully reviewed but simply listed under "Other" are included on the basis of their reputation, but in the time we were assembling this book we were simply not able to visit that property personally.

Many of the inns included in this list are notable properties belonging to Select Registry Inns, the Bed and Breakfast Association of Virginia, and/or Bed and Breakfasts of the Historic Shenandoah Valley. Some belong to all three.

Be sure to book early in fall and spring, ask for detailed directions from your planned route, and ask very specific questions about access. The fall "leaf season" also coincides with college football and parent weekends, making it imperative to plan ahead at that time. Early May blossoms with buds and college graduates, bringing another sweep of relatives and sightseers to the Valley. But rooms are available if you look, even in "high seasons," especially outside the major college towns. Be forewarned, however: Some inns impose two-day minimum-stay requirements during those times.

When the directions line of our information block reads "Call for directions," it means that there are a variety of routes, depending on which road you're taking, or that the path from the main road involves many turns. Innkeepers will be happy to direct you.

Inquire about access for the handicapped, especially where it has been designated as "limited." Many of the older buildings in the Valley have limited access. In some cases the dining rooms are open to easy entry, but there are stairs to the rest room area or narrow rest room doors. In other cases, limited accessibility may mean that there is a single step to negotiate going into the building. Be specific about your needs.

Well-known year-round resorts in the Valley include the world-famous Homestead, Massanutten, and Bryce resorts. (Just outside the boundaries of the book are The Greenbriar and Wintergreen; see sidebar on page 148.) Most of these resorts now offer timeshare units with complete kitchens as well as short-term hotel-style rooms. Each offers its own array of activities for guests of all ages. They make great bases for a one-week or longer stay, especially if you want to combine a visit to the Valley with golf or skiing.

Camping is discussed in Chapter Four, *Outdoor Recreation*.

SHENANDOAH LODGING NOTES

RATES

All rate ranges are based on rates posted at the time of writing, without discount. Rates can change at any time. Many of the inns offer discounts for longer stays and off-season stays. Rates are sometimes increased during fall foliage season or in May, when spring flowers and college graduations abound. Many also offer AARP, AAA, and other discounts. Be sure to ask when you book.

Rates quoted do not include tax imposed by the state on a per-night basis. We use the following scale to give you an idea of the rates we were quoted when researching the book:

Inexpensive	Up to $75
Moderate	$76 to $125
Expensive	$126 to $175
Very Expensive	Above $175

AMERICAN PLAN

Some of the inns require the inclusion of an American Plan or Modified American Plan — a package of some meals, all meals, or just breakfast and dinner — during high season. Some require it all the time.

MINIMUM STAYS

Many also require two-night stays on weekends during the spring or fall leaf seasons. Often, however, if you call at the last minute and they have an opening they will override the minimum rule. The hotels listed do not have a minimum. The resorts in the area often have a two-night minimum stay and, for their timeshare units, sometimes have a one-week minimum.

DEPOSITS AND CANCELLATIONS

Most of the properties require at least a credit card number to hold a room, and many impose a partial cancellation fee or require a full night's payment for cancellation within 24 hours. The ones with the most stringent policies in this regard are usually the smallest establishments, where a cancellation at the last minute means losing a good portion of the planned income for that night. Be sure to ask about the cancellation policy when you make your reservation.

OTHER CONSIDERATIONS

Most of the properties do not allow pets, although a few will do so for an additional fee. Be sure to ask first. If you're traveling with a pet and want to stay somewhere that does not accept pets, most can recommend nearby kennels.

While it is true that most inns do not accept children, this is changing. Many that say they do not accept children will consider a child over age 12, so always inquire. Most of the inns charge an additional per-person fee if you have a third person in the room, child or adult.

Many of the inns are jumping on the no-smoking bandwagon. If you are a smoker, inquire when you make your reservation as to the inn's policy in this regard.

You will notice that some of the inns in the mountain counties do not have street addresses. This is not an omission. The towns do not consider it necessary to have numbered street addresses, as folks just pick up their mail at the post office.

BOOKING

Most of the properties can be booked by phone or online. Timeshare exchange units are often booked through large international membership groups, or you can call the resort directly to inquire about units that are left open for rental rather than exchange.

Resorts on the Border

The Greenbriar (800-453-4858; www.greenbriar.com; 300 W. Main St., White Sulphur Springs, WV 24986) is a world-renowned resort nestled on 6,500 acres in the scenic Allegheny Mountains in West Virginia. The Greenbrier offers more than 50 activities, including three championship golf courses, a new golf academy, a gallery of fine shops, and a host of traditional amenities that have distinguished this resort for more than 200 years. Reservations may be made through the Web site or by phone.

Wintergreen Resort (800-266-2444; www.wintergreenresort.com; PO Box 706, Wintergreen, VA 22958) also has much to offer visitors and is just a short hop over the Blue Ridge, just beyond Waynesboro and the counties included in the scope of this book. The resort offers a Rees Jones golf course, health spa, summer music festival, and tennis camps, proving that skiing is not the only entertainment option in the mountains. This 11,000-acre property is a true four-season resort.

FREDERICK, CLARKE, AND WARREN COUNTIES

Winchester

HISTORIC FULLER HOUSE INN

Innkeeper: Richard Otam. 540-722-3976, 877-722-3976. www.bedandbreakfast.com (go to Winchester VA or Fuller House Inn). stonsoup@shentel.net. 220 W. Boscawen St., Winchester, VA 22601. Follow signs for downtown. Parking in rear.
Price: Expensive.
Credit Cards: MC, V.
Handicap Access: No.
Special Features: Decisions on children and pets on case-by-case basis.

There are only three rooms in this inn, but this property is worth noting because of its premier downtown location: It is only two blocks from the historic walking mall.

The rooms are decorated with period décor reflecting significant epochs in the town's history: Colonial, Civil War, and Victorian. Portraits, bedspreads, and other antique linens enhance décor. The Colonial Room is the most expensive of the three because it offers a private bath and porch, but it goes fast despite its higher cost.

The rooms are comfortable and furnished with all amenities, including hairdyers, coffee and tea makers, and cable TV. Breakfast is taken to rooms in a basket each morning.

Host Richard Otam designs and builds English country furniture and kitchens. Most of what you see in the rooms is not handmade by him, but gathered lovingly by the owner, Debra Johnson, who also owns Stone Soup Gallery. (See Chapter Seven, *Shopping*.)

LONG HILL BED AND BREAKFAST

Innkeepers: Rhonda and George Kriz.
540-450-0341, 866-450-0341.
www.longhillbb.com.
longhillbb@longhillbb.com.
547 Apple Pie Ridge Rd., Winchester, VA 22603.
From downtown, take Rte. 522 and make right onto Apple Pie Ridge Road. Go 0.9 mile; Long Hill driveway is on the left. Call for directions from other points.
Price: Moderate. (Corporate and long-term rates on request.)
Credit Cards: AE, D, MC, V.
Handicap Access: Partial. No outdoor ramp, but several entries without steps. Bathroom sinks will accommodate wheelchairs. Showers have handrails.
Special Features: No pets; children on a case-by-case basis.

This inn is a modern home, built in the 1970s and remodeled lovingly into an inn by Rhonda and George Kriz. The incredible entranceway boasts wrought-iron gates and stained glass retrieved from a church in Richmond. Other architectural details salvaged from various old homes grace the inn throughout.

The home also showcases the couple's extensive antique collection, including kitchen and household items. Of particular note is the dining room sideboard, a square rosewood piano, circa 1840s. The spacious nature of the house allows easy flow among the public spaces while the décor creates "nooks" of privacy for guests.

Each of the three rooms has a modern bathroom and its own control for heat. The library and a Jacuzzi are available for guests, as is the outdoor pool (in season, of course). The downstairs recreation room, which runs the entire length of the house, has a jigsaw puzzle under way at all times and a 1920s-era regulation-size pool table ready for play.

The grounds are carefully landscaped into a series of gardens that provide private space for guests. Seclusion and peace can be found in the butterfly and bird garden or alongside the fish pond.

Be sure to wake up hungry to enjoy George's breakfast specialties: fruit compote, Long Hill breakfast pie, caramel French toast, or blueberry/raspberry coffeecake. With just a bit of notice they will make your meal early in the day and accommodate special dietary needs.

Rhonda Kriz is a native of the area. Her grandfather was a judge and his desk sits in the library. Singer Pasty Cline took her wedding vows standing in front of it!

Berryville

BATTLETOWN INN

Innkeeper: Leo Bernstein, owner.
540-955-4100, 800-282-4106.
www.battletown.com.
battletown@battletown
.com.

You can't miss this inn, right on the Main Street of Berryville. There are 12 rooms, each with a private bath, some with Jacuzzi. Renovations with antiques have returned the inn to its early years of elegance, but rugs in the main area were a bit threadbare at the time of our last visit.

102 W. Main St., Berryville, VA 22611.
Price: Inexpensive.
Credit Cards: AE, D, MC, V.
Handicap Access: Limited.
Special Features: No pets; children OK.

The building was erected in 1809 as a private home for the daughter of the town's founder. In 1946 it became an inn. Mary Murray operated the inn's restaurant for 35 years, establishing its reputation for fine southern Virginia food.

The Gray Ghost Tavern, a small room between the entry and formal dining room, was added in 1997. Folks can enjoy local wines at the bar and food from the dining room in its more informal setting. While sitting at the bar, expect ghost stories to whirl about you. It is reputed that one of Confederate Colonel John Mosby's men haunts the house — perhaps you'll even see him yourself!

Col. John Mosby

Colonel John Singleton Mosby was a confederate raider during the Civil War. This dashing officer was born in Edgemont, Virginia, on Dec. 6, 1833. He was expelled from the University of Virginia for shooting another student in a duel and, while languishing in jail as punishment, he took up the practice of law.

He was not a secessionist, but felt it necessary to support his "mother" state when war called him to choose sides. He became adept at roiling Union forces, disrupting supply lines, and escaping into the fogging Virginia evenings, earning him the nickname "The Gray Ghost."

Mosby also had a definite flair for the flamboyant, which was particularly evident during a raid that occurred on March 6, 1863. Mosby and a mere 29 men rode boldly into Federal-occupied Fairfax and proceeded directly to the courthouse, where Mosby captured a sleepy, nightshirted Union General Edwin H. Stoughton.

While Mosby was a frequent visitor in this area, his is not the ghost of the stories about the Battletown Inn. Local lore has it that a Confederate soldier, upset because his lover left him to be with a Union soldier, hanged himself in the tavern area while it served as a temporary Civil War hospital.

Stephens City

INN AT VAUCLUSE SPRING
Innkeepers: Neil and Barry Myers.
540-869-0200, 800-869-0525.
www.vauclusespring.com.
mail@vauclusespring.com.
231 Vaucluse Spring Ln., Stephens City, VA 22655.
North of Winchester; call for directions, as there are several twists and turns from each main road.

This inn is a meticulously restored 18th-century building, its name taken from the French country retreat of the great romantic poet Petrarch. Current owners and innkeepers Neil and Barry Meyers bought the house of colonial-era Valley lawyer Gabriel Jones, who had bought the house in 1785 from a family of local artists, the Chumleys. The Chumleys lived in a modern house on the property that also has been made over for guest use.

Even a short visit to the property makes it easy to see why it was named for a poet's retreat — the

Price: Expensive to Very
  Expensive. Two-night
  minimum required on
  weekends, but you can
  call to check availability
  for a single-night stay.
Credit Cards: MC, V;
  personal checks accepted.
Handicap Access: One
  room; breakfast/dining
  area not accessible.
Special Features: No
  children or pets.

magic of the site acts as an inspiring muse. A paved parking lot makes it easy to store your car and then simply imagine that you're visiting in the days of the pioneers.

The six manor-house rooms and the others are all air-conditioned and have private baths. The Jones Room on the top floor of the manor house offers the best view (the poet's muse worked best for me there). It also has a queen-sized four-poster bed, a Jacuzzi, and bedroom and bathroom fireplaces. Actually, each of the 15 rooms has a working fireplace.

For those who can't bear to leave this mountain retreat, the inn serves a prix fixe supper on Friday night and dinner on Saturday night. While relaxing in the lounge next to the breakfast room, guests can browse through the story of the inn's restoration, documented photographically by the current owners and in several magazine articles.

Front Royal

CHESTER HOUSE
Innkeepers: Phillip Inge,
  Allen Hamblin, and
  Barbara Hamblin.
800-621-0441, 540-635-3937.
www.chesterhouse.com.
mail@chesterhouse.com.
43 Chester St., Front Royal,
  VA 22630.
Take the Front Royal exit
  from I-66 and follow signs
  for downtown.
Price: Moderate to
  Expensive.
Credit Cards: AE, MC, V.
Handicap Access: Yes.
Special Features: Golf
  packages available. Two-
  night minimum required
  during certain times of
  the year. No pets, but
  innkeepers can
  recommend excellent
  kennel nearby. Children
  accepted on a case-by-
  case basis.

This incredible find, built in 1905 by Charles Samuels, an international lawyer and prominent local citizen, is just a few steps away from the Belle Boyd House, the shops, and the restaurants in the heart of town.

The inn's two acres of gardens and mountain views offer plenty of opportunity for bucolic musing. In the terraced gardens, arbors of wisteria, a fish pond, fountains, Italian garden statuary, and a half-acre of historic boxwoods combine to form a floral refuge.

The outdoor statuary and many of the inn's design elements are original to the builder. Samuels ordered the marble work and statues from the Continent, and had local craftsmen work the wood to replicate the elegance of the Italian-style manor homes he had admired while abroad.

The rooms of the main house are warm and comfortable, and each has a private bath. The sitting room is fitted out as an early 20th-century parlor and contains many books on Front Royal history and plenty of information on the interesting Mr. Samuels. The more formal living room of the home holds a baby grand piano as well as numerous antique collectibles. The poured concrete garden house, now a guest accommodation with Jacuzzi, makes this one of the area's more unique properties.

Complimentary soft drinks, beer, wine, sherry, homemade cookies, and full breakfasts complete the inn's hospitality. Specialty items such as "mile-high popovers" and cinnamon brown sugar pancakes are among the more popular breakfast offerings.

WOODWARD HOUSE ON MANOR GRADE
Innkeepers: Joan and Bob Kaye.
540-635-7010, 800-635-7011.
www.acountryhome.com.
woodhouse@rmaonline.net.
413 S. Royal Ave., Front Royal, VA 22630.
From town, head south on Main Street. A few blocks out you'll see the house perched high on a hill on your right.
Price: Moderate to Expensive; 2-night min. May, Jun., Oct.
Credit Cards: All major.
Handicap Access: No.
Special Features: Children OK; no pets.

This hilltop 1919 restoration by innkeepers Joan and Bob Kaye offers a wonderful view of the mountains and town from its brick-pillared porch.

Driving up, look for the small row of shops, including a charming antique store, that mark the way. The drive is steep, but the short climb is worth it and parking is on a level patch of ground. Your reward is a 1920 house that has been made over into a terrific little B&B.

The Kayes have filled the home with collectibles and hand-painted furniture. Especially lovely is Joan's quilt collection. Each room's bed is festooned with a different selection from her assortment, many gathered locally. She also uses the quilts to decorate in other rooms.

Each room comes with a private bath, cable TV, air conditioning, and radiator heat. All are tastefully furnished with period pieces and decorated to give a warm and welcoming look.

The Tea Pot Pub (nonsmoking) and room next door are nice places to relax. Complimentary wine, beer, and nonalcoholic beverages are available.

The inn calls its morning meal a "skip-a-lunch breakfast" and its crown jewel. Certainly the selection of fruits, cereals, eggs most anyway, omelets, French toast, waffles, pancakes, and Joan's homemade muffins give you the energy needed to take advantage of the area's activities — hiking, rafting, golf, horseback riding, biking, shopping, and sightseeing in town.

KILLAHEVLIN BED AND BREAKFAST INN
Innkeeper: Susan O'Kelly.
800-847-6132, 540-636-7335.
www.vairish.com.
kilhvln@shentel.net.
1401 N. Royal Ave., Front Royal, VA 22630.
Continue through town on North Royal Avenue.
Price: Expensive to Very Expensive.

This 1800s inn is listed on the National Register of Historic Places and the Virginia Landmarks Register. Not only is the building lovely, it is located on a former Civil War encampment site where two of Colonel John Mosby's rangers were hanged.

The original owner/builder was an Irish baron. In 1990, Susan O'Kelly discovered the property and found it the ideal place for someone of Irish descent to set up innkeeping. She calls it "Virginia's Little Bit O'Ireland."

Credit Cards: AE, CB, D, DC, MC, V.
Handicap Access: Limited.
Special Features: Inquire about children; no pets.

This historic house sits on top of a hill with a wonderful view, and its wood-paneled halls and stained glass windows reflect the skill of local craftspeople. The guest rooms have been remodeled, and there are two private cottages (totally modern) in back. The "Blue Room" faces sunset over the mountains.

O'Kelly also has created a little Irish pub in a back corner of the first floor, replete with windows that look out onto the mountain, and a TV, dartboard, and cribbage for those who like to keep their eyes on other entertainment. The bar is stocked (including Irish beer on tap!) and all drinks are free for guests.

Guests who enjoy the inn's homemade sweets can take home what O'Kelly calls a "sweet memory" (for $20) in its own collectible tin.

LACKAWANNA BED AND BREAKFAST
Innkeepers: Philip and Sandra Charles.
877-222-7495, 540-636-7945.
www.lackawannabb.com.
stay@lackawannabb.com.
236 Riverside Dr., Front Royal, VA 22630.
Call for directions. There are a number of twists and turns from various main roads.
Price: Moderate.
Credit Cards: AE, MC, V; personal checks accepted.
Handicap Access: No.
Special Features: No pets; children over 10 permitted.

If a view of the famous Shenandoah River is of prime importance, then perhaps this 19th-century Italianate home with 11-foot ceilings and a wraparound porch facing the river is the place for you. Located just outside of town, the Lackawanna Bed and Breakfast is nestled on two acres between the North and South Forks of the Shenandoah. ("Lackawanna" means "meeting of the waters" in the Delaware Indian language.)

This large Victorian home, built by Dorastus Cone, owner of the Riverton Mills, retains period appearance inside with lace curtains and period furniture. Each of its two bedrooms has a private bath. Your own canoe is welcome or you can rent nearby.

Middletown

WAYSIDE INN
540-869-1797, 877 869-1797.
www.waysideofva.com.
7783 Main St., Middletown, VA 22645.
I-81 Exit 302 to Valley Pike (Rte. 11); follow signs for Middletown.
Price: Moderate to Expensive.
Credit Cards: AE, D, DC, MC, V.

Middletown's tiny Main Street boasts antique shops, a potato chip factory, restaurant, theater, tiny store, church, and this inn, all just a few minutes away from Cedar Creek Battlefield/Belle Grove Plantation. (See Chapter Three, *Cultural Attractions*.)

This historic site has been entertaining folk since the time of George Washington. (Be sure to see the oldest part of the house, which dates back to the 1790s.) In the 1960s, a Washington, D.C., financier

Shenandoah2000

Middleton's Wayside Inn has been entertaining travelers in style since the time of George Washington. The inn often offers special packages for those who want to attend the nearby Wayside Theatre.

Handicap Access: Limited (some rooms).
Special Features: No pets; children OK (no cribs available).

and antique collector bought the building and restored and refurbished the inn. Its 24 antique-furnished rooms and suites range in style from Early American to Empire to Victorian. Décor includes canopied beds, English, French, and Oriental antiques, brocades, chintzes, silks, and other accoutrements of bygone eras.

This is also a wonderful place to make part of a package. Couple a stay with a play at the Wayside Theatre just down the street, or with a sumptuous dinner at the inn. (See listing in Chapter Six, *Restaurants, Food Purveyors, and Wine*.)

OTHER AREA INNS

Berryville has two B&Bs worth noting: Sandy Sowada's **Lost Dog** (540-955-1181; www.thelostdog.com; sandy@thelostdog.com; 211 S. Church St.), and Betsy and Ruth Pritchard's **Smithfield Farm** (540-955-4389, 877-955-4389; www.smithfieldfarm.com; info@smithfieldfarm.com; 568 Smithfield Ln.).

Another of the area's award-winning inns also houses one of the area's five-star restaurants: **L'Auberge Provencale** (800-638-1702; Rte. 2, PO Box 203, White

Post, VA 22663). Alain and Celeste Borel successfully blend the charm and delicate flavors of their homeland of Avignon, France, with the sweet hospitality and wonderful ingredients of the Shenandoah. Their fantastic food is discussed in Chapter Six, *Restaurants, Food Purveyors, and Wine*. Dinner is open to outside diners, but the sumptuous breakfast is for guests only.

SHENANDOAH COUNTY

Strasburg

The Hotel Strasburg retains much Old World charm but offers modern comforts, including many suites complete with Jacuzzi and some of the best dining in town!

Shenandoah2000

HOTEL STRASBURG
Innkeepers: Gary and Carol
  Rutherford, owners.
800-348-8327, 540-465-9191.
www.hotelstrasburg.com.
thehotel@shentel.net.
213 Holliday St., Strasburg,
  VA 22657.
Take Strasburg exit from I-
  81; follow signs for
  downtown.
Price: Moderate to
  Expensive.
Credit Cards: AE, D, DC,
  MC, V.
Handicap Access: In dining
  room only.
Special Features: Children
  OK; no pets.

This 1890s hotel just a few blocks from Main Street has been a landmark in the area for years. Not all of their rooms and suites are in the main Victorian building, however. The Rutherfords increased availability by buying up small surrounding homes and making them into suites. Each of the accommodations enjoys a private bath and several have a Jacuzzi.

The hotel is within walking distance of the Strasburg Emporium antique market, and the hotel itself is decorated with antiques from a wide range of periods. Most are for sale, making it a shop and lodging all in one. And despite its antique appearance, the hotel's conference facilities and banquet area can serve up to 80 people, making it an ideal site for a small wedding or meeting.

The three dining rooms and lounge in the main building also serve up some of the area's best food. (See listing in Chapter Six, *Restaurants and Food Purveyors*.)

Woodstock

The Seven Bends

If you climb the Woodstock Tower, you can see the seven bends of the Shenandoah River. The hike to the tower is less than one mile round-trip from downtown Woodstock. Call the Shenandoah Tourism Office, 888-367-3965, or the Lee District Office of the George Washington National Forest, 540-984-4101, for more information.

CANDELWICK INN, LCC
Innkeepers: Sharon and Dennis Pike.
540-459-8008; 703-435-9606 during the week.
www.candlewickinnllc.com.
candlewickinnllc@hotmail.com.
127 N. Church St., Woodstock, VA 22664.
Turn down any side street. Church St. runs parallel to Main.
Price: Moderate to Expensive.
Credit Cards: MC, V; personal checks accepted.
Handicap Access: Not in bathrooms, but there are two first-floor rooms.
Special Features: No children or pets.

This circa-1831 home on the National Register of Historic Places has been lovingly restored by Fairfax County schoolteacher Sharon Pike and her husband, Dennis. The décor is enhanced by their collection of antique teacups and other china, and a wonderful old player piano in the parlor. (Guests are permitted to select from their collection of piano rolls to make their own evening entertainment.) At five o'clock, the innkeepers serve lemonade on the veranda. Guests can sip while listening to church chimes or simply enjoy the porch swing as the sun sets into the mountain.

There are five guest rooms, all with private bath (including one suite with a Jacuzzi). Two of the smaller rooms — the Alpine and the Shenandoah — are located on the first floor.

Leave your car parked as you walk about the shops, pubs, and eateries of tiny Woodstock. Exploring her neighboring towns of Edinburg and Mount Jackson will require a short drive — ten minutes or so — but not much more exertion than that.

For photos of the inn, try these Web sites: www.innsite.com./inns/A005367.html or www.bbonline.com/va/candlewick.

THE RIVER'D INN
Innkeepers: Diana Lurey and Dan Fauver.
800-637-4561, 540-459-5639.
www.riveredinn.com.
innkeeper@riverdinn.com.
1972 Artz Rd., Woodstock, VA 22664.

When the Shenandoah River rises, covering the Valley's low-water bridges, the locals say you are "river'd in." Hence the name of this inn, where you can fish or simply luxuriate in a wonderful setting.

The great stone fireplace of the main room is not your only chance to warm up by wood-fired embers

Call for directions.
Price: Moderate to Very
  Expensive; some
  discounted weekend
  specials.
Credit Cards: AE, CB, D,
  DC, MC, V.
Handicap Access: Yes.
Special Features: No pets;
  children on a case-by-case
  basis.

**THE INN AT NARROW
  PASSAGE**

Innkeepers: Ellen and Ed
  Markel.
540-459-8000, 800-459-8002.
www.innatnarrowpassage
  .com.
innkeeper@innatnarrow
  passage.com.
Rte. 11 South, PO Box 608,
  Woodstock, VA 22664.
I-81 Exit 283 to Rte. 11,
  south for 2 miles. Inn is
  on left, just past Narrow
  Passage Creek. Turn left
  at sign pointing to
  Chapman Landing Rd.
Price: Moderate.
Credit Cards: D, MC, V.
Handicap Access: One
  room.
Special Features: Children
  OK; no pets.

on a chilly morning or evening. Each of the three dining rooms has a distinctive fireplace and every room comes equipped with a working fireplace as well. More than 70 works of art by travel photographer Steve Ember and others are on exhibit here.

The inn has a full bar and offers full breakfast for guests, dinner on the weekends, and lunch Thursday through Saturday. Dinner is open to the community.

This historic building has been lovingly updated so that all of the rooms are air-conditioned and most have private baths. Although the inn is just off Rte. 11, its location by the river and the enveloping trees and shrubs give it the appearance of being far out in the country.

The site of the inn is a favored river ford for early pioneers, a point of narrow (and shallow) passage. The oldest section of the inn was built around 1740 for the convenience of travelers on what was then the Great Wagon Road. Travelers threatened by Indian attackers who knew they would have to slow down to cross the river found protection behind the inn's thick walls.

During the Civil War, the inn's strategic location made it a natural to be Stonewall Jackson's headquarters during part of the Valley Campaign. Many historians claim that it was while he was staying at the inn that Jackson commanded Jedediah Hotchkiss to "Make me a map of the Valley." You can even ask to stay in the room Jackson used.

The inn is only a short drive (two miles) from Edinburg, where the famous Harry Murray's Fly Shop is located. If your pleasure is visiting battlefields, you will find yourself well located for events at Cedar Creek or New Market, and only five minutes by car from both the Shenandoah and Naked Mountain Vineyards.

The price range quoted above is for two in the room, and includes breakfast. An extra person in the room is an additional $10 per night. Some weekends a two-night stay is required.

Basye

BRYCE RESORT
540-856-2121, 800 821-1444.

This four-season resort has an 18-hole golf course designed by Ed Ault, skiing (even grass skiing

www.bryceresort.com.
bryce@bryceresort.com.
PO Box 3, Basye, VA 22810.
12 miles west of Mount
    Jackson (and I-81) via Rte.
    263.
Price: Moderate to
    Expensive.
Credit Cards: MC, V.
Handicap Access: Some
    rooms are accessible, but
    be sure to inquire in
    advance.
Special Features: Children
    OK; no pets. Two-night
    minimum on condo units.

in the summer), a 45-acre lake and horseback riding on-site.

Winter visitors are rewarded with six slopes, equally divided among various ability levels. In addition, there are two teaching/beginner areas and a special learn-to-ski program for children age 4 to 8.

During warmer weather, guests can enjoy water sports, tennis, golf (miniature and regular), and hiking trails. Great fishing, paddleboats, and canoes on Lake Laura round out the pleasures of the site.

Activities are geared to all ages, and there are many family-friendly versions of boating, trail rides, fishing, and other adventures for resort guests. The concierge desk also helps guests find local sources for their enjoyments.

The resort's restaurant offers great views and good food. Coleman's Basye Bistro and Bistro Express offer a place to order pizza, hot wings, and shrimp — major food groups for golfers and skiers.

Bryce is a prime place to stay if you want modern accommodations for the Shenandoah Valley Music Festival in Orkney Springs (see Chapter Three, *Cultural Attractions*). It also provides a great base for exploring the western part of Shenandoah County, which offers a lot of natural beauty and the joy of uncovering small-town antique stores, crafts, good food, and hospitality.

**ORKNEY SPRINGS
    HOTEL, SHRINE MONT**
540-856-2141.
shrine@shentel.net.
221 Shrine Mont Circle,
    Orkney Springs, VA
    22845.
Price: Inexpensive.
Credit Cards: None.
Handicap Access: No.
Special Features: Children
    OK; no pets.

The Shrine Mont property and hotel are owned by the Episcopal Diocese of Virginia and used as a retreat center. Each summer it becomes the home of heavenly music and the Shenandoah Valley Music Festival that has been held there every year since 1962.

This historic property has not been updated much since the diocese bought it (942 acres for $1.2 million) in 1979. The oldest section of this 19th-century structure listed on the National Register of Historic Places was built in 1853 and is called the Maryland House.

The property acreage is open for walking, hiking, bird watching, and viewing the fabled mineral springs. (Do not drink from them.) Those nearby springs have been a draw since the days when the Native Americans roamed the area.

OTHER AREA INNS

Sky Chalet in *Basye* (877-867-8439; skychalet@skychalet.com; 280 Sky Chalet

Ln.), **The Widow Kip's Country Inn** in *Mount Jackson* (800-478-8714; www .widokips.com; widokips@shentel.net; 355 Orchard Dr.), and **Cross Roads Inn Bed and Breakfast** in *New Market* (540-740-4157; www.crossroadsinnva.com; freisitz@shentel.net; 9222 John Sevier Rd.) have earned good reputations.

PAGE COUNTY

JORDAN HOLLOW FARM INN

Innkeepers: Gail Kyle and Betsy Maitland.
888-418-7000, 540-778-2285.
www.jordanhollow.com.
jhf@jordanhollow.com.
326 Hawksville Park Rd., Stanley, VA 22851.
Call for directions.
Price: Expensive to Very Expensive.
Credit Cards: AE, CB, D, DC, MC, V.
Handicap Access: One room.
Special Features: Children welcome in family rooms; no pets (except they board horses).

The inn is across from Hawksbill Park, looks up onto the mountains, and is surrounded by horses on its own 150 acres. You can even arrange to bring your own to this restored colonial farm.

Jordan Hollow has seven suites and nine rooms — all large and luxurious, each with its own special "personality." Innkeepers Gail Kyle and Betsy Maitland say that the Horse Fantasy Suite (queen bed, garden view) is a favorite of their guests. Each suite also has a two-person hydro-massage tub.

The carriage house is the check-in location and a place to congregate for a game of chess, a glass of wine, or a sample of one of the many microbrews on hand.

Rates include a full gourmet breakfast for two daily. The inn also offers activities such as wildflower walks and trail rides. These are often offered as packages with the room, priced per couple. Some packages include a meal either at The Farmhouse restaurant (on-site), or a picnic or room service catered by The Farmhouse. Food is fresh, local, and superb!

MIMSLYN INN

800-296-5105, 540-743-5105.
www.svta.org/mimslyn.
mimslyn@shentel.net.
401 W. Main St. (Rte. 211), Luray, VA 22835.
Call for directions.
Price: Moderate. (Note: Breakfast is not included except for special packages.)
Credit Cards: AE, D, MC, V.
Handicap Access: Yes.

The Mimslyn Inn looms over the road from the top of a hill, its long driveway leading to what appears to be an oversized Southern mansion. The original house on this site, known as "Aventine," was moved to Court Street. The new, oversized structure, built by the Mims family in the 1930s, was designed to be a small hotel or inn.

Almost all of the inn's interior and exterior features are Virginia-made. The bricks were fired in Glasgow, the bathroom ceramic tile was made in Roanoke, and the roof slate came from Buckingham.

Special Features: Children OK; pets accepted at an additional charge of $20 per pet.

An impressive oversized porch (complete with rocking chairs) sets the stage for an equally impressive lobby — stunningly large with polished floors. The dining room and desk are on the left and a massive fireplace is on the right. A curved wooden staircase is the centerpiece.

Mimslyn Inn's 49 rooms include three king suites, five queen suites, and six family suites. All are decorated with colonial-style furniture and are outfitted with single, double, queen-, or king-sized beds. Be sure to let them know which style you want.

The inn also boasts an old-fashioned solarium, a *de rigueur* element for luxury properties of the '30s. On the basement level is a traditional gift shop and a gallery that carries P. Buckley Moss art, including several prints that feature the inn.

You'll need your car to get back into town, but you can stroll the 14 acres of the inn itself to your heart's content, enjoying its wonderful landscaping and the local birds that inhabit it. Or you can simply sit on the porch and watch the mountains beyond Rte. 211 change color as the hours creep toward sunset.

The inn serves lunch and dinner daily and offers a fine Sunday brunch. These are open to the public and the seasonally changing menu includes local venison, chicken, and other delights prepared by the chefs. Lunch and Sunday brunch are usually buffets.

WOODRUFF INNS & RESTAURANT

Innkeepers: Lucas and Deborah Woodruff.
540-743-1494, 866-937-3466.
www.woodruffinns.com.
woodruffbnb@rica.net.
138 E. Main St., Luray, VA 22835.
Price: Moderate to Expensive; discounts for weekdays sometimes available.
Credit Cards: AE, D, MC, V; personal checks accepted.
Handicap Access: In restaurant only.
Special Features: Pets and children under 12 in riverfront properties only.

There are five properties in the Woodruff Group — the yellow Victorian Inn in the center of town is where the main dining rooms are located and where guests check in for all the properties. In this building, incredible crystal chandeliers, windows salvaged from a church, and plush red and purple can be found at every turn. Tons of pillows rest on low-slung settees, where guests can enjoy cream sherry and chocolates.

The Woodruff House, an 1882 structure, acquired a rooftop Jacuzzi in the course of its restoration. It's part of an ultraromantic fireside suite.

The rest of the properties include guest rooms decorated in French Country style in the 1890s Rose House, and suites in two riverfront homes: the Shenandoah River Cabin and the Shenandoah River Cottage. The latter offer an unfettered view of the night sky and mountains, along with a river-view hot tub to compensate for the short drive back to the main building for dinner. All rooms have their own fireplace and morning coffee service.

The inn prides itself on its afternoon tea, a delightful English tradition that has taken root in Luray in grand fashion. When savoring the delicate pastries at teatime, you'll be glad to know that the same gourmet hands will cook your morning's full breakfast.

The hands belong to owner Lucas Woodruff, who has been a chef for more than 20 years. His dinners are four- or five-course affairs that feature fresh seasonal items prepared with classic French and New American techniques. For more on Woodruff's fine dining, see Chapter Six, *Restaurants, Food Purveyors, and Wine.*

ROCKINGHAM COUNTY

JOSHUA WILTON HOUSE
Owners: Craig and Roberta
  Moore.
540-434-4464, 800-2WILTON.
www.joshuawilton.com.
info@joshuawilton.com.
412 S. Main St.,
  Harrisonburg, VA 22801.
Price: Moderate.
Credit Cards: AE, DC, MC,
  V.
Handicap Access: In
  restaurant only.
Special Features: No pets;
  no children under 8.

This wonderful old Victorian inn is just a few steps away from the Main Street entrance to James Madison University. For this reason as well as for its superb food and wonderful rooms, reservations are difficult to come by and prized when they are secured. It is one of our favorite (albeit expensive!) places to eat in "the burg," as the JMU students often call Harrisonburg. (Chapter Six, *Restaurants, Food Purveyors, and Wine.*)

There are five lovely guest rooms in the inn. All rooms have a private bath and are furnished with period antiques and local art. Room One overlooks the gardens and patio, and Room Two offers the option of a cozy fireplace. But Room Four — in the turret — is one of the most often requested rooms in the house. The spacious room holds a four-poster Victorian bed and armoire, and inside the turret itself is a sitting area.

The inn's small size means it fills very fast, especially on holiday weekends and special university weekends, as well as during leaf season and spring apple time. Rates include a sumptuous breakfast for two from one of the best kitchens in the county. Jump on the opportunity to take an American Plan or Modified American Plan with your stay, since reservations in the restaurant can be hard to come by.

**STONEWALL JACKSON
  INN BED AND
  BREAKFAST**
Innkeepers: Robin Lambert,
  Michelle Gumbs, and
  Wayne Engel.
540-433-8233, 800-445-5330.
www.stonewalljacksoninn
  .com.
info@stonewalljacksoninn
  .com.

During the 1864 march of Union troops down the Valley, most of Harrisonburg was put to the torch. In rebuilding, locals — including the builders of this structure — turned to the nearby stone quarries.

This inn, a restored 1885 blue stone mansion, is full of upscale comforts. Its owners are former James Madison University professors, so they're attuned to the needs of those who want to come and

547 E. Market St.,
  Harrisonburg, VA 22801.
Price: Moderate. Discounts
  for weekday stays.
Credit Cards: AE, D, MC, V.
Handicap Access: Limited.
Special Features: No pets;
  inquire about children.
  No two-day minimum on
  weekends.

do business with the university, as well as travelers who want to enjoy the local area's Amish crafts and wonderful scenery.

A stained glass window greets visitors by the door. The entry hall is also enlivened with watercolors, most by Rachel Goodman, a former student of the owners. Most of the original watercolors are for sale. In addition to Goodman's work, the owners display a broad collection of P. Buckley Moss prints (some for sale).

When guests arrive, tea or sherry and snacks are served in the dining area or garden. The inn is on a main road, but the garden is in the back of the property and secluded, so the effect is to distance oneself from the hubbub. Smoking is restricted to outdoor areas only.

Décor in the rooms (named for Civil War generals of both sides) is mostly Victorian period. The inn's namesake room, the most expensive one in the house, is a suite that includes a lovely window-side seating area.

Each of the 10 guest rooms is sound-insulated and climate-controlled and has a private bath, cable TV, data port hookup, and refrigerator. A daily gourmet breakfast is as likely to include ham and grits as smoked salmon with caviar. You can order ahead to have a romantic dinner for two served in the small but quite elegant dining area or in your room.

It should come as no surprise that the inn has received many awards, including "The Best B&B Near a University" and one of the "Country's Top 15 B&B/Country Inns" in Arrington's *Bed & Breakfast 2003 Book of Lists*.

CAVE HILL FARM BED AND BREAKFAST

Innkeepers: Jennifer
  Dowling, manager, and
  John L. Hopkins III,
  innkeeper.
540-289-7441, 888-798-3985.
www.cavehillfarmbandb
  .com.
info@cavehillfarmbandb
  .com.
9875 Cave Hill Rd., PO Box
  27, McGaheysville, VA
  22840.
Price: Expensive.
Credit Cards: AE, D, MC, V.
Handicap Access: No.
Special Features: Children
  OK; no pets.

Many bed and breakfasts strive to incorporate some of the feeling of staying in a "real" home with the convenience, comfort, and luxury of a boutique hotel. The Cave Hill Farm property achieves this easily because it *is* such a property.

The house and grounds have been owned by the same family for more than 200 years. A few years ago, the family decided to open this pre-Civil War mansion to the public. They contracted with an architect to provide each of the rooms with a private bath, ensured that all fixtures were updated, and then hired a professional innkeeper to assist them in the day-to-day operation of the enterprise.

No matter which room you stay in, you'll have a great view of the mountains. Many antiques in the common areas and guest rooms, all named for family members, are original to the house. Antique farm equipment is displayed in a small museum in the basement of the building.

The 400-acre farm is still a working enterprise, with dairy cows and turkeys in one section and designated walking paths for guests in others. The front area of the property and other areas close to the house exhibit the more genteel side of country living: an herb garden, a large magnolia, and a 150-year-old walnut tree. Roses, irises, and peonies are among the old flowers that offer up their fragrance as you walk up the path or relax on the front porch.

Breakfast is the only regular meal served. It includes both simple and elegant features such as homemade breads, "morning cakes," and amaretto peaches.

A small parking lot sits next to the cave in the side of the hill that gives the property its name. Over the years, the owners have found Native American and Civil War relics in the stream that flows by and into the cave. The site is just ten minutes from town and two minutes from the main road, but it seems a world away.

MASSANUTTEN RESORT
800-207-MASS,
540-289-9441.
www.massresort.com.
masresort@aol.com.
1822 Resort Dr.,
McGaheysville.
Mail: PO Box 1227,
Harrisonburg, VA 22801.
Price: Moderate to
Expensive.
Credit Cards: AE, MC, V.
Handicap Access: Yes.
Special Features: Children
OK; no pets. Many units
have full kitchens and
rent by the week.

Massanutten has a great reputation for skiing, but it is truly a four-season resort, with wonderful golf facilities (27 holes and nine more on the way), tennis, swimming, and more. The resort's staff also can arrange for other special activities, such as horseback riding, mountain biking, fishing, or tours of the area.

The resort offers eight different types of accommodations, from simple hotel rooms (140 on-site) to condo units and entire townhouses. Room rates vary by season and type. Timeshare owners at other resorts exchange into Massanutten through Resort Condominium International; they have a separate entrance to the resort and different fees.

Though Massanutten has two restaurants on-site, management often brings in another restaurant to host a special meal (such as a wine dinner) in its new recreation facility. Even the arts get a turn at Massanutten, with live theater and occasional arts and crafts events.

The wooded hills and walkways of the resort are home to a great deal of wildlife. The surroundings are lovely, but, as in any part of the Shenandoah, be sure to watch for deer while you are driving in early morning or twilight.

AUGUSTA COUNTY

Churchville

THE BUCKHORN INN
540-337-8660.
www.thebuckhorninn.com.

The Buckhorn Inn has been open for guests since 1811, when it was called the Buckhorn Tavern. In 1854, Stonewall Jackson and his wife passed the

Joan Leotta

At the Buckhorn Inn you can stay in the same room that Stonewall Jackson and his wife used.

info@thebuckhorninn.com. 2487 Hankey Mountain Way, Churchville, VA 24421.
On Rte. 250 just west of Staunton.
Price: Inexpensive.
Credit Cards: MC, V.
Handicap Access: In dining room only.
Special Features: No pets; children on case-by-case basis.

night here. You can request the same room they had.

Period antiques from Civil War times through the '20s grace the décor, and P. Buckley Moss has done a print of the place, cementing its spot in the pantheon of locally important buildings. The current innkeepers, the Daly family, consider themselves stewards of the inn rather than owners.

Each comfortably appointed room has a separate bathroom, and the two-room suite boasts a Jacuzzi. A side porch overlooks George Washington National Forest.

The grounds are somewhat limited, but that porch is a great place to sit and watch the world go by in the late evening. Churchville itself is very well located, too, especially if you're interested in Staunton and want to go from there into the mountain counties. (In the stagecoach era, the inn had a reputation for gambling and attracted high rollers traveling Route 250 on their way west to the famous spas in Hot Springs.)

The Daly family opens its wonderful restaurant on weekends for lunch and dinner for both guests and the public. (Chapter Six, *Restaurants, Food Purveyors, and Wine.*) Breakfast is only for Buckhorn guests, however, and is included.

Staunton

Courtesy of Frederick House

The Frederick House, in the heart of Staunton, welcomes visitors in its main building and offers restored rooms with great views of Staunton and the surrounding mountains.

FREDERICK HOUSE HOTEL
Innkeepers: Joe and Evy Harman.
540-885-4220, 800-334-5575.
www.frederickhouse.com.
stay@frederickhouse.com.
28 N. New St., Staunton, VA 24401.
Price: Moderate to Very Expensive. Corporate discounts offered.
Credit Cards: AE, D, DC, MC, V.
Handicap Access: No wheelchair access.
Special Features: Children OK; no pets.

This 23-room hotel, a Select Registry Inn, was formed by ingeniously combining and remodeling several buildings. Its core buildings were constructed between 1810 and 1910, and their redesign, combined with the town's hilly terrain, resulted in features such as terraced gardens and private entrances for some of the rooms.

All of the beautiful rooms have private baths and are furnished with both period pieces and modern amenities. Ten of them are suites.

The main building on New Street is the location of the breakfast room/tearoom, and is large enough to be used for small meetings. The tearoom is also a delightful place to enjoy a gourmet breakfast, which is included in the price of the room. (Teatime is not included in the room price and is open to the public, so make a reservation!)

The hotel is within walking distance of Mary Baldwin College, Blackfriars Theatre, and many wonderful restaurants in downtown Staunton. Guests should also leave time to explore Frederick House's winding hallways, which have been made into miniature art galleries.

The author seated on the steps of the Belle Grae Inn in Staunton. The food is as delicious as the setting is lovely.

Joan Leotta

BELLE GRAE INN
Innkeeper: Michael Organ.
888-541-5151, 540-886-5151.
www.bellegrae.com.
rejuvenate@bellegrae.com.
515 W. Frederick St.,
    Staunton, VA 24401.
Take Staunton exit from I-81
    or I-64 and follow the
    signs for downtown.
Price: Moderate to
    Expensive.
Credit Cards: AE, MC, V.
Handicap Access: Yes.
Special Features: No pets;
    children over 12 OK.
    Conference facilities for
    40.

This is another multiple-building inn. Restoration of the main building and several of its Victorian neighbors has resulted in 17 rooms (including suites) in this top-of-the-hill property.

Because of the varied sorts of homes that have been added to the inn, the size and shape of rooms varies. Not all rooms offer the same amenities. There are fireplaces in all and hot tubs in some. If you need a sports fix but are assigned a room without a TV, one is available in the lobby for all guests.

The first floor of the main property is home to the restaurant and breakfast room. Large picture windows afford spectacular views over the rooftops of lovely Staunton into the heart of the mountains. What's more, the buildings that comprise the inn are just a few blocks away from everything you want to do in Staunton, so you can park your car and forget about it.

During certain times of the year guests are required to stay on a Modified American Plan, which means taking dinner at the inn. Staunton has many good restaurants, so you may be tempted to groan at this requirement. Don't. The food here is wonderful. Folks flock in from all over to sample the wonderful entrees and other creations available at one of two seatings. Lamb shanks on a recent evening were braised and balanced with a succulent wine sauce.

Nice touches, such as a plate of cheese and fruit, greet guests in their rooms, and a full wine and cheese reception is held in the tearoom and garden promptly at 5pm.

SAMPSON EAGON INN

800-597-9722, 540-886-8200.
www.eagoninn.com.
eagoninn@rica.net.
238 E. Beverley St.,
Staunton, VA 24401.
Take Staunton exit from I-81
or I-64, then follow the
signs for Gypsy Hill area
of downtown.
Price: Moderate.
Credit Cards: AE, MC, V.
Handicap Access: Limited.
Special Features: No
children or pets.

This house was once the site of the workshop and living quarters of a 19th-century blacksmith and wheelwright, and the grounds of the place once took up the whole block, including land that is now Gypsy Hill Park.

Inside the 1840s mansion (the blacksmith apparently did quite well!) there are many cheerful surprises. The five guest rooms are meticulously restored and furnished to the time of the blacksmith founder, with just a few exceptions. The wainscoting was added in the early 20th century, as was the porch, but you wouldn't want to give up the porch to have 19th-century authenticity. The gardens, though much smaller now than when the house was built, are still secluded and dense enough to provide a small retreat for visitors.

Teatime and breakfast are more than a simple experience at the Sampson Eagon. The owner is a true gourmet and knowledgeable about many of the area's fine eating establishments — both in Staunton and those that are worth a drive out of town. A sample of one of the inn's more delectable offerings is on the Web in the form of a recipe for chocolate cake with Kahlua.

TWELFTH NIGHT INN

Innkeepers: Juliette and John
Swenson.
540-885-1733 for reservations;
540-885-4213 to reach a
guest.
www.12th-night-inn.com.
stay@12th-night-inn.com.
402 Beverley St., Staunton,
VA 24401.
Price: Moderate to
Expensive.
Credit Cards: AE, MC, V.
Handicap Access: No.
Special Features: Children
OK; no pets. Discounts
on Blackfriars Theatre
tickets if purchased when
booking the room.

Juliette Swenson, originally from Bath, England, and husband John, a Connecticut native, are veteran B&B owners. Taking over this three-guest-room inn is their fourth such endeavor.

The inn's décor is Shakespearean, which fits in nicely with the hosts' own English/English-American antecedents. Each room's walls are hung with original art by Juliette's family and her own works, as well as a variety of locally made or Shakespeare-inspired items.

The house itself is a 19th-century prairie-style home designed by local architect T.J. Collins in 1904. It includes a wraparound porch and wonderful landscaped garden, and is just a few steps away from the town's main shopping, eating, and theater district.

Juliette serves many of her own homemade jams at breakfast (full on week-ends, continental during the week), and offers a cookbook, *Foods for Love*, trad-ing on her own name's Shakespearean connection. Her little book is sold at the theater as well as at the inn and various other shops in town.

The "Act I" room is recommended for guests with children because it holds a double sofa bed. "Act II's" elegant nautical/Shakespearean theme, not to men-tion its cable TV, makes it a favorite of sports fans. The smaller "Olivia's Gar-den" room is also charming. It keeps its garden/Shakespeare connection with framed prints of Anne Hathaway's cottage and gardens, as well as a view of the inn's own landscaped garden and waterfall.

ROCKBRIDGE COUNTY

SUGAR TREE INN
Innkeepers: Terri & Henry
  Walters.
800-377-2197, 540-377-2197.
www.sugartreeinn.com.
innkeeper@sugartreeinn
  .com.
PO Box 10, Rte. 56, Steeles
  Tavern, VA 24476.
Call for directions from I-81
  Exit 205.
Price: Moderate to
  Expensive.
Credit Cards: AE, D, MC, V.
Handicap Access: Limited.
Special Features: Pets OK;
  ask about children.

This secluded mountain inn on 28 acres is the inn of choice for bird-watching devotees and other nature lovers. The secluded location high up in the Blue Ridge Mountains means that sightings of rarer species are frequent. Sunset views are incredible since no city lights interfere.

Owners Terri and Henry Walters have plenty of information to offer on hiking and local sights. My friends usually combine the romance of the trails, hiking, and birding with carriage rides in nearby Lexington (less than an hour away) and theater in Staunton.

There are nine rooms, two suites, and 11 private baths. You can eat at the inn or go into Lexington or tiny Vesuvius for meals. Meeting planners love the combination of isolation-without-isolation and the fact that you can book for up to about 25 people.

This inn closes for January and February. (Note: As this went to press, the Sugar Tree Inn was up for sale.)

Raphine

DAYS INN
888-254-0637, 540-377-2604.
584 Oakland Circle,
  Raphine, VA 24472.
From I-81 or I-64 south, take
  Exit 205 and turn onto
  Rte. 606. Proceed to top of
  hill.

There are 67 rooms in this little property, which sits approximately equidistant between Staunton and Lexington. Room rates vary by season, but the rates are usually lower than the local B&Bs. We stum-bled on it because everything else around was booked during a recent leaf season.

The structure is new (1999), but built with the faux colonial/Georgian style that is so popular

Price: Inexpensive to Moderate.
Credit Cards: AE, CB, D, DC, MC, V.
Handicap Access: Yes.
Special Features: Children OK, pets OK at an additional charge of $10 per pet.

among large properties in Virginia. If you're traveling during summer, the outdoor pool is an amenity you might enjoy.

Ask for a balcony room so that you can enjoy the sunset view, no matter the time of year. The incredible palate of purples and pinks and blues, even with the light buzz of traffic from below, makes this a worthwhile stop.

Raphine itself is a good location if you want to get up early and go see the Cyrus McCormick Farm, which opens at 8:30. Also nearby are Wade's Mill, Rockbridge Winery, and Buffalo Springs Herb Farm. The knowledgeable desk staff will help you map out an itinerary to nearby sights.

The restaurant in the motel is the exception to the rule of "ordinary" chain hotel restaurants. Kathy's of Raphine serves standard fare for breakfast and lunch, and then comes to wonderful life with dinner. (Chapter Six, *Restaurants, Food Purveyors, and Wine*.) The wine list is amazing and full of local specialties. The food is varied and, believe it or not, the restaurant's specialty is oysters — fresh from Virginia's coast!

Lexington

THE HAMPTON INN COL. ALTO
Hampton Inn Lexington- Historic District
540-463-2223, 800-HAMPTON.
www.hampton-inn.com/ hi/lexington-historic.
401 E. Nelson St., Lexington, VA 24450.
Take Exit 188B from I-81 and follow signs for downtown.
Price: Expensive to Very Expensive in B&B part of the property; Moderate in the regular inn.
Credit Cards: AE, CB, D, DC, MC, V.
Handicap Access: Yes.
Special Features: Children OK; no pets.

This stop is far from a standard chain hotel, yet it's not quite a traditional bed and breakfast, either. The manor house portion of the building is an almost-200-year-old home, fully restored, with ten guest rooms. The furniture consists of skillful reproductions and the bathrooms are modern, complete with robes, etc.

One of the rooms is on the first floor and is partially accessible. For others who choose to stay in one of the hotel's modern rooms because a handicap makes a B&B impractical, the manor house is open for tours — a nice option.

Breakfast is served in the rooms for the B&B folks, and there is a different breakfast room for hotel guests just behind the inn. The reception area for both the inn and the hotel is in the hallway of the manor house.

The rest of the hotel is skillfully added on behind the house — plain but nice rooms, very modern, and a conference center, all low enough so as not to besmirch the 19th-century appearance of the house when you approach. Carriage tours of the city make the hotel a regular stop.

Joan Leotta

The Maple Inn is a restaurant as well as an inn.

LEXINGTON HISTORIC INNS
Alexander-Withrow House, McCampbell Inn, Maple Hall
Owners: The Peter Meredith Family.
Host: Don Fredenburg.
877-463-2044 (for all three properties).
11 N. Main St., Lexington, VA 24450 (Alexander-Withrow House and McCampbell Inn).
3111 N. Lee Highway, Lexington, VA 24450 (Maple Inn).
Price: Moderate to Very Expensive.
Credit Cards: D, MC, V.
Handicap Access: No.
Special Features: No pets; inquire about children.

This group of properties bills itself as a specialist in weddings and other private parties. Unlike some other groupings, these three are not adjacent to one another. Guests can choose to stay either at the **Maple Hall** location six miles outside of Lexington (see second half of this entry), or at one of the two town properties, **Alexander-Withrow House** and **McCampbell Inn**. The town properties are in the center of the historic district and within walking distance of practically everything you would want to see.

THE ALEXANDER-WITHROW HOUSE AND McCAMBELL INN

The Alexander-Withrow building was one of the few town structures — maybe the only one — to survive a disastrous 1796 fire. This same inn provided accommodations for Richard Gere and Jodie Foster while portions of the movie "Sommersby" were filmed here.

Withrow is a five-suite establishment. Each suite has accoutrements such as a Jacuzzi and, of course, the convenience of stepping out into old Lexington at anytime.

Built by John McCampbell in 1809, the McCampbell Inn's center section started out as John's home and later was expanded to become the Central Hotel. The McCampbell Inn has 14 individual rooms and two suites. Each is carefully furnished and includes wet bars and all modern conveniences. The McCampbell is the location of the breakfast room for both downtown properties. Again, step out into the street and you're within walking distance of VMI, Washington and Lee University, numerous shops, and many wonderful restaurants.

MAPLE HALL

This 1850 plantation home sits on 56 rolling acres six miles north of Lexington on Route 11. Its columned veranda is a spectacular place to look out onto the mountains. The halls are paneled with a rich, dark wood, and the sitting room and dining areas are richly and comfortably furnished. Just behind the main house are two cottages with all-new suites inside.

The quiet charms of the restaurant (open to the public) make it an ideal place for a quiet, romantic evening. (See Chapter Six, *Restaurants and Food Purveyors*, for more on the menu.) Conference facilities for 40 and a swimming pool also add to the enjoyment at Maple Hall.

APPLEWOOD INN AND LLAMA TREKKING
Innkeepers: Linda and Christian Best.
540-463-1962, 800-463-1902.
www.applewoodbb.com.
inn@applewoodbb.com.
Buffalo Bend Rd., PO Box 1348, Lexington, VA 24450.
Not far from Rte. 11 exit for Lexington; call for precise directions.
Price: Moderate to Expensive.
Credit Cards: AE, MC, V.
Handicap Access: Limited; call for details.
Special Features: Pets and children OK; inquire about availability.

Tucked along a ridge between the Blue Ridge and the Short Hills of the Alleghenies, Applewood Inn adds an Andean twist to this corner of Shenandoah. Seven llamas live here, and you can see them frisking across a field from the porch and balcony that run alongside the guest rooms here, or visit them in their barn. In mild weather, you can also take them on a two-hour trek across this tucked-away property; a llama with a name like Ethan Allen or Chaos will tote your provisions.

As for the inn itself: think contemporary cedar, lined with windows and replete with passive solar energy. Appalachian-style quilts cover the beds and flowers surround the outdoor pool. Settle in on comfy gingham or plaid furniture in the common room to catch a video or read from the assortment of books shelved here, or take advantage of the 'fridge, microwave, and range top in the kitchen.

Four guest rooms range from the "European Room," with French doors leading to the deck and its private hot tub, to the cozy (but less fancy) "Autumn Room." Other rooms offer Vermont Castings stoves or whirlpool tubs. All in all, a very comfy place with a contemporary style that makes it cool, too.

Rates for a guided llama trek over parts of the 36-acre property vary by season. At the time of this writing the rate for guests was $12 for adults and $10 for children 6 to 12. Nonguests can ride but pay more. The inn will provide a picnic lunch for guests for a small fee. The inn can also arrange Lime Kiln theater tickets during their season.

Shenandoah2000

The Natural Bridge Hotel is one of the grand old auto touring hotels. The original burned and the current building was reconstructed in 1963.

NATURAL BRIDGE INN AND CONFERENCE CENTER
800-533-1410.
www.naturalbridgeva.com. /hotel.html.
info@naturalbridgeva.com.
15 Appledore Ln., PO Box 57, Natural Bridge, VA 24578.
Price: Inexpensive to Moderate.
Credit Cards: AE, D, DC, MC, V.
Handicap Access: Limited.
Special Features: Children OK; no pets.

Natural Bridge Hotel is a grand property in the style of the 1930s. The first hotel on the location was built in 1828. The current incarnation — overlooking the caves, bridge, and other nearby attractions — was rebuilt in 1963 after an earlier structure burned down. Its secluded mountain setting, though just a few minutes from I-81, is worlds away.

The marble lobby is a true bit of elegance and a wonderful way to welcome guests.

As for accommodations, rooms are small but well-appointed and many have balconies that look out onto the mountains. Rates vary by season, day of the week, room size, and view. Mountain views and balconies are a bit more but worth it. (Be sure to check the Web site for summertime specials, which offer mountain-view rooms at bargain prices on selected dates.) There are still separate cottages (open seasonally) for rent as well.

The absolute quiet that seizes this normally bustling spot late at night and when the tourists are gone in mid-afternoon leaves you alone with the mountains and the stars. Truly spectacular and a good value for the price.

OTHER LEXINGTON LODGINGS

The Lexington area is a hotbed of B&B activity. Among your choices are:

Llewellyn Lodge (800-882-1145; www.llodge.com; 603 S. Main St.); **Brierley Hill** (800-422-4925; www.brierleyhill.com; 985 Borden Rd.); **Magnolia House Inn Bed and Breakfast** (540-463-2567; www.magnoliahouseinn.com; 501 S. Main St.); and **The Stoneridge Bed & Breakfast** (800-491-2930; www.webfeatinc.com/stoneridge; Stoneridge Lane).

Just outside of Lexington, try **Cottage Farm B&B** in *Buena Vista* (800-895-7457; www.cottagefarm.com; 3147 Glasgow Highway); **Oak Spring Farm** in *Raphine* (800-841-8813; www.oakspringfarm.com; 5895 Borden Grant Trail); and **The Hummingbird Inn** in *Goshen* (800-397-3214; www.hummingbirdinn .com; 30 Wood Lane).

ROANOKE COUNTY

Roanoke

Although one of the newest cities in the Valley, Roanoke boasts one of the area's grandest historic urban properties, the Hotel Roanoke. This beautiful hotel has been restored to its former grandeur while being outfitted with all the appurtenances of modern comfort.

HOTEL ROANOKE
540-985-5900, 800-222-TREE.
www.hotelroanoke.com.
110 Shenandoah Ave.,
   Roanoke, VA 24016.
Price: Moderate to Very
   Expensive.
Credit Cards: AE, DC, MC,
   V.
Handicap Access: Yes.
Special Features: Children
   OK; no pets. Conference
   facilities and ballroom.

This historic 1890s hotel is now run by the Doubletree chain and Virginia Tech University in a partnership that provides comfort and luxury for guests and training for students in hotel management. This means you get chocolate chip cookies (a Doubletree trademark) *and* the cheerful efficiency of young adults learning the hospitality trade.

The hotel was built in 1882 during the heyday of railroad fortunes and is a vital part of Roanoke's railroad history. The imposing wooden structure has a Tudor look to the outside that make it one of the city's most recognizable landmarks. Its gardens

Courtesy Hotel Roanoke

The Hotel Roanoke was built in the late 19th century by the railroad and displays the grandeur of those days. Today the hotel is run by Virginia Tech and Doubletree.

and carefully landscaped walkways and driving areas add to the elegant appearance of the exterior.

Inside it is festooned with fabulous chandeliers and the large rooms, thick rugs, and rich art that are associated with the grand hotels of the past. All of this makes it easy to understand why the Hotel Roanoke is still considered one of the most elegant places in town to entertain. What's more, it's truly *in town* — it's a short walk from the hotel to the Center Square shops, theaters, and museums.

Presidents, millionaires, movie stars, and other luminaries have spent the night here. In the earliest days, guests came by train and were brought to the hotel by carriage. Today's guests usually drive up to check in and then park their car. A pedestrian walkway carries guests safely to and from the hotel.

Dining options within the hotel include the ultra-elegant Regency Dining Room or the lighter fare of the Pine Room Pub. The historic murals of The Palm — this is where you take breakfast or tea — provide relaxing interior views.

The addition of a conference center in recent years adds to the hustle and bustle of the place, but modern touches do not detract from its stately beauty in any way.

OTHER ROANOKE PROPERTIES

The Patrick Henry Hotel (800-303-0988, 540-345-8811; www.patrickhenry-roanoke.com; 617 S. Jefferson St.) has 117 rooms on 10 floors and is also within walking distance of downtown. Magnificent chandeliers hang from 30-foot-high ceilings in the lobby. Many rooms come with kitchenette. **Maridor Bed & Breakfast** (800-631-1857, 540-982-1940; www.bbonline.com/va/maridor; 1857 Grandin Rd.), a short drive from downtown and highly recommended, has five choices ranging from $105 to $145. Henry Foster and Jim and Sue Given are the innkeepers. **The Wyndham Roanoke Airport** (540-563-9300, 800-WYNDHAM; 2801 Hershberger Rd. NW) is used by many of the parents at Roanoke College and Hollins University. Check this Web site if all of the choices are full: www.visitorscentral.com/Roanoke.

Catawba

The **Down Home Bed and Breakfast** (540-384-6865; www.downhomebb.com; 5209 Catawba Valley) is located between Roanoke and Salem in Catawba. Its environment is distinctly rural, great for hikers and nature lovers, but it's also close enough to the city so that you can zip in for part of the day. The B&B boasts a library of hiking literature and proximity to several trails, including Dragon's Tooth and McAfee's Knob, along with its full breakfast and private-bath rooms.

Salem

Salem is often used as an overflow town for those visiting nearby Radford University and Virginia Tech, so their special-event schedules, combined with Roanoke College's, can affect room availability here. But don't worry about it — Salem, Roanoke, and Lexington are close enough to each other that any one of the three can easily be used as a base for visiting the other two.

Among the many chain hotel offerings is the **Comfort Inn** (540-387-1600, 800-228-5150; www.choicehotels.com; 151 Wildwood Rd.; I-81 Exit 137 to Rte. 540). This is a basic property with a microwave, refrigerator, and VCR in every room. You can walk to some shops.

If you want to be within walking distance of the antique shops and restaurants on Main Street in Salem, you may wish to stay at the **Inn at Burwell Place** (540-387-0250; www.burwellplace.com; burwellplace@yahoo.com; 601 Main St.). There are two suites and two rooms, all with private bath, and two of the beds are four-posters. The décor is varied in period but lovely with dark woods predominating. The inn's prices range from Moderate to Expensive.

Check **www.metrotravelguide.com** for Salem if you need other choices.

THE MOUNTAIN COUNTIES

HIGHLAND COUNTY

Monterey

CHERRY HILL BED AND BREAKFAST
Innkeepers: Rich and Linda Holman.
540-468-2020 (day), 540-468-1900 (evening).
www.cherryhillbandb.com.
secrets@ntelos.net.
Mill Alley, PO Box 530, Monterey, VA 24465.
Rates: Moderate.
Credit Cards: AE, D, MC, V.
Handicap Access: No.
Special Features: No pets; inquire about children.

The renovation of this Victorian-style house has taken it from worn to cheery. Built in 1900 by John A. Whitelaw, the home retains its wonderful porch and has a great garden with a large lilac bush on the corner to mark the coming of spring.

All three rooms have a queen-sized bed and private bath. The largest room is the "Highlander Suite," which is really two rooms joined by a bath (claw-foot tub and a shower). The sitting area offers a wet bar and small library, and a large bedroom has its own sitting area, bay window, and private entrance.

The décor of the inn reflects the Holmans' wonderful taste and love of art. From the porch, guests can relax in rocking chairs or a porch swing while enjoying a breathtaking view of the mountains. All the while they are but a few steps away from the best places in town to eat and shop.

HIGHLAND INN BED AND BREAKFAST
Proprietors: Gregg and Deborah Morse.
888-466-4682, 540-468-2143.
www.highland-inn.com.
highinn@cfw.com.
Main St., Monterey, VA 24465. Call for directions.
Price: Inexpensive to Moderate. Inquire about midweek specials.
Credit Cards: AE, D, MC, V.
Handicap Access: Limited.
Special Features: Children OK; inquire about pets.

Highland Inn was built in 1904 to lodge tourists escaping from the summer heat of nearby cities. Prominent guests in its early days included Harvey Firestone, Henry Ford, and John Philip Sousa.

The inn's architectural glories included a two-level porch, which it retains today. A 1919 fire did some damage to the original structure, which held 30 small rooms, but repairs were made and the hotel continued. Air conditioning, however, signaled the demise of this great mountain inn and many others.

The advent of air conditioning meant it was no longer necessary to escape to the mountains. Nevertheless, renovation began in 1979, and today's owners operate the inn to provide Victorian charm to those who want to escape the reach of modern life but retain modern conveniences. All 18 of the guest rooms have bath and cable, but no telephone (unless you have a cell phone with you). There is still no air conditioning, and the cool mountain breezes still ensure that it isn't needed.

Each room is furnished with antiques and all of the rooms have full shower tubs. Three also have claw-foot tubs and three rooms have been made into suites.

Breakfast and solitude are hallmarks of the inn. The Monterey dining room, open Wednesday through Saturday evenings and for Sunday brunch, features the culinary style of Executive Chef Brian Mungle. Samples from the menu include Tuscan-style pesto torte, a double-cut pork chop stuffed with ricotta and mushrooms with blackened cream sauce, grilled rainbow trout with fennel béarnaise, and caramel praline ice-cream cake. The menu varies to ensure freshness. (Chapter Six, *Restaurants, Food Purveyors, and Wine*.)

ANOTHER PLACE TO STAY

Debora Ellington (540-474-5137) has a lovely two-bedroom apartment above the **Ginseng Mountain Store** in ***Blue Grass*** for rent on a nightly, weekly or monthly basis. The unit is moderately priced and has a Jacuzzi in the bath and a complete kitchen. Nightly rentals get breakfast. (Read more about Ginseng Mountain Store in Chapter Seven, *Shopping*.)

BATH COUNTY

Warm Springs

The Inn at Gristmill Square, a popular place to stay in Warm Springs, also boasts a wonderful restaurant in the restored mill.

Joan Leotta

INN AT GRISTMILL SQUARE
Innkeepers: The McWilliams Family.

There has been a mill on this site in the heart of Warm Springs continuously since 1771. The current mill building was erected in 1900 and operated until 1971, when it became the home of the Waterwheel Restaurant. The inn was created in 1972, utiliz-

540-839-2231.
www.gristmillsquare.com.
Grist@va.tds.net.
PO Box 359, Warm Springs,
   VA 24484.
Head west from Rte. 220
   onto Rte. 619 (Court
   House Hill); proceed 500
   yards to inn on right.
Price: Moderate to
   Expensive.
Credit Cards: D, MC, V.
Handicap Access: No
   wheelchair access.
Special Features: Children
   OK; no pets. Tennis and
   outdoor pool; thermal
   pools nearby.

ing five original 19th-century buildings, and what was the old blacksmith shop now holds a country store.

The property boasts 17 unique and spacious guest rooms, each with its own bath and many with working fireplaces. Several of the rooms are really suites with two rooms and private bath. A wonderful basket of fruit and cheese welcomes each guest, and the treats continue each morning with the delivery of a complimentary continental breakfast.

Spa facilities are nearby. The Jefferson Pools are a short drive from the inn, but The Homestead resort owns them now. If you just want to take a peek you can drive down during business hours, but if you want to soak up the whole experience, make a reservation through the inn or by calling The Homestead directly (800-838-1766).

Gristmill Square guests also have an "in" for use of The Homestead's famous Cascades golf course, and the inn carries plenty of brochures on birding and other area delights. Warm Springs itself is a lovely place to spend some time. See Chapter Seven, *Shopping,* for information on the art gallery and other shops, and Chapter Three, *Cultural Attractions,* for notes on the library and courthouse.

ANDERSON COTTAGE
Innkeeper: Jeanne Bruns.
540-839-2975.
www.bbonline.com/va/
   anderson.
JeanBruns@webtv.net.
Old Germantown Road, PO
   Box 176, Warm Springs,
   VA 24484.
Price: Moderate.
Credit Cards: None;
   personal checks accepted.
Handicap Access: No.
Special Features: Inquire
   about children and pets.

This 200-year-old building has been in Jeanne Bruns' family since 1870. Prior to becoming an inn, it served as an 18th-century tavern, a girls school, a summer inn, and a farmhouse for a local family. Bruns is a great source of information about both the house and the area.

Two buildings make up the farmhouse: an older log cabin and a newer clapboard structure. The 1820 brick kitchen is now a separate guest cottage. There are five rooms for guests (four in the house and one in the cottage). The main house is deemed inappropriate for small children, but Bruns says the Kitchen Cottage is fine for families.

Only breakfast is served, but guests are allowed to use the kitchen in the main house to prepare picnics and store snacks. Cottage guests have their own full kitchen.

The main house is closed during the winter; only the Kitchen Cottage is open December through March. Maid service and breakfast supplies (not the meal itself) are provided during that time. Regular B&B operation resumes in March.

No smoking is allowed inside the historic building, which is a short walk from the Warm Springs Mineral Baths and the Garth Newel Music Center.

Hot Springs

THE HOMESTEAD
800-838-1766, 540-839-1766.
www.thehomestead.com.
Homestead.info@ourclub
.com.
Rte. 20 (Main St.), PO Box
   2000, Hot Springs, VA
   24445.
Call for directions.
Price: Expensive to Very
   Expensive.
Credit Cards: All major.
Handicap Access: Yes.
Special Features: Children
   OK; no pets. Spa, tennis,
   shuttles, movies, fitness
   center, afternoon tea, on-
   site shopping, golf,
   KidsClub.

The Homestead is not simply a place to stay. It is an *experience*.

Since its founding in 1766 by Thomas Bullett, a friend of young George Washington, The Homestead has entertained the august of every era in American history.

The Homestead was acquired by Dr. Thomas Goode in 1832 and then by J.P. Morgan, who replaced the old structures with new ones in 1892. Thomas Edison was one of the early guests in the "new" buildings. At about that same time a bathhouse was built over the famous pools used by Thomas Jefferson. (For a fee, you too can relax in their soothing warmth.)

Golf came to the property in that same turn-of-the century time with the construction of the first six holes of The Old Course. The first tee of The Old Course, which is still in use today, enjoys the historic distinction of being the oldest first tee in continuous use in America. Golf continues to be on the leading edge at The Homestead, and a draw for the greats of the game as well as anyone who has the fee and wants to try his luck. The resort's Cascades Course has hosted seven USGA golf championships, among others.

At the end of the 20th century, the Pinehurst Company began another restoration of this historic resort to ensure that future guests would enjoy the highest level of pampering that modern technology could provide. This commitment continues today.

Most stays here are on a Modified American Plan, which means that you have breakfast and dinner at the inn. This is no hardship at The Homestead unless you have an aversion to good food. Because the rates include food, they are generally quoted per person, per night, based on double occupancy, rather than per room. There can be additional charges for children, upgraded room features, and extra adults.

You can save by booking a discount package (especially in November, January, or February, except for Valentine's Day weekend) or by going during the week. The Web site, www.thehomestead.com, offers specials on a regular basis.

Even if you're paying top dollar, staying here is worth it and a way to experience the pampering that some of the wealthiest and most powerful in America have experienced.

Just off of the bustling and elegant lobby is the President's Lounge. On the walls of the lounge hang the portraits of the 15 presidents who have visited The Homestead — including George Washington, whose term predated the resort.

He likely visited the grounds on one of his trips west and, even if he didn't walk this precise tract, his friendship with the resort's founder certainly merits him a place in its history.

Off to the right of the lobby is an indoor avenue of lobby shops, a carpeted runway of delightful spots that form a gauntlet for your wallet.

The Homestead's KidsClub is second to none in the fun department. Jam-packed with innovative, exhilarating activities in a top-notch facility, it's no wonder The Homestead was ranked among the top five family resorts by *Travel and Leisure* magazine. KidsClub requires an additional fee and serves children as a sort of camp by the whole- or half-day with crafts, storytelling, and other programs.

The food is briefly discussed in Chapter Six, *Restaurants, Food Purveyors, and Wine*. Again, it would take pages and pages to do justice to the range and quality of the offerings. The best way to summarize would be to say that the food is of the elegance and variety of a landlocked cruise ship.

OTHER BATH COUNTY PROPERTIES

Millboro's **Fort Lewis Lodge** (540-925-2314; www.fortlewislodge.com) and *Warm Springs'* **Meadow Lane Lodge** (540-839-5959; www.meadowlanelodge .com) are two other recommended properties. The Fort Lewis Lodge is a very expensive, historic, rustic lodge on a 3,000-acre estate. Meadow Lane Lodge is a small, in-town B&B.

ALLEGHANY COUNTY

Covington and *Clifton Forge* are easily reached in a day-trip while staying in Highland County or Bath County, or while on the way from those two locales to Staunton or Roanoke. An overnight stay was not *de rigueur* for me, but if you wish to stay in either location, there are a number of chain accommodations and several inns available. Among them is **Milton Hall** (877-764-5866; 207 Thorny Ln., Covington), a five-room Gothic Victorian (circa 1874). **Firmstone Manor** (800-474-9882; 6209 Longdale Furnace Rd., Clifton Forge) is an inn with five rooms and one suite hosted by Charles Towle and Barbara Jarocka. Firmstone Manor is near Longwood Lake and just a short drive from the heated springs and other recreation and shopping opportunities of the area.

CHAPTER SIX

Everything from Soup to Nuts

RESTAURANTS, FOOD PURVEYORS, AND WINE

Courtesy of Willson-Walker Restaurant

Lexington's Willson-Walker House serves excellent food that blends the best of tradition, local products, and modern presentations.

Early European settlers and African slaves combined their own food preferences with what they learned from Native Americans to develop crops that would flourish and provide solid income for life in the Shenandoah Valley. Their culinary skills, hospitality, and hard work turned the area into a thriving farmland community. At the time of the Civil War, fields of wheat and many grain mills dotted the countryside, earning the Valley the nickname "Breadbasket of the Confederacy."

Today the Valley is known for fruit (primarily apples and peaches), trout, poultry, fine beef, exotic meats such as buffalo and emu, dairy products, corn, poultry, herbs, and top-notch vegetables. The bounty of the Valley is also packaged in the form of candies, jellies, and jams.

Virginia hams are cured just outside the Valley, so many purveyors carry them and they grace the table in many area restaurants. Pork in general regularly takes center stage on local menus, often in the form of barbecue.

The fine raw materials and beauty of the Valley continue to attract fine chefs to the area. Today's visitors can sample not only traditional Southern preparations of the region's bounty, but also a wide variety of ethnic preparations from Brazilian to Thai, Italian to Indian, German to Nouveau American. New places to eat and shop for food sprout up as regularly as the Valley's crops.

As for the grape, Virginia's wineries number more than 80 now — up from just a handful only 20 years ago. The farm wineries of the Shenandoah Valley and some other nearby wineries of note are listed in a section at the end of this chapter along with referrals to Web sites and phone numbers that will help you plan a Napa-style tour of Virginia's wine country. Fall is a particularly great time to visit since wineries are in full gear for harvest and are readying their best production for the annual Governor's Cup Competition.

A NOTE ON PURVEYORS

Chain grocery stores are listed only when they are one of few options. Check local phone books for Food Lion, Kroger, Giant, and Wal-Mart stores. Travelers are rarely more than 30 minutes away from a major grocery store in any part of the Valley.

Pick-your-own and other orchards listed are those on the Virginia Department of Agriculture list (800-284-9452; www.vdacs.state.va.us or www.virginia apples.org/pick-your-own). During "season" (April through October), signs for these and other farms appear, and roadside stands pop up on all of the secondary roads in the Valley.

Apples are the most common side-of-the-road crop. The most common Valley varieties are Paula Red, Ginger Gold, Gala, Red and Golden Delicious, Rome, York, Winesap, Stayman, Granny Smith, and Fuji. Commonly found varieties of peaches grown in the commonwealth include Harbelle, Red Haven, Sun High, Loring, Blake, and Biscoe. Farm markets are another good source for the Valley's fresh produce. In a few places, the signs for the stands are even visible from I-81.

Many of the orchards grow peaches, berries, pumpkins, corn, and other items as well as apples, and some even allow visitors to pick their own, in season. Call ahead to find out what is in season and whether or not you should bring your own containers. October is often a time for pumpkins and fall festivals, including hay rides, at many of the farms.

In stores, if you want something that represents Virginia, look for products marked with a red check in a blue box. That designation, "Virginia's Finest," means that the produce is recognized by the Virginia Department of Agriculture as an edible emissary for the Old Dominion. **Shop Virginia's Finest** (800-

284-9452; www.shopvafinest.com) at the Virginia Department of Agriculture & Consumer Services gives the names of these products and locations where you can purchase them.

Several take-out only or primarily take-out restaurants are listed under purveyors rather than in the dining section.

USING THIS SECTION

The team of folks sampling restaurants include trusted sources and friends familiar with the Valley, our son Joe's Virginia Tech fraternity bothers and their adviser, Don Riley, Elizabeth Lloyd, and writer friends (including Dan Casey and Allison Blake), relatives of writer friends, and our daughter, Jennie, and her friends at James Madison University.

When selecting a restaurant, be sure to note the times of services as well as days open and meals served. Some restaurants in the Valley still serve meals only during specific times. A recent trend toward eliminating lunch service has been sweeping the Valley, too, so be sure to call ahead if you are determined to try lunch at a specific spot.

Always inquire about handicap accessibility, especially where it has been designated as "limited." Many older buildings in the Valley have difficult access. In some cases the dining rooms are open to easy entry, but there are stairs leading to the rest rooms or narrow rest room doors. In other cases, limited accessibility may mean that there is a single step to negotiate going into the building. Be specific about your needs.

The establishments are listed from north to south in county groupings, first the dining establishments we were able to review, then a few others that were highly recommended but not reviewed, then the food purveyor section. Within each county segment, the first part of each food purveyor section is produce farms and farm markets, alphabetically. The second is food establishments and shops (including specialized farms such as buffalo, goat, or deer farms). They are listed by town, north to south.

The guide to cost in eating establishments is based on these parameters, which include appetizer, entrée, and dessert:

Inexpensive	Up to $15
Moderate	$16 to $30
Expensive	$31 to $40
Very Expensive	Over $40

Credit cards are abbreviated as follows

AE — American Express	DC — Diner's Club
CB — Carte Blanche	MC — MasterCard
D — Discover	V — Visa

FREDERICK, CLARKE, AND WARREN COUNTIES

Winchester

ONE BLOCK WEST
540-662-1455.
www.1blockwest.com.
25 S. Indian Alley.
Open: Tues.–Sat.
Price: Moderate for lunch,
   Expensive for dinner.
Cuisine: Modern
   International with an
   emphasis on
   Mediterranean.
Serving: L (11–2), D (5–8
   approx.).
Credit Cards: AE, DC, MC,
   V.
Handicap Access: Yes.

This restaurant's décor and stylish food preparation fit well with its art gallery neighbors. Chef Brian Pellatt crafts even ordinary items with luscious artistry and serves them in a gallery-like setting complete with white walls and polished woods.

Before opening his own restaurant, Pellatt cooked at the Jockey Club in Washington, D.C., and for the Ashby Inn in nearby Paris. Mixed grill of lamb and a napoleon of mozzarella and tomato are two of his specialties. Salmon may be served "Portuguese" style or char-grilled with artichoke barquille. Potatoes are straw-sized and wonderfully crisp. The chef's tasting menu, offered regularly, allows guests to sample a wide variety of wonderful items from this kitchen at a fixed price.

The wine list is not long, but it is a wonderful selection of French, Spanish, and California libations. In addition, the list includes many dessert wines and a large selection of ports.

Reservations are recommended for weekends, especially during the town's First Friday celebrations or Apple Festival.

On weekend evenings, diners at Winchester's Violino restaurant often enjoy a strolling violinist as well as outstanding Italian cuisine.

Courtesy Violino Restaurant

VIOLINO RISTORANTE
ITALIANO
540-667-8006.

Lunch at Violino allows sampling the exquisite Italian food in smaller portions, while dinner reservations allow diners to experience larger portions, more

www.nvim.com/violino.
181 N. Loudoun St.
Open: Daily except Sun.
Price: Moderate to
    Expensive.
Cuisine: Italian.
Serving: L, D.
Credit Cards: AE, D, DC,
    MC, V.
Handicap Access: Yes.

selections, and music. On Friday and Saturday evenings, a violinist roams among the tables.

Although chicken, fish, and vegetarian entrées are well represented in its repertoire, veal reigns supreme at this restaurant. Northern Italian émigrés Franco and Marcella Stocco transform simple veal dishes into celestial delight by using top-quality ingredients, recipes from their home provinces, and a genuine concern for what the customer will want. The result melts in your mouth.

Fish dishes are another good choice. Many of the menu's fish selections are local. The preparations are classic Italian and the entrées are light, moist, and delightful.

Appetizers are varied but the portions are large. If your appetite is only medium-sized, try a salad as a first course. They are light and much more than a few shreds of lettuce.

The hospitality shows the best of Italian and Valley tradition. Don't be surprised if a salad simply "shows up" at your place (at no additional charge) simply because the owners think your dinner would be more enjoyable with one.

The house wine list is mostly Italian, a surprise in the middle of Virginia's wine country, but not a disappointment since the choices complement the food quite well.

With all this going for it, it should come as no surprise that reservations are strongly recommended for Violino.

TUCANO
540-722-4557.
12 S. Braddock St.
Open: Mon.–Sat.
Price: Moderate to
    Expensive.
Cuisine: Brazilian.
Serving: L (Mon.–Fri.
    11:30–2), D (Mon.–Sat.
    5–10).
Credit Cards: AE, D, MC, V.
Handicap Access: Partial.

My Brazilian friends swear by Tucano — finding it worth the hour-plus drive from the D.C. suburbs for dinner. This restaurant is also open for lunch, a less-expensive way to sample its wide array of Brazilian food, including meat trays and fejoida, Brazilian black bean stew. Tucano's rendition will compare well to any other Brazilian restaurants; the spicing is just right.

Service is thoughtful and the waiters will be glad to help you order from among the many dishes. If you see a number of items that seem Iberian or Continental, even Italian, don't be surprised. Brazil is home to many immigrant groups, notably the Portuguese and, in many cities, the Italians.

The restaurant is medium-sized — about 50 tables — and fills up at lunch and dinner. It is well located for a walk around the Old Town area and is a fun place to stop.

DAILY GRIND
540-662-2115.

There are three Daily Grind locations in the Winchester area. This review applies to the Loudoun

3 S. Loudoun St.
Open: Daily.
Price: Inexpensive.
Cuisine: American.
Serving: B, L, D, light snacks.
Credit Cards: MC, V.
Handicap Access: Yes.

St. restaurant, but other locations are similar in their offerings. We found the coffee and pastry excellent, but the sandwiches only ordinary. This is a good light lunch or snack and beverage spot.

In addition to a wide variety of coffees by the drink (or to take away by the pound of bean) and a counter full of interesting candies, they offer European sodas. These are made the old-fashioned way, with syrup flavors (mostly natural) and the addition of soda water. They are a light and refreshing alternative.

Since many of the restaurants in the area observe strict serving hours — that is, they close after lunch until the dinner hour — mark this spot for those times when your stomach isn't operating on the standard of an 11–2 lunchtime.

Other locations in Winchester:

33 E. Piccadilly St.; 540-678-1600.
3035 Valley Ave., Suite 101; 540-678-9957.

CORK STREET TAVERN
540-667-3777.
8 W. Cork St.
Open: Mon.–Sat. 11am–1am, Sun. noon–10.
Price: Inexpensive to Moderate.
Cuisine: American-Southern.
Serving: L, D.
Credit Cards: AE, CB, D, MC, V.
Handicap Access: Yes.

The tavern is practically next door to the George Washington Office Museum. Although one can picture GW stopping by after a hard day at the French and Indian War, the tavern is not old enough to have hosted him.

Nevertheless, its wood-paneled interior and specialty burgers and ribs are favorites with locals and visitors alike. The old wooden bar has high stools and a TV for sports fans. Service is often slow, especially during the lunch rush, so be patient — but rest assured, it's worth the wait, especially for those ribs!

Front Royal

STADT KAFFEE
540-635-8300.
www.stadtkaffee.com.
300 E. Main St.
Open: Daily.
Price: Moderate.
Cuisine: German.
Serving: L (Sat. only), D daily.
Credit Cards: AE, CB, DC, MC, V.
Handicap Access: Yes.

This restaurant's décor makes it feel like a transplanted rural German café, harking back to the region's German settlers. The walls are dark wood, and square windows are adorned with window boxes and delicate lace curtains. Elegant woodcarvings and an occasional Black Forest-style clock confirm its German focus, as does its distinctly German menu. All of this is more than window-dressing, though; the German language papers on the counter confirm the site as a center of activity for the local German-American community.

During the day, the windows let in plenty of light, as befits a bustling community center. In the evening, with tables lit by candle, the atmosphere turns romantic. At either meal, the food takes a starring role. German may translate into hearty, but it is never plodding or heavy here.

Specials are listed on a chalkboard — take note. These generally offer good value and showcase seasonal items. For instance, luncheon spinach crêpes are an outstanding spring special — light enough to float off the plate, but in a generous serving of two. The accompanying potato salad was a vinaigrette-based delight.

Regulars seem to favor the selection of sausages and other German pork and veal specialties. The plates are full but light enough to permit indulgence in the scrumptious-looking German desserts.

Lunch is busy, but it should be no problem getting a table. Dinner is another matter — if you're going on a weekend, reserve! The service is friendly and attentive and, all appearances to the contrary, no passport is required.

The interior of the Royal Dairy Bar in Front Royal has a 1950s style with booths and a Formica soda bar. The menu is a throwback to the 1950s as well — with treats to delight modern visitors.

Joan Leotta

ROYAL DAIRY ICE CREAM BAR & RESTAURANT
540-635-5202.
241 Chester St.
Open: Daily.
Price: Inexpensive.
Cuisine: American.
Serving: B, L, D.
Credit Cards: None.
Handicap Access: Yes.

The best of the 1950s is preserved in the décor, menu, and friendly service of this spot. The restaurant's wonderful low, L-shaped counter with vinyl-covered swivel stools runs the length of a long, rectangular dining room. Booths with high, wooden-backed benches and vintage Formica tables line the window side of the building. Either seating location provides a wonderful view of the entire place thanks to the mirror-lined wall behind the counter.

This culinary time machine is great for enjoying world-class ice cream as well as fine, light salads or hearty, 1950s-style sandwiches, meat loaf, fried chicken, and other homey delights. Breakfast offerings include pancakes and a full range of egg dishes from over-easy to omelets.

The wonderful breakfasts, lunches, or home-style dinners smell and look great, but there are many who save all their calories for Royal's fantastic ice-cream creations — gooey sundaes, gut-busting banana splits, root beer floats. When faced with that cornucopia of dairy riches, however, don't forget the pure delight of a scoop of plain ice cream in a bowl.

JALISCO MEXICAN RESTAURANT
540-635-7348.
510 S. Royal Ave.
Open: Daily.
Price: Inexpensive.
Cuisine: Mexican.
Serving: L, D.
Credit Cards: AE, MC, V.
Handicap Access: Yes.

The stucco walls, décor, and south-of-the-border music at Jalisco create a picture-perfect postcard version of a Mexican hacienda and make this a fun spot to visit for lunch or anytime, especially with a large group.

But no matter what your taste in décor or music, go for the excellent food. It's not that you'll find dishes you haven't heard of before. The special charm of Jalisco is that it offers things you *think* you know, cooked with layers of flavor you didn't know were possible in such simple fare. Items ordered elsewhere in Tex-Mex stand-alone and chain establishments are way better here. A luncheon order of chile rellenos tasted as if someone's mother had been waiting in the back to prepare them. No grease, lots of taste. Even the salsa was wonderful — a deep chipotle-style creation with a smoky, dusky flavor that was sweet, sharp, and mellow all at once!

If you want to try this restaurant you'd be wise to go with a crowd so you can share and sample many different menu items. The service is attentive, just the right speed, and steeped in true hospitality. The commitment to guests even extends to take-out. Those ordering items to go will find that the chips and salsa served at the table before dinner show up in the carry-out bag as well.

There are other Jalisco restaurants in Virginia, each individual in its approach. This one is a truly yummy spot.

THE APPLE HOUSE
540-635-2118, 800-462-1867.
www.applehouseva.com.
4675 John Marshall Hwy.,
  Linden.
Open: Mon. 8–5, Tues.–Sun.
  8–7.
Price: Inexpensive.
Cuisine: American
  barbecue.
Serving: B, L, D.
Credit Cards: MC, V.
Handicap Access: Yes.

Here, at I-66 Exit 13, hard and nonalcoholic Alpenglow cider came into the world. These days, bottled ciders in a variety of flavors and apple-themed gift items (see Chapter Seven, *Shopping*) take up the right side of the tiny building wedged behind a gas station.

Inside on the left are ten or so tables with oilcloth table coverings and plain, vinyl-cushioned chairs. Service is at the counter whether you're eating in or taking out. But don't be fooled by plain appearances. Some of the best barbecue in the state passes over that counter.

Those who want to try one of their apple doughnuts should be sure to make this an early morning breakfast stop. Hot from the fryer, the doughnuts are light, nongreasy, and lightly flavored with apple and cinnamon. These cakes sell out regularly — and early in the day!

The barbecue (pork or beef) tastes as though it has a hint of molasses in it (but the recipe is a secret), making it different from what is served in most of the surrounding area. For a barbecue lunch it can't be beat. They sell it by the plate (sandwich alone or a platter with coleslaw) or by the pound.

Middletown

WAYSIDE INN
540-869-1797.
www.alongthewayside.com
/dining.asp.
7783 Main St.
Open: Daily.
Price: Moderate.
Cuisine: American,
   Continental.
Serving: L, D.
Credit Cards: AE, D, DC,
   MC, V.
Handicap Access: Limited.

Since the late 18th century, this inn has been serving hungry travelers with good cheer, good food, and those little extra touches that make you know you've stumbled upon a culinary jewel.

The menu tends to simple dishes well, even elegantly, prepared — chicken, roasted and grilled meats, pan-seared fish. Even a basic Cobb salad is served with élan. Each fresh and tasty element of the salad — ham, egg, cheese — is carefully cut into bite-sized pieces and arranged in a fan about the cut lettuce in the center.

The wine list offers a nice selection, including many local wines by the glass or the bottle.

The wood-paneled rooms with fireplaces, antique furniture, and paintings revive the colonial-era atmosphere, and the inn still hosts overnight guests. (See Chapter Five, *Lodging*.) Be sure to ask to explore the small room in the back that was part of the original inn when George Washington stopped by. If you're planning an outing to the Wayside Theatre, call the inn to arrange a pre- or post-theater dinnertime.

Berryville

BATTLETOWN INN
540-955-4100, 800-282-4106.
www.battletown.com.
102 W. Main St.
Open: Tues.–Sun.
Price: Moderate.
Cuisine: American, Southern.
Serving: L (Wed.–Sat.), D
   (Tues.–Sat.), SB.
Credit Cards: AE, D, MC, V.
Handicap Access: Yes for the
   restaurant, no for the
   rooms at the inn.

The bar in the center of the inn has been serving brews and food since 1809, making this one of the most historic stops among the various Valley eateries. The inn enjoys a good reputation for adding a soupçon of the unexpected to classic Southern fare. For example, Virginia ham might be paired with a honey-mustard bourbon; apple-wood smoking enhances pork loin; and crab cakes are fully crab and fully flavorful with a tomato tarragon hollandaise sauce. Lunch sandwiches continue the same flair. Chicken club, for example, comes with Brie.

Sunday brunch choices include prime rib with eggs, an eggs Benedict that comes with a crab cake, and pecan French toast — mmmmm. Peanut soup, a Virginia standard, can be gritty, but here the rendition is light and smooth — tasting of peanut, but not reeking of it.

The wine list does homage to the wares of local vineyards and the waiters are knowledgeable. All of this and rum buns to die for! While waiting for brunch, the waiter will likely set one on your plate. Such hospitality is common to the inn that is operated under the auspices of the Wayside Foundation of American History and Arts, and is a popular gathering place for local folks.

The original building (now part of the tavern) was put up in 1809 by Sara Stribling, the daughter of Benjamin Berry, for whom the town was later named. When the building became an inn it was called Battletown Inn for the original name of the village, a roadside stop where tavern brawls and fights were common. Garden club parties are far more likely guests today.

OTHER AREA RESTAURANTS

One of the area's five-star restaurants is a French inn, **L'Auberge Provencale** (800-638-1702; www.laubergeprovencale.com; Rte. 2, White Post). The food here is a trip to France and the reading of the list of awards in the hallway builds up a sense of anticipation for a meal that is, by all accounts, met and often surpassed. Dinners are prix fixe and are served from 6–10:30 Wed.–Sun. A recent menu included a napoleon of roasted tomatoes, peppers, zucchini, tomatoes, and fresh herbs (from their own herb garden) as a side or appetizer course, and a lobster-crab cake entrée with ginger lemon aioli.

Winchester's **Café Sofia** (540-667-2950; Rte. 11 just south of Winchester), a favorite of TV weather forecaster Willard Scott, is an expensive eastern European restaurant known for its goulash and delicate dessert palichintas (light crepes with a variety of fillings).

FREDERICK, CLARKE, AND WARREN COUNTY FOOD PURVEYORS

Farms and Farm Markets

High Hill Farms (540-667-7377; hillhigh@shentel.net; 933 Barley Ln., Winchester) Owner Wendy Wright's farm can be reached from I-81 Exit 310 (call for details). Open 10–5 on weekends with group tours during the week. Apples from September through October. Halloween brings haunted hay rides and a pumpkin patch. This farm also sells mums, straw bales, cider, homemade pies, bread, and its famous pumpkin fudge pie.

Marker-Miller Orchards (540-662-1391; www.markermillerorchards.com; jm farmer@shentel.net; 3035 Cedar Creek Grade, Winchester) John and Carolyn Marker's farm is also at Exit 310 off I-81 (call for details). Farm open Jul.–Nov., Mon.–Fri. 9–6, Sat. 9–4. On the second weekend of October there is a festival

Apples are a staple fruit crop of main delight in this part of Virginia. The Winchester Apple Festival (first weekend in May) is *the* place to try apple pie, apple this, and apple that. The Web site www.virginiaapples.org offers this recipe alternative to the usual apple pie or cake. It originated with the Williams family and is reprinted with permission of virginiaapples.org

Apple Squares
By Mary Williams and Helen Williams Smith

1 large egg	½ cup margarine	1 tsp. vanilla
1 cup flour	½ cup brown sugar	1 cup apples, diced
1 tsp. baking powder	(less 1 tablespoon)	½ cup chopped pecans
¼ tsp. salt	½ cup sugar (less 1	
1 tsp. cinnamon	tablespoon)	

Melt butter and mix with both sugars and the egg.
Mix the dry ingredients, flour, baking powder, salt, and cinnamon, then add to the liquid and beat until smooth.
Stir in nuts and apples and mix well.
Pour into an 8" square glass pan and bake for 35 to 40 minutes.

The original Williams Orchard Apple Squares recipe came from Helen Williams Smith, an extension agent for Rappahannock County. She gave the recipe to Mary Williams, owner of the Williams Orchard. This dessert is so popular Mary gave some thought to selling the apple squares, but the family always ate them before they could get to market! Mary recommends using the Virginia York apple for the recipe, but you can also use either a Winesap or a Golden Delicious apple.

with crafts, apple-butter making and bluegrass music. A wide variety of fruits and vegetables are grown here: apricots, apples, plums, green beans, pears, pumpkins, and ornamental corn.

Nichols Farm (540-869-1258; 1832 Chapel Rd., Middletown) Take Exit 302 from I-81 and follow signs from Middletown. The Nichols family opens the farm from mid-Sept.–Oct., Mon.–Sat. 9:30–5. Primarily apples and pumpkins.

Richard's Fruit Market (540-869-1455; 6410 Middle Rd., Middletown) Take Exit 307 from I-81. Open Aug.–Nov., Sat. 8:30–6, Sun. 10–6. A peach festival on the third Sunday in August and an apple harvest festival on the fourth Saturday in September, both with bluegrass music, food (home-cooked dinners!), and family fun. Some hard-to-find varieties of apples — Idared, Grimes Golden, and others. Peach varieties include Harbelle, Red Haven, Sun High, Loring, Blake, and Biscoe. Pumpkins in season along with sweet cider, country hams, jelly, local honey, and fall mums.

Rinker Orchards (540-869-1499; 1156 Marlboro Rd., Stephens City) Exit 307 off I-81 (call for details). This orchard is open Apr.–Oct., daily 10–6. Farm furnishes containers and welcomes children. First crop of year is asparagus. Raspberries ripen from mid-April through June and apples begin in August. Pumpkins and cider fill out the bins in fall.

Shawnee Springs Market (540-888-4164; lisa@shawneesprings.com; 6656 N. Frederick Pike, Cross Junction) At I-81 Exit 317 (call for details). Open year-round for individual visits and tours, 6am–9pm daily except Christmas Day. Their own brand of preserves, "Shawnee Springs," is available in apple, peach, pumpkin, pear, apricot, peach-raspberry, strawberry-peach, cherry, and unsweetened apple butters. They sell Virginia hams and an array of gift products and gift items, including stationery and fireworks. Fresh items from Silver Queen corn in July to peaches in August to apples in mid-September. Early spring bedding plants, too.

Virginia Farm Market (540-665-8000; 1881 N. Frederick Pike, Winchester) One mile north of Winchester on Rte. 522. The big red barn is open daily Apr.–Dec.; hours vary by season, so call in advance. Lizer's Farm Market, on-site, features homemade pies, preserves, and jelly (with and without sugar). Virginia sugar-cured country hams and jug-your-own fresh-squeezed cider are offered Sept. 15–Oct. 31, as is Pumpkin Land. Farm is also open for tours. Peaches (Red Haven, Topaz, Early Glow, Harbrite, Sun High, Loring, Blake, Biscoe, Crest Haven, Jefferson, Redskin, and Elberta); apples (Rambo, Cortland, Greening, Lodi, and others); pumpkins, corn stalks, gourds, painted pumpkins, and Indian corn are also available.

SHOPS AND OTHER FOOD ESTABLISHMENTS

Winchester

Brown Bag Sandwich Shop (540-667-3473; flashpage.tripod.com/brown_bag_sandwich_shop.htm; 13 W. Boscawen St.) All carry-out or delivery, but if sandwich lunches are your favorite, join the long line, call in your order, or send it via the Internet. Owner Linda Dehaven is a master of sandwich art. You can try peanut butter and jelly for $1.35, a perfectly yummy cheese melt with fresh tomato for not much more, or the Dagwood Club stuffed with chicken salad, lettuce, tomato, bacon, and yummy melted cheese (one of the priciest at $3.50). *Southern Living* magazine has written up this tiny spot.

Murphy's Beverage (540-723-9719; 167 N. Loudoun St.) The Friday-night wine tastings are a good introduction to the shop and to a spectrum of Virginia selections. The shop will make up baskets of Virginia-made goods and goodies — prices vary widely, but you can start at around $20 (plus shipping).

Old Town Sweet Shop & Candy Bouquets (540-662-5002; 156 N. Loudoun St.) Homemade chocolate and fudge are the highlights here, but candy, candy, candy, and ice cream of all kinds are also available. Cones and fudge available at the counter.

Linden

The Apple House (540-635-2118, 800-462-1867; 4675 John Marshall Hwy., Linden) Located at Exit 13 off I-66. Open daily Mon. 8–5, Tues.–Sun. 8–7. Hot barbecue, doughnuts, and a variety of ciders. See listing under "Restaurants."

Front Royal

Gourmet Delights (540-635-8610; 204 E. Main St.) Gift baskets and Virginia-made products. Lots of interesting candy items.

J's Gourmet (540-636-9293, 800-742-6421; 206 S. Royal Ave.) Great selection of wines and gourmet food items and the baskets that can make them into wonderful gifts. Locally made products as well as international taste delights.

Berryville

Smithfield Farm (877-955-4389; www.smithfresh.com; 568 Smithfield Ln.) This is a place to stop if you're carrying a cooler! Free-range eggs, pork, veal, and beef raised organically. Internet and phone orders accepted.

Clarke County Farmer's Market (540-955-4463; town parking lot on S. Church St.) May–Oct., Sat. 9–12. Local farm produce.

Middletown

Route 11 Potato Chip Factory (800-294-SPUD; www.rt11.com; Rte. 11) This small wooden building is one of the world's great snack food factories. The fantastic vegetable chips produced here range from fiery hot to Chesapeake crab, from standard salt and vinegar to barbecue and special vegetable chips. Both the factory and the store are open to the public Fri. and Sat. Many Valley stores sell the chips, and you can also purchase them by mail.

SHENANDOAH COUNTY

Strasburg

HOTEL STRASBURG
540-465-9191, 800-348-8327.
213 S. Holliday St.
Open: Daily.
Price: Moderate to
  Expensive.
Cuisine: American with
  Continental touches.
Serving: B (Sat.–Sun. only;
  hotel guests get
  continental breakfast
  Mon.–Fri.), L, D.
Credit Cards: AE, CB, D,
  DC, MC, V.

A wonderful menu of local, seasonal fare, traditional Virginia specialties, and Continental favorites awaits. The ambience and food of the Strasburg combine to make it a place equally delightful for a business lunch or a romantic dinner.

The antiques in the dining room, lace table coverings, and lovely china give the feel of having stepped into another era. Portions display Virginia hospitality and even the simplest chicken or fish dish sings due to the freshness of the ingredients.

Try to save room for dessert. The pies are

Handicap Access: Yes for dining, no for accommodations.

homemade and sport delicate crusts and fantastic fresh fruit fillings. Peach pie calls for a celebration!

Woodstock

SPRING HOUSE TAVERN
540-459-4755.
www.jesara.com.
325 S. Main St.
Open: Daily.
Price: Inexpensive to Moderate.
Cuisine: American Southern.
Serving: L, D.
Credit Cards: AE, D, DC, MC, V.
Handicap Access: Yes.

The front of Spring House Tavern has just a few tables and a carry-out counter, but the back of the restaurant is a warren of cozy little booths and tables just right for crowds of two, four, or six to converse and enjoy good, hearty food.

A fan club could be formed from those who order the clam chowder, any one of the standout overstuffed sandwiches, or the ribs that appear on both the lunch and dinner menus. This eatery also has a nice wine and beer selection.

Spring House serves up local conviviality as well as good food. Service was friendly and attentive. Dinner specialties often include local fish. It is open late, which also makes it a gathering place for those who want to linger over a casual dinner.

Edinburg

SAL'S ITALIAN BISTRO
540-984-9300.
125 S. Main St.
Open: Daily.
Price: Inexpensive for lunch, Moderate for dinner.
Cuisine: Southern Italian.
Serving: L, D.
Credit Cards: MC, V.
Handicap Access: Yes.

Sal's gets really crowded at lunch. The menu is ambitious and innovative with a definite southern Italian accent. Sandwich standouts include succulent subs and wraps — particularly tempting choices include the meatball sub or a flavorful chicken wrap full of white meat.

Italian specialties such as calzone and stromboli are made in Sal's own kitchen and add delectable variety to what would otherwise be a standard pizza list. All of the seafood is served over linguini and comes with soup and salad.

Veal and chicken dishes are available in many of the same preparations. This means that those who fear veal Marsala's cholesterol can select chicken Marsala and enjoy the same depth of rich, sweet Marsala contrasting with lightly breaded meat and a hint of pepper — with less cholesterol.

New Market

SOUTHERN KITCHEN
540-740-3514.
9576 S. Congress St.
Open: Daily.

When you're through hunting for bargains or out-of-print gems at Paper Treasures Bookstore across the street, Southern Kitchen is where to find out-of-this-world fried chicken.

Shenandoah2000

Looking for a place right out of the '50s with great fried chicken? Try the Southern Kitchen in New Market.

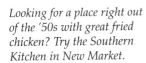

Price: Inexpensive.
Cuisine: American-
    Southern.
Serving: B, L, D.
Credit Cards: D, MC, V.
Handicap Access: Partial.

Counters and Formica tables holding paper placemats with facts about "The Old Dominion" complete the '50s atmosphere. It's definitely old-fashioned, but that's a high compliment in reference to this eatery. It means an emphasis on quality ingredients and simple preparation. Fried items are never greasy.

Sausage biscuits and gravy take a starring role on the breakfast menu. The lunch and dinner menus are practically the same and, although patrons say everything is good, it's the fried chicken that stands out. The restaurant serves some of the best fried chicken I have *ever* tasted. How do they fry it so that it is moist and delicious on the inside, crisp on the outside — and seemingly greaseless? That is a mystery for the ages.

Tableside jukeboxes are reasonably priced for each song, although a bit heavy on the country, but who cares when you're savoring the fantastic fried chicken?

Meringue pies are homemade here, but the berry ones are not. Go for the lemon meringue if it's available. Fluffy light meringue tops dense, tart filling on a flaky crust. Oh, and did I mention the fried chicken?

OTHER EATERIES

Shenandoah County has several other restaurants recommended by locals, including Strasburg's historic **Old Mill** (540-465-5590; on Rte. 11 just outside Strasburg), which offers dinner Thursday through Saturday and a Sunday afternoon buffet. **Cristina's Mexican** (540-465-5300; 348 E. King St., Strasburg) serves lunch and dinner daily. **Lucio's Ristorante** (540-856-8082; 1894 Fairway Dr., Basye) is an informal alternative for those staying in the far western part of the county, as is the **Restaurant at Bryce Resort** next door (540-856-2121, 800-821-1444; 1982 Fairway Dr., Basye).

SHENANDOAH COUNTY FOOD PURVEYORS

If you stop for some homemade goat cheese at Green Haven Farm in Woodstock, you may also get to meet the goats!

Joan Leotta

FARMS

Blue Ridge Dairy Farm (540-436-9194; 480 Harrisville Rd., Toms Brook) Exit I-81 at Toms Brook. Call for exact directions and hours. It's pick-your-own for blueberries, apricots, raspberries, and cherries in season, which runs June through September.

Swover Creek Farms (540-984-8973; swover@shentel.net; 4176 Swover Creek Rd., Edinburg) Take the I-81 Woodstock exit, but call first to get additional directions. Lynn St. Clair sells homemade jams and breads and offers pick-your-own strawberries in their short season, and blackberries, raspberries, and various vegetables as they ripen from June through the end of the season.

SHOPS AND OTHER FOOD ESTABLISHMENTS (INCLUDING ANIMAL FARMS)

Strasburg

The Daily Grind (540-465-3406; 160 N. Massanutten St.) Serves up great coffee, pastries, and related food items. Mostly carry-out.

Virginia Memories (540-465-8755; www.virginiamemories.com; vagifts@shentel .net; 160 N. Massanutten St.) If it's a food product made in Virginia, you can put it into a gift basket here. Order online after your trip to the Valley if you decide you can no longer live without Alpenglow.

Woodstock

Woodstock Farmer's Market (540-477-9470; Main and Mill Sts., Woodstock) A source for farm-raised produce and occasionally venison and fresh eggs from the county's fallow deer farm. May–Oct., Sat. 8–12.

Green Haven Farm (540-459-3783; Woodstock) Call for precise directions from I-81's Woodstock exit. This is a great place to stop for homemade cheese — you need to call ahead if you want to sample some fresh-made goat's ched- dar. It tastes like a fine Italian pecorino, which is made from sheep's milk. The goats are raised as a part-time venture, so the family may not be home or have cheese ready unless you call. Don't worry about needing to coincide with their schedule. They will leave the cheese in a cooler on the porch and you can leave a check in their box. If they're home you may even get to meet the goats!

Jerome

Bowers Buffalo Farm (btowers@shentel.net; Alum Springs Rd. in Jerome, near Edinburg) For more information on the farm and/or buffalo, contact them by e-mail. Buffalo has been called the "original health food" (higher in protein, yet lower in fat, cholesterol, and calories than most other meats, including poultry and some kinds of fish). It tastes good, too — like tender beef, no gamy taste.

Basye

Deauville Fallow Deer Farm (540-856-2130; deer1@shentel.net; 7648 Crooked Run Rd.) Owned by Alex and Gail Rose. Open Fri.–Mon. 10–4. This is the Roses' home. Call or write ahead for a visit at any time other than the posted hours, and if you're visiting any time other than Jun.–Sept., call to confirm even those hours. It lies a couple of turns and about five miles past the Bryce Resort entrance, so ask for directions, too. Deauville Fallow Deer Farm spe- cializes in a type of deer has been used for food since ancient times. You can order this lean and mild venison in many cuts, but it's more than a butcher shop. The deer live in a lovely setting, and children are encouraged to visit and pet them. Another great attraction on the farm is the many types of hens and their colorful eggs.

Lacey Spring

Shenandoah Fisheries, Inc. (540-433-2395; PO Box 276, Lacey Spring) If you want to catch rainbow trout with surety or just purchase some for your freezer, this is a place to stop. Check with them by phone before going if you're planning to fish.

PAGE COUNTY

Luray

THE VICTORIAN INN RESTAURANT
Part of the Woodruff Inn Collection
540-743-1494,
866-WDRFINN.
www.woodruffinns.com.
woodruffbnb@rica.net.
138 E. Main St.
Open: Daily.
Price: Moderate to Expensive.
Cuisine: International Fusion.
Serving: B (guests only), L (selected weekdays), D (Wed.–Sun.); afternoon tea 3–4.
Credit Cards: AE, D, MC, V.
Handicap Access: Yes.

The décor is a heady mix of Victorian-era dark woods and rich violet and pink damask curtains and cushions. Two stained glass windows (from churches that had been torn down) grace the ends of the dining rooms on each side of the formal entry hall.

Once settled into a table and accustomed to the romantic opulence, it's time to take a look at the menu. Chef Lucas Woodruff creates wonderful specials to showcase seasonal vegetables and superb-quality meats and fish. Woodruff's adroit use of spices and blending of flavors makes his fusion cuisine a delightful and memorable dining experience. Choice of a four-course prix fixe and à la carte menu offers appetizers such as Brie with berry sauce and crab cakes, and main courses such as Dijon rack of lamb (with Cabernet sauce) and a spicy jambalaya served with smoked ham.

The wine list includes specialty bottles from Virginia's Barboursville Winery under the inn's own label. California and French wines round out the selections. There are some especially interesting offerings of Barboursville dessert wines.

Long one of the most elegant places in Luray to plan a dinner, the inn began a lunch service in the fall of 2002.

All guests at the inn receive a complimentary tea, and the public is welcome to join them — for a fee, of course. There are two levels of tea available to the public: regular afternoon tea, which includes a panoply of luscious baked goods, and the full English tea with sandwiches, pastries, and other little delicacies. Reservations required.

MIMSLYN INN
800-296-5105, 540-743-5105.
www.mimslyninn.com.
mimslyn@shentel.net.
401 W. Main St.
Open: Daily.

The dinner menu at Mimslyn includes Southern specialties and dishes with a continental flair. Goat cheese crostini and fried oysters with apple ginger chile sauce are among some of the more interesting appetizers. The main courses are local fare and Southern mainstays with flair that often include items

Price: Moderate.
Cuisine: American Southern.
Serving: B, L, D, SB.
Credit Cards: AE, D, MC, V.
Handicap Access: Yes.

like appetizer rainbow trout with an oyster cornbread stuffing, sautéed breasts of chicken with brandy applesauce, and ham steak with red-eye gravy.

Sunday brunch is an extravagant buffet of luncheon and breakfast foods, including waffles, omelets, roast beef and pork, fruits, and seasonal dishes.

The dining room itself is large and windowed. The high ceilings and dark wood furniture recall the more prim and proper dining customs of the '30s and '40s, when women wore white gloves and hats to all such places and men never forgot to pull out the ladies' chairs.

A MOMENT TO REMEMBER
540-743-1121.
www.luray.net.amomentto remember.
55 E. Main St.
Open: Daily.
Price: Inexpensive.
Cuisine: American.
Serving: B, L, D.
Credit Cards: MC, V.
Handicap Access: Yes.

Conveniently located right across from the Luray-Page County Chamber of Commerce, this is a great place to plan out your attack on Luray's sights. While there, sample the fine sandwiches, fabulous pastry (the bran muffins are sinfully delectable), and great coffee. Breakfast and lunch items are served all day.

Hot sandwich choices include veggie options, and the mesquite-grilled chicken salad is quite good. Desserts are mostly espresso creations named for exploring caves. They sound and look yummy and are large enough to share.

Imported beer and wine accompany the live music on most Friday and Saturday evenings, along with an occasional dinner special in addition to the usual light fare of salads, sandwiches, and soups. An open mic on the first and third Friday of each month awaits those who are brave enough to try. Call ahead to find out about the music if you're planning to go in the evening.

This is a good place to sip a cappuccino, a chai tea, or even a basic American cup of coffee while you sort your purchases from Luray's downtown shops. Bonus! If you're in need of a book, there are several shelves of used books for sale (courtesy of Bank Street Books).

Stanley

THE FARMHOUSE RESTAURANT
At Jordan Hollow Farm Inn
540-778-2285, 888-418-7000.
www.jordanhollow.com.
jhf@jordanhollow.com.
326 Hawksville Park Rd.
Open: Daily.
Price: Expensive.
Cuisine: American Modern/ Southern.

In the Valley of the Stars the food and ambience here rates a Milky Way's worth of stars!

The restored over-100-year-old farmhouse restaurant showcases all-American, fresh food served up in unique and tantalizing creations. Despite the long drive, they took the governor here for a reception when he gave the graduation speech at James Madison University in Harrisonburg.

The farm's own herb garden is the source for many

Serving: D (B for guests only), SB.
Credit Cards: AE, CB, D, DC, MC, V.
Handicap Access: Yes.

of the seasonings. Local trout often graces the menu and should not be missed. Local goat's cheese often appears in side dishes and carefully crafted appetizers whose beauty is bested only by their taste. The main courses are equally intriguing.

The only caveat about the menu is that the wine and microbrew lists are so long and tempting that you might want to book a room rather than attempt the winding roads after a large meal. If you're not staying and want to drive to and fro in daylight, think about their Sunday brunch as a way to sample their taste delights. Be sure to reserve in advance.

OTHER EATERIES

Luray's two ice cream parlors are well worth trying, but are open only during the summer: **Tastee Freeze** (540-743-6916; 402 W. Main) and **Dippin' Dots** (540-743-4777; Hwy. 211 W.). In addition, these Luray restaurants were recommended by several locals: **Dan's Steak House** (540-743-6285; www.restaurant .com/danssteakhouse; 8512 Hwy. 211 W.) and **Brookside Restaurant** (800-299-2655, 540-743-5698; 2978 Hwy. 211 E.).

FOOD PURVEYORS

Luray

Farmer's Market (540-743-5511) At least one vegetable stand sets up daily in summer and fall under the town mural near the Luray-Page County Chamber of Commerce on Main St. Some vegetables are local and some are brought in from Pennsylvania Dutch country.
Dodie's Donuts (540-843-0674; 1428 Hwy. 211 W.) An old-fashioned doughnut shop. Don't count the calories, just enjoy.
La Dama Maya Herb and Flower Farm (540-743-4665; 1755 Hwy. 340) Maureen Messick is the owner of this wonderful spot to purchase herbs and visit. Herb and flower plants, dried flowers, herb shop, gardens, festivals, and classes. Open Apr.–Dec., Wed.–Sun. 10–4.

ROCKINGHAM COUNTY

Harrisonburg/Dayton/Bridgewater/McGaheysville

JOSHUA WILTON HOUSE AND RESTAURANT
540-434-4464, 888-2WILTON.

This restaurant's popularity is based on the excellence of the food and its proximity to campus.

Shenandoah2000

Harrisonburg's Joshua Wilton House is one of the area's culinary delights.

www.joshuawilton.com.
info@joshuawilton.com.
412 S. Main St.,
   Harrisonburg.
Open: Tues.–Sat. 5–9.
Price: Expensive.
Cuisine: Continental.
Serving: D, SB (B for those
   staying at the inn only).
Credit Cards: AE, DC, MC,
   V.
Handicap Access: Yes for
   restaurant, no for inn
   rooms.

(Be sure to make reservations if you want to eat here, especially on special university weekends; check the JMU and EMU calendars.) Dining on the patio is generally easier to obtain, but the air does get chilly out there. The rooms of the first floor are intricately set up so that tables, while close together, still retain a feeling of privacy. The watercolors on the wall (for sale) are by local artists.

The daily menu creations of Chef Mark Newsome include unique and tasty renditions of local trout, lamb, exquisite beef, and a wonderful array of side vegetables. Appetizer choices may include chorizo sausage-stuffed quail, grilled and served over a cinnamon-scented risotto, or sage-flavored trout stuffed with prosciutto. Main course selections such as grilled duck breast accompanied by stewed lentils, sun-dried tomato chutney, and lemongrass with ginger sauce are often among the items that can be selected from the prix fixe menu.

The wine list has over 100 choices, many local and quite good. Portions are ample but not overwhelming. You also can order wine "flights" — several tastings of different varieties of a type of wine (several Chardonnays, for example) — or a wine menu that offers a glass of the "just right" pairing of wine for each course of the prix fixe meal.

The inn's pastry chef, Neal Beaver, creates sugary subtleties that range from a chocolate terrine (a milk and white chocolate mousse served with raspberry sauce) to homemade ice creams (mango even!) served with sesame cookies.

PARGO'S SPIRITED FOODS
540-433-5000.
1691 E. Market St., Harrisonburg.
Open: Daily.
Price: Moderate.
Cuisine: American.
Serving: L, D.
Credit Cards: AE, D, DC, MC, V.
Handicap Access: Dining room yes, bar and lounge no.

OK, it's a chain. But it's fun and consistently good! The appetizer list is long and it's easy to make a meal by ordering two appetizers instead of an appetizer and a main course. Soup and salad options abound as well. Basic meat, salad, or fish entrées with special touches are always available. My family likes the bourbon-soaked specialties the best, especially the salmon.

The children's menu is extensive too, and diversionary coloring mats or other items are always on hand in case there is a long wait. Quality and service are consistently good.

Because of the extensive variety, if one person wants to eat lightly while another in our party is in the mood for a sandwich and the third wants a full dinner, this is a great place to select. (Reservations on weekend evenings are a good idea.)

TASTE OF THAI
540-801-8878.
919 S. High St., Harrisonburg.
Open: Daily.
Price: Inexpensive to Moderate.
Cuisine: Thai.
Serving: L, D.
Credit Cards: All major.
Handicap Access: Yes.

The Thai food explosion has hit Harrisonburg in a big way. This is one of two good Thai restaurants in town. My daughter and her friends favor pad Thai noodle, a signature dish of Thai cuisine done with delicious simplicity here. Jennie adds: "The green curry is also great, and serving sizes are large enough for two people to split one main course. It is a little more expensive than the Thai Café (see below), but the atmosphere is more formal and the dining area is larger with larger tables in the back that are good for birthday celebrations."

THE THAI CAFÉ
540-433-2201.
182 Neff Ave., Harrisonburg.
Open: Tues.–Sun.
Cuisine: Thai, Vietnamese.
Price: Inexpensive to Moderate.
Serving: L, D.
Credit Cards: D, MC, V.
Handicap Access: Yes.

The Thai Café, a small, family-run operation, serves a variety of reasonably priced Thai and Vietnamese foods in an informal setting. Our daughter and her friends prefer the Vietnamese specialties here, particularly the chicken pho. Pho is served with lime and cilantro and comes in eight varieties.

Green curry with shrimp or tofu is another popular choice, particularly with vegetarians. Jennie also adds, "My favorite appetizer item is the spring rolls made from rice paper and filled with clear rice noodles, shrimp, and vegetables — steamed, not fried."

Jennie warns that the curry comes a bit on the spicy side, but is not too over-powering. Chiles on the menu itself mark the heat of various entrées and are very accurate. If you find yourself in the opposite situation, you can add some of the hot chile sauce that you find on the table. (And if you like it, you can buy a bottle to take home at the deli next door.)

BLUE STONE INN
540-434-0535.
9107 N. Valley Pike,
　Harrisonburg.
Open: Tues.–Sat.
Price: Moderate.
Cuisine: American seafood,
　steak.
Serving: D.
Credit Cards: MC, V.
Handicap Access: Limited.

The blurb in the tourist bureau material describes the cuisine at this restaurant as simply "seafood and steak." But let me tell you, you would be wise to delve more deeply.

This is widely considered one of the best restaurants in the area. For that reason, the spot is always crowded. JMU professors and the rest of the local Harrisonburg crowd fill the booths and tables, every day of the week. Reservations are recommended.

The offerings seem basic, but the treatment of the basics with a deft touch is what takes the food to a higher level. Surprisingly, for a restaurant so land-locked, some of the best dishes are on the seafood side of the house. One of the standards and favorite items on the menu is their grilled trout stuffed with crab-meat. This dish blends the best of Virginia's seafood from the Tidewater area with the trout pulled fresh from the Valley's mountain streams and trout farms.

There is also a long list of beers to choose from here, and the wine list offers many Virginia selections.

The relaxed atmosphere of tables and booths in the wood-paneled room that used to be a hunting lodge make it a comfortable place to unwind. It is well worth the bit of a drive from JMU. Not too many of the students frequent the place, so while it is noisy it is not boisterous, and if you're over 30 you'll feel quite at home here. The décor includes walls full of '50s-era pictures of local customers enjoying their meals.

The service is great — most of the wait staff has been there for a long time and is quite knowledgeable about the offerings on the menu. I couldn't fit in dessert, but noticed that the cakes and pies were flying by to other diners with more hearty appetites. Mark this as a "must" if you are in the area.

OTHER EATERIES

There are several other good, recommended Harrisonburg eateries. Two Indian restaurants frequented by many students are the **American Indian Café** (540-433-1177; 91 N. Main St.) and the **Bombay Courtyard** (540-442-7166; 1588 S. Main St.). The **Boston Beanery Restaurant & Tavern** (540-433-1870; 1625 E. Market St.) is a good place for lunch or a snack. **Calhoun's Restaurant and**

Brewery (540-434-8777; 41 Court Sq.) is a local brewpub frequented by students and locals. The **Outback Steakhouse** (540-438-0190; 261 University Dr.) has an outpost in Harrisonburg, as does the **Texas Steakhouse** (540-433-3650; 1688 E Market St.).

ROCKINGHAM COUNTY FOOD PURVEYORS

Harrisonburg

This is a large town. There are a number of chain grocery stores sprinkled throughout, including **Food Lion**, **Kroger**, and **Wal-Mart Supercenter**. The stores and markets listed below sell fresh or rarer items.

FARMS AND FARM MARKETS

Harrisonburg/Dayton

Dayton Farmer's Market (540-879-9885; 42 S. Dayton) More than 20 shops with everything from barbecue to toys. Great local cheese, and an open-air seasonal section with vegetables as well. Closed Sun.

Harrisonburg Farmer's Market (540-433-1676; W. Water St.) Produce, baked goods, and even some organic produce. Herbs and cut flowers round out the selection. Open mid-Apr.–Thanksgiving, Tues.–Sat. 7–1.

Timberville

Bowman Fruit Sales, Turkey Knob Farm Market (540-896-3079; Rte. 881) Take I-81 Exit 264 to Rte. 211 west to Rte. 881 and go 2 miles; market is on right. Open Sept.–Dec. (Another stand operated by these folks can be found at the Harrisonburg Farmer's Market.)

Shenville Creamery and Garden Market (540-896-6357, 877-600-7440; www .shenville.com; creamery@shenville.com; 16094 Evergreen Valley Rd.) Take I-81 Exit 264, then head west on Rte. 211) Open Mon.–Sat. The best homemade soft cheeses, fresh milk, and old-style candies that you have ever tasted! Take a cooler and plan to eat their ice cream on-site, too! Mmmmm!

SHOPS AND OTHER FOOD ESTABLISHMENTS

Harrisonburg

Asian Market Thai Food Store (540-438-1119; 182 Neff Ave.) Thai and other Asian food ingredients. Great Thai chile pepper sauces, too — the same kind served in The Thai Café next door. Also offers plastic "Chinese" dinnerware.

Mr. J's Bagels and Deli (540-564-0416; 1635 E. Market St.) This is a basic bagel shop and deli. Good place to stop if you want something quick or if you want to take home a dozen freshly made bagels.

Cinnamon Bear Bakery and Deli (540-433-2867; 600 University Blvd.) This is the antidote to the common supermarket bakery. Yummy delights aimed at both the local population and the hoards of hungry college students in the area.

Elkton is also home to a branch of the Coors Brewing Company (540-289-8000). At the time of this writing they were no longer giving tours, although you may find references to that in some older tour books.

AUGUSTA COUNTY

Churchville

THE BUCKHORN INN
540-337-8660.
thebuckhorninn.com.
info@thebuckhorninn.com.
2487 Hankey Mountain
  Hwy. (Rte. 250).
Open: Weekends only,
  except for guests.
Price: Moderate.
Cuisine: Italian.
Serving: L (Sat. only), D
  (Fri.–Sun.).
Credit Cards: MC, V.
Handicap Access: Limited.

The modern back room of the inn is a banquet hall for tour groups and large receptions. The front part of the house, the older part of this 1830 inn, is decorated and furnished much as it was when Stonewall Jackson and his wife stayed here.

The Buckhorn Inn is repositioning itself under new owners, the Daly family, as a place to go for dinner. Among its Italian dishes, the Daly family specializes in out-of-this-world veal — delicate, flavorful, and oh so fresh!

Shrimp bisque and stuffed portabella mushrooms along with baked Brie with raspberry sauce tempt the palate, as do other appetizer choices. Entrées include lasagna, the standby surf and turf, and a wide variety of preparations that showcase that high-quality veal, from simple piccata to the heady sweetness of veal Marsala and more.

The dining room of the inn welcomes families, especially for dinner. The proximity to Staunton makes this a good place to mark for eating, even if you can't stay here. Be sure to call for a reservation. At the time of this writing the inn served dinner on weekends only.

Staunton

BELLE GRAE INN
540-886-5151, 888-541-5151.
www.bellegrae.com.
rejuvenate@bellegrae.com.

The Belle Grae is a landmark cluster of beautifully restored Victorian homes dating from 1870 to the early 1900s. The restaurant is in the main building. Many locals join guests to dine in the spa-

515 W. Frederick St.
Open: Wed.–Sun.
Price: Moderate to
    Expensive.
Cuisine: Continental.
Serving: D (Breakfast and
    tea for those staying at the
    inn).
Credit Cards: AE, MC, V.
Handicap Access: Yes.

cious rooms that overlook the lights of the town. Others enjoy one of the cozier nooks near one of the first-floor fireplaces or in a softly lit wood-paneled room.

If you're staying at the Belle Grae you'll want to make a dinner reservation as soon as you reserve your room. During the leaf season or other heavy tourist times in the area, innkeeper Michael Organ may require that you dine with them to get a room (Modified American Plan). Don't complain — consider it a guaranteed reservation!

A guest's culinary experience starts with a complimentary afternoon tea or cocktail hour. Weather permitting, this snack of light hors d'oeuvres and drinks will be held in the Azalea Courtyard. Organ uses the occasion to introduce guests to his plan for the evening meal. He previews choices from the prix fixe menu and records your choice of options — choice of seatings, and dessert before theater or after, for example.

The dinner menu varies seasonally and features local, simple food artfully prepared. We had lamb shank, which was tender and delightful and came with a choice of lovely and delicious side dishes. The salads are imaginative and served with light dressings.

We loved the option of being able to put our dessert off until we returned from the theater so we didn't have to rush to make the show. We walked slowly down the hill to the Blackfriars Playhouse (see Chapter Three, *Cultural Attractions*) on a warm fall night. After enjoying some of the best Shakespeare on this side of the Atlantic, we returned with just enough appetite after the uphill walk to do justice to the cheesecake that awaited us.

**PAMPERED PALATE
    CAFE**
540-886-9463.
26 and 28 E. Beverley St.
Open: Mon.–Sat. 9–5:30.
Price: Inexpensive to
    Moderate.
Cuisine: American and
    Greek.
Serving: B, L.
Credit Cards: DC, MC, V.
Handicap Access: No.
    (Downstairs accessible,
    but dining and rest rooms
    upstairs are not.)

This is the place to go for a quick, light lunch or a quick, not-so light but very delicious sandwich. The menu offerings include sandwiches, salads, or hot platters with quiche-of-the-day and soup and salad. Vegetarians will find plenty to choose from. My personal favorites are the Greek salad and the delicious turkey and veggie wraps served in the restaurant's trademark baskets.

The tiny "bistro" tables are the perfect spot from which to watch the activity on the busiest shopping street in downtown Staunton while enjoying their wonderful pastries. High tea is served occasionally; call for details.

L'ITALIA
540-885-0102.

Emilio Amato, a native Italian, has been cooking up veal, chicken, and pasta delights for the

www.litaliarestaurant.com/
home2.html.
23 E. Beverley St.
Open: Daily except Mon.
Price: Moderate to
Expensive.
Cuisine: Italian.
Serving: L, D.
Credit Cards: AE, CB, D,
MC, V.
Handicap Access: Limited.

Shenandoah crowd for the past seven years. We gave the menu a workout on a recent visit with a party of ten — on graduation weekend, when the place was *sooo* crowded. The kitchen crew and the wait staff performed expertly. Appetizers, including calamari and salads large enough to be a small meal in themselves, were served in generous portions.

L'Italia has some of the best veal in the Valley, and it's prepared in imaginative versions of traditional Italian presentations. The veal Siciliana is veal paired with eggplant. Veal rolls with asparagus and a Marsala cream sauce are also luscious. The meat is so tender you can cut it with a fork!

Seafood dishes come with a side of pasta with a flavorful southern Italian-style marinara sauce, redolent of basil and oregano. Pasta entrées also show a delicate hand with sauces and an imaginative touch in pairings.

Lunch specials are a nice way to try the restaurant's deft hand — salad and soup combos and lunchtime pasta are reasonably priced and served in smaller portions. The wine list is mostly Italian with a nice though small selection of Virginia wines as well.

The Pompeii Lounge upstairs, besides acting as bar/gathering place for the beyond-college-age set, also has dining rooms available for larger dinner parties (minimum of 15) at no additional charge.

**THE BEVERLEY
RESTAURANT**
540-886-4317.
12 E. Beverley St.
Open: Mon.–Fri. 7–7, Sat. 8–3.
Price: Inexpensive to
Moderate.
Cuisine: American,
Continental.
Serving: B, L, early D. Tea
served Wed. and Fri. 3–5
by reservation only.
Credit Cards: V, MC.
Handicap Access: Limited.

This little spot is always filled for lunch, and tea reservations fill up quickly, too. Tea is a delightful experience, complete with scones and cream and lemon curd.

The basic menu items of sandwiches, soups, salads, and quiches are prepared with a delectable élan. Dieters take note: If you are saving up calories by skimping elsewhere, this little eatery is the place to indulge in a caloric spree. Actually, I have begun to have dreams of the entire stretch between Staunton and Lexington as a veritable pastry heaven due to both the number and variety of universally excellent cakes, cookies, pies, and assorted goodies that can be found there.

WRIGHT'S DAIRY-RITE
540-886-0435.
www.dairy-rite.com/
index.html.
346 Greenville Ave.
Open: Daily.
Price: Inexpensive.

Rev up the time machine — oh, wait, you don't have to! Just drive over to Wright's Dairy-Rite. Pull your car up into a parking spot and speak into the "phone" at your very own order stand. The waitress zips out and serves you in your car with a hook-on tray — a scene right out of *Happy Days*.

Wright's in Lexington is a place you can still pull up and obtain 1950s-style service in your car — and enjoy 1950s-style milkshakes and burgers.

Joan Leotta

Cuisine: Diner.
Serving: L, D.
Credit Cards: AE, D, MC, V.
Handicap Access: Yes.

The star of the menu is the Superburger (two beef patties with cheese and lettuce, topped with their special sauce). The Monsterburger is an even bigger version of the Superburger.

It is theoretically possible to order one of their absolutely luscious burgers with a soft drink. But why would you (unless you are lactose-intolerant) when you can order a real milk shake here? These are just thick enough to be creamy but not so thick that you can't suck it up through the straw. Most of the locals recommend strawberry, but the vanilla is also superb. You can order your milk and milkshakes plain or malted here — another throwback to the '50s.

The Wright family did not seek to make themselves an independent landmark. Mr. Wright started his own place with his own special sauces and shakes when he couldn't get in on the chain movement. Many of those early chains are gone, but Wright's recently celebrated its 50th anniversary at the same site, with the same angular '50s-style signs, same great service, and same great food.

MRS. ROWE'S
540-886-1833.
www.mrsrowes.com.
mrsrowes@intelos.net.
74 Rowe Rd.
Open: Daily. Early closings
   Oct.–Mar.; call ahead
   during those months.
Price: Inexpensive.
Cuisine: American.
Serving: B, L, D.
Credit Cards: D, MC, V.
Handicap Access: Yes.

This is one of the area's storied spots. Locals rave about it. Reviewers rave about it. The food is simple, ample, though a bit on the bland side. The pastry cases in the front proudly display their specialty pies and cookies, and many folks were leaving with a box or bag of this or that bakery item. Our sampling of the cookies and cherry pie found them a bit bland, but the local audience obviously enjoys the character of the food.

Stuarts Draft and Waynesboro

SCOTTO'S TRATTORIA
540-337-5000.
2691 Stuarts Draft Hwy.,
   Stuarts Draft.
and
540-942-8715.
1412 W. Broad St.,
   Waynesboro.
Open: Daily.
Price: Moderate.
Cuisine: Italian.
Serving: L, D.
Credit Cards: AE, D, MC, V.
Handicap Access: Yes.

The menu offers lots of variety and serves high quality all around. The secret is that each of these dishes involves using good ingredients and treating them with the simple elegance that is at the heart of Italian cooking.

But the star dish here is the pizza. The absolutely wonderful, crispy, thin-crust pizza is brushed with an aromatic, oregano-filled sauce and topped with an abundance of cheese (the real stuff!) dripping off each slice. Two other popular specialties are fried ravioli and ziti.

The décor reveals that the restaurant maintains a close relationship with the local community — the walls are covered with thank-you notes from school groups and sports teams that have either toured the restaurant or been sponsored by it. It's not a fancy place, but it has a comfortable, fun atmosphere and the food is wonderful.

OTHER AREA EATERIES

These other good places to eat in Staunton have been recommended by a number of folks: **Boston Beanery Restaurant & Tavern** (540-868-5555; 1311 Greenville Ave), **Depot Grille** (540-885-7332; 42 Middlebrook Rd.), and **The Pullman Restaurant** (540-885-6612; 36 Middlebrook Ave.).

AUGUSTA COUNTY FOOD PURVEYORS

Farms and Farm Markets

Andre Viette Farm & Nursery (800-575-5538; 994 Long Meadow Rd., Fishersville) Open Apr.–mid-Dec., Mon.–Sat. 9–5, Sun. 12–5. Check them out for edible flowers and herbs. High-quality perennials also for sale.

Chester-Cestari Farms (540-337-7282; wool@chesterfarms.com; 3581 Churchville Ave., Churchville) Open Mon.–Sat. 9–5. Special events here are really a lot of fun. We attended a pumpkin fest and had a great time. This is the place to go if you want a specially woven wool blanket or if you want to buy high-quality American lamb. The lamb comes in sealed packages and can be shipped overnight to your home. A free Wool Fair in April — shearing of hundreds of sheep, wool carding, dyeing and spinning; horse- and tractor-drawn wagon rides; home-cooked food. Free Pumpkin Fest in October — same activities as Wool Fair plus rides to the pumpkin patch for pick-your-own pumpkins. Educational tours of farm and wool mill available.

The Golden Kernel (540-249-4813; 1752 Weyers Cave Rd., Grottoes) Carroll and Linda Swartz specialize in growing sweet corn (hence the name of the farm) and pumpkins. Harvest time is a great time to go since they offer hay rides. In addition to their own produce, their farmstand also includes bulk foods, cheese, meat, and local crafts. They are open year-round, Mon.–Sat. 10–6. Call before going to see if there is anything in the field for picking or if things are only available at the stand.

Staunton-Augusta Farmers' Market (Contact "Market Master" Jeff Ishee at 540-332-3802 or info@emarketfarm.com; Wharf parking lot, downtown Staunton) Open Apr.–Oct., Sat. 7–12. This is a producers-only market featuring vegetables and fruits grown in the area. Among the bounty, hungry shoppers also can find items such as garlic, fresh and dried flowers, honey, eggs, baked goods, meats, poultry, vinegars, herbs, and plants. Unlike many markets that are only collections of stands, this one also offers food-oriented entertainment. Chefs give demonstrations, they hold an old-fashioned harvest festival, give hay rides, and even sponsor occasional breakfasts and bake sales for nonprofit civic groups. New additional midweek location with many of the same vendors and activities in *Verona*, Apr.–Sept., Wed. 2–6. Contact market master for details and directions.

Waynesboro Farmer's Market (540-942-6705; wddi@waynesborova-online .com; 503 W. Main St., Waynesboro) This market is open May–Oct., Sat. 7–12, and adds an evening session Jun.–Sept., Tues. 5–8. The additional evening hours are not all that's unique about this market. This is a real community-centered organization with produce, crafts, flowers, baked goods, and art coming from local sources. They even offer county fair-type events such as a children's tomato-growing contest and seminars on flower arranging or growing roses.

Wenger Grape Farms (540-943-4956; wengerd@cfw.com; 4094 Stuarts Draft Hwy., Waynesboro) Open Mon.–Sat., 8–dark. This is where you can pick grapes — Concord and Niagara, two old-fashioned varieties that are wonderful to eat and great to use to make jam and grape pies. Fresh grape pie is also a New York State wine country specialty, but once you've tasted one you'll want to place it in your pantheon of great dessert recipes.

SHOPS AND OTHER FOOD ESTABLISHMENTS

Staunton

La Tienda Hispana (540-574-3233; 2411 W. Beverley St.) Lots of Goya products. Great place to pick up the fixings for your own versions of Mexican, Central and South American specialties.

Joan Leotta

The Virginia Made Shop just outside of Staunton is a great place to purchase Virginia ham, peanuts, locally made soaps, and handcrafts.

Waynesboro

Virginia Made Shop (540-886-1833; 54 Rowe Rd., adjacent to Mrs. Rowe's) This shop carries a wide array of edible merchandise designated with the Virginia's Finest checkmark, meaning that these peanuts, jellies, jams, honeys, and candies are good enough to be food ambassadors for the Old Dominion. Handmade soaps and body creams are among the better-known nonedible products found in the Virginia Made Shop.

ROCKBRIDGE COUNTY

Raphine

KATHY'S OF RAPHINE
540-377-5299, 540-377-5288.
584 Oakland Cir.
Open: Daily.
Price: Inexpensive.
Cuisine: American Southern.
Serving: B, L, D.

We were surprised when the locals suggested this spot for dinner. After all, it's the restaurant in the Comfort Inn, a motel chain. Ahhh, humility. Don't judge a restaurant by the vinyl or a menu by the distance from the sea — that's the lesson we learned.

Credit Cards: AE, D, MC, V.
Handicap Access: Yes.

We had a wonderful meal here. In addition to great food, they had an amazing wine list, an entire page long with many Virginia wines as well as the standard California choices. Several are from the award-winning Rockbridge Vineyard just up the road.

One of their specialties is fried oysters, and they're really worth ordering. The oysters are fresh and wonderful, and the breading is light and airy — no grease, even though they're fried. Other offerings that rate a try include trout served in various ways. The meat dishes include barbecue, fried chicken, ham, and steaks. Veggies are fresh-tasting and delicious.

There are nightly specials, too. Trust the kind and attentive wait staff to suggest what is especially great that night.

You may not associate this sort of restaurant with romance. But the view from the large window at Kathy's offers one of the most romantic in the Valley — a full backdrop of the mountains. This view is wonderful in the morning and afternoon, and rises to breathtaking heights at sunset. The ability to experience heart-shaking beauty in an otherwise ordinary-looking place, and discovering an ordinary place that serves extraordinary food with extraordinary service — those traits are the hallmark of the Valley itself.

Note: There are two other Kathy's restaurants in the Valley. They are affiliated, but locals assure me that this is the one with the magic touch in the kitchen!

Fairfield

WHISTLE STOP CAFÉ
540-377-9492.
33 Soapy Place.
Open: Tues.–Sun.
Price: Inexpensive.
Cuisine: Italian-American.
Serving: B, L, D.
Credit Cards: D, MC, V.
Handicap Access: Yes.

Great Italian and simple American food is served in a simple setting with trains running around the restaurant's perimeter on an overhead platform. Soups may include Italian wedding as well as traditional vegetable. Great sandwich selections include subs and calzones.

There are lots of different choices for meat-eaters and vegetarians alike. Whatever you order, follow it up with one of their wonderful desserts — especially the ice-cream dishes or the pie. But watch out!

If you eye a piece of the homemade pie on your way in you may want to order it with your dinner — especially on Sundays, when the pies sometimes run out.

Lexington

MAPLE HALL
877-463-2044 (for Maple Hall and for its two related properties); 540-463-4666 for dining reservations only.

The Maple Hall dining room is widely known among locals as the place to go when you know Chef Robert's sausage roll is on the menu. It's listed as an appetizer, but if you order it, prepare to share.

The menu changes with the seasons, so don't set

www.lexingtonhistoricinns
.com.
311 N. Lee Highway, six
miles north of Lexington.
Open: Daily.
Price: Moderate.
Cuisine: Continental with
some American regional
touches.
Serving: D (B for guests
only).
Credit Cards: D, MC, V.
Handicap Access: Yes.

**THE WILLSON-WALKER
HOUSE**
540-463-3020.
www.willsonwalker.com.
30 N. Main St.
Open: Tues.–Sat. 11:30–2:30,
5:30–9 (closed Sat. lunch
Jan.–Mar.).
Price: Moderate for lunch,
Expensive for dinner.
Cuisine: American with an
emphasis on Virginia.
Serving: L, D.
Credit Cards: AE, D, MC, V.
Handicap Access: Yes.

your heart on the stuffed shrimp appetizer (Gulf shrimp, feta cheese, and prosciutto), the steak Diane or the French rack of veal. Instead, call ahead or just wait to see what simply wonderful surprises the current menu holds. Do be sure to make reservations, though. The locals find the dark wood interiors and soft lighting as wonderful a complement to this exquisite food as do visitors, so the dining room does fill up!

For a fine dinner or a great lunch, step into this 1820 classic revival townhouse, restored to its pre-1911 look. This is a place where atmosphere is part of the draw and one simply hopes that the food lives up to the surroundings. Fortunately for those who love food as well as history, the Willson-Walker lives up to all expectations. Their $5 lunch is a legend in the area and a wonderful way to sample the kitchen without stretching your budget.

Reservations are recommended for both lunch and dinner, and the menu changes daily, based on what is freshest at the time. But one word of warning: This place is seductive. The chef creates wonderful American nouveau creations with regional accents. If you aren't sticking to the $5 lunch, you might try the chicken Caesar, the Reuben, or the crab cakes. Soups change daily, and for those who can't leave the diet behind, the menu lists the Weight Watchers point value next to each dish.

Dinner entrées include unbelievably delicious beef (local!) topped with blue cheese under the name "Piemontese Ribeye." Free-range chicken (when available) is my choice. True free-range chicken has a unique flavor, and this one-of-a-kind taste is further heightened by the skill of Willson-Walker's chef. Vegetarian entrées are prepared to order upon request.

Casual dress is OK at lunchtime and on the veranda at dinner; otherwise, this is a coat-and-tie place. It's worth the extra effort to have dinner here, though leaving room for dessert is difficult!

SOUTHERN INN
540-463-3612.
www.southerninn.com.
geohuger@southerninn.com.
37 S. Main St.
Open: Daily.
Price: Moderate.

The atmosphere here is casual, but the food is elegant. Proprietors George (chef) and Sue Ann Huger produce contemporary, seasonal dishes utilizing local produce, meats, and other products; the menu varies with what is the best available food.

Cuisine: Updated American.
Serving: L, D, SB.
Credit Cards: AE, D, MC, V
Handicap Access: Yes.

Waiters clad in black and white await diners at this longtime Lexington landmark.

Fancy sandwiches, salads, and grilled pizzas fill the luncheon menu alongside entrées like pasta, or a stuffed portabella mushroom (and a nod to down-home cuisine in the form of meatloaf). The Reuben shows the chef's special touch with corned beef, braised red cabbage, and Swiss on marble.

Look for larger-sized versions of the luncheon dishes for dinner, along with seafood (pan-seared sea scallops, sautéed mahi-mahi) or steaks and poultry. Don't miss the locally grown sautéed greens side dish (ask what they are first!). Chef salad is also a treat — a different-each-day creation of their chef.

OTHER EATERIES

Lexington is one of those special places — small but sophisticated. The eateries in Lexington and nearby reflect that sophisticated style. In addition to the places we reviewed, these others have been recommended:

The **Blue Heron Cafe** (540-463-2800; 4 E. Washington St.) is a natural food eatery that is open for lunch only during the week and for dinner on Friday and Saturday only. Another good lunch spot is **City Subs & Steaks** (540-464-SUBS; 159 S. Main St.), especially for Philly cheese steaks. They also deliver.

Pool tables, karaoke, and entertainment are the big draws at **BJ's Oasis** (540-464-4483; 18 E. Nelson St.). **The Palms** (540-463-7911; 101 W. Nelson St.) is a bit more upscale and a good place to try a fancy burger at dinner. **Kenney's** (540-261-2592; 1518 Magnolia Ave.) serves foot-long hot dogs and burgers with their own special sauce. **The Inn at Union Run** (540-463-9715; 325 Union Run Rd.) is an elegant eatery with a nice wine list.

Many other fine eateries are outside of Lexington, but still within Rockbridge County. **Mill Creek Café** (540-997-5228; Rtes. 39 and 42, Goshen) is known for its home-style cooking. At the Natural Bridge try the **Colonial Dining Room** (540-291-2121; 15 Appledore Ln.) for breakfast, lunch, or dinner — large selection, homey food. The **Sugar Tree Inn Restaurant** (800-377-2197; Rte. 56, Steeles Tavern; see also Chapter Five, *Lodging*) offers the splendid scenery of the Blue Ridge as a backdrop for its gourmet candlelight dinners served on Friday and Saturday nights by reservation only. Caveat: Closed Jan. and Feb.

ROCKBRIDGE COUNTY FOOD PURVEYORS

FARM MARKETS

Buena Vista Community Market (540-261-2880; Magnolia St., Buena Vista) The fresh fruit, vegetable, and plant market is small — generally not more than eight or ten vendors. It's located in the downtown section of Buena Vista

May–Sept., Sat. 8–1. The Chamber of Commerce sponsors occasional special events and music here, too. Take the Buena Vista exit from I-81 and follow signs for downtown.

Shops and Other Food Establishments

Buena Vista

Buena Vista Bakery (540-261-1970; 118 W. 21st St.) Open Tues.–Fri. 7–5; Sat. 9–2. Home-baked goods, fresh bread, homemade desserts, and sandwiches. Specials include cream puffs, cinnamon rolls, and Southern-style bread pudding.

Lexington

Caroline's Bakery (540-463-5691; 8 N. Main St.) This is a great place to stop in to pick up a box lunch, but the pastries and breads are the standout items to order. Breads are a local favorite and the varieties available each day are posted. The pastries include cookies, gooey bear claws, and cinnamon rolls. Their pecan rolls are without peer — large, nutty, and flavorful.

Cocoa Mill Chocolate Co. (540-464-8400; 115 W. Nelson St.) Wine-infused chocolates and truffles of all types their specialty — take them up on their offers to taste. These chocolates are especially divine because they are freshly made. We took home a box of truffles with liquors and a box of wine chocolates full of a delightful red wine from Rockbridge Vineyard. There are also slabs of milk and dark chocolate that serve as greeting cards and chocolates in a variety of fun shapes. The shop has been written up in many gourmet magazines and it deserves all the praise it gets!

Fun Foods and Accessories (877-473-4433; www.funfoodsforyou.com; 6 E. Washington St.) Lots of candies and things. If you want unique food favors for a party, this is the place. Opening a tearoom soon.

Healthy Foods Market (540-463-6954; 110 W. Washington St.) Complete line of vitamins, herbs, and homeopathic products. Fine selection of fresh local produce, too. This is an especially good place to stop if you use a variety of herbs and spices and just want a small amount — they sell them in bulk.

Lexington Coffee Roasting Co. (540-464-6586, 800-322-6505; 9 W. Washington St.) Fresh roasted coffees, espresso, and frozen drinks. They have things to eat, too: fresh bagels, muffins, and pastries. Open Mon.–Fri. 7:30–5:30, Sat. 8–5, Sun. 9–2.

Virginia Born and Bred (540-463-1832; www.vabornbred.com; 16 W. Washington St.) Some of the best in wines and foods made in Virginia are here for you to take home.

Washington Street Purveyors (540-464-WINE; 9 E. Washington St.) Fine wines, cigars, microbrews, imports, brewing supplies, gourmet snacks, hot sauces, and accessories. Great selection of Virginia wines.

Raphine

Buffalo Springs Herb Farm (540-348-1083; www.buffaloherbs.com; Raphine Rd.) Open Apr.–mid-Dec., Wed.–Sat. 10–5; also Sun. 1–5 in Apr., May. Even if you aren't into herbs, you'll enjoy simply seeing the grounds and barn on this 18th-century farmstead.

Wade's Mill still operates and sells stone-ground grains of several types. Upstairs is a gourmet kitchen store.

Shenandoah2000

Wade's Mill (540-348-1400; www.wadesmill.com; 55 Kennedy) Take Exit 205 from I-81, then head west on Rte. 606. Open Apr.–mid-Dec., Wed.–Sat. 10–5; also Sun. 1–5, Apr., May, Sept.–Dec. only. This water-powered gristmill is on the National Register of Historic Places, and it's something to see, even if you aren't fascinated by mills. The Valley was the breadbasket of the state and the old South before the Civil War. Seeing the mill in operation and tasting some of its production (buckwheat, bread flour, cornmeal, and more) are tangible reminders of a way of life gone by. You can purchase hand-ground flours of various types.

BOTETOURT AND ROANOKE COUNTIES

Roanoke is a gourmet food lover's delight. It would take an entire book to even begin to cover them all. We've selected just a few to put here for review and have listed a few others known to be great. For more information, consult a diner's guide to the city or one of the many e-guides to the city available online.

Roanoke

NAWAB INDIAN CUISINE
540-345-5150.
www.nawabonline.com/index2.html.
118A Campbell Ave. SE # E.
Open: Daily.
Price: Inexpensive to Moderate.
Cuisine: Indian.
Serving: L (Mon.–Fri. buffet; Sat.–Sun. from menu), D.
Credit Cards: AE, D, MC, V.
Handicap Access: Yes.

Not only is the food here wonderful, the service is exceptional! The cuisine of India offers much more than a few curries. In fact, the term Indian cooking is an umbrella term for a variety of types of cooking from all of the Indian regions. At Nawab, the Arora family serves primarily the food of their native Punjab region, which includes the wonderful clay-baked tandoor meats and a wide variety of vegetarian dishes as well as curry.

Everything is à la carte. We put ourselves in the hands of the capable waiter and he guided us through a set of dishes that met our desire to try a variety of things without over-ordering. You may want to order a soup or a light course, but be sure not to overlook the flat breads. All of the food can be adjusted from mild to hot to meet your palate's needs, and various chutneys can complement the flavor of just about any item.

You don't need to be an expert in Indian food to know that what you are getting here is simply wonderful! Even the smallest item was perfection itself. The mulligatawny soup is especially superb, a delicate and flavorful rendition of the Indian standard. Some dishes are deceptively rich, but don't worry — the restaurant is used to giving out boxes for leftovers.

The attention to detail exhibited in the delicate flavors of the food and the thoughtful service are, doubtless, what account for the fact that Nawab has enjoyed top billing among Roanoke's restaurants for some time.

The Arora family owns six other restaurants throughout the area. Besides the one we tried in Roanoke there are branches in Virginia Beach, Norfolk, Newport News, and Williamsburg; Huntington, West Virginia; and Winston-Salem, North Carolina.

CARLOS BRAZILIAN AND INTERNATIONAL FOOD
540-776-1117.
4167 Electric Rd.
Open: Wed.–Fri. 11:30–2; Mon.–Sat. 5–9:30.
Price: Moderate to Expensive.
Cuisine: Brazilian, Italian, Continental.
Serving: L, D.
Credit Cards: AE, MC, V.
Handicap Access: Yes.

The Roanoker magazine has rated Carlos the city's top restaurant for several years running. It's not hard to see why. (The fact that a Brazilian and an Indian restaurant duel for the top spot in this Virginia town is a testament to the refined palates of the populace.)

Carlos is a white tablecloth restaurant suitable for a business lunch or a romantic dinner. The easy hospitality of the staff makes even those in more casual attire feel quite welcome. The restaurant recently moved from its downtown location to the busy commercial, more suburban Electric Road, home to many of Roanoke's shopping malls and other fine restaurants. As a result, decisions about hours of operation were in flux at the time of this writing. But the chefs moved along with the restaurant and my Roanoke informants assure me that the food remains outstanding.

The fejoida, a traditional black bean stew, is wonderful here, as is another Brazilian staple, "Frango Tropical," a chicken dish sautéed with fruit.

Plates of vegetables, veal, chicken, and pasta look lovely and taste great. Also available are a vast array of Brazilian-style grilled meats and several delicious vegetarian entrées (seasonal).

The folks at Carlos have a knack for taking the freshest items of the season and presenting them in ways that reflect well on all of the international cuisines represented in their heritage.

SALTORI'S
540-343-6644.
202 Market Sq.
Open: Daily.
Price: Moderate.
Cuisine: American with Italian accents.
Serving: L, D.
Credit Cards: AE, D, MC, V.
Handicap Access: Yes, downstairs.

Look at the posted menu and you'll see that it offers a balance of sandwiches and salads with a little Italian flair to them.

Saltori's has tables on the first floor grouped around a large wooden bar and open metal stairs to an upstairs that was closed when we visited. In earlier incarnations the upstairs was a cigar bar. Today it seems to be a haven for jazz music on weekend evenings.

Luncheon specials include several tasty salad and sandwich combinations. The dinner menu adds Italian specialties — mostly pastas — to the list while keeping the price moderate. I haven't tried them, but if they follow the line of treatment that is given to the simple salads and focaccia sandwiches, they will be tasty and imaginative.

MILL MOUNTAIN COFFEE & TEA
540-342-9404.
112 Campbell Ave. SE.
Open: Daily.
Price: Inexpensive.
Cuisine: Light fare and pastries.
Serving: B, L, D.
Credit Cards: MC, V.
Handicap Access: Limited.

Mill Mountain has local flavor that you won't want to miss. Artists, businesspeople, and tourists alike hang at the big oak bar or sit and read newspapers at the tables. This is also *the* place to go after a dinner on the Square or between shops and museums if you're seeing the sights. It opens early and closes late and is open seven days a week.

They roast their own coffee and serve the finest quality teas here. The lattes are delicious, the pastries a constant temptation, and the sandwiches delectable. European/Italian sodas also are available.

Even the décor is irresistible, with handmade chairs that are a delight to sit in as well as lovely to behold.

Mill Mountain has several locations. The atmosphere is the most fun at the Center in the Square site listed here, but the offerings are equally delicious in all locations.

CHICO AND BILLY'S PRESTIGIOUS PIZZA AND PASTA PALACE
540-772-4454.
3334 Brambleton Ave.
Open: Daily.
Price: Inexpensive.
Cuisine: Italian.
Serving: L, D.
Credit Cards: D, MC, V.
Handicap Access: Limited.

There are only about a dozen tables in the restaurant, and they fill up fast at all hours. It's worth the wait, or you can take your "pie" home or call for delivery (within a few miles). Those who choose to dine-in can enjoy a glass of wine or beer with dinner.

Though they do serve pasta, the restaurant confirms that folks order pizza more than anything else. The most popular version is pepperoni, but these geniuses of dough and topping will prepare your pizza with anything you want. For example, white pizza is on the menu and is most often ordered with spinach and sun-dried tomatoes. No matter what you decide on — pizza, calzones, or pasta — it's all made to order here, where homemade means great flavor.

Chico and Billy's changed hands in April 2002, but the new owner has pledged to keep the recipes, especially the pizza, the same. Rumors abound that expansion to at least one other spot may occur, but assurances accompany all rumors that the quality is inviolable. Mangia bene!

THE COFFEE POT BARBEQUE AND GRILL
540-774-8256.
2902 Brambleton Ave.
Open: Mon.–Sat.
Price: Inexpensive.
Cuisine: Barbecue.
Serving: L (buffet Mon.–Fri.), D.
Credit Cards: D, MC, V.
Handicap Access: Limited.

Ask anyone in town and they'll be able to give you directions to the little log cabin with a log-and-chink coffeepot on top, just outside of downtown. It houses what many claim is the best North Carolina-style barbecue in Roanoke. (North Carolina-style usually means barbecue made with a vinegar-based sauce.)

Built during the 1930s, The Coffee Pot is one of the last true old roadhouses from that era that remains in operation anywhere in the country. The building has even been designated a National Historic Landmark.

Current owner Carroll Bell says most roadhouses, the places folks drove to "out of town," were torn down when cities expanded and their rustic ambience didn't blend in with the new cityscape. But The Coffee Pot persisted, and customers can read its history in a flurry of articles that lines the walls.

Bell took it over in the '80s and turned it to barbecue. Pulled pork is the mainstay, but Bell reports her lunch buffet also has beef barbecue, chicken, and her secret coleslaw, a non-mayonnaise-based side dish. Except for the buffet, the same menu reigns all day and into the night.

And as with the roadhouses of old, The Coffee Pot sees all walks of life at its tables at various times of day. It's a great place for people-watching.

THE NEW YORKER DELICATESSEN & RESTAURANT
540-366-0935.
2802 Williamson Rd.
Open: Daily except Monday.
Price: Inexpensive
Cuisine: Deli.
Serving: L, D.
Credit Cards: None; cash only.
Handicap Access: Yes.

One friend called this spot the home of the best overstuffed sandwich and sub, a Roanoke institution, and a great family restaurant.

There are about 160 seats here, but they also do a heavy take-out business, especially at lunch, thanks to their reputation for making *everything* from scratch and for searching near and far for the best quality deli meats. Their sandwiches are overstuffed — with the best.

Their wonderful kosher-style sandwiches and salads have been served up from this same spot for more than 44 years. The deli is also open on Sunday, when many of Roanoke's other eateries are closed.

THE ROANOKER RESTAURANT
540-344-7746.
2522 Colonial Ave. SW.
Open: Mon.–Thurs. 7–7, Fri.– Sat. 7–10, Sun. 8–9.
Price: Inexpensive.
Cuisine: American Southern.
Serving: B, L, D.
Credit Cards: MC, V.
Handicap Access: Yes.

While any meal here treats hungry folks to good, honest Southern cooking, breakfast is the real draw, especially on Sundays. Since 1941 Roanokers have been lining up on Sunday mornings here, where you can savor a fine and full Southern breakfast until 11am.

Among the most popular offerings (although an entire menu of possibilities awaits) are the wafer-thin ham slices served with red-eye gravy and biscuits. Or perhaps you'll choose the Crafton special (named after the founder), which is two eggs, two pieces of bacon, red-eye gravy, and biscuits. Or maybe your taste runs to the special named for his brother, Charlie: two pancakes, sausage, and that wonderful gravy.

The helpful staff serves lunch from 11:30 and dinner from 4:30 daily, but you can order egg dishes — including omelets and breakfast meats (ham, sausage, bacon) and of course biscuits — all day long. And although the restaurant is not downtown, it's easy to find, just off 581's Colonial Avenue exit between Tower Mall and Virginia Western Community College.

STEPHEN'S RESTAURANT
540-344-7203.
2926 Franklin Rd. SW.
Open: Mon–Thurs. 5–9 (last seating), Fri.–Sat. 5:30–9, last seating at 9. Closed Sun.
Price: Moderate to Expensive.

Owner and chef Stephen Foster describes himself as self-taught, but he grew up in the restaurant business from his early days in Mississippi. He discovered a talent for the cuisine of neighboring Louisiana and carried that talent with him when he founded Stephen's in Roanoke in 1987.

His restaurant is housed in a contemporary two-story building with a wrought iron fence in the courtyard. The inner space, also enhanced with

Cuisine: Fresh seafood with emphasis on southern Louisiana dishes.
Serving: D.
Credit Cards: AE, D, DC, MC, V.
Handicap Access: Yes.

wrought iron, is divided up into smaller dining rooms to offer privacy.

The menu offerings are guided by the season. "I'm known for my seafood combinations, my sauces, and my south Louisiana dinner," Foster says.

It's no surprise that the combinations are so popular. They include things like rockfish Diane — fresh fillet with scallops, crab, and a Diane sauce.

He also serves a variety of fish fillets over a bed of caramelized Vidalia onions enhanced with the presentation of other veggies, depending upon what is fresh from the sea and the garden.

Other creations include a red-eye cream sauce over crab, combinations of peanut-encrusted pork tenderloin with fried jumbo shrimp, and chicken prepared whatever way the muse leads him, recently a hard-cider and butter sauce. Desserts include blackberry sorbet, pecan brittle cream anglaise, and fresh pecan torte.

OTHER ROANOKE EATERIES

Other fine places to eat spring up regularly in Roanoke. Here are some additional suggestions that we did not have time to more fully research, but that have been deemed by friends to be well worth a visit.

Fantastic service and great food is served at the Patrick Henry Hotel's **Hunter's Grille** (540-345-8811, 800-303-0988; 617 S. Jefferson St.). This elegant dining spot is known for its steak. The ladies' luncheon is also a standby here, and many clubs and functions (showers, weddings, etc.) use the Grille because the ambience is great and the food is always good.

The Hotel Roanoke (540-985-5900, 800-222-TREE; 110 Shenandoah Ave.) offers an elegant "power breakfast" in its **Pine Room,** and its very expensive **Regency Room** regularly wins awards as one of the most romantic places to go out to eat. **Arzu** (540-982-7160, 213 Williamson Rd. SE) is the place for good food, great service, and a great wine list. **First Street** (540-343-0179; 309 Market St. SE) has great happy hour drinks, convenient location, and above-average food.

Angler's Café (540-342-2436; 310 Second St. SW) is known for great lunches that are moderately priced.

Salem

MAC & BOB'S
540-389-5999.
316 E. Main St.
Open: Daily.
Price: Moderate.
Cuisine: American (steaks, seafood).

In addition to a long list of drinks, sandwiches and salads, they also serve pizza and great burgers here. No matter what you order, the food is well prepared.

With such good appetizers it's hard to save room for dessert, as good as those looked. Be sure to

Serving L, D.
Credit Cards: MC, V.
Handicap Access: Yes.

order wings if you like them — theirs are among the best in the area, spicy and a perfect crispness to the skin.

An eclectic mix of people and a general level of excitement infuse this spot. It's located right across from Roanoke College, so professors and students are often chatting at various levels of intensity around the room. The locals recommended this place as the number one spot and we were not sorry to have followed their recommendations.

MACADO'S
540-387-2686.
209 E. Main St.
Open: Daily.
Price: Moderate.
Cuisine: American.
Serving: L, D.
Credit Cards: AE, MC, V.
Handicap Access: Yes.

There are several locations of this restaurant in both Roanoke and Salem. The décor at this particular branch is fun — very eclectic — and the sandwiches are great! The menu offers a range of foods from pasta to chicken to burgers and salads. It's also a great spot for drinks and wings, lunch or dinner. The restaurant has won awards in the Roanoke area for its desserts, but the entrée portions are so big that you might not make it that far.

OTHER SALEM EATERIES

Also highly recommended in Salem is the **Sake House** (540-986-1207; 141 Electric Rd.), a great place for fresh sushi. The restaurant's pedigree includes a list of awards. It's open for lunch and dinner and has a tearoom as well as a sushi bar. **Mill Mountain Coffee & Tea** (540-342-9404; 112 Campbell Ave.) has spread into Salem, so if you became addicted to their coffees, teas, and pastries in Roanoke, now you can get a fix while antiquing in Salem.

BOTETOURT AND ROANOKE COUNTY FOOD PURVEYORS

Farm Markets

Botetourt County

Ikenberry Orchards (540-992-6166; 2557 Roanoke Rd., Rte. 220, Daleville) Mark and Ben Ikenberry open the orchard daily and extend the hours during the summer. Apple butter, cider, preserves, and country ham round out their offerings. Seasonal offerings include apples — Red Delicious, Golden Delicious, Jonathan, York, Winesap, Stayman, and Rome — peaches, sweet corn, assorted other summer veggies, pumpkins, and Indian corn.

Roanoke & Roanoke County

Fresh fruit and vegetables from nearby farms are available at the Historic Roanoke City Farmer's Market.

Roanoke Valley Convention and Visitor's Bureau

Historic Roanoke City Farmer's Market (540-342-2028; chrish@downtown-roanoke.org; all over Market Square) This is the oldest continuously operating open-air market in Virginia. It opens Mon.–Sat. at 7am and stays open all day, though some booths close earlier than others. There are almost 60 stalls offering fruits, vegetables, home-baked goods, and local preserves. This is not a producer's market, which means you can find things grown outside of the area, including exotic fruits. The yellow and white striped awnings are a happy harbinger of morning — grab a cup of coffee at Mill Mountain Coffee & Tea on Campbell and then walk through the stalls. The market also sponsors several activities, including a chili cook-off on the first Saturday in May, and is central in the town's *Dickens of a Christmas* celebration held on the first three Friday evenings each December.

Jamison Orchard (540-774-5537; 5635 Grandin Rd. Extension) This has been a family farm since 1875, and it's now practically in the city, just one mile west of Rte. 419 near the Oak Grove School. Open Mon.–Thurs. 9–6, Fri. 9–7, Sat. 9–4; closed Sun. The farm sells its own fruits and veggies and makes up gift baskets. They also sell local cheese, honey, apple butter, peach butter, and homemade hard candies. Among their fruits, the stars are apples, peaches, and nectarines.

Salem

Salem Farmer's Market (540-375-4098 for "Market Master" Beth Carson; Main and Broad Sts.) Runs Apr. 1–Dec. 1, Mon.–Sat. dawn till dusk. The market is a sheltered, 25-stall setup that features home-grown or homemade products. They include baked goods, jams, honey, flowers, specialty items, and, at the right time, Christmas greenery. They also use the market to anchor several outdoor festivals, including an art show in May, a farmer's festival in July, and Olde Salem Days in September.

Vinton

Vinton Farmer's Market (540-983-0613; vintonmemorial@aol.com; 204 Lee Ave.) Open Mon.–Sat. during daylight hours and Sun. 12–6. They have a special Market Day on the first Saturday of each month with events such as a gospel concert in July and bluegrass concerts May–Aug. Shoppers can find a large variety of fresh produce, baked goods, plants, and crafts. Vendors often set up as well.

SHOPS AND OTHER FOOD ESTABLISHMENTS

Roanoke

Asian Pacific Market (540-563-0986; 5221 Williamson Rd. NW) Assorted items that will please the palate and stock the kitchen of anyone wanting to cook Asian specialties.

Good Things on the Market (540-343-2121; Market Square) This is a fun spot to stop, full of luscious goodies, including jams and jellies and Virginia wines.

Lee & Edwards Wine Merchants (540-343-3900; lande@rev.net; 309 S. Jefferson St.) They advertise themselves as the premier wine and food shop in southwest Virginia. Certainly their climate-controlled cellar does feature a wide variety of Virginia and other wines. They offer the equipment needed to brew up a small batch of microbrew beer or wine at home and they carry a wide line of food products that have earned the Virginia's Finest designation. Open daily 10–6.

Nuts and Sweet Things (540-344-3717; 32 Market Square SE) We stopped in here to purchase some of their delightful chocolates and found that they also offer yummy homemade fudge and a wide variety of wrapped candies to tempt passersby.

On the Rise Bread Co. (540-344-7715; 303 Market St. SE) Good breads — crusty European-style. Not cheap, but worth it!

Roanoke Wiener Stand (540-342-6932; 25 Campbell Ave. SE) This shrine to the humble hot dog is open every day but Sunday for lunch (until about 3). Located in the heart of the action at Center in the Square, this purveyor serves cooked dogs, not raw, but is listed in the purveyor section since there is no sit-down area. This doesn't seem to bother half of Roanoke, which seems roughly the number of folks who line up to take these delicate meat-on-bun creations back to their office or, on nice days, to eat while resting on one of the nearby park benches.

Salem

Heartland Bread Co (540-387-4034; 30 W. Main St.) This national chain offers wonderful breads and rolls and assorted sweet baked goods. A yummy spot to stop.

Salem Donut (540-389-4938; 100 E. Fourth St.) You like doughnuts homemade? Tired of big brands in a box? Then this is the place for you. Leave the calorie counter at home.

THE MOUNTAIN COUNTIES

HIGHLAND COUNTY RESTAURANTS

Monterey

ROYAL PIZZA AND SUBS
540-468-3333.
Rtes. 220 and 250.
Open: Daily except Sun.
Price: Inexpensive.
Cuisine: Pizza/Deli.
Serving: L, D.
Credit Cards: MC, V.
Handicap Access: In dining area only.

Their sandwiches are popular and the subs substantial, but the pizza by the slice is a standout. They offer a choice of red sauce or white pizza with more than a dozen different possible toppings. Chewy crust, piquant (with oregano) sauce, and quality cheese make this a find — soul food for Italians in the Virginia mountains. This little restaurant (part of a gas station) becomes one of the town's social centers on Saturday evenings, complete with live music, and has been a mainstay of the community since the mid-1990s.

HIGH'S RESTAURANT
540-468-1600.
Main St.
Open: Daily 7–7.
Price: Inexpensive.
Cuisine: American Southern.
Serving: B, L, D.
Credit Cards: None.
Handicap Access: Limited.

This is a great spot for lunch or just for pie. High's serves up simple food — salads and sandwiches and a few entrées — except when it comes to dessert. Then the kitchen produces exceptional offerings that sound simple, but are raised to a level of elegance and delectable wonder. One of the best lemon meringue pies came from their kitchen — light meringue, dense tart filling, and nice crust.

The Formica tables were packed at lunch so I ate at the counter and the service was great. Save the inn across the street for a more elegant supper; if it's simple but good and surroundings don't count, mark this one with a star!

OTHER EATERIES

Other recommended eateries in Monterey are the restaurant and tavern at the **Highland Inn** (540-468-2143, 888-INN-INVA; www.highland-inn.com; highinn @cdw.com; Main St.). The inn is open to the public for dinner and Sunday brunch only, and I was not able to sample a meal here. But every local person and many of the other nearby innkeepers recommended it as a great place for dinner. Chef Lisa Jamison's offerings are tantalizing. The inn's **Monterey Dining Room** and **Black Sheep Tavern** (casual dining on Thursday nights and Friday and Saturday lunch from 11:30–2) serve food from the same kitchen. The buffet nights are a local favorite. The à la carte menu includes crab-stuffed mushrooms, "pride of the mountains" steak, cilantro lime chicken, and Highland County rainbow trout among the dinner offerings. The luncheon menu at the tavern is pretty much soup, salads, and sandwiches, moderately priced. Desserts feature maple pecan pie (this is maple syrup country!) and tollhouse pie. Small but select wine list with Virginia and California wines both well-represented.

BATH COUNTY RESTAURANTS

Hot Springs

ELLIOTT'S RESTAURANT
540-839-3663.
Main St.
Open: Tues.–Sat 11:30–2;
  Tues.–Thurs. 5:30–9,
  Fri.–Sat 5:30–9:30; closed
  Sun. and Mon.
Price: Moderate to
  Expensive.
Cuisine: American.
Serving: L, D.
Credit Cards: MC, V.
Handicap Access: Yes.

Karen Diamond, area resident and a fan of good dining, highly recommends this restaurant. It's easy to find Elliott's — anyone can tell you where it is despite the town's lack of street addresses. What's more difficult is getting a table (be sure to reserve on a weekend) and making your choices from their incredibly delightful menu.

The Elliotts hail from California and they have brought their California flair with veggies and light foods to Virginia. Lunch can begin with a bruschetta of sun-dried tomatoes and Gruyere cheese or a salad of mixed greens with bacon shiitake vinaigrette. For an entrée, try prawns with scallions, a sandwich of grilled portabella or turkey on ciabatta, or a crab cake sandwich with asagio cheese. Desserts often include lemon cheesecake or a raspberry and lemon sorbet, and there are even more choices at dinner.

Dinner can begin with flatbread and pesto or crab cakes and a puff pastry filled with three different mushrooms (portabella, oyster, and shiitake). Salad lovers can order spinach salad with sautéed pears and walnuts. Other choices include sea bass or grilled pepper beef. Portabella mushroom lasagna fulfills their claim of care for vegetarians, while oven-roasted duck breast with port wine reduction and sun-dried cherry and apple chutney fulfills the promise of "something that uses Virginia ingredients, but with a Western flair." The wine list also includes local selections.

OTHER EATERIES

Also in Hot Springs you will want to try **Sam Snead's Tavern** and the other eateries of **The Homestead** resort (540-839-7989; www.thehomestead.com; Hot Springs).

For a number of years, Sam Snead's Tavern has also been a part of The Homestead. We have listed it separately because it is outside of the hotel complex and because of its great golfing décor and associations. All those who struggle with the small dimpled ball will want to take at least a drink if not a lunch here. Its paneled walls, golf ambience, and fine food (especially the trout almandine) make this a popular place.

Of course the big gorilla of restaurants in Hot Springs is the complex of eateries in The Homestead. And if you're staying there, you're probably staying on the American Plan (all meals included) or the Modified American Plan (breakfast and dinner), which doesn't leave much room for eating out. But who needs to? The Homestead's food has been celebrated as one of its assets since the resort opened in the 19th century, and there are a large number of dining options there to suit the moods and whims of its guests. These are: **Café Albert, Cascades Club, The Mountain Lodge Restaurant**, **Casino Club Restaurant**, the main **Dining Room**, **1766 Grille**, and the **Player Pub**. Each one has a different personality and menu, and can be previewed on The Homestead Web site or by calling the resort.

Warm Springs

WATERWHEEL RESTAURANT
Inn at Gristmill Square
540-839-2231.
Rte. 619.
Open: Daily 6–9pm.
Price: Expensive.
Cuisine: American and Virginia specialties with Continental touches.
Serving: D.
Credit Cards: D, MC, V.
Handicap Access: Yes in dining room, no to wine cellar and rest room.

Dinner at the Waterwheel Restaurant — the restored gristmill portion of the inn complex — is open to all, and many locals and guests of other inns drive here for dinner. Though there is more than one seating on weekends, be sure to make reservations, even on a weeknight and especially in leaf season. The tiny **Simon Kenton Pub** provides shelter and libations to those waiting for their table.

Seasonal offerings dominate the menu. Trout, since it comes from a local fish farm, is almost always available. Pecan-encrusted trout is a specialty, as is duck in a lovely tart cherry sauce. Accompanying vegetables are carefully selected and artfully prepared. Desserts also feature local produce, often in the form of cobblers.

The long wine list includes selections from many local wineries. The restaurant has an interesting tradition of allowing guests to hop down the two little steps and rummage about in the wine cellar themselves! The bottles are stored in various well-labeled nooks and crannies beneath the old wheel in what was once the mechanical room of the mill.

The ambience of distant tables, many in little nooks (some near a fireplace) makes this a prime locale for a romantic dinner. Service is superb.

ALLEGHANY COUNTY RESTAURANTS

Clifton Forge

Whether you take the train or come by car, Clifton Forge, home of the C&O archives, is a wonderful spot to visit. The downtown is not large, but there are several lovely shops and places to eat. Locals recommended Victor's for pizza, subs, or an Italian dinner, Michel Café for a nice French dinner, and the Club Car for a great lunch. Since lunch was what we sought, we went to the Club Car.

CLUB CAR SHOP AND DELI
540-862-0777.
clubcarva@aol.com.
525 Main St.
Open: Daily except Sun.
Price: Inexpensive.
Cuisine: Deli.
Serving: L.
Credit Cards: AE, D, MC, V.
Handicap Access: Yes.

The Club Car serves delightful sandwiches made with Boar's Head deli meats, a sign of top quality, on fresh, crusty rolls. Patrons order food at the counter and they bring it to your small, garden-style table.

Pastries are rich, homemade, and worth every calorie! As for liquids, there are a great number of sodas, specialty coffees, and teas to choose from. They sell wine, but not for consuming in the deli.

The deli is also a food purveyor and vendor of a number of decorative kitchenware items ranging from pans to baskets to tea towels. Some of the unique kitchen items were the exact same or at least eerily similar to some I had seen at The Homestead's shops — but at almost half the price!

The Club Car is also happy to make up a gift basket of Virginia's Finest products or Big Fat Jerry's Seasoning, or enroll you in their coffee or tea of the month club should you so desire.

OTHER EATERIES

Other eateries of note in *Clifton Forge* include **Michel Café and French Restaurant** (540-862-4119; 424 E. Ridgeway), which was recommended as a romantic place for dinner, **Bella Pizza and Pasta** (540-862-4548; 418 East Ridgeway), and **Douthat Lakeview** at Douthat State Park (540-862-8111).

Covington

Cucci Pizzeria (540-962-3964; 566 E. Madison St.) They are closed on Sunday, but otherwise provide a good eating option if you happen to stop in Covington, a large industrial town with a small historic center. Good pizza at good prices.

MOUNTAIN COUNTY FOOD PURVEYORS

HIGHLAND COUNTY FOOD PURVEYORS

Bolar

Southernmost Maple Products (540-468-2682; Rte. 607, HCR 2, Box 380) Mike Puffenbarger says he operates the southernmost maple-tapping and sugar-making operation in the United States. Stop in to buy syrup and candy; during the festival times, you can watch them make it!

McDowell

Sugar Tree Country Store and Sugar House (540-396-3469; www.sugartree countrystore.com; sugartree@intelos.net; Rte. 250) Lots of maple products and candies. (See Chapter Seven, *Shopping.*)

Monterey

Highland County Market (540-468-1922; highcent@cfw.com; Spruce St.) Betty M. Mitchell is the director of the market, which meets at the community center and is open mid-Jun. through early Oct., Fri. 2–5. The list of what they sell is amazingly long and includes locally grown veggies, apples, plants, and flowers; homemade baked goods, including breads, cakes, and cookies; and homemade jams and jellies, candy, goat cheese, and barbecue sauce. This market even offers local meats, maple syrup, and barbecue. And for those who are looking for something just a bit different, you can shop here for locally produced dog biscuits. They also sell handmade soaps and crafts. The market is a highlight of the Hands & Harvest Festival on Columbus Day weekend and the Maple Festival on the second and third weekends in March.

Ginseng Mountain Farm and Store (540-474-3663; Rte. 220, six miles north of Monterey in Blue Grass) Honey, local maple syrup, and homemade hams and jellies are the goods that have this spot from Chapter Seven, *Shopping,* in this section as well. Owner Deborah Ellington also sells lamb during the fall. The sheepskin goods in the shop come from her own herd.

Virginia Trout Company (540-468-2280; Rte. 220, north of Monterey) Open

Mon.–Fri. 8–4, Sat.–Sun. 9–4. They hatch 'em and raise 'em so you can fish for your own or buy them frozen.

BATH COUNTY FOOD PURVEYORS

There are a number of fine delis and small markets in the area. To find a large market you need to drive to Covington. The **Duck-In Deli and Market** (540-839-3000; downtown Hot Springs) is a great place to pick up little items. For gourmet food, try the **Homestead Market** (540-839-7845; Hot Springs) just across from the spa parking lot. The market carries so many different gourmet chocolates it's impossible to list them all. Also, fine teas, wonderful lunch meats and cheeses, jellies and jams, and other fine items for snacks or to take home as gifts.

ALLEGHANY COUNTY FOOD PURVEYORS

The town of Covington is the home of the area's large chain supermarkets; you can locate them in the phone book. For special items, see the Club Car Shop and Deli in Clifton Forge listed under "Restaurants."

WINERIES

Joan Leotta

Shenandoah Valley is home to many award-winning wines.

A visit to the Shenandoah (or anywhere else in Virginia) would hardly be complete without a trip to at least one of the state's more than 80 farm wineries.

There are five wine-growing regions in the commonwealth of Virginia. As defined by the state's tourism office, the Shenandoah Valley touches wineries in the Shenandoah, Central, and tip of the Southwestern wine regions. Each region includes different microclimates, but many of the same varietals are grown all over the state.

Early efforts to produce wines in Virginia began almost as soon as the Jamestown settlers stepped off the boat in 1607. But even illustrious gardeners such as Thomas Jefferson, George Washington, and Philip Mazzei had trouble getting imported vines to take root and concluded that the future of American wine lay in American grapes. By the mid-1800s a small but fine Virginia wine industry was winning international awards with wines from the Norton grape, still grown in the state.

Virginia's vineyards were trampled and burned in the constant to and fro of both blue and gray during the Civil War. The economic and social climate of World War I, the Great Depression, Prohibition, and World War II further diminished wine production until, by 1950, only 15 Virginia acres were recorded in grape cultivation.

In the early '60s and '70s, as many dairy farms were being transformed into tract housing, interest in wine revived. Over the next 20 years, the wine industry exploded until, by the end of 2000, Virginia was the 11th-largest wine producer in the United States.

The *Virginia Wine Gazette,* a free newspaper produced by Cort Publishers in Rhode Island and the Virginia Wine Marketing Program (800-VA-VINES; www.virginiawines.org; PO Box 1163, Richmond, VA 23218), is available free at information centers and wineries. It carries reviews and articles on topics such as the bouquet of Viognier and new devotion to Riesling. Serious oenophiles will want to dip into other sources such as Faye Weems' new book, *Virginia Wineries: Your Complete Tour,* published by Richmond's Auburn Mills Ltd. For an in-depth study of the area's wineries, their history, and wines, you can turn to *Touring East Coast Wine Country* by Marguerite Thomas (Berkshire House, 2002). Thomas, a wine critic, interviews the vintners and offers a frank assessment of their products. Many Virginia wineries carry these publications.

Whatever your preference, when visiting wineries in the Shenandoah Valley, you will likely find these three things wherever you go: incredibly good wines, hospitable winery owners, and superb scenery.

VISITING THE WINERIES

Hospitality is still a treasured virtue in the Shenandoah, and winemakers are truly happy to welcome you to their property. Winery tours, tasting room visits, and on-site festivals are three of the most frequent activities at Virginia's wineries besides actually making and marketing the wine. Many wineries also offer their spectacular settings for rent for meetings, weddings, and other events. Most tours last from 30 to 40 minutes.

The tasting room experience is about a lot more than sampling wine. Especially in the smaller wineries, we often end up talking with the owner and winemaker, both of whom are usually great sources for restaurant information, tidbits about local shops, and even places to stay.

In addition to selling a nice array of wine paraphernalia, many tasting room gift shops are also outlets for local art and crafts (even homemade soap), as well as for local food products such as boutique cheese and local honey.

Free still outnumbers fee for tastings at most Valley wineries, but staff costs are forcing more to change. Our information is as up-to-date as possible. Opening days and hours vary widely from winery to winery. In general, the busiest touring season runs from April to October, and you can be *fairly* sure of finding even small winery owners at home and offering tours and tastings on weekends during those months. Larger wineries are usually open during the week as well, although many of even the largest close on Tuesdays. The best advice is to call ahead at all times, especially for the smaller vineyards. Always call ahead if you are a group of eight or more. And when calling, be alert that some area codes in the Charlottesville area (804) are in the throes of change.

You'll notice that the bunch-of-grapes road sign often points the way to wineries. But since wineries themselves have to pay for those signs, some don't place them, so don't think you're wrong if your directions are good but you don't see a sign. Wineries located on more winding back roads usually have them. There is a wonderful link on the Web site www.virginiawines.org that gives detailed maps of the small nests of roads around the wineries.

The wineries listed below are in the Shenandoah, within a short drive of the Valley, or just off one of the main roads you will likely be using to enter or exit the Valley. The inclusion of those outside of the strict geographic boundaries of this book is purely a personal choice. For a complete listing of wineries in the Valley, check the Virginia Wineries 2003 Festival and Tour Guide (www.virginia wines.org) and Marguerite Thomas' *Touring East Coast Wine Country.*

WINERIES

Afton Mountain Vineyard (540-456-8667; 234 Vineyard Lane, Afton, VA 22920) Open Mar.–Dec., Wed.–Mon. 10–5. Wines: Chardonnay, Gewürztraminer, Cabernet Sauvignon, Riesling, and Pinot Noir. No tasting fee. Snack items sold. Closed on major holidays. Other times, call. Inquire for large groups.

Chateau Morrisette (540-593-2865; www.thedogs.com; PO Box 766, Meadows of Dan, VA 24120; near Milepost 1717 on Blue Ridge Parkway) Tastings are $2 per person year-round, Mon.–Thurs. 10–5; Fri.–Sat. 10–6; Sun. 11–5. Closed Thanksgiving, Christmas, and Veterans Day. Wines available include Pinot Noir, Chardonnay, Vidal Blanc, and more.

Passport

The **Virginia Wine Marketing Board** promotes visits to wineries through its passport. Participating wineries stamp your passport for all visits during that calendar year. At the end of the year, return the stamped passport (a minimum number of stamps is required) to the Virginia Wine Marketing Office for a prize. Many of the Shenandoah wineries participate. To obtain a passport, call 800-828-4637 or download one from www.virginiawines.org.

Deer Meadow Vineyard (540-877-1919, 800-653-6632; dmeadow@shentel.net; 199 Vintage Ln., Winchester VA 22602) Mar.–Dec., Wed.–Sun. 11–5 or call for appointment. Wines for tasting include: Chardonnay, "Afternoon of the Fawn," Chambourcin, and "Golden Blush." No food. No tasting fee.

Fincastle Winery (540-591-9000; www.fincastlewine.com; 203 Maple Ridge Ln., Fincastle, VA 24090) This family winery owned by David Sawyer, Georgia Classey, and Richard Classey opened to the public in May 2003. Visitors are welcome Sat. and Sun. 1–6 and by appointment until the harvest time of Sept./Oct. or until they sell out of their current stock. They offer Cabernet Sauvignon, Chardonnay, and Cabernet Franc. There is no tasting fee and no food sold at the winery.

Guilford Ridge Vineyard (540-778-3853; 328 Running Pine Rd., Luray, VA 22835) Wines: Bordeaux and Beaujolais-style wines and a crisp white blend called Pinnacle. Stage, picnic grounds. Tasting fee is $3 per person. Reservations required; open only for groups of eight or more.

Hill Top Berry Farm & Winery (434-361-1266; www.hilltopberrywine.com; hill top1@intelos.net; 2800 Berry Hill Rd., Nellysford, VA 22958) Open Apr.–Jan., Wed.–Sun. 11–5. Call for other times. They specialize in fruit wines and are also open for picking your own fruit in season. No tasting fee. Some snacks.

Landwirt Winery LLC (540-833-6000; www.valleyva.com/landwirt.html; land wirt@shentel.net; 8223 Simmers Valley Rd., Harrisonburg, VA 22802) Open Apr.–Dec., 1–5 weekends only. Open other times by appointment. They offer Chardonnay, Riesling, Pinot Noir, Cabernet Sauvignon, and Cabernet Franc. No tasting fee. No food.

Linden Vineyards (540-364-1997; www.lindenvineyards.com; linden@crosslink .net; 3708 Harrels Corner Rd., Linden, VA 22642) Open Dec.–Mar., weekends 11–5; Apr.–Nov., Wed.–Sun. 11–5. No groups. Their wines include Chardonnay, Sauvignon Blanc, Bordeaux-type reds. No tasting fee. Some food items for sale.

Naked Mountain (540-364-1609; www.nakedmtn.com; PO Box 131, Markham, VA 22643) Tastings Jan.–Feb., weekends only 11–5; Mar.–Dec., Wed.–Sun. and selected Mon. holidays 11–5. Wines to taste are Chardonnay, Riesling, Sauvignon Blanc, Cabernet Sauvignon, and Cabernet Franc. No tasting fees except for groups over ten. Light fare.

North Mountain Vineyard and Winery (540-436-9463; www.northmountain-vineyard.com; wine@northmountainvineyard.com; 4374 Swartz Rd., Maurertown, VA 22644) Take Exit 291 off I-81. Open Mar.–Nov., Wed.–Sun. 11–5; Dec.–Feb., weekends 11–5. Closed Christmas and New Year's. Winery building is quite lovely — modeled after a European-style farmhouse. Wines to sample include Chardonnay, Riesling, Claret, Chambourcin, and Cabernet Sauvignon. No tasting fee. No food.

Oakencroft (434-296-4188; www.oakencroft.com; fwr@oakencroft.com; 1486 Oakencroft Ln., Charlottesville, VA 22901) Tours and tastings Mar. weekends 11–5; Apr.–Dec., daily 11–5. Wines to taste include Countryside White, Countryside Red, Chardonnay, Cabernet, and Merlot. Tasting fee is $1 per person, $3 per person to keep glass. No food.

Oasis (800-304-7656, 540-635-7627; www.oasiswine.com; oasiswine@aol.com; 14141 Hume Rd./Rte. 635, Hume, VA 22639) Tours and tastings year-round, daily 10–5. Closed Thanksgiving, Christmas, and New Year's. The winery also operates a gourmet restaurant on-site, offers catering, and has a large meeting space. In addition, Oasis conducts limousine and yacht tours of Virginia wine country. Wines that can be tasted at their location are two types of Chardonnay, Riesling, Gewürztraminer, two styles of Cabernet Sauvignon, Merlot, Meritage, and Brut Champagne. Fee is $3 per person, which includes a keepsake glass. Full restaurant.

Other Spirits

Whiskey lovers need not travel to Kentucky for a sample. The commonwealth's own legal brew, Copper Fox, made by former financial planner Rick Wasmund, is sold in state (ABC) liquor stores and can be sampled at the factory in Sperryville (540-987-8800; 7 River Ln., Sperryville, VA 22741). Call for tasting hours; they vary.

Peaks of Otter Winery (540-586-3707, www.peaksofotterwinery.com; appleseed @earthlink.net; 2122 Sheep Creek Rd., Bedford, VA 24523) Open Aug.–Nov., daily 8-5. Other times by appointment. Fruit wines take center stage here — apple, berry, cherry, and peach, among others. Apple/chile pepper wine along with jellies, ciders, fruit butters, and an on-farm vacation rental also vie for visitor interest. No tasting fee. No food.

Rappahannock Cellars (540-635-9398; www.rappahannockcellars.com; 14437 Hume Rd., Huntly, VA 22640) Open daily 11:30–5, 11:30–6 on Sat. Wines on-site are Chardonnay, Cabernet Franc, Viognier, Cabernet Sauvignon, and Vidal Blanc. Tasting fee of $3 includes glass. Free tours. No food.

Rebec Vineyards (434-946-5168; www.rebecwinery.com; 2229 N. Amherst Hwy., Amherst, VA 24521). Tours daily 10–5. This five-acre winery, listed as a historic landmark, is known for its annual garlic festival as well as its wines. Wines offered include Chardonnay, Sweet Briar Rose, Landmark White, Autumn Glow, Sweet Sofia, Gewürztraminer, Riesling, Merlot, Viognier, and Pinto Noir. Tasting fee only for large groups. No food.

Shenandoah2000

The award-winning Rockbridge Vineyard offers tours and tastings to visitors year-round.

Rockbridge Vineyard (888-511-WINE, 540-377-6204; www.rockbridgewine.com; rocwine@cdf.com; 30 Hill View Ln., Raphine, VA 24472) Take Exit 205 off I-81. Open year-round, Wed.–Sun. 11–5 (except Thanksgiving and Dec, 24, 25, 31 and Jan. 1). Their wines come under two labels — DeSheil (their premiums) and Rockbridge. Types include Vignoles, Traminette, Vidal Blanc, De Chaunac, Chambourcin, Pinot Noir, White Riesling, Chardonnay, and Bordeaux Reds. No tasting fee. No food.

Rose River Vineyards and Trout Farm (540-923-4050; Rte 648, Syria, VA 22743) Open Apr.–Nov., weekends 11–5. In addition to the wines, you can design your own label and roam their 177 acres, including trout pond. (Trout farm and pond open Mar.-Oct., weekends only.) Wines of the house include Cabernet Sauvignon, Chardonnay, Riesling, Mountain Peach, Mountain Pear, and Mead. No tasting fee. No food.

Sharp Rock Vineyards (540-987-9700; www.sharprock.com; darmor@sharprock .com; 5 Sharp Rock Rd., Sperryville, VA 22740) Tastings Mar.–Dec., Fri.–Sun.

afternoons until 5 and by appointment. B&B on-site. The wine list here includes Sauvignon Blanc, Chardonnay, Cabernet Franc, Malbec, and Cabernet Sauvignon. Tasting fee $2. Light fare available.

Shenandoah Vineyards (540-984-8699; www.shentel.net/shenvine; shenvine @shentel.net; 3659 S. Ox Rd., Edinburg, VA 2824) Take Exit 279 off I-81. Tastings daily 10–6 (10–5 Dec.–Feb.) Closed Thanksgiving, Christmas, and New Year's. Their wine list includes Cabernet Sauvignon, Merlot, Chardonnay, Riesling, and Chambourcin. No tasting fee. Light fare available.

Smokehouse (540-987-3194; www.smokehousewinerybnb.com; smokehouse@ tidalwave.net; 10 Ashby Rd., Sperryville, VA 22740) Tastings and tours Feb.–Dec., weekends 12–6. Closed Thanksgiving and Christmas. Otherwise call for appointment. No fee. Sells sandwiches, light lunch. This is the place to try that medieval specialty, mead. They also make and sell English-style hard ciders and other unusual Old World historic beverages. The 19th-century log cabin on-site also functions as a B&B. The tasting room is fun just to see — it has a thatched roof.

Spotted Tavern Winery/Dodds Cider Mill (540-752-4453; Rte. 612/Hartwood Rd., PO Box 175, Hartwood, VA 22471) Tours and tastings Apr.–Dec., weekends 12–4. Other times call for appointment. This is Virginia's only winery and cider mill. They use an antique cider press. Their wines include Stonehouse White, Dodd Brothers Sparkling Cider, and Moonbeam Virginia Hard Cider.

Valhalla (540-725-WINE; valhallawines.com; Valhalla@AOL.com; 6500 Mt. Chestnut Rd., Roanoke, VA 24018) Open early Apr.–mid-Dec., Sat. 12–5, Sun. 1–5. Wines are aged in a cave 60 feet underground. They include Syrah, Viognier, Cabernet Sauvignon, Merlot, and Sangiovese. Tasting fee is $2 per person, includes glass. No food.

Veritas (540-456-8000; www.veritaswines.com; 145 Saddleback Farm, Afton, VA 22920) Open Wed.–Sun. 10–6 (10–5 in Nov., Dec.) and by appointment. This is a place to try Cabernet Fran, Merlot, Traminette, and Chardonnay.

White Hall Vineyards (434-823-8615; www.whitehallvineyards.com; Sugar Ridge Rd., White Hall, VA 22987) Their wines include Pinot Gris, Soliterre, Gewürztraminer, Cabernet Franc, Cabernet Sauvignon, Merlot, and Chardonnay. No fee. No food.

Wintergreen Winery (434-361-2519; www.wintergreenwinery.com; 462 Winery Ln., PO Box 648, Nellysford, VA 22958) Near Wintergreen Resort, on the site of historic Highview Plantation. Winery and gift shop open Apr.–Oct., daily 10–6; Nov.–Mar., daily 10–5 except for Thanksgiving, Christmas, and New Year's Day. They offer their signature Black Rock Chardonnay, Chardonnay, Three Ridges White, Thomas Nelson White, Cabernet Sauvignon, Riesling, Blush, and a raspberry dessert wine. No fee. No food.

CHAPTER SEVEN
It's in the Bag
SHOPPING

The Valley is a great place to find hand-crafted items.

When the going gets tough . . . the tough, the tender, and anyone who enjoys browsing and buying head for the Shenandoah. It's a great place to discover unique antiques, quality crafts, traditional pottery, furniture, metalwork, and fine art.

Even the most ardent minimalist will find it hard to escape the Valley with only photos, and long after the suitcases have been unpacked, Shenandoah souvenirs will remind visitors of the beauty of the land and the skill of its artisans.

Some of the best antique hunting can be done along Route 11 and Interstate 81, also known as Antique Alley, but that's certainly not the only shopping pastime in the area. Those spectacular mountain sunsets and river sunrises attract many talented artists, and potters turn out exhibit-quality vases, plates, bowls, and more. A lot of fine furniture is made in the Valley, too, especially around Harrisonburg.

While the area's spectacular beauty inspires its artists, the intellectual life of the Valley blooms at its many colleges and universities, and they in turn provide live-in customers for the wonderful (non-chain!) bookstores of the area.

Please note that this is not an exhaustive list of places to shop, just my picks. One of the joys of travel in the Shenandoah is the constant uncovering of new and exciting places. Let us know when you discover something spectacular that we haven't included here.

PLANNING YOUR SHOPPING SPREE

This section is arranged geographically, county by county, subdivided into Web sites, malls, and then an alphabetic list of flea markets and individual stores, including antique shops, specialty stores, and galleries.

Most Valley merchants will accept major credit cards and some even take personal checks, though flea markets may be cash only.

Unless stated otherwise, stores in the Valley are open from 10 to 5 weekdays and from 11 to 4 on Saturdays. Sunday openings are another story. Stores that are not located in malls may not open at all on Sunday, even in Roanoke. If you're really counting on visiting a certain store, phone ahead, especially on Sundays. During winter, call ahead even on weekdays. In the low tourist times, many stores are closed on Monday, and some take Tuesday off as well.

Flea markets are a weekend tradition turned into an art form here. Their goods come in varying degrees of usability, from nearly perfect to almost falling apart. Bargaining is often a valuable tool. Most are open only on weekends — which may or may not mean Friday, depending on the market. Some of the flea markets do not have contact numbers, and for those you can call the local tourism office. (See Chapter 8, *Information*, for numbers.)

FREDERICK, CLARKE, AND WARREN COUNTIES

Winchester

First Friday, held the first Friday of each month except January and May, is a special time for shoppers and other revelers in old town Winchester. Even the art galleries stay open until 9, and refreshments and live music can be found at venues throughout the walking-friendly downtown.

WEB SHOPPING

www.visitwinchesterva.com/shopping/shp_town.htm.
www.antiqueinfo.com/states/virginia/winchester.htm.
www.svfleamarket.com/directions.htm.
www.americanantiquities.com/shenandoah.html.
www.winchesterva.com/antiques.html.

MALLS

Apple Blossom Mall (540-665-0201; www.shopsimon.com; 1850 Apple Blossom Dr.; I-81 to Rte. 50) Anchor stores include JCPenney, Sears, and Belk's, a Southern-based department store with a nice line of clothing and more. There are 80 specialty stores, a six-screen movie house, a children's play area, a food court, and several chain restaurants.

Creekside Village (1712 Handley Ave., south of Winchester in Kernstown) This mall is located on Rte. 11, almost next to one of the battlefield sites. Creekside offers a variety of specialty stores and businesses, including clothing and collectible shops. Store hours vary.

Delco Plaza (540-662-6778; 170-S Delco Plaza; corner of Millwood Pike and Rte. 522, between Front Royal and Winchester) Food Lion, Big-Lots, Jo-Ann Fabrics, a fitness center, dry cleaner, a movie theater, video store, and hair salon.

Millwood Crossing (540-662-5157; 381 Millwood Ave.) This mall offers antique stores specializing in furniture, pottery, glass, toys and dolls, books, quilts, and more. Special focus on Country French furniture. The mall itself is a destination to see since it was once an apple-packing house. A Civil War dressmaker is located here, too.

Valley Avenue Flea Market and Consignment (540-722-6768; 1000 Valley Ave., Winchester) Be sure to save time to shuffle through the items here, particularly the ever-changing consignment pieces.

SHOPS

Blind Faith (540-678-1140; www.blindfaithent.com; 148 Loudoun St.) Choose from more than 500 kinds of acoustic or electric guitars, the most in Winchester, according to owner Tony Cobberly. This shop is also a regular entertainment venue for First Fridays.

Dancing Fire Gallery (540-722-2610; 15 E. Boscawen St.) They sell both built and wheel pottery along with unusual crafts, many local. Potter/owner Leslie Malone teaches classes and sells her own work here as well. Especially fun to visit on First Fridays, when Malone often coordinates food, entertainment, and product offers.

The Doll Boutique (540-667-8835; 33 S. Loudoun St.) If you collect dolls, you'll want to stop here.

The Door Mouse (540-722-0746; 11 N. Loudoun St.) A fun place to shop for unique children's gifts and clothing.

Gallery One Creative Framing and Art (540-662-0233; gallery1@shentel.net; 19 E. Boscawen St.) High-quality framing and the work of local artists, including Jim Holmes and Don Black.

Jubilee Gallery (540-662-2210; 15 Indian Alley) This wonderful shop features the work of artist-owner Bill Whiting and others. Trompe l'oeil paintings on the alley wall guide you to its doors. Hours vary, so call first.

Joan Leotta

This trompe d'oeil riding stable on the outside of a building entertains shoppers in downtown Winchester.

Joanne Happ Gallery (540-678-5525; 135 N. Loudoun St.) Open Thurs.–Sat. 10–4 or by appointment. Happ is described as a realist — the detail in her work is photographic. Oil paintings and prints are available here and many other places around town.

Kimberly's Gifts & Fine Linens (540-662-2195; 135 N. Braddock St.) I admit a weakness for linens, but who wouldn't want to relax on sheets that begin at a 206 thread count and go up to 1,000? European and American linens of the finest quality.

Knit 1 Perl 2 (540-662-6098; 29 W. Boscawen St.) Open Wed.–Fri. 10:30–4:30, Sat. 10:30–1:30. Knitting fans will want to stop at this one — lots of good supplies.

National Wildlife Catalog Outlet (540-535-0801; 2039 S. Pleasant Valley) Open Mon.–Fri. 9–9, Sat. 9–7, Sun. 11–5. If you like animal and bird motifs (and bargains), you must stop at this gem of an outlet.

Old Town Stained Glass Gallery (540-667-9560; 161 N. Loudoun St.) Stained glass and pretty custom creations, plus lessons and supplies to make your own.

Rainbow's End Used Books (540-665-0334; 9 W. Boscawen St.) This sliver of a store often spills out onto the sidewalk with a display of special bargain books. Stack upon stack to delight bibliophiles of many interests.

Shenandoah Arts Council (540-667-5166; 2 Cameron St.) This arts management organization gives grants and sells work by local artists on-site.

Stone Soup Gallery (540-722-3976, 877-722-3976; 107 N. Loudoun St.) This restored house calls itself a showcase of talent. I found the historic building a great place to browse for antiques, survey original pottery by owner Debra Johnson, and peruse Civil War artifacts. British House of Iron accessories and other quality gift items also await.

Wilkins Shoe Center (540-667-5600, 888-737-5967; www.wilkinshoe.com; 7 S. Loudoun St.) Open Mon.–Thurs. 9:30–6, Fri. 9:30–8, Sat. 10:30–5. This is the Nordstrom of the Shenandoah! More than 30,000 shoes in many sizes. They tend to the classic and are hard to beat for fit.

Winchester Antiques and Collectibles (540-667-7411; 1815 S. Loudoun St.) Nice collections and selections. Many antique linens and glass for sale on last few visits. The selection shifts with time.

Winchester Book Gallery (540-667-3444; www.winchesterbookgallery.com; bookgall@shentel.net; 185 N. Loudoun St.) Two floors of books and book-related gift items. The store has an especially nice selection of children's books and Civil War material, including a lot of local Civil War history. Owners Shannon Gemma and Allison Major also have created a special section featuring works of former area resident Willa Cather.

Linden

The Apple House (540-635-2118, 800-462-1867; 4675 John Marshall Hwy.) Between Winchester and Front Royal, I-66 Exit 13, just into Warren County. This is where Alpenglow cider was invented. Soft and hard varieties here and a huge selection of apple-themed gifts.

Berryville

Gold Leaf, Ltd. (540-955-0383; GoldLeaf@shentel.net; 26 E. Main St.) This retail gift shop carries a wide variety of collectibles, including Fenton Art Glass, BRIO toys, and cast-iron doorstops. Best of all, the second-floor Christmas shop is open year-round.

Mrs. White's Quilt Shop (540-955-2383; 35 E. Main St.) A fun store with quilts of all sizes and lots of quilted items for the house.

Front Royal

WEB SHOPPING

www.ci.front-royal.va.us/shopping.htm.

SHOPS

Blue Ridge Arts and Crafts Council (540-635-9909; www.blueridgearts.org; 301 E. Main St.) A place to shop and view some of the area's best art. Particularly good for pottery, sculpture, and paintings.

Fretwell's Café and Gift Shop (540-622-6066; 205 E. Main St.) Open Mon., Wed.–Fri. 11–9, Sat. 9–9, Sun. 10–5. A place to sustain both body and kitchen — lots of delicious things to eat and stylish culinary items. Shenandoah-made skin care products and birdhouses share shelf space with national-brand collectibles such as Boyds Bears.

Front Royal Antiques and Flea Market (Rte. 522 Bypass between Quality Inn and Rte. 55) An outdoor venue with more than 100 booths. Open Saturday, Sunday, and holidays spring–fall. More great browsing.

Goldsmith's Fine Jewelry (540-636-2935; 218 E. Main St.) Antique and estate jewelry. The window display is often filled with a tantalizing selection.

Heaven Sent Shoppe (540-622-2060; 216 E. Main St.) Gifts, Bibles, and religious books plus Amish crafts, furniture, and food items. Fresh fudge and homemade ice cream in season.

Indoor Flea Market (540-635-5827; www.warrencountyfair.com; Warren County Fairgrounds, a short drive from downtown) Open Sat.–Sun. 9–5, except Aug., when fair is in residence. Lots and lots of "stuff." Great browsing.

Middle of Main Antique Emporium (540-636.7787; www.midmain.com; 213 E. Main St.) Lots of dealers under one roof — biggest in the Old Town area. It might take a while to find what you want, but you also might find a treasure you didn't know you wanted until you saw it here.

Mountain Mystic Trading Company (540-635-6318; 215 South St.) If you were a child of the '60s you'll recognize the selection in this store. Novelties, crafts, and lots of candles.

Royal Oak Bookshop (540-635-7070; 207 S. Royal Ave.) Collectible volumes and more for the book enthusiast. A short drive from the downtown area, but it's worth the trip.

Shen-Valley Flea Market at Double Tollgate (540-869-7858; www.svfleamarket .com; Rte. 522 just north of Rte. 340/Rte. 277 intersection) Open year-round, Sat.–Sun. from 7am on. Calls itself the area's largest flea market. Free parking and a carnival atmosphere. Bargains and treasures of all sorts.

Tariq Oriental Rugs, Inc. (540-636-3566; www.tariqorientalrugs.com; 213 E. Main St.) You might not expect to find imported luxury carpets in the mountains of Virginia, but be happy they're here! Wonderful place to browse for exotic floor coverings. Knowledgeable staff.

Middletown

The Carpetbagger (540-869-7732, 888-840-1865; www.thecarpetbagger.com, sales@thecarpetbagger.com; 7805 Main St.) Period clothing and handmade 18th-century carpetbags by Bob Porter, a.k.a. "Bag Maker to the Stars."

Sperryville

Nearby **Sperryville** isn't really in the area covered by this book, but it's just over the line and easily reached. If you were a *Dukes of Hazard* fan, you'll want to go just a smidge out of your way to find **Cooter's Place** (888-414-7714; www.cootersplace.com; cootersplace@hotmail.com; 11691 Lee Hwy.). Nearby, the **Sperryville Emporium** (540-987-8235; www.enterit.com/sperryville8235/; 11669 Lee Hwy.) offers custom wood furniture and Virginia hams all in one place!

SHENANDOAH COUNTY

Strasburg

This used to be the center of pottery-making in the young United States. Now the town sells vintage pottery and vintage everything else.

Bygones (540-665-8900; Bygones22657@yahoo.com; 137 E. King St.) Antiques.

Shenandoah2000

The Great Strasburg Antique Emporium is an antique hunter's paradise — many vendors under one roof.

Civil War Relics (540-465-4090; 309 N. Massanutten St.) This is the place for bullets, belt buckles, buttons, books, prints, and other collectibles from the Civil War.

The Great Strasburg Antique Emporium (540-465-3711; 160 N. Massanutten St.) This was one of the first antique stores to offer many dealers under one roof. Prices are open to bargaining. I once saw someone buy four Limoges boxes for $20 each here. Lots of glass and Civil War-era photos, too.

Green Acres Antiques (540-465-4702; 131 N. Massanutten St.) Assorted antiques.

Heirloom Emporium (540-465-2627; 110 N. Massanutten St.) Assorted antiques.

Strazburg Mineral Gallery and Rock Haus (540-465-8777; www.multistone intl.com/special/visit.htm; 135 S. Holliday St.) Showroom hours Tues.–Fri. 10–6, Sat. 12–5. This is a wholesaler with retail sales in the showroom, so always call ahead to make sure the showroom is open. Equipment for rock hounds and a fantastic array of minerals and stones to buy. Also carries beads.

Sullivan's Country House Antiques (540-465-5192; 1395 John Marshall Hwy.) General antiques, including a lot of furniture.

Woodstock

Baskets of Distinction (540-459-4908; 521 N. Main St.) This is a great place to order baskets of Virginia products and find all sorts of interesting little gifts and craft items. It's here instead of under food because of the large number of gift items, but it was a close call!

Celia's Shop (540-984-8576; 23123 Senedo Rd.) Antiques are stacked about in a home-like fashion. Furniture for sale as well as small odds and ends. Just a short hop from downtown.

Jacklyn's Gifts and Collectibles (540-459-6385; 319 S. Main St.) Good selection for browsing. It's an items-stocked-to-the-rafters sort of organization.

Valley Treasures (540-459-2334; 660 N. Main St.) Open Mon.–Thurs. 10–6, Fri.–Sat. 10–8, Sun. 12–6. It seems small yet boasts of 75 booths. A great spot to browse or buy. Some of the booths hold merchandise in a "rougher" state.

Edinburg

Beyond the Moon (540-984-3634; 102 S. Main St.) If you don't find something among the old items, you might enjoy some of the modern collectibles or fine art on hand. Old stained glass and architectural antiques a specialty.

Edinburg Village Shops (540-984-9785; lyncrum@shentel.net; 127 S. Main St.) In a turn-of-the-century house one can browse a collection of pottery, prints, paintings, handcrafted furniture, and fabric accessories. Fine array of places to buy gifts — locally made art, crafts, and gift items from many sources.

Flea Market (Landfill Rd. just outside of town) A great place to find bargains. Fri.–Sun. 8–5.

Collecting: A Local Artist's Fame

One of the artists in the Edinburg Village Shops is local resident and potter Lynne Crumpacker (540-984-9785). Crumpacker's creations are a testament to the fact that beauty of form and function are not exclusive, and that inspiration comes from both necessity and the joy of nature.

"Sometimes I just create a piece because I need one and I feel that if I need it others probably do, too," she explains. That was the thought behind her narrow, window-ledge watering can, a favorite item in the store. Sometimes nature inspires first and the item follows. For instance, after years of watching sleek crows outside her kitchen window, Crumpacker finally found a function for their form in the shape of a toothpick holder.

Since 1989, on the occasion of Edinburg's annual Ole Time Festival (usually the third weekend in September), she creates a limited edition, signed, numbered, and dated pottery piece. Each year she keeps the "identity" and number of the items a secret. People start lining up before daybreak on the Saturday of the festival for a sale that begins at 9am and ends when the coveted pieces are gone. The early creations are showing up in auctions now, offering a chance for those who missed a year to fill in their collections.

Murray's Fly Shop (540-984-4212; www.murraysflyshop.com; murrays@shentel.net; 121 Main St.) Harry Murray is known throughout the Valley for his equipment and wisdom. You can visit the Web site and request a catalog if you can't get there in person. This is the place to go if you want fishing equipment and the lowdown on the best places to use it.

The Watchful Tiger (540-984-9600; www.thewatchfultiger.com; 201 N. Main St.) Bills itself as a purveyor of fine and fanciful fashion for feminine "fizzeek." Casual and elegant items share the same space — a lot of unique patterns, imported accessories, and batik. The best part: These unusual creations are available in sizes 6 through 24.

Mount Jackson

The Art Group (540-477-4131; tag@shentel.net; 5906 Main St.) Local, national, and international artists in a wide variety of media. Resident artists include a furniture painter, oil and watercolor artists, and photographers. The Art Group building has display windows fronting Rte. 11, the main street of Mount Jackson and the main thoroughfare of the Shenandoah Valley. Art classes available.

Flea Market (Fridays by the bridge on Rte. 11 just outside Mount Jackson) A very eclectic collection. This particular flea market is my favorite, thanks to the setting and the market "master," who will bargain on higher-priced goods but not on items under $5.

The Mount Jackson Art Group is one of many artists' cooperatives in the Valley.

Shenandoah2000

Nostalgia Mart (540-477-9709; 5946 Main St.) Large variety of used books and paper ephemera, but this spot is only open Fri.–Sun. 10–5 and closes Dec. through June.

S&L Past and Present Collectibles (540-477-3100; 5991 Main St.) Open Tues.–Thurs. 9:30–5, Fri.–Sat. 9:30–6, closed Mon. If you're hunting antiques during the week, try this shop.

New Market

Antiques by Burt Long (540-740-3777; PO Box 806, 3455 Old Valley Pike; Exit 264 off I-81 to Rte. 11) This has the added advantage of being only two miles from the exit, so you can shop easy-off/easy-on.

A Basket Case (888-757-4438, 540-740-4438; msnvder@shentel.net; 187 E. Lee Hwy.) This shop stays open until 7 daily and welcomes children, who will no doubt be attracted to many of its collectible animals. It's also a great place to shop for cards to go with those gifts. Located in a historic area.

Bedrooms of America (540-740-3512; 9386 Congress St.) Store and museum combination. Building was used by General Jubal Early as a headquarters during the Civil War. Room after room of bedroom furniture from the 17th century to the modern period alongside a great selection of dolls, gifts, furniture, and clocks for sale.

Luminations and Luxuries (540-740-9492; 9395 S. Congress St.) If you're a fan of fancy candles, you might want to stop here. They also carry homemade soaps.

Packrat Willy's Antiques & Collectibles (540-740-4300; packrat1@shentel.net; 9394 S. Congress St.) A large collection of china looms in the front window. This is a place to sort through — don't expect a quick in and out.

Paper Treasures (540-740-3135, 800-410-3135; www.papertreasuresbooks.com/left.html; rlewis1@rica.net; 9595 Congress St.) Open weekdays 10–6 or later, Sat.–Sun. until 8. Closed Thanksgiving, Christmas, and New Year's Day. This former car dealership is now a glass-front book emporium of the first quality. Probably one of the largest used bookstores in the Valley: Over 250,000 books and paper ephemera are neatly cataloged in row upon row of sheer bibliophile heaven! Seekers also can hunt online at www.abebooks.com/home/paper treasures. There is a fine collection of Civil War-related books and a large children's section. If you're selling items, call to make an appointment.

Timberville

Art Studio Pottery (540-896-4400; 346 Endless Caverns Rd.) Joan Cordner's hand-thrown luminaries financed her children's college educations. Her delicate colors and glazes on bowls and other pottery are worth the visit. In the charming log home that acts as studio, shop, and dwelling, Cordner also carries fine pottery crafted all over the state and elsewhere in the United States — mostly potters she knows personally. A good place to go for the unusual piece, including large entry-hall-sized items.

PAGE COUNTY

Luray

Bank Street Books (888-661-2665, 540-843-0690; 201 W. Main St.) Used and new books. Owner JoAnn Fargo, a former D.C.-area resident, has retreated to the beauty of the Luray area to apply her long years of urban library experience to a bookshop of her own. Nice selection. Open Friday and Saturday only. Bibliophiles can browse a small portion of the stock on other days at **A Moment to Remember** café at 55 E. Main St.

Bren's (540-743-9001; 24 E. Main St.) The first thing you notice upon entering is the huge display of Burt's Bees Products. These natural products are wonderful and not easy to find in stores. A large selection of the latest in Crabtree & Evelyn and estate jewelry as well.

Copper Kettle (540-743-6060; www.copper-kettle.com; 10 E. Main St.) Antiques, gifts, crafts, and work by local artists. They also have a large variety of seasonal produce and plants. Open Sundays.

First Forest Furniture and Millwork (540-743-2051; 15 Campbell St.) John Coleman, a master with fine woods, creates furniture from your fancy (or his) —

anything you want to serve your needs. His furniture-cum-sculpture is housed behind The Warehouse Art Center, right by the train tracks downtown.

Luray Antique Depot (540-743-1298; 49 E. Main St.) Open daily 11–5 or later. Great place to hunt for that special something. These folks go far for antique brass hardware and trunk fittings, and they also do art and frame restoration, lamp repairs, and cane seat replacement. The parking lot fills up with fruit and vegetable vendors in the summer.

Mill End Country Crafts (540-743-5653; www.lurayvirginia.com; stevek@shentel .net; 424 E. Main St.) Lots of Civil War prints.

Mountain Memories (540-743-7333; 4 E. Main St.) This shop is closed Tuesday and Wednesday, but if you catch it open you'll find furniture (including a great selection of metal-topped tables from the '30s), old jewelry, and dolls.

Trompe L'oeil Train Station

Local artist Jennifer Bradt (if you're lucky you might find some her work at **The Warehouse Art Center**; see below) is the town's very own muralist. I came upon her right behind the Visitor Center, where she was painting a wonderful mural of a train arriving at the Luray depot. Her work is popping up all over. A local girl who returned to town after attending art school in Columbus, Ohio, Bradt's talent is appreciated by many. Contact the Visitor Center (540-743-3915; 46 E. Main St.) if you want her to do a mural for you.

This N That (540-743-5810; 16-18 E. Main St.) An old variety store that now is a center for display cases full of links to the past. Each item has been carefully sorted and tagged, and things are displayed well. A huge selection of Depression glass and a wide selection of old comics, books, and toys were the highlights for me on a recent visit. The store is large enough to accommodate furniture and also has two walls full of oil paintings and prints. The paper selection is good, too — an entire display case full of tourist postcard packets, among other items.

Virginia Gift Shop (540-743-4022; 24 E. Main St.) Collectibles from many sources, lovely local craft items, Department 56 pieces, and modern jewelry are seamlessly integrated in the stock at Bren's (see above).

The Warehouse Art Center (540-843-0200; www.warehouseartcenter.com; dmayes@shentel.net; 15 Campbell St.) A changing array of art in a fun spot: a real warehouse by the tracks. Experimental and ultramodern art along with comforting views of nature and the mountains. Wide range of media — watercolors, sculpture, oils, acrylics, photography, and more.

Stanley and Shenandoah

Shenandoah General Store (540-652-2003; 119 Maryland Ave., Shenandoah) A place for gifts, crafts, and a variety of services — even dry cleaning and cell phone sales!

Stanley Gift Shop at Jordan Hollow Farm (540-778-2285; 326 Hawksbill Park Rd., Stanley) Tiny but unique. If you stop here, look over the collection of great horse-inspired items.

ROCKINGHAM COUNTY

Mauzy

This old stagecoach stop at Mauzy just over the border in Rockingham County has been converted into a delightful shopping destination.

Shenandoah2000

Shops at Mauzy (540-896-9867, 866-222-9173; www.mauzyshopping.com; 10559 N. Valley Pike) Just off I-81 at Exit 257, 12 miles north of Harrisonburg. Open Mon.–Sat. 10–6, Sun. 12–6. The building itself is worth stopping for. The large white structure, with its second-story porch, was an early-1800s stagecoach inn, then an ice house, and so on. The outbuildings on the property are fun to peruse as well. Everything from Civil War marbles (they were found under the cobblestones of Fredericksburg) to handmade local crafts and unique items from all over the world is for sale. But leave time to browse — the order of the items is not intuitive.

Harrisonburg/Dayton /Bridgewater

MALLS

Rolling Hills Antique Mall (540-433-8988; 779 Market St., Harrisonburg) Take Exit 247B off I-81, then head west on Rte. 33. Open Mon.–Sat. 10–6, Sun. 1–6. More than 50 dealers have set up in this location. Lots of paper goods and

Civil War items. Of special interest if you collect postcards — they claim to have 100,000. I know there were *a lot!*

Silver Lake Mill (540-879-3582; www.silverlakemill.com; outside Dayton) Take Exit 240 or 245 off I-81 to Silver Lake Rd. Open Thurs.–Sat. 10–5. You'll see the silo and know you're there. The mill offers ceramics, unique children's gifts, handmade furniture, stained glass, and unique gift items. The site also has a display of its mill history, from its founding in the 18th century until it was burned by Custer during the Civil War. The renovated mill is open for tours on Thursday and Friday.

Valley Mall (Rte. 33 E., Harrisonburg) This mall has 90 stores and a food court. Big stores include JCPenney, Leggett's, and Wal-Mart. Also has many national chain clothing stores that college kids enjoy. One unique shop is the Blue Ridge Nature Shop, which offers local art and Virginia-made products among its varied crafts.

SHOPS

Blue Ridge Pottery (800-826-4846; www.blueridgepottery.com; Rte. 33 E. 14 miles from Massanutten) Open daily except closed Mondays in March. This is the place to go if you want to see pot-making on a wheel, and to take a one-day class if you have time. Be advised: The ride from Massanutten is deceptively long. Those two miles past Skyline Drive aren't hard, but it takes a lot longer because you go up and over the mountains.

Changing Seasons Gift Shop (540-433-9627; 4090 Evelyn Byrd Ave., Harrisonburg) Look for a fine gift shop in the location of the old Shotsie's Christmas Attic.

Coin and Gift Shop (540-434-1938; 136 W. Elizabeth St., Harrisonburg) Antiques and collective jewelry, watches, and gold and silver coins are for sale in this shop right in the center of town. A lot of fun for browsing and a must for coin collectors.

Cupp Basket and Supply (540-289-5197; 9714 S. East Side Hwy., Elkton) Open Tues.–Thurs. and Sat. 9–12, Wed. and Fri. 9–5. Just outside of Harrisonburg is a superb homemade basket source. Cathy Cupp's workmanship is wonderful and she offers classes, too. The shop is also a good stop for those who like to make their own gift baskets.

Dayton Farmer's Market (540-879-3801; Rte. 42, Dayton) Just a few miles south of Harrisonburg. Open Thurs.–Sat. 9–6. Food, odd spices, and lots of crafts. Mennonite-baked goods and jams and jellies. Of the small stalls, two of my favorites are Early American Tin Lighting and a branch of the store called 10,000 Villages that has crafts from the Third World (www.villages.ca/). Shopping in this boutique chain provides income to folks living in substandard conditions. The products are first-rate and often unusual.

Gift and Thrift Shop (540-740-0300; 227 N. Main St., Harrisonburg) A true thrift shop with some unique jewelry and a branch of the 10,000 Villages store connected. Great spot to find unusual imported gifts.

Stop in at one of the many shops inside the Dayton Farmer's Market for wonderful cheese and meats, Mennonite baked goods,Virginia produce, and candies and spices by the ounce.

Shenandoah2000

Harper's Lawn Ornaments (540-434-8978; www.harperslawnornaments.com; Exit 251 off I-81 to Rte. 11 S.) Open Mon.–Sat. 8:30–5; also Sun. 1–5 May–Aug. This is the place in the Valley for those who like large ceramic people and animals on their lawn. Many more types and sizes than found elsewhere.

McHone Jewelry (540-433-1833; www.mchonejewelry.com; 75 S. Court Sq., Harrisonburg) Excellent selection of estate jewelry. The owner seems to have an eye for the unique.

Patchwork Plus (540-879-2505; www.sew200.com/patchworkplus; Rte. 42 S., Dayton) Open Mon.–Wed. 9–5, Thurs.–Sat. 9–6. Classes, supplies, and staff that can give knowledgeable help. If the quilt museum in Harrisonburg inspires you to take up the craft, you may want to come here to purchase the necessary items to get started.

Shenandoah Heritage Farmer's Market (Rte. 11 just south of Harrisonburg) Open Mon.–Fri. 10–6, Sat. 9–6. In addition to crafts and Mennonite jellies, this one has a Civil War memorabilia booth. Antique and Amish-made furniture, too.

Suter's Handcrafted Furniture (800-252-2131, 540-434-2131; www.suters.com; suters@suters.com; 2610 S. Main St., Harrisonburg) Solid cherry, mahogany, and walnut in many styles, all handcrafted. This is high-end furniture, well worth the visit if you're in the market.

Troy Miniature Shoppe (540-828-3983; 201 N. Main St., Bridgewater) This is one of the best sources in the Valley for dollhouse makers and other users of miniatures. Sells Twinkling Treasures hand-painted miniatures, among other items.

Mount Crawford (Between Harrisonburg and Staunton)

Green Valley Bookstore/Book Fair (800-385-0099, 540-434-0309; www.gvbook fair.com; 2192 Green Valley Ln.) Take Exit 240 off I-81, go east on Rte. 682 for

1.5 miles, look for Green Valley sign, turn left onto Rte. 681. Springs up like mushrooms after a rain — usually six times a year for two weeks each time. When they are open this is the largest bookstore on the East Coast. Mostly new books. Call or check Web site for schedule.

AUGUSTA COUNTY

Fisherville

Andre Viette Farm and Nursery (800-575-5538; www.viette.com; Rte. 608) Open Mon.–Sat. 9–5, Sun. 12–5 for a tour of the gardens or to shop. Call for a schedule of the free lectures and tours of the tremendous varieties grown here. My favorite time to visit is during the annual day lily festival. Various other flower varieties are feted throughout the year.

Quail Hill Herb Shoppe (540-941-8891; Rtes. 250 and 608) A place for serious herbalists, with high-quality medicinal herbs and homeopathic remedies.

Staunton

The shops in the Wharf historic district in Staunton include art galleries, wine boutiques, and antique stores.

Shenandoah2000

Staunton has five separate historic districts and two distinct (both wonderful) downtown shopping districts — **Beverley Street** and **The Wharf** (no water — it's a refurbished railroad depot). Both of these areas are also replete with restaurants. The Wharf shops are within a one-block radius of each other and only a few blocks from the Beverley Street area. The listing below is alphabetical.

Back Porch Potter (540-885-2323; 126 S. Lewis St.) Majolica pottery and many other eye-catching creations — very European in design. Call for hours and to see if the owner will be throwing when you're there. Very reasonable prices for unusual, whimsical pieces.

The Book Stack (540-885-2665; 1 E. Beverley St.) Nice selection of modern titles and a fair number of good used books. There are works by local authors and hard-to-find Civil War books as well.

Byers Street Housewares (540-887-1235; 12 Byers St.) Open Mon.–Sat. 9:30–6, Sun. 11–4. This store offers unique kitchen goods as well as traditional lines, a nice selection of Virginia taste treats, and a great supply of wine racks and wine paraphernalia. This is a serious kitchen store.

Celebrate (540-885-0300; 134 E. Beverley St.) Across from the Dixie Cinema and around the corner from a Shakespearean theater, this shop sells memorabilia related to the bard. Also offers wonderful gift items and a full array of party supplies ranging from kid-party basics to fine tea items.

Crown Jewelers (540-885-0653; 6 E. Beverley St.) Reproduction items, silver, silver plate, and pewter. Stop in and check out their "sparklies," new and old. The staff will take the time to discuss how a watch will look with a certain outfit or whether the gift is right for a baby or bride you know.

Once Upon A Time (540-885-6064; onceuptime@lycos.com; 25 W. Beverley St.) Open Mon.–Fri. 10–5 and by appointment. The windows of this shop draw you right in. Even if you're not a clock collector, it's hard to resist at least browsing in this shop, with its myriad takes on time. The shop also repairs European and American watches and clocks. Proprietors Dean and Irene Sarnelle are conscious of the unique nature of their talents in today's throwaway world and try to accommodate client needs.

Rachel's Quilt Patch (540-886-7728; www.rachelsquiltpatch.com; 40 Middlebrook Ave.) This is a great place to go if you're a quilter — for supplies, lessons, or to admire the work of masters. Various quilted household items abound as well. Rachel's also offers doll patterns and accepts online orders.

Rock Paper Scissors (540-886-4309; 110 E. Beverley St. B.) Open Tues.–Sat. 11–5. Goods include handmade jewelry, and paper and textile art. Definitely unique creations.

Staunton Station Pottery and Gifts (540-887-0011; 38 Middlebrook Ave.) This tiny Wharf-area shop is a nest of handmade pottery, including Leslie Moyer's designs. The shelves are also bedecked with clusters of collectibles, including Annalee dolls, nativity sets, Santas, and angels.

Sunspots by Designs in Copper (540-885-8557; www.sunspots.com; 202 S. Lewis St.) Open Mon.–Fri. 10–5:30, Sat. 9–5, Sun. 11:30–4. If you want to redecorate your garden, save time for this store. Metal and hand-blown glass bird feeders and suncatchers dominate the store, which has a large sales room. There are on-site demonstrations, as well as a choice of seconds for the artistic-minded on a budget.

Three Sisters (540-886-6488; 10 S. New St.) Open Mon.–Sat. 1–5. Upper-crust used clothing (Talbots, Dana Buchman, etc.) and jewelry. This place is fun! The antique jewelry is mostly good "junk" jewelry from the early and mid-20th century. Carve out some time for their hard-to-resist selections, including many earrings — clip-ons as well as posts.

Trains and Hobbies (540-885-6750; 123 W. Beverley St.) Antique trains, train motif gifts, and Lionel stock (both pre- and post-1969) share space with modern items such as Thomas the Tank Engine pieces in this tiny but popular shop. Magazines and items to build dioramas and scale layouts for trains are also sold here.

Trout Studios and Gallery (540-885-3208; 162 Greenville Ave.) Outside of the major shopping area, near Wright's Restaurant. The prices aren't cheap, but the creations are one-of-a-kind objects. These perfume bottles, vases, paperweights, and other objects of daily use will become some of your favorites.

The Wharf Antiques (540-885-5200; 14 Byers St.) Open Mon.–Tues. 11–5, Thurs.–Sat. 11–8, closed Wed., call first on Sun. Joseph Miska's good taste in what he selects is evident everywhere. The items change according to what he finds, but there is usually a little bit of everything to choose from.

White Swan Gallery (540-886-0522; 107 E. Beverley St.) A wonderful collection of sophisticated works done primarily by local artists — turned wooden bowls, pottery, watercolors, photographs, acrylics. Beware: Locals shop here too, and if you pass something up it may not be there when you go back. The store also stocks note cards by many of the featured artists.

Churchville

Chester Farms (877-ONE-WOOL; www.chesterfarms.com; 3581 Churchville Rd., Rte. 250) Lamb and sheepskin rugs and wool blankets. Festivals often held on the grounds — magnets for local crafters — and there are often discounts on the wool goods.

Verona

The Factory Antique Mall (540-248-1110; www.factoryantiques.com; 10 Lodge Ln.) This is one of those destination-shopping spots: furniture, Civil War-era items, books, pottery, glassware, and a lot more.

Waynesboro

MALL

Village Factory Outlets (540-949-5000; 601 Shenandoah Village Dr.) There were just a few outlets open when we visited; Levi and Dockers and Jones of New York were among those we saw.

Shops

Artisans Center of Virginia (540-946-3294; www.artisanscenterofvirginia.org; 601 Shenandoah Village Dr.) A wide range of juried traditional and contemporary craft by Virginia artists. Located next to the factory outlets.

P. Buckley Moss Museum (540-949-6473, 800-430-1320; 150 P. Buckley Moss Museum Dr.) Just south of Exit 94 off I-64. Open Mon.–Sat. 10–6, Sun. 12:30–5:30. Full selection of prints and original works available on the museum's lower level.

Rockfish Gap Outfitters (540-943-1461; www.rockfishgapoutfitters.com; 1461 E. Main St.) Before you set out to do any outdoor sport in this part of Virginia, check in with the Rockfish Gap folks — not just for equipment, but for know-how and tips.

Shenandoah2000

Creativity inspired by the beauty of the Valley is on display and for sale at Waynesboro's Shenandoah Valley Art Center.

Shenandoah Valley Art Center (540-949-7662; 600 W. Main St.) Fine local crafts — wood, pottery, metal, enamel, jewelry, housewares, and more. A different artist is featured each month.

Virginia Metalcrafters (540-949-9400; 1010 E. Main St.) Metalworking used to be practiced far and wide in the "furnaces" of the mountains. This is one of the few still practicing the old arts of the forge. You can watch the crafters at work from an upstairs window; just don't go at lunchtime (12–1). Those distinctive "W" Williamsburg hotplates are made here. Especially tempting are the seconds (hard to see why they were rejected) and discontinued items. Even first-quality items are discounted.

ROCKBRIDGE COUNTY

Raphine

Wade's Mill Kitchenware (540-348-1400; www.wadesmill.com; 55 Kennedy) Exit 205 off I-81, then west on Rte. 606. Open Apr.–mid-Dec., Wed.–Sat. 10–5; also open Sun. 1–5 in Apr., May, Sept.–Dec. Great kitchen goods imported from France. See listing under "Rockbridge County Food Purveyors" in Chapter Six as well.

Lexington

Lexington's downtown shops provide a wide variety of charming items from furniture and antiques to gifts, food items, art, books, and crafts. The area is also bustling with students and the shops that cater to them.

Artisans on Washington Street (540-464-3625; www.artisansinlex.com; 22 W. Washington St., Lexington) This place has handcrafted jewelry, pottery, and photography. Prices are very moderate for professional art. It is a cooperative, so the artists themselves take turns manning the gallery sales.

Artists in Cahoots (540-464-1146; www.artistsincahoots.com; 1 W. Washington St.) A cooperative of county artists, which means many of the artists are on-site sharing cash-register duties and talking to the customers about their art.

The Best Seller (540-463-4647; 29 W. Nelson St.) New, used, and children's books. Charming store, great selection.

The Bookery, Ltd. (540-464-3377; 107 W. Nelson St.) New and used books. Buy, sell, trade. Out-of-print searches and good selection of Civil War and local history books.

Cocoa Mill Chocolate Co. (540-464-8400; 115 W. Nelson St.) Wine-infused chocolates and truffles of all types are a specialty of the owners. Take them up on their offers to taste.

Francesca's Antiques (540-464-1400; www.francescas-antiques.com; 5 W. Nelson St.) Wonderful array of goods!

Fun Foods and Accessories (877-473-4433; www.funfoodsforyou.com; 13 S. Main St.) This is the place to shop for fancy wedding favors, parties, and student care packages.

Healthy Foods Market (540-463-6954; 110 W. Washington St.) Lexington's only juice bar and a wonderful place to buy herbs and spices by the ounce. Offers a variety of organic foods, goat's milk, homemade cheese, and free-range eggs. Homemade soaps and other products as well.

Lexington Antiques (540-463-9519; 25 W. Washington St.) This shop has the most interesting displays in its windows. Closed Sunday.

Pappagallo (540-463-5988; 23 N. Main St.) Classic ladies shoes, clothing, and accessories — very preppy, very stylish.

Reel Time Fly Fishing (540-462-6100; www.reeltimeflyfishing.com; 23 W. Washington St.) A great place to stop if you're interested in fishing.

Second Story Bookshop & Lexington Historical Shop (540-463-6264; 19 S. Randolph St.) New, used, and rare books. Good selection of Civil War books and local history here, too.

The Shenandoah Attic (540-464-8383, 800-483-4072; victorianparlour@shenan doahattic.com; 17 S. Main St.) This is the place to find Virginia-made products. I stocked up on the local honey, but you'll also find throws, pottery, Yankee Candles, gourmet foods, lighthouses, and other fun products.

Stonewall Jackson House Gift Shop (540-463-2552, 8 E. Washington St.) Framed prints, T-shirts, sweatshirts, postcards, and other special Lexington gifts. Great selection of books on the Civil War.

University Sportswear (540-464-3000; 15 W. Washington St.) Washington and Lee and VMI sportswear, gifts, and accessories. The place to buy gifts for alums and indulge in a little preppy sportswear for yourself.

The Victorian Parlour (540-464-8888, 800-483-4072; victorianparlour@shenan doah.attic.com; 23 S. Main St.) An abundance of Victoriana here — lace, tapestries, porcelain, crystal, and jewelry. Shop here for small birthday gifts, hostess gifts, and unique but elegant wedding and shower gifts.

Virginia Born & Bred (540-463-1832; 16 W. Washington St.) Fine gifts made in Virginia, gourmet food and wines, and custom-made gift baskets.

Outside of the city, try this venue for antique shopping:

Valley of Virginia Antiques (540-464-4138; www.antiquesvirginia.com, antiques va@rockbridge.net; 3459 Lee Hwy.) Rtes. 11 and 716, six miles north of Lexington. Check on the hours before you visit. More than 4,500 square feet of showroom space that includes furniture, linens, glassware, and even garden items.

Natural Bridge

Natural Bridge Gift Shop (540-291-2121; in the Natural Bridge gatehouse) Postcards, sportswear, and books featuring the Natural Bridge. Twelve miles south of downtown Lexington; take Rte. 11 south. The selection of tourist and gift items is wonderful.

ROANOKE COUNTY

Roanoke

As befits a town that has big-city elegance, small-town friendliness, and a lively historic center, Roanoke offers great antique shopping, several large malls with a variety of contemporary shops, plus other intriguing shops both downtown and just outside of town. This listing gives some general information on the malls and antique shops in the area, and lists a number of the more unique shops downtown and near downtown. If antiques are your interest, be sure to pick up the *Antique Dealer's Directory* at the visitors bureau (114 Market St.), check it out online at www.sundaydriver.com, or call 540-989-8328 and ask for the *I-81 Route 11 Corridor Guide*.

MALLS

Roanoke Antique Mall (540-344-0264; www.roanokeantiques.com; rmall1@ aol.com; 2302 Orange Ave. NE) Open Mon.–Sat. 1–6, Sun. 12–6. Variety, variety, variety! Everything from lamps to linens, buttons to toys, watches to whatchamacallits. At least one stall with antique books and maps.

Tanglewood Mall (703-989-4685; 4420-A Electric Rd. at Rtes. 419 and 220) Most stores open Mon.–Sat. 10–9, Sun. 1–6. There are 122 stores and a food court. One store to note here is Blue Ridge Mountain Sports Outdoors (540-774-4311), a local source for maps and other gear to get you into the mountains for hiking, water sports, etc. The New Mountain Mercantile features local arts and crafts and the To The Rescue Museum is inside the mall.

Towers Shopping Center (540-982-6791; 2235 Colonial Ave. SW) There are 11 places to eat in this mall, including a Baskin-Robbins and a bakery, Heartland Bread. Java the Hut and Wildflour Café are two other good places to eat. There is also a Kroger, photo stores, and jewelers.

Valley View Mall (540-563-4000; www.valleyviewmall.com; 4802 Valley View Blvd. at I-581 and Hershberger Rd.) Open Mon.–Sat. 10–9, Sun. 12–6. There are 111 stores in this mall, including Hecht's, JCPenney, Leggett's, and Sears.

SHOPS

B&D Comic Shop (540-342-6642; 802 Elm Ave. SW) This is a well-stocked place for collectors. Call ahead if you have items to sell.

Binaba (540-345-7064; 120 E. Campbell St.) African items imported from several countries — a wonderful selection that's moderately priced. Textiles and wonderfully decorated salad bowls, plates, and trays. Lots of items here for gift-giving and home décor.

Black Dog Salvage (540-343-6200; blackdog@rev.net; 1809-B Franklin Rd. NW) Located a mile from the center of town. Open Mon.–Sat. 9–5. Salvaged architecture open to the public, not just the trade. Haggle if you will — the occasional stained glass window and other wonderful details come in here and will give your home the charm of a historic building.

Blue Ribbon Boutique (540-345-3553; 208 Market St. SE) Basic gift shop but with lots of fun items — definitely a winner!

Cricket Creek (540-343-5309; 108 Market St. SE) More wonderful fun things to look at, bring home to friends, or use to decorate your home.

Farmer's Market (540-342-2028; Market Square) Booths of produce open Mon.–Sat. 7–5.

Gallery 108 (540-982-4278; 108 Market St.) Located within the Farmer's Market, but keeps more retail store hours. This is an artists' cooperative with wonderful pottery, etchings, jewelry, sculpture, oils, and acrylics. They also do framing.

Gift Niche (540-345-9900; 101 Market Sq. SE) Part of the market — small, but well-stocked with unique items.

Lee and Edwards Wine Merchants (540-343-3900; lande@rev.net; 309 S. Jefferson St.) A wide variety of wines from all over the world and tastings every Sat. from 11–6 and on the first Tuesday evening of each month. You can also join their wine or beer of the month club. (If you live out of state, check your local laws.) They also offer a beer tasting on the last Thursday of every month. Knowledgeable staff.

Orvis (540-345-3635; www.orvis.com; 19 Campbell Ave SE) Orvis' fine classic clothing for women and accessories to die for are in abundance here. A complete line of outdoor equipment also graces this store.

Paper Memories (540-774-1881; 3212 Brambleton) Great selection of used books and ephemera.

Science Museum Sales Shop (540-342-5725; 1 Market Sq. SW) Even if you don't stop at the science museum, you'll want to peruse their wide variety of items that help kids and adults explore the universe in a logical and lovely way. Closed Sun.

Too Many Books (540-985-6469; 1330 Grandin Rd. SW) Large selection of used and new books. A lot of history offerings, some collectibles.

Twists & Turns (540-345-0884; 129 Campbell Ave. SE) You can order custom designs in iron furniture, or choose from a number of "standard" designs in over 100 finishes. In addition to chairs, they make wrought iron and glass tables, tea carts, and many other items for home and garden. This is definitely furniture as art.

Wertz's Fine Gifts & Pottery (540-982-1192; 209 Market St. SE) The pottery is the best thing here. Be sure to stop by and check it out.

Salem

The downtown offers many possibilities, and Main Street is one giant antique emporium. The listings below are my favorites.

Antique Lamp Shop (540-389-3183; 1800 W. Main St.) The name says it all.

Auntie Em's Antiques & More (540-389-2294; 514 W. Main St.) Good variety of antiques.

Christopher Gladden, Bookseller (540-389-4892; 211 S. College Ave.) Antique books, maps, and other items.

The Gilded Lily (540-387-5096; 17 S. Broad St.) Antiques, including linens. Furniture and books, too.

Givens Books (540-986-1103; www.abebooks.com/home/chip53/; 1641 E. Main St.) Chip and Susan Givens stock about 35,000 used and new books at this location. Call if you have something to sell to them; buying is done by appointment.

Olde Salem Framing & Gallery (540-389-4553; 201 E. Main St.) Original art, prints, and framing.

Quilts and Crafts (540-387-0339; 208 E. Main St.) Collectibles and antique quilts.

Salem Market Antiques (540-389-8920; 1 W. Main St.) The wide selection makes this a good place to stop.

Virginia Showcase Antiques (540-387-5842; 4 E. Main St.) Antique toys and more.

Wright Place Antique Mall (540-389-8507; wrightpl@gateway.net; 27 W. Main St.) Lots of choices!

Vinton

This town enjoys a wide reputation for antiques. These are the two spots that rank highest on most lists for shoppers in the area:

Vinton Antique Mall (540-344-6847; 107 S. Pollard St.) A large selection of goods.

Walnut Avenue Antiques (540-342-5922; 6 Walnut Ave.) Great variety of items.

THE MOUNTAIN COUNTIES

HGHLAND COUNTY

McDowell

Sugar Tree Country Store and Sugar House (540-396-3469; www.sugartree countrystore.com; on main road, PO Box 19) The name of the store honors the original name of the town, Sugar Tree Grove, which was later changed to honor a popular governor. This store is a great place to shop and a fun place to watch the sugaring process (actual trees or sugar camps are a few miles away). The sap is brought in and processed in a small space during the Highland County Maple Festival. Most of the sugar camps do not demonstrate the process after the festival, but you can see the processing equipment here and at the Maple Museum. Be sure to ask which syrup is their own. Other gift items include wonderful pottery made by local potters and the owners' daughter.

Monterey

One of the things you notice here is the lack of street addresses. Folks get their mail at the post office — no need for addresses. Everyone knows where everything is, so just ask!

Field Books (540-468-3339; Main St.) Used and rare books, paper ephemera, stamps, and graphics. The Fields also do bookbinding and repair, but call ahead. When they're traveling or tired, the store is closed.

Gallery of Mountain Secrets (540-468-2020; Main St.) This is a wonderful place to stop and shop. Owned by the proprietors of the Cherry Hill Bed and Breakfast, this gallery has art and art-quality craft items made in the mountains and nearby. The watercolors, photography, and hand-turned wooden bowls are most tempting.

Ginseng Mountain Store (540-474-5137; U.S. Rte. 220, 6 miles north of Monterey in Blue Grass) Usual hours are Thurs.–Sun. 12–5:30, but be sure to call. They will often open to accommodate visitors if they have sufficient notice. The soft sheepskin rugs or covers are made from their own sheep. (They also sell whole and half lambs in the fall!) There are pottery gifts, wooden Christmas ornaments, and food items, including a homemade marinade. The owner is a potter, and her own work is sold along with that of other high-quality potters from around the Northeast. They have an array of delicate and beautiful beeswax Christmas ornaments, and some exquisite handmade wooden kitchen items.

BATH COUNTY

Millboro

Millboro General Store (540-997-9497; Main St.) This store was once a train depot. Now it's the definitive country store where locals play checkers on the front porch and an eclectic array of goods and services awaits within. This one has a game room and all sorts of handcrafted gifts and little food items.

Bacova

The famous Bacova mats and mailboxes are made here, but the factory is no longer open for tours.

Bacova Gallery (540-839-2399; Main St.) Open Thurs.–Sat. 10–5, longer in summer; call ahead. An old church now filled with art — this is not a place to seek out bargains. Some European works, and many 19th- and early 20th century artists. Mission and rustic furniture, too.

Warm Springs

Dean Cottage Den (540-839-3326; Rte. 645) Owner Jean Elliott puts together a sprightly collection of wonderful local art items and fantastic gifts from all over. This little gem is located just across from the Inn at Gristmill Square. Call to be sure it's open.

Warm Springs Gallery (540-839-2985; Rte. 645) Gordon and Barbara Ferguson own the gallery, which is an elegant sales venue for watercolors, pottery, prints, and jewelry, most by local artists.

Hot Springs

The Homestead (800-838-1766; www.thehomestead.com/welcome/ shopping.asp; see Chapter Five, *Lodging,* for primary information) is a world-class resort where shopping is a world-class activity. There are shops inside the hotel (**The Tower Corridor**), alongside the hotel (**Cottage Row**), and in the **Village** just outside the property. All of the merchandise is worthy of browsing and all items have price tags that reflect the high quality of the merchandise. The list of all shops is on the Web site above. Some of my favorites are listed below — I've left the rest for you to discover on your visit.

COTTAGE ROW:

Quilts Unlimited (540-839-5955) Handicrafts and quilts.

FiddleSticks (540-839-7420) Toys and an ice-cream parlor conveniently located next to The Homestead's KidsClub.

THE TOWER CORRIDOR:

1766 Shop (800-838-1777) All sorts of memorabilia of your stay at The Homestead.

The Classic Bath (800-838-1777) Each of the spa pools also has a gift shop. This one goes beyond — if you use it in a tub or shower, you will find it here!

The Homestead Collection (800-838-1777) You admired the furnishings at The Homestead? Then this is the place to determine if you want to buy reproductions of same to take home.

The Master's Gifts (540-839-GIFT; www.themastersgifts.com; Rte. 220) This shop, outside of the Homestead group, offers a wide variety of items, including some local crafts. Here you will find Williamsburg pottery, golf-themed gift items, and Virginia specialty foods.

Mustoe House Antiques and Gallery (540-839-2272; Rte. 2) Call ahead for hours since the gallery keeps a seasonal schedule. The building itself is interesting — an old log house that is now on the register of Virginia Historical

Landmarks. In 1998 its current owners took over and turned it into a show-place/shop for antiques, including architectural items and sporting antiques.

Pampillonia Jewelers (540-839-2832) Tiffany jewelry, clocks, and gifts.

Healing Springs

Healing Springs Antiques (540-839-2348; down Route 220 from Hot Springs) Call for an appointment to see their local primitive antiques and folk art collection.

ALLEGHANY COUNTY

Covington

The Accessory Place (540-962-5666; 916 Monroe Ave.) Open Mon., Tues., Thurs., Fri. 10–6, Sat. 10–2. Amish-made specialties and other items for the home.

Clifton Forge

MALL

Clifton Forge Antique Mall (540-862-7123; 528 Main St.) Open daily; call for hours. Lots of vendors of various antique specialties. Eclectic and fun!

SHOPS

Alleghany Highlands Arts and Crafts Center (540-862-4447; 439 E. Ridgeway St.) Open May–Dec., Mon. –Sat. 10:30–4:30, Sun. 12–4 closed Sun. and Mon. Jan.–Apr. This is a wonderful spot to buy crafts, watercolors, oils, acrylics, pottery, and woodwork done by some of the area's many artists.

Chesapeake and Ohio Historical Society (540-862-2210; 800-453-COHS; 312 W. Ridgeway St.) If you want train memorabilia, this is the place to stop. Basic business hours, but call ahead to be sure they'll be open for shopping or research.

Club Car (540-862-0777; 429 E. Ridgeway St.) Great kitchen accessories — some of the same brands as Homestead shops but for less.

Rosie's Collectibles (540-862-2999; 507 E. Ridgeway St.) Lots of items for collectors of various sorts. Antiques and crafts, too.

CHAPTER EIGHT

Helpful Hints
INFORMATION

Joan Leotta

Everywhere in the Shenandoah signs impart information on historic events. Here, at Fort Edward Johnson in Highland County, are Confederate breastworks. From this point you can see where the Battle of McDowell was fought.

We offer here a modest compendium of useful information, designed to make your stay in Shenandoah country as comfortable as can be. The following topics are covered:

Note: The information is given by county and counties are listed from north to south with mountain counties following. Information that covers more than one county, or is easier to use if presented alphabetically, will be so presented.

AMBULANCE/FIRE/POLICE

Dial **911** to request an ambulance, report a fire, or obtain help in an emergency anywhere in the area. If you need other, nonemergency information, call one of the numbers below.

VIRGINIA STATE POLICE

Clarke, Frederick, and Warren Counties: 540-662-3313.
Page and Shenandoah Counties: 540-743-5442.
Rockingham County: 540-434-8593.
Augusta County: 540-885-2142.
Botetourt and Rockbridge Counties: 540-291-2548.
Roanoke County (Cities of Roanoke and Salem): 540-375-9500, 800-542-5959.
Alleghany, Bath, and Highland Counties: 540-863-4416.

COUNTY SHERIFFS

Alleghany County: 540-965-1770.
Augusta County: 540-245-5333.
Bath County: 540-839-2375.
Botetourt County: 540-473-8230.
Clarke County: 540-955-1234.
Frederick County: 540-662-6162.
Highland County: 540-468-2210.
Page County: 540-743-6571.
Roanoke City: 540-853-2941.
Rockbridge County: 540-463-7328.
Rockingham County: 540-564-3800.
Shenandoah County: 540-459-6100.
Warren County: 540-635-4128.

CITY POLICE

Berryville: 540-955-3863.
Buena Vista: 540-261-6171.
Clifton Forge: 540-863-2513.
Covington: 540-962-2236.
Front Royal: 540-635-2111.
Harrisonburg: 540-434-2545.
Lexington: 540-462-3705.
Roanoke: 540-853-2203.
Salem: 540-375-3010.
Shenandoah: 540-652-8193.
Staunton: 540-332-3845.
Waynesboro: 540-942-6675.
Winchester: 540-665-5623.

AREA CODES

At press time, all of the Shenandoah Valley is in the **540** area code. In early 2003 some areas just outside the counties in this book changed. We have tried to include the updated area codes in all cases.

BOOKS ABOUT THE SHENANDOAH

The following is a select list of books about the Shenandoah Valley and Virginia, with particular emphasis on the Civil War.

Local bookstores have a number of small pamphlets on interesting aspects of life in the Valley, but there are also a number of books. Many can be found on the Web at www.shenvalleyweb.com/amazon.

HISTORY

Armstrong, Richard L. *Battle of McDowell.* H. E. Howard, 1990. A 121-page reissue of the original 900-plus-page volume on the topic. Good detail for Civil War buffs.

Clark, Champ. *Decoying the Yanks: Jackson's Valley Campaign.* Time Life Civil War Series, 1985. Hardcover, 176 pp.

Editors of Time Life Books. *Shenandoah 1862 (Voices of the Civil War, Vol. 10).* Time Life Books, 1998. Hardcover, 180 pp.

Eicher, David. J. *Civil War Battlefields: A Touring Guide.* Taylor Publishing Co.,

The Rockbridge County Courthouse is one of the places you might want to visit to do genealogical research.

Shenandoah2000

1995. Paperback, 228 pp. One entire chapter is devoted to the Valley. Very detailed information on the battles — an essential.

Hildebrand, John R. *Iron Horses in the Valley: The Valley and Shenandoah Valley Railroads, 1866-1882.* White Mane Publishing Co., 2000. Paperback, 160 pp. If you're a railroad buff, you may find this one indispensable — especially for its 24 pages of photos of old trains on two Virginia lines.

Krick, Robert K. *Conquering the Valley: Stonewall Jackson at Port Republic.* Louisiana State University Press, 2002. Paperback, 608 pp. Pricey at $25, but used copies of the older editions can be purchased for less than $10 and it is in libraries.

Martin, David G. *Jackson's Valley Campaign: November 1861 – June 1862.* Da Capo Press (Great Campaigns Series), 1988. Hardcover, 256 pp. Out of print, but available used and in libraries.

Tamer, Robert G. *Stonewall in the Valley: Thomas J. Stonewall Jackson's Shenandoah Valley Campaign, Spring 1862.* Stackpole Books, 2002. Paperback, 624 pp. This new edition is more than a reissue. It contains new insights as well.

Webb, Garrison. *Amazing Women of the Civil War.* Rutledge Hill Press, 1991. Paperback, 228 pp. An excellent section on Belle Boyd.

Wheeler, Richard. *Sherman's March: An Eyewitness Account.* HarperCollins (Harper Perennial Library), 1991. Paperback, 241 pp. Puts together a loose collection of eyewitness accounts. Fascinating and horrifying at the same time.

NATURE AND OTHER NONFICTION

Gildart, Bert, and Jane Gildart. *Hiking Shenandoah National Park.* Globe Pequot Press (Falcon Imprint), 1998. Paperback, 160 pp. Includes maps organized by the three park districts: north, central, and south.

Gupton, Oscar W., and Fred G. Swope. *Wildflowers of the Shenandoah Valley and Blue Ridge Mountains.* University of Virginia Press, reprint ed. 2002. Paperback, 224 pp.

Heatwole, John L. *Shenandoah Voices: Folklore, Legends, and Traditions of the Valley.* Howell Press, 1997 (2nd edition). Hardcover, 148 pp. Not strictly nonfiction — lots of fiction in this one, too. Very expensive, even on Amazon, but libraries own it.

Reeder, Carolyn, and Jack Reeder. *Shenandoah Heritage: The Story of the People Before the Park.* Potomac Appalachian Trail Club, 1995. Paperback, 87 pp.

Suter, Scott Hamilton. *Shenandoah Valley Folklife* (Folklife in the South Series). University Press of Mississippi, 1999. Paperback, 104 pp. Recipes, folklore, and more. A bit academic at times, but good.

BIOGRAPHY

Biographies of the major players — Belle Boyd, Stonewall Jackson, and Robert E. Lee — are plentiful and widely available through Barnes and Noble and Amazon, and at the sites that honor them. We can only touch on a handful here.

Boyd, Belle. *Belle Boyd in Camp and in Prison.* Louisiana State University Press, 1998. Paperback, 200 pp. Belle Boyd's memoir of her activities as a spy in the Shenandoah Valley during the Civil War, first published in 1865.

Farwell, Byron. *Robert E. Lee: A Biography.* W.W. Norton, hardcover ed. 1995, paperback ed. 1997, 472 pp.

————. *Stonewall: A Biography of General Thomas J. Jackson.* W.W. Norton, paperback ed. 1993, 448 pp.

Freeman, Douglas Southall. *Lee.* Scribner, paperback ed. 1997, 656 pp. A one-volume condensation of Freeman's definitive four-volume biography.

Morris, Roy, Jr. *Sheridan: The Life and Wars of General Phil Sheridan.* Vintage Books, 1993. Paperback, 464 pp.

Nolan, Alan M. *Lee Considered: Robert E. Lee and Civil War History.* University of North Carolina Press, hardcover ed. 1991, paperback ed. 1996, 231 pp.

Robertson, James I. *Stonewall Jackson: The Man, The Soldier, The Legend.* Simon & Schuster, hardcover ed. 1997, paperback ed. 1999, 998 pp. The gold standard among biographies of Jackson.

Scarborough, Ruth. *Belle Boyd: Siren of the South.* Mercer University Press, 1997. Paperback, 212 pp.

Sheridan, Philip. *Personal Memoirs of P.H. Sheridan: General United States Army.* Da Capo Press, 1993. Paperback, 986 pp. A two-volume CD-ROM version is also available from Digital Scanning, Inc. Both are very expensive.

Thomas, Emory M. *Robert E. Lee: A Biography.* W.W. Norton, hardcover ed. 1995, paperback ed. 1997, 472 pp.

Wittenberg, Eric J. *Glory Enough for All: Sheridan's Second Raid and the Battle of Trevilian Station.* Brassey's, 2001. Hardcover, 352 pp.

CLIMATE, WEATHER, & WHAT TO WEAR

The seasonal temperature variations in the Shenandoah depend on altitude as well as north-south orientation. In winter, the mountain ranges boast wonderful ski facilities, and snow can appear high or low, anywhere from Winchester to Roanoke. But you're much more likely to find snow and ice on the roads in winter in the northern and mountain counties than in the lower, more southerly counties. Carry a sweater at all times — and an umbrella. To obtain an accurate weather report for your Valley visit, go online to www.virginia.org /site/weather.asp. Roadside conditions are available by dialing 511, a Valley-wide information number.

The temperature variations along the almost 300-mile length of the Valley are most profound in spring and fall. If you were to drive from Winchester to Roanoke without stopping during spring, the progress of blooms would take you from early buds to full blossoms as you head south. Similarly, fall foliage colors begin at the northern heights of the mountains and in the cooler Frederick-Clarke County areas, and unfold more slowly and last longer as elevations decline and you progress south.

Cool days and cooler nights are typical in autumn. Cool mornings, warm afternoons, and cool evenings are typical in spring. Even in summer, hot days may have cool evenings. Beware of fog in the mountains at dusk and dawn from autumn through late spring and after heavy summer rains.

Summer is hot throughout, except for higher elevations, and humidity ranges from horrible to tolerable. The coolest spot in summer is underground — in the caves of the valley, where it is always around 50 degrees

Winter is not rugged in the valley; even the ski areas seem to enjoy gentle snows. But the damp cold can be pervasive, especially in the early morning and at night.

HOSPITALS AND OTHER EMERGENCY CARE

By dialing **911** you can obtain emergency medical care. For other, non-emergency help, contact a nearby hospital and ask for the name of a physician and/or the name and location of a nearby pharmacy. Call 800-422-8482 or 540-981-7641 for a **physician referral service** in the southern part of the Valley. The services listed below are listed strictly for your convenience, to provide a point of reference for each county. They are not recommendations for care.

Frederick, Clarke, and Warren Counties

Surgi-Center of Winchester (540-536-8934, 1860 Amherst St., Winchester; Urgent Care: 540-536-2232, 607 E. Jubal Early Dr., Winchester).
Warren Memorial Hospital (540-636-0300; 1000 N. Shenandoah Ave., Front Royal).

Shenandoah and Page Counties

Shenandoah Valley Health Services (540-459-2000; 762 S. Main St., Woodstock).
Page Memorial Hospital (540-743-4561; 200 Memorial Dr., Luray).

Rockingham County

Rockingham Memorial Hospital (540-433-4266; 235 Cantrell Ave., Harrisonburg).

Augusta County

Augusta Medical Center (540-332-4000, 540-932-4000, 800-932-0262; 96 Medical Dr., Fishersville) Serves Staunton and Fishersville.

Rockbridge County

Stonewall Jackson Hospital (540-462-1200; 1 Health Circle, Lexington).

Roanoke County (also serves Botetourt)

Roanoke Community Hospital (540-985-8000; 101 Elm Ave., Roanoke).
Roanoke Memorial Hospital (540-981-7000; Belleview at Jefferson St., Roanoke).

<u>*Salem*</u>

Lewis-Gale Medical Center (540-776-4000; www.lewis-gale.com; 1900 Electric Rd., Salem).

<u>*Mountain Counties (and Botetourt)*</u>

Alleghany Regional Hospital (540-862-6011; www.alleghanyregional.com; PO Box 7, Low Moor).
Bath County Community Hospital (540-839-7000; Rte. 220, PO Drawer Z, Hot Springs).
Highland Medical Center (540-468-3300; PO Box 490, Monterey).

INFORMATION FOR TRAVELERS WITH DISABILITIES

Virginia publishes *Virginia Travel Guide for Persons with Disabilities*. Call 800-742-3935 or TDD 804-371-0327 for a free copy. People with hearing impairment may access the toll-free number for a free guide by calling the relay service in their state.

Check out this and other brochures at www.virginia.org/site/main.asp?referrer=publications, or call 800-VISIT-VA. The Web site www.vadsa.org also offers information you will find helpful. Another good Web site for travelers with disabilities is www.access-able.com.

LATE-NIGHT FOOD AND FUEL

Many of the grocery chains in the Valley operate at least one 24-hour store. Check the local phone directory for a listing. The 24-hour **Kroger** and **Wal-Marts** are within a short drive of most of the cities in the Valley.

Gas stations up and down I-81 and I-64 are open late, many 24 hours to accommodate the flow of commercial traffic in the area.

On Skyline Drive, gas is available in season during the day at three locations: **Elkwallow Wayside** (mile 24.1), **Big Meadows Wayside** (mile 51), and **Loft Mountain Wayside** (mile 79.5). Otherwise, fuel up before you enter the park.

Most of the gas stations on the major roads have small-to-large food/snack areas as well as gas pumps. In the mountain counties, the concept of 24-hour service (except for towing and medical emergencies) is not much in evidence.

Most places close in the evening, so collect your snacks and put fuel in the car before you head in.

LIBRARIES

The Shenandoah region has many libraries, and most store materials for genealogical research. (Appointments are usually necessary to access the genealogical files.) Hours vary widely, and many of the smaller libraries are not open on Sundays or holidays. Be sure to call ahead if you plan to use a library for genealogical research.

Local tourism offices and chambers of commerce can provide information on smaller libraries. The listing below provides the phone number for the main library in a county/regional library system and its included areas. Call (or e-mail) the main library to see if there is a branch in the place you are visiting or, if you're doing research, where the records you're seeking are kept.

Frederick, Clarke, and Warren Counties

Shenandoah2000

The Handley Library in Winchester is a good place to search the area's genealogical records.

Handley Regional Library (540-662-9041; www.hrl.lib.state.va.us/handley; 100 W Piccadilly St., Winchester).

Clarke County

Clarke County Library (540-955-5144; 36 E. Main St., Berryville).

Warren County

Samuels Public Library (540-635-3153; www.shentel.net/library/samuels; 538 Villa Ave., Front Royal).

Shenandoah County

Shenandoah County Library (540-984-8200; www.shenandoah.co.lib.va.us; scl@shentel.net; 514 Stoney Creek Blvd., Edinburg) Serves Edinburg, Bayse, Orkney, Mount Jackson, Strasburg, and New Market.

Page County

Page County Public Library (540-743-6867; 100 Zerkel St., Luray).
Massanutten Regional Library (540-434-4475, 800-594-BOOK; www.mrlib.org; 174 S. Main St., Harrisonburg) Serves Rockingham County, too.

Augusta County

Augusta County Main Library (540-949-6354; www.lib.co.augusta.va.us; 1759 Jefferson Hwy., Fishersville).
Staunton Library (540-332-3902; 1 Churchville Ave., Staunton).

Rockbridge County

Rockbridge Regional Library (540-463-4324; www.rrlib.net; 138 S. Main St., Lexington) Serves Buena Vista, Lexington, Glasgow, Goshen, and Bath and Rockbridge Counties.

Botetourt County

Botetourt County Library (540-473-8339; 11 Academy St., Fincastle) Serves Buchanan, Blue Ridge, and Fincastle.

Roanoke (County & City) and Salem

Blue Ridge Library (540-977-3433; 28 Avery Ave., Roanoke).
Roanoke County Library (540-853-2475; 706 S. Jefferson St., Roanoke).
Roanoke County Public Libraries (540-772-7507; www.co.roanoke.va.us/library/rcplhome/AreaLibraries.htm; 3131 Electric Rd. SW, Roanoke).

Salem Library (540-375-3089; salemlibrary.info; 28 E. Main St., Salem).

Mountain Counties: Highland, Bath, Alleghany

Highland County Library (540-468-2373; www.highlandlibrary.homestead.com/index.html; hcpl@highlandcounty.org; 10 Water St., Monterey) Smallest state-supported library in the commonwealth.

Bath County Regional Library (540-839-7286; www.lib.rang.gen.va.us; Courthouse Hill, Warm Springs).

Clifton Forge Public Library (540-863-2519; www.ci.clifton-forge.va.us/library.htm; 535 Church St., Clifton Forge).

Alleghany Highlands Genealogical Society (540-962-1501; yorkylvr@intelos.net; 605 Dolly Ann Dr., Covington) The society has its own library; call for appointment.

Charles P. Jones Memorial Library (540-962-3321; www.covington.va.us/about_us/library.htm; 406 W. Riverside St., Covington).

UNIVERSITY LIBRARIES

Each of the colleges and universities in the Valley has a library. Often their specialized resources are open to outside researchers by appointment. The list below shows those Valley academic libraries that maintain an online presence. Full information on these colleges is given in Chapter Three, *Cultural Attractions*.

Bridgewater College (www.bridgewater.edu/departments/library).
Eastern Mennonite University (www.emu.edu/library).

Roanoke College in Salem is one of the many colleges and universities along the I-81 corridor in the Valley.

Courtesy Roanoke College

James Madison University (www.lib.jmu.edu).
Liberty University (www.liberty.edu/resources/library).
Roanoke College (www.roanoke.edu/library).
Shenandoah University (www.su.edu/library/index.htm).
Virginia Military Institute (www.vmi.edu/library).
Washington and Lee University (www.wlu.edu/~hblackme/sum95/lib1.html).

NEWSPAPERS, MAGAZINES, AND OTHER MEDIA

Virginia has a long history of local journalism. While you can also readily find the *Wall Street Journal, USA Today, The Washington Post* and *The New York Times* in most of the larger towns of the Valley, especially the university towns, local papers are a good source of information and should not be ignored. In addition to the listings below, most of the jurisdictions publish periodic advertising and local history papers that are available in tourism offices throughout the state.

WEB MAGAZINE

Shenandoah Valley Magazine (www.shenandoahvalleyweb.com).

WEB PAPER

Shenandoah Valley Herald online (www.dnronline.com/svh.html).

MAJOR DAILY PAPERS

The papers are listed north to south.
The Winchester Star — Winchester; www.winchesterstar.com.
The Page News & Courier — Luray; www.pagenewsonline.com.
Daily News-Record — Harrisonburg; www.dnronline.com.
The Daily News Leader — Staunton; www.newsleader.com.
The News-Virginian — Waynesboro; www.newsvirginian.com.
Virginian Review — Covington; www.alleghanyhighlands.com.
Roanoke Times & World News — Roanoke; www.roanoke.com.

NONDAILY NEWSPAPERS (PRINT ON VARYING BASIS)

News Leader — Staunton; www.newsleader.com.
Rockbridge Weekly — Lexington; www.rockbridgeweekly.com.
The News-Gazette — Lexington; www.thenews-gazette.com.
Blue Ridge Business Journal— Roanoke; www.roanokebiz.com.
Clarke-Times Courier — Berryville; www.clarketimescourier.com.

MAGAZINES

Blue Ridge Country (540-989-6138; www.blueridgecountry.com; 3424 Brambleton Ave. SW, Roanoke, VA 24018) Covers several states.

The Roanoker (800-548-1672; www.theroanoker.com; 3424 Brambleton Ave. SW, PO Box 21535, Roanoke, VA 24018. Devoted to Roanoke. Especially helpful for its dining guide.

RADIO

Tuning your automobile radio in the Valley will likely bring you a country music station — or two or three. But there are other stations broadcasting in the Valley. Reception is good up and down the center part of the Valley, difficult in the mountain areas.

The listing below is a sampler of stations whose broadcasting originates in the Valley, grouped by format

Talk Radio

Winchester: WNTW (610 AM).
Harrisonburg: WSVA (550 AM).
Lexington: WREL (1450 AM).
Roanoke: WFIR (960 AM).

Country

Winchester: WUSQ (102.5 FM).
Lexington: WREL (96.7 FM).
Covington: WIQO-FM (100.9 FM).

Mixed Music

Woodstock: WAZR (93.7 FM).
Luray: WMXH (105.7 FM).
Covington: WKEY (101 AM).

Nostalgia

Front Royal: WFTR (95.3 FM).

Public Radio

Harrisonburg: WMRA (90.7 FM); WXJM (88.7 FM).

Roanoke: WVTF (89.1 FM).
Monterey: WVLS (89.7 FM).

Religious

Winchester: WTRM (91.3 FM).
Harrisonburg: WEMC (91.7 FM).
Roanoke: WRXT (90.3 FM).
Salem: WPAR (91.3 FM).

Rock

Front Royal: WFQX (99.3 FM).
Winchester: WINC (92.5 FM).
Vinton: WJJS (106.1 FM).

ROADSIDE SERVICE

Roadside service — even 24-hour service — is widely available along I-81, a major trucking route, and along I-64. We have listed at least one 24-hour towing service in each county. In the more populated counties there are many such services, which can be located in the phone book. If there is no answer at one of these listings, call the nearest police authority. Your toll-free automobile club number should be able to provide you with local references as well. The county listings are alphabetical by county. Please remember: A listing of a repair shop or towing service here does not constitute an endorsement or recommendation.

Alleghany

Covington Tire (540-962-3988; 1015 S. Monroe, Covington) Towing and many repairs, but not on engines.
Dewey's Engine (540-962-3255; 609 W. Chestnut, Covington) Towing 24 hours.

Augusta

Drumheller's 24-Hour Towing and Repair (800-542-8384, 540-953-8401; 1211 Richmond Rd., Staunton, and 2101 W. Main, Waynesboro) Phone numbers reach an operator who covers both locations.
Junior's 24-Hour Towing and Auto Repair (540-943-7070; Rte. 340, Stuarts Draft).

Bath

Jerry's Wrecker Service (540-839-2801, if no answer call 540-839-2500; Warm Springs).

Ralph Riener's Service (540-839-5211; Warm Springs) No tow.

Botetourt

Arrington's Auto Repair and Towing (540-992-3985; 3966 Lee Hwy., Troutville). **Fleshman's Service** (540-992-2206; 2927 Simmons Dr., Cloverdale) No tow.

Clarke

Berryville Auto Parts (540-955-1292; 107 Main St., Berryville)

Frederick

Bob's Used Cars and 24-Hour Towing (540-542-1110; 1467 Front Royal Pike, Winchester).

Highland

Gas and Go (540-396-3487; Main Street, McDowell) Latest gas; open until 10pm. **Hunters Auto Park** (540-468-2329; Monterey) Towing 24 hours. **Hines Street Service and Repair** (540-468-2329; Monterey). **Meryl's Auto Park** (540-398-3428; McDowell).

Joan Leotta

Autumn décor festoons the Shenvallee Creamery in Timberville, a great place to stop for Valley-made cheese and other products any time of year.

Page

Bill Turner, Inc. (540-743-3338; 1203 E. Main St., Luray) No towing.
Freeze's Towing and Auto Repair (540-743-4095; 1018 E. Main St., Luray).
Foltz's Auto Repair (540-743-6177; 633 E. Main, Luray) Towing, too.

Roanoke

Boyd's Auto Repair (540-387-1067; Salem) Towing 24 hours.
Carr's Garage (540-387-9665; 42 Hurt Ln., Salem).
Robert Young's (540-982-3809; 210 Carver Ave. NE, Roanoke) Towing 24 hours.
Salem Fast Towing (540-293-2926; 3838 W. Main St., Salem).

Rockbridge

Auto Towing and Repair (540-463-9600; 23 Johns Way, Lexington) Towing 24 hours.

Rockingham

Jenkins Automotive and Tire (540-434-4409; 90 E. Gay St., Harrisonburg) Repairs only.
Layman's Towing and Repair (540-434-0691; 701 Jefferson St., Harrisonburg).

Shenandoah

New Market Exxon Service Center (540-740-3623; 9378 N. Congress, New Market) At night and on holidays, call 540-740-8426.
Town and Country Towing (540-459-5900; 18852 Old Valley Pike, Woodstock) Towing 24 hours.

Warren

Park's Automotive (540-636-3278; 232 S. Royal Ave., Front Royal).
Precise Automotive (540-636-4040; 425 S. Royal Ave., Front Royal).

TOURIST INFORMATION

You can order more than twenty different brochures and the *Virginia Travel Guide* by calling 800-VISIT-VA or through the Web site at www.virginia.org/site/main.asp?referrer=publications.

Many of the smaller towns also are developing their own Web sites.

Listed below are the primary tourist offices followed by several Web sites and other sources for specialized information on topics of interest, notably the Civil War.

TOURISM AND OTHER HELPFUL OFFICES

Winchester — Frederick County

Winchester-Frederick County Convention and Visitors Bureau (540-450-0097; www.winchesterva.org; slamb@winchesterva.org; 1360 S. Pleasant Valley Rd., Winchester, VA 22601).
Winchester Chamber of Commerce (540-662-4118; www.winchesterva.org; Kurtz Business Centre, 2 N. Cameron Ave., Winchester, VA 22601).

Front Royal — Warren County

Front Royal Department of Tourism (540-635-5788, 800-338-2576; www.ci .front-royal.va.us; visitfr@shentel.net; 414 E. Main St., Front Royal, VA 22630).

Berryville — Clarke County

Berryville-Clarke County Chamber of Commerce (540-955-4200; www.clarke chamber.com; 101 E. Main St., Suite 2, Berryville, VA 22611) Also contact www.co.clarke.va.us for brochures and to see latest events.

Luray — Page County

Luray-Page County Chamber of Commerce (540-743-3915, 888-743-3915; www .luraypage.com; pagecofc@shentel.net; 46 E. Main St., Luray, VA 22835).

Shenandoah County

Shenandoah County Tourism (540-459-6227, 888-367-3934; 600 N. Main St., Suite 101, Woodstock, VA 22664).

Harrisonburg — Rockingham County

Harrisonburg-Rockingham Convention and Visitors Bureau (540-434-2319, 540-433-1497; www.hrcvb.org; hrcvb@planetcomm.net; 10 E. Gay St., Harrisonburg, VA 22802).
Harrisonburg-Rockingham County Chamber of Commerce (540-434-3862; www.hrchamber.org/about/index.html; 800 Country Club Rd., Harrisonburg, VA 22802).

Staunton —Augusta County

Greater Augusta Regional Chamber of Commerce (540-949-8203; www.augusta chamber.org; chamber@cfw.com; 732 Tinkling Spring Rd., Fishersville, VA 22939).
Staunton Convention and Visitors Bureau (540-332-3865, 800-342-7982; www .stauntonva.org; troubetzkoyss@ci.staunton.va.us; 116 W. Beverley St., Second Floor, Staunton, VA 24401).

Lexington — Rockbridge County

Lexington-Rockbridge County Visitor Center (877-453-9822, 540-463-3777; www.lexingtonvirginia; lexington@rockbridge.net; 106 E. Washington St., Lexington, VA 24450).
Lexington-Rockbridge Chamber of Commerce (540-463-5370; www.lexrock chamber.com; chamber@lexrockchamber.com; 100 E. Washington St., Lexington, VA 24450).

Botetourt County

Botetourt County Chamber of Commerce (540-473-8280; www.bot-co-chamber .com; bccoc@rbnet.com; 13 W. Main St., Fincastle, VA 24090).

Roanoke County

Roanoke Valley Convention and Visitors Bureau (540-342-6025, 800-635-5535; www.visitroanokeva.com; 114 Market St., Roanoke, VA 24011).
Roanoke County Chamber of Commerce (540-983-0700; www.co.roanoke.va.us; 212 S. Jefferson St., Roanoke, VA 24011).
Salem Visitors Center (540-375-4044; www.salemciviccenter.com or www.visit-salemva.com; 1001 Boulevard, Salem, VA 24153).

Bath, Allegheny, and Highland Counties

Alleghany Highlands Chamber of Commerce (540-962-2178; www.alleghany highlands.com; ahchamber@aol.com; 241 W. Main St., Covington, VA 24426).
Alleghany County Chamber of Commerce (540-862-4960; 501 E. Ridgeway, Clifton Forge, VA 24422).
Bath County Chamber of Commerce (800-628-8092, 540-839-5409; PO Box 718, Hot Springs, VA 24445).
Highland County Chamber of Commerce (540-468-2550; PO Box 223, Monterey, VA 24465).
Western Highlands Travel Council — Covers Alleghany, Bath, and Highland Chambers of Commerce. Meets at the Bath County Chamber. Contact number moves according to which of the three counties chairs the council.

TOPICAL LISTINGS

O ther important tourism listings follow. Some are located outside the Valley, but serve the Valley among other areas.

Appalachian Trail Conference (304-535-6331) This group is located in West Virginia but has information on the entire trail.

Bed and Breakfast Association of Virginia (540-672-0870; www.bbav.org) The association publishes a membership directory divided by region. Reservation number: 800-934-9184.

Blue Ridge Parkway Association (828-670-1924; www.blueridgeparkway.org; tomhardy@blueridgeparkway.org; 199 Hemphill Knob Rd., Asheville, NC 28802).

Shenandoah National Park (540-999-3500; www.nps.gov/shen/home.htm; 3655 US Hwy. 211 E., Luray, VA 22835).

Shenandoah Valley Travel Association (540-740-3132; www.svta.org; jim@svta.org; 277 W. Old Cross Rd., New Market, VA 22844).

Virginia State Park Reservation Number (800-933-PARK).

Virginia Association of Convention and Visitors Bureaus (434-386-9686; www .vacvb.com; etdovel@aol.com; 3741 Woodside Ave., Lynchburg, VA 24503).

Virginia Civil War Trails (888-CIVIL-WAR).

Virginia Department of Transportation (24-hour highway help hotline: 800-367-7623).

Virginia Hospitality & Travel Association (804-288-3065; www.vhta.org; 2101 Libbie Ave., Richmond, VA 23230).

Virginia State Parks (Virginia Department of Conservation and Recreation: 804-786-5045; www.dcr.state.va.us; 203 Governor St., Suite 213, Richmond, VA 23219).

Virginia Winery Festival and Tour Information (800-828-4637).

In addition to these organizations, you'll find many sites on the Blue Ridge and Skyline Drive at **www.BlueRidgeSkyline.com**.

Virginia operates welcome centers on major roadways entering the state. From these you can obtain maps and brochures on a variety of attractions in the commonwealth. One of these centers is located in the Valley, in Covington: **Covington Welcome Center**; 540-559-3010; I-64, One Welcome Center Dr., Covington, VA 24426.

STILL MORE SITES

www.state.va.us — Official Web site of the commonwealth.

www.virginia.org — This site has a weather link for finding out what's going on weather-wise in the area (www.virginia.org/site/weather.asp), a kid's page, and a special guide for international visitors. You can also use this Web site to request the current issue of the state's travel guide.

www.mosbyheritagearea.org/heritage.html — The area around Clarke County eastward into Faquier and Loudoun Counties is where General John Singleton Mosby led the Union troops on a merry chase up and down the roads. These were his haunts and markers appear around the county noting concentrations of Mosby activity. There is also a brochure available that tells about the area; obtain one through the Clarke County Web site: www.co.clarke.va.us.

www.cvco.org/tourism/histrich — This site is especially for history buffs.

TOURS

You want to visit a wild cave? Travel by motorcycle, horse, or alpaca? Need a guide so that you can drive to the best spots in your own car? Here are some of the tour companies that live and work in the Valley:

Highland Adventures (540-468-2722; PO Box 151, Monterey, VA 24465) Canoes, wild caves, rock climbing, and picking wild food — all of this and more for folks of all ages.

City Life: Civil War Auto Tape Tour of Lexington (540-464-1100; PO Box 2, Lexington, VA 24450) A one-hour cassette leads you on a driving tour to 14 locations in and around Lexington. Inexpensive and an automatic souvenir as well.

Lexington Carriage Co. (540-463-5647; 106 E. Washington St., Lexington, VA 22450) Ride through the streets much the same way the Civil War-era greats of the town would have ridden around with their families.

Shenandoah Mountain Touring (540-434-2087; www.mtntouring.com; mountaintouring@aol.com; 135 S. Main St., Harrisonburg, VA 22803) The tour office is located inside the **Shenandoah Bicycle Company** (540-437-9000; www.mtn touring.com/htm/main_index.htm) Tours range from mountain bike training to one-day trips into the countryside to five-day overnighters. This group's specialty is the George Washington National Forest and the mountainous areas within.

Motorcycle Tour Company of Virginia (540-234-9797; www.mctourva.com; austin@mctourva.com; PO Box 293, Hampden-Sydney, VA 23943). If you like the feel of the open road and tour with a motorcycle — either your own or a rental — then you'll want to put a star by this listing. Guided tours for those on their own cycles as well as those who rent. They provide helmets, you provide all other safety gear. You do need a motorcycle license.

Old Virginia Tours, Inc. (800-685-7265, 540-377-2110; www.oldvatours; gary@old vatours.com; 12 Wachovian Way, Raphine, VA 24472) Old Virginia's specialty is interpretations at major historic sites. Options include one- and three-hour tours of Staunton, Lexington, Winchester, and environs. Lots of choices. Call or check the Web site for details.

Driving and Walking Tour — Pamphlets to help you find your own way around the principal sights are available for many of the towns. Because of their popularity, more of the locales are developing them. Check with the local tourism office and ask if there are any driving or walking tour pamphlets available.

IF TIME IS SHORT

It's hard to select highlights in the Shenandoah Valley because the region offers so many different activities: outdoor recreation, cultural events, shopping, and the exploration of historic sites, just to name a few.

I-81 is the fastest way to connect the north and south points of the Valley and it too is scenic, even though trucks often obscure the scenery. Within a daytrip's distance of the major entry points into the Valley are most of the activities you would want. In fact, there is no part of the Valley where you cannot combine wineries, caves, battlefields, outdoor fun, and more in just a few days. As for when to visit — the answer is anytime!

Driving on and to and from Skyline and the Blue Ridge is very time consuming. Select a short segment if your time is limited, and research ahead of time which hikes and other activities you want to enjoy. There are many entry points and exit points on both roads, so you can take a few hours to enjoy the splendors of those roadways and still have plenty of time for the rest of the Valley.

Every time of year reveals a different facet of the Shenandoah's splendor. The deep reds and yellows and oranges of autumn, and the pale pinks and lavenders of the redbud dogwood and lilacs of spring are the best known seasons in the area. But not to be missed are the starker beauties of winter, when dark trees are outlined against velvet skies and layers of white snow as skiers "shoosh" by on glistening slopes. Or the deep, full greens of summer, which provide a lush backdrop for warm days spent visiting the Shenandoah's many attractions.

If you're pressed for time, stick to the sights close to I-81, but keep this book handy. Once you've been to the Shenandoah, you'll want to return and explore further.

Index

LODGING BY PRICE CODE

Inexpensive	Up to $75
Moderate	$76–$125
Expensive	$126–$175
Very Expensive	Above $175

AUGUSTA COUNTY

Inexpensive
The Buckhorn Inn, 163

Moderate
Sampson Eagon Inn, 167

Moderate–Expensive
Belle Grae Inn, 166
Twelfth Night Inn, 167

Moderate–Very Expensive
Frederick House Hotel, 165

BATH COUNTY

Moderate
Anderson Cottage, 178

Moderate–Expensive
Inn at Gristmill Square, 177

Expensive–Very Expensive
The Homestead, 179

FREDERICK, CLARKE, AND WARREN COUNTIES

Inexpensive
Battletown Inn, 149

Moderate
Lackawanna Bed and Breakfast, 153
Long Hill Bed and Breakfast, 149

Moderate–Expensive
Chester House, 151–52

Wayside Inn, 153
Woodward House on Manor Grade, 152

Expensive
Historic Fuller House Inn, 148

Expensive–Very Expensive
Inn at Vaucluse Spring, 150
Killahevlin Bed and Breakfast Inn, 152

THE MOUNTAIN COUNTIES

Inexpensive–Moderate
Highland Inn Bed and Breakfast, 176

Moderate
Cherry Hill Bed and Breakfast, 176

Expensive–Very Expensive
Jordan Hollow Farm Inn, 159

PAGE COUNTY

Moderate
Mimslyn Inn, 159

Moderate–Expensive
Woodruff Inns & Restaurant, 160

ROANOKE COUNTY

Moderate–Very Expensive
Hotel Roanoke, 173

ROCKBRIDGE COUNTY

Inexpensive–Moderate
Days Inn, Raphine, 168
Natural Bridge Inn and Conference Center, 172

RESTAURANTS BY PRICE CODE

RESTAURANTS BY CUISINE

CITIES AND TOWNS OF THE SHENANDOAH

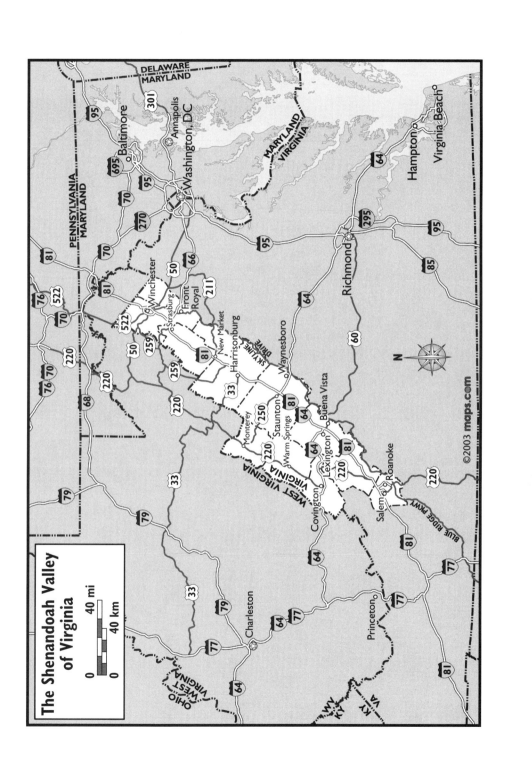

The Shenandoah Valley of Virginia

©2003 maps.com

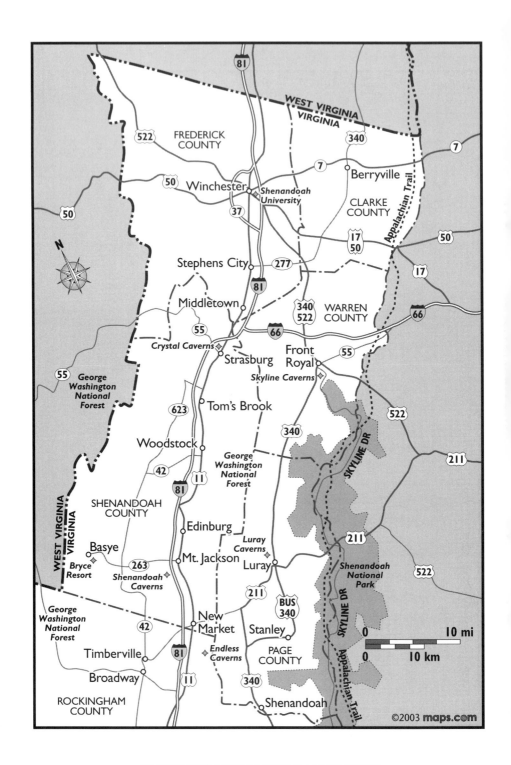

NORTHERN SHENANDOAH VALLEY

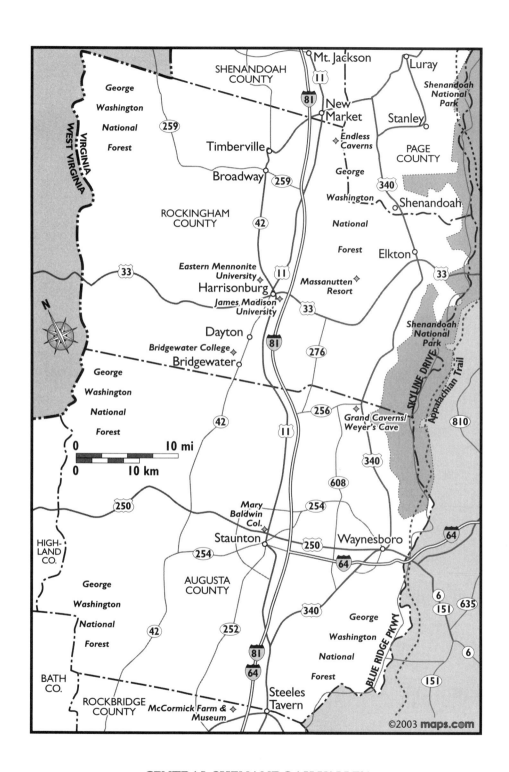

CENTRAL SHENANDOAH VALLEY

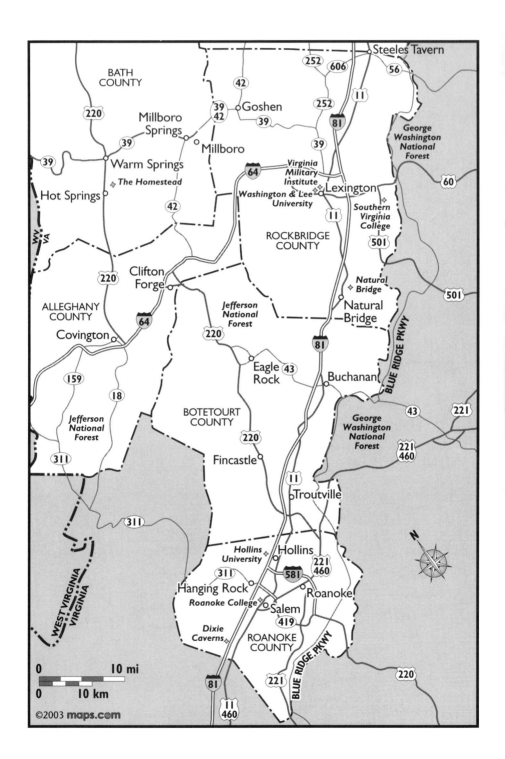

SOUTHERN SHENANDOAH VALLEY

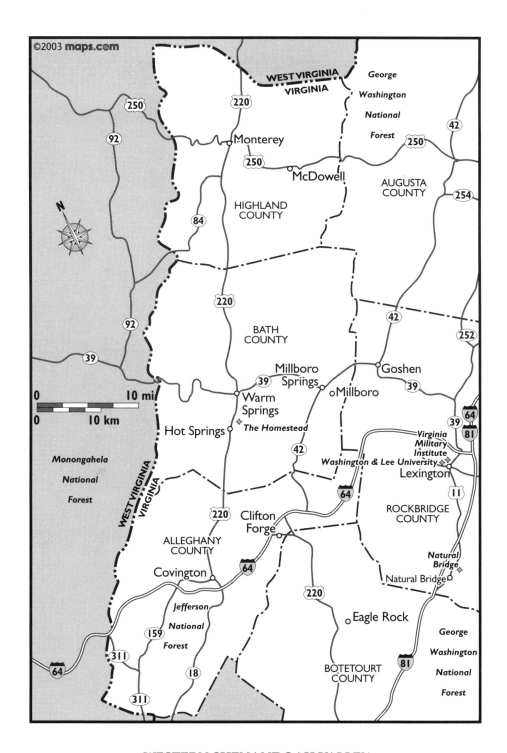

WESTERN SHENANDOAH VALLEY

About the Author

Joan Leotta's love affair with the Shenandoah, "Land of the Daughter of the Stars," began at the age of twelve. For the past quarter-century, she has lived on the edge of the region, making forays into the heart of the Valley for vacation, a dinner or an afternoon hike. She has covered its festivals, fairs, shops, and restaurants in her travel writings, which have appeared in the *Washington Post, Women's Day, Stars and Stripes,* and the American Automobile Association regional magazine. Joan is also a storyteller who performs Shenandoah Valley and other folklore for schools libraries, museums, fairs, and festivals all over the East Coast. (Over the years the area's geographic highs and lows have become a metaphor for the Valley's impact on the joys and sorrows of her own life.) Her latest performance project is a one-woman show based on the exploits of Belle Boyd, a Confederate spy who lived in Front Royal during the Civil War.

Joan Leotta and her husband live in Burke, Virginia.